Perception of Reality and the Fate of a Civilization

Molly,
I don't despair about the future when I see the gentleness & sweetness of your strength at work.
~~Love~~
Dick

Perception of Reality and the Fate of a Civilization

Ordinary People as Virtual Pioneers in Critical Times

Richard J. Robertson

Copyright © 2003 by Richard J. Robertson.

Library of Congress Number:		2003092533
ISBN:	Hardcover	1-4134-0650-5
	Softcover	1-4134-0649-1

All rights reserved. No part of this book may be reproduced or transmitted in any form or by any means, electronic or mechanical, including photocopying, recording, or by any information storage and retrieval system, without permission in writing from the copyright owner.

This book was printed in the United States of America.

To order additional copies of this book, contact:
Xlibris Corporation
1-888-795-4274
www.Xlibris.com
Orders@Xlibris.com
18808

Contents

Acknowledgements 9

Chapter 01

Introduction 11

PART I
A Critical Juncture in History

Chapter 02
EARTH IN RUINS AND
    CIVILIZATION IN DECLINE? 35

Chapter 03
FAILING SOLUTIONS? 56

Chapter 04
CONJECTURES ABOUT CAUSES 78

Chapter 05
SPENGLER ON THE DECLINE
    OF WESTERN CULTURE 100

PART II
How First Principles Evolve:
The function of Behavior

Chapter 06
THE ENGINE OF
    CULTURAL DECLINE 131

Chapter 07
HISTORY AND
   THE CONTROL OF PERCEPTION 145

Chapter 08
HIERARCHY OF PERCEPTIONS AND EVOLUTION OF IDEAS .. 170

PART III
Open Loop and Closed Loop Systems

Chapter 09
A MORE TECHNICAL EXPOSITION OF FEEDBACK CONTROL
   SYSTEMS 197

Chapter 10
INADEQUACY OF LINEAR LOGIC 222

Chapter 11
ROLE OF CONTEMPORARY PSYCHOLOGY IN THE LOSS OF
   ACCOUNTABILITY 249

Chapter 12
BIOLOGICAL BASE AND
   CULTURE PARADIGMS 267

Chapter 13
SOCIETY AS
   QUASI-CONTROL SYSTEM 282

Chapter 14
REORGANIZATION:
   INDIVIDUAL AND SOCIETAL 306

PART IV
*Virtual Pioneers:
Ordinary People in
Times of Crisis*

Chapter 15
INDIVIDUALS AND CIVILIZATIONS 331

Chapter 16
THE POWER OF
    ORDINARY PEOPLE 358

Chapter 17
PERCEIVING THE FUTURE 376

Chapter 18
INDIVIDUAL STRATEGIES:
    THE MICRO LEVEL 414

Chapter Notes 437

Bibliography 461

Appendices 475

Author Index 481

Subject Index 485

Acknowledgements

I began this book while a professor of psychology at Northeastern Illinois University. I owe many thanks to my department and our chairperson, Peggy Condon, for the support to introduce my own introduction to psychology using Perceptual Control theory and conduct the studies that I have been fortunate enough to pursue. I also express my appreciation to Bill Powers for his life long devotion to a better understanding of the nature of behavior and for putting research in it on a sound experimental basis, one that merits the respect of "hard science" investigators. Besides Bill there are many other members of the Control Systems Group whose insights and techniques have enlarged my fund of knowledge about and interest in human systems of many levels of organization. Quite a few of them are cited throughout the book.

In addition I want to laud the "Hutchins Plan" of the University of Chicago College where I came to appreciate the interconnectedness of the fields of knowledge as well as the relation between human action, civilization and history. I especially note two fellow students, philosophers Art Olsson and Fred Wranovicks, whose insights and attitudes encouraged me in looking for the broad picture, the most inclusive view of any subject at hand.

Another group to whom I owe many insights and much personal growth are my colleagues in the profession of psychotherapy, especially those in the American Academy of Psychotherapists—most of all the members of my "family group" in the Academy.

Finally, last but not least I owe much to my wife, Vivian, who put up nobly with my erratic schedule, unavailability, writing, rewriting endlessly as it seemed.

Obviously, none of the above is responsible for the failures and deficiences of the project.

Chapter 01

INTRODUCTION

When a ship is sinking there comes a time when it's "every man (or woman) for himself." In the end of the twentieth century, experts[1] of all sorts have been claiming that Western Civilization is sinking. Not that that is new; prophecies of doom are as old as the hills, however there are increasing signs that the condition of Western Civilization is severely worsening. Critics, like Patrick Buchanan(2002)as one recent example, see the United States unraveling internally and as a world power and economic force, taking the West down with it. Many financial experts advise one to get off the ship, seemingly oblivious of the fact that there might be no alternative plane upon which to light. Ecological experts see the world in danger of being made unlivable for humans, by humans. A flood of writings of this genre aim to arouse us to the danger but can't agree about what to do about it.

It seemed difficult to maintain any great fervor for reform with the prosperity of the last decade, but things have begun to look more critical with the recent economic plunge, the catastrophe of 9/11, and the clash of Islamic and Western cultures all around the earth. Even before the bad news began coming at the end of the last century many serious writers argued that the prosperity of the last decade was ephemeral, momentarily serving to mask the buildup of deep stresses in our civilization. Admittedly many of the scare scenarists are pitchmen selling dubious remedies such as off-shore investments and havens. Still their messages reflect the views of more serious writers. A succinct and telling picture is drawn by Krippner, Mortifee and Feinstein (1998) using the fate of Easter Island culture as a metaphor for what is happening in the earth at present:

> Countless cultures around the world have disappeared.... Easter Island... is unique because of... isolation from its neighbors... 1600 years ago the island's first settlers, explorers from Polynesia, found themselves in a pristine paradise .... They multiplied and prospered.... Eventually, as the island's population grew... the forests were cut more rapidly than they regenerated.... In time the absence of wood for sea going canoes reduced the fish catches, while erosion and deforestation diminished crop yields .... When the Europeans arrived ... the once-fertile island was barren and desolate. Its remaining inhabitants... were heirs to a once greater society that had degenerated into violence, starvation, and cannibalism.[2]

Is this a cameo of the future of all of us? Krippner et. al. go on, "Humanity may not act in time to prevent the decimation of the rain forests, fossil fuels, arable land, and ocean fisheries .... But there is a crucial difference between us today and the ill-fated Easter Islanders: They had no books or histories of other doomed societies ... and this information can save us." (Ibid.)[3] In order for the information to save us there must be concerted action informed by innovative thinking and uncompromised leadership. That implies effective cooperation and governance. But that is just what is in question at this point in history.

When government proves ineffective in dealing with major, long term problems of society ordinary people increasingly *are* on their own. My desk is littered with unsolicited invitations to move out of the United States to some more livable place, or to invest in foreign (non Western) enterprises. The self-proclaimed gurus behind these advertisements want to show you how to survive, leaving the "suckers" behind, although it is hard to see the merits of their strategy if, in fact, it is the world that is sinking. Still their arguments and blandishments are occasionally thought provoking, if only for the short term. While they are mostly rich, global-oriented individuals there are also common citizens who seem to have lost faith in government, seeing it as controlled, by impractical "liberals" or greedy, earth-hating "conservatives"—depending upon their political leaning. How does an ordinary person evaluate the presumed facts of these critics and, most importantly, decide what actions to take if he begins to lose faith in the stability of our culture? Are we observing a genuine decline in civilization or a paradigm shift in our conception of the nature of physical and social reality on earth?

I believe those issues are one and the same. As we progress through the ensuing chapters you can see how the very existence of such Jeremiahs and their dire warnings is itself a sort of evidence. Let me give a parallel from the high days of the Roman empire. Aldo Schiavone, in his book *THE END OF THE PAST*: Ancient Rome and the Modern West (2000) sets out to answer the question, Why did the historical course of the West contain within itself the greatest catastrophe ever experienced in the history of civilization—[the fall of Rome]? To set the stage he begins by reporting a speech for a ceremonial occasion by a rising Greco-Roman rhetorician Aelius Aristides (143 or 144 A. D.) that

> the skillful stage managers of the imperial court . . . staged [to] display . . . unconditional approbation that surrounded the power of Rome . . . and that represented the most unequivocal ~legitimization of ~Rome's supremacy . . . [to support the view that] they were living in a latter-day golden age . . . or at least in a state of unprecedented well-being and comfort.

Schiavone wants us to understand that this performance had some quality of whistling in the dark.

> But in order to understand Aristides' assessment in its fullest sense, we must attempt to situate our text against an even larger background. The optimism just described was not the only component of the sensibilities of the era. . . . Even as this rosy image was establishing itself among the members of the ruling class of the empire-especially in the provinces and the court . . . the old Italian nobility . . . was already beset with difficulties and problems [and] a veil of uneasiness, perplexity, and anxiety was beginning to fall over the consciousness of many people in these same aristocracies, gradually coming to rest on their souls. From our vantage point, we can identify [that] in this distant welter of emotions. . . [was] something resembling a disjoined, or at least ambivalent, perception of the world. (ibid.)

The parallels with our own times are not hard to find. Consider the cover of the May 13, 2002 *Business Week*, Wall Street—How corrupt is it? In the following chapters I will cite further instances, from the commonplace to the broad scale, of anxiety about the future of our times. As I consider the problem with finding reliable experts on the vital questions

I am disheartened at the way they contradict each other.[4] Some are persuasive enough on specific points to cause me to worry about the future of my grandchildren. I do what I can in the immediate present. I support various save-nature causes, and I make a few investments hoping to preserve my modest resources from inflation and the tax man. But, even those seemingly worthy acts come into question by experts who maintain that support for a particular solution could actually be harmful, if it is the wrong solution.

The lack of even basic consensus about what the problems are might explain why so many solutions in recent decades seemed to fail. Are the efforts of all of us scrambling to maximize our own well-being canceling out each others' efforts to save the world? Have we in the global society lost the ability to cooperate effectively on the grand scale? In the view of some this, itself, is a sign of cultural degeneration. I am not satisfied with the explanations for the decline of Western Civilization given by some of the most vociferous critics currently, nor with their proposed remedies, but I do agree with their gloomy conclusions—to an extent. More about that later.

What do we mean by terms such as *decline* of a civilization and *corruption* of a culture? This requires consideration of how social action (behavior) works. I propose that we will gain a better understanding of these major social developments by examining how the behavior of individuals functions in the evolution of cultural changes. Although the actual facts about the state of nature and the state of civilization require carefully constructed research,[5] we ordinary people depend largely on the popular media for the information upon which we form attitudes and take action. Thus, it is all important whether those in control of that information identify their interests with those of the rest of us, or indeed, have abandoned the common people of their countries or—maybe even worse—don't know what they are doing.

The views given by the media all over Western Civilization continually present events and incidents suggesting that we are in a state of cultural, moral and ecological degeneration. Statistics on murders show an increasing number over the last decades in the U. S., and even the recent downturn is against a baseline far higher than in generations past;[6] a recent trial of two ten year old children for murdering a toddler in England shocked that nation before similar events began to become almost commonplace. Massacres by children in the U. S. are becoming repeated horror stories; national wars and revolutions in former Yugoslavia and the Soviet Union, Asia, and Africa and the Middle East are proving impervious to control by the U. N. Countries recently independent of the former Soviet Union are flirting with dangerous nuclear installations because they have no alternatives for power, or because they feel insecure about the instability in Russia. A flood of reports from environmental societies like The Sierra Club keep warning of the degradation of world environments by irresponsible multi-national corporations and third world governments.

There has always been turmoil in various places around the world. How is the present situation different? Let me consider *corruption* from my point of view as a psychologist. What so frequently drives kids crazy in chaotic, abusive or degenerate environments is the inconsistency, the unreliability, the arbitrariness that we term hypocrisy in adult affairs. When the growing child can not form any consistent view of the rules and reality that obtains in his or her surroundings it predisposes to the development of the opportunism and impulse drivenness characteristic of the psychopath. Even in households where this tendency is limited to what we call a "normal" extent, I believe that the extraordinary appeal of violence in our media reflects the underlying frustration and irritations of the child who represses the more overt acting out of such tendencies. Adults from such environments show more convoluted versions of this condition.

From the opposite point of view, that of the dominant figure, this kind of chaos is created when the one with greater power determines each encounter to his own advantage, whether by formulating rules *ad hoc* to his benefit, by imposing brute force to overrule any rules that were thought to exist, or by deception—convincing the inferior that he will benefit by accepting conditions that are to his disadvantage. You can find examples of each of these types of transactions in the daily news. What all have in common is that those with most power do not honor any system or set of principles or values that could overrule their opportunism in any particular instance. That is what corruption means. You can not count on your common sense understanding of the constitution, the law, the promise implied in a contract or the word of another, or, ultimately, your perception of reality.

Since the Enron scandal broke there has been a parade of other companies charged with misleading the public, their constituents and the government as to what really was going on in their business. Employee pensions have been diverted to insiders' pockets. Communities have been despoiled by corporations that guaranteed jobs in return for tax benefits or eminent domain proceedings only to welsh on their promises. Stockholders are routinely fleeced of earnings by executives giving the funds to each other while the corporations go bankrupt.

It is not hard to view the increasing voter apathy that one sees in national elections in the light of legislators increasingly beholden to the rulers of corporations rather than their constituents—and hence *not doing anything about these disgraceful perversions of business practice.*

It is true that most of the actions involved will go unpunished or even unresolved because they were not illegal in terms of laws, which after all, we have come to see as sometimes written just to enable such aberrations. Nevertheless in the common sense of ordinary people these actions are *crimes* despite not being illegal. The outcome that is developing is beginning to show many parallels with the case of the Roman Empire when the senate had become a pool of wealthy but impotent individuals increasingly isolated from and indifferent to the unemployed and unmotivated mass of the common people in the street. At the same time one can find further parallels between the battles of multinational corporations and those of the robber barons who fought over the turf of the Roman Empire after its collapse. There was no governing authority to impose rules of conflict and limits to outrages, and the same seems to be coming to be the case today. No wonder that such entities find themselves too enmeshed in struggles to survive in the unregulated psychopathic atmosphere of much of contemporary global business to worry about what effect they might be having on the physical or moral environments on this earth.

This could persuade one that the western world is on its last legs. But, worst of all, the remedies appear not to be working, or in some cases accentuate the problems. My aim in this book is to address the reader who concurs in the view that our civilization is in trouble, whether or not it is in fact collapsing—and that proposed remedies, on the national and international level, need remediation themselves. Further, that we are already looking at the "every man for himself" condition of ships of state coming apart at the seams. The crisis is viewed variously as technological, moral, political, and socio-psychological. The root causes are attributed to increasing pressures resulting from growing human populations and uncontrolled degradation of the biological environment by industrial processes of previous centuries that are only beginning to be addressed in the more advanced countries. This may be true. Yet it is human decision-making that determines the effects we have upon this earth, and the on-going processes of decision-making by all of us is the ultimate tool for whatever changes can come about. It is the thinking behind human behavior, then, that is the ultimate source of the problem, and hopefully, the solution.

It seems that contemporary politics and planning is stuck—caught in non-functioning processes. Conservative writers like Bork (1996) and Buchanan (2002) see it as corruption—the loss of moral standards fostered by liberal philosophy starting especially in the revolts of the '60s. Liberal writers see it as the greed and hypocrisy of the ruling class. Both have a point, but they are phenotypic explanations, to use a biologic analogy. We need a more profound explanation, a genotypic approach.

What one can accomplish depends upon what he or she will try. What she or he will try depends upon what he or she believes is possible, and desirable. What is not thought possible is never attempted. Thus, the conception of reality held, individually and collectively, most ultimately determines the conditions in which persons, groups and nations live. It goes without saying that theories of reality can be more or less realistic. The theories of physical reality that were developed during the last few hundred years have permitted technological development of a world that would be unimaginable to people living at the beginning of this era. But, the discordance between the current environment—increasingly determined by technology rather than nature—and the environment to which human nature (as presently conceived) is suited, leads some people to see modern civilization as a net loss, as witness the contemporary growth of "back to nature" movements. The upsurge of religious fundamentalism within the Christian and Muslim religions might be a psychological counterpart of such yearning for simpler, more "natural" living conditions.

At the same time the conception of human nature formulated four hundred and fifty years ago by Descartes has undergone no fundamental change in spite of a great accumulation of facts about social relations and the biology of the brain. I will argue that a major reason for the failure of reform measures of all sorts lies in a misunderstanding of how human behavior works. They fail by repeated attempts to solve problems by promulgating actions instead of goals. That results from a lack of understanding that properly constructed control systems act automatically to realize their goals, and that we humans can understand ourselves and our behavior better in terms of thinking of behavior as the functioning of intentional-control systems.

Cultural regression can not succeed in the long run. The other alternative is to advance on the psychological and political fronts to keep step with technological advances. The foundation for new ways of thinking is already being laid, albeit modestly so far, in the cybernetic revolution of the 1940s. A new view of human nature is currently emerging—resulting from a closer examination of how humans "work." Beginning about the middle of the 20th century the concept of a living organism has begun to change drastically. From being a kind of reflex machine built to react mechanically to stimuli from the environment, as described around 1650 by Descartes, it is coming to be understood as a system, in continual transactions with its environment, working to keep environmental conditions within limits required by internal specifications for survival of the organism. I will examine the positive and negative contributions of human actions in these terms as I review the critiques of the current crisis and the problems of world civilization, seen by many, major western writers.

Part I examines the concerns of many writers about the current state of the world: That there is evidence of a dwindling of Western power and influence. Then, that this decline of power is synonymous with a decline of Western Civilization itself. Next, I consider conjectures as to the causes of this decline, tentatively accepting Spengler's (1918, 1926) thesis that the history of a culture is the drawing out of the implications of its initial assumptions about reality. And further, that there is a tendency for the process to deteriorate over time as the most fruitful implications are developed and "used up." Continuing from this thesis I examine how major movements in human attitudes arise as ordinary people begin to see things in new ways after coming to the conclusion that old views no longer work. The potential for creating new forms of human organization follows in that process.

Part II is devoted to examining the process of deterioration of social and moral structures in terms of the dilemmas individuals struggle to cope with in the increasing complexity and inconsistency of our culture. In Part III I first present a semi technical sketch of the most well developed modern view of how behavior works. I go on to argue that the traditional conception is, itself, one of the basic ideas of Western culture whose utility has expired. It has become one more obstacle to innovative thinking about the problems of society. Then I begin to explore how the newer approach can lead to different ways of thinking about reality. Finally in Part IV I argue the role of ordinary people in eventually reforming the structure of society, based upon new conceptions of the nature of reality, and how the very process of surviving difficult times contributes to the evolution of culture or its transformation into new forms.

This is not basically a psychological treatise, even though I approach the subject from my own background as a psychologist. I do not maintain that the solution to all our problems is simply a better understanding of how behavior works. We clearly need to find better ways to devote human energy and human creativity to both technological and human problems. I do maintain that the Cartesian paradigm of "stimulus and response" predisposes a kind of linear logic which lends itself poorly to attempts at holistic approaches to large scale issues (or individual behavior, too, for that matter). We all have implicit theories about behavior that affect how we understand and deal with each other as we endeavor to collaborate on getting out of personal as well as world predicaments. To begin to understand behavior as a control process will reform this thinking.

Chapter two will review in some detail the dire predictions about where the world is heading and the ebb and flow of argument about how critical the situation is. In addition to the abstract, statistical arguments of Jeremiahs such as Lester Brown and Paul and Anne Ehrlich and their opponents such as Julian Simon, I examine the persistent flood of journalistic articles and reports the majority of which lean to the side of pessimism.

Then in chapter three I report the views of many serious writers that attempts at solutions to system-wide problems—whether environmental, political or economic—are failing to meet their objectives. I will examine the possible sources of failure in terms of complexity and the paralysis that results from opposing interests and values and set the stage for the argument that complexity and paralysis result from the drawing out of initially effective assumptions about virtue and reality to speciously logical but convoluted ends. Then we shall consider the mood of anxiety and frustration on the part of writers who, I believe, present and represent the workings of these tangled views as they influence what serious readers are coming to think.

As individuals we live and act in the world consisting of our perceptions and beliefs. The average citizen forms attitudes and takes action in terms of his or her subjective impressions, while only a small minority of people—experts in given areas—are constrained by hard facts in their decision making. In our present circumstances this means that a significant number (even at times a majority) of us are acting on views promulgated by the molders and purveyors of opinion. Major among such views is that many things aren't working right any more, and this despite the apparent good times that were supported by our, previously, booming economy. The fears persist because of the anxious pictures we get from so many media sources and the recent decline in the economy.

In chapter four I shall review the arguments that the persistence of large scale problems is evidence of limitations in ways of thinking that, in turn, suggest the beginnings of over ripening of the basic premises of Western Civilization. Different writers such as Lucaks (1970), Kennedy (1987) and Davidson and Rees-Mogg (1997), and others, agree that it is in decline but offer different views of the cause. Lucaks is more inclined to the idea that old ways of thinking are inadequate to current problems, whereas Kennedy presents a view identifying economic and geopolitical competition, while Davidson/Rees-Mogg propose that revolution in technology—especially as affecting the projection of power—is the major driving force in the emergence of new, and decline of prior, forms of civilization. Still, the common threads in their arguments suggest a convergence on the view that current ways of pursuing solutions to major problems are beginning to stagnate and deteriorate. Western Civilization is either undergoing disintegration of its major structures or a paradigm shift in which traditional values and ways of perceiving—and conceiving of—reality are being transformed into something about which we can only vaguely guess.

Another group of writers see a decline in moral fiber and attribute it to a social evolution which is culminating in a tendency toward dissolution of personal ties, anomie and mediocrity. The shared criticism is that Western social structure and the capacity for confident judgment is deteriorating. It goes to suggest that our present Western ways of thinking might well be proving inadequate or incomplete for dealing with the increasingly complex problems of society as well as for confronting the challenge of other societies emerging on the world scene. The main issue, then, is to understand how—if this is the case—it comes about.

That interest led me to re-examine in Chapter Five Oswald Spengler's (1918) thesis that there are basic premises informing the structure of any civilization and that when all the major implications of the basic principles are coming to be fully drawn out the ability for innovation declines. Newer implications drawn from the basic logic begin to go around in circles. Our current perception of failing attempts at solutions of major problems can be understood in this light. This condition ultimately sets the stage for other sets of basic assumptions about reality to make their bid on the world stage. This view has an interesting parallel in Thomas Kuhn's (1970) thesis that the history of science has played out through a series of revolutions of fundamental principles, which he calls *paradigm revolutions*. Using this terminology one can argue that we are in the midst of not one but several paradigm revolutions in not only science but culture as well. The question of whether our civilization is in decline and another is ascendant might be more nearly meaningless than unpredictable in terms of the paradigm shifts that may be underway.

It will help to approach the entire discussion from the point of view of an individual trying to understand the future for both intellectual and practical reasons. I believe that social "forces" on whatever scale are the sum total of a multitude of individual actions and hence, the decisions that individuals make, make the final difference. How does a private person who is not a member of any of the circles of power and influence decide what to do, whom to believe for the information needed to decide what to do? And what can you do about it—whatever you decide to believe? One view seems to be that an ordinary person can't do anything about the ultimate course of his or her life; that social forces, or historical forces, or economic forces carry us all along like the proverbial guy on the river without a paddle.

An opposite view is that such "forces" are just abstractions from observations of the net results of millions of decisions and actions by individual human beings. I subscribe to the latter view, with qualifications. As an illustration of the way in which paradigm shifts occur through the actions of multitudes of ordinary people and can overturn conventional ways of thinking and acting—as it were, over night—I could cite two such spontaneous revolutions in our present era: the sexual revolution of the 1960's and the rapid shift in public sentiment against tobacco companies in the 1990's. Nothing significant had changed in the establishment scenario or publicly held values about what should be considered moral and appropriate sexual behavior. Yet, within the short span of a decade or so latent pressures suddenly burst into the open and behavior—such as committed cohabitation—that had for centuries been viewed as immoral, suddenly spread like wildfire. Even some conservative, establishment churches rapidly found it OK to accept into, or continue membership of, people living out of wedlock—something that would have been rejected only a decade or two before.

Another example would seem to be the emergence of opposition to the use of tobacco in the last decade despite powerful advertising campaigns and the long-held bondage of a majority of the U. S. congress to the tobacco companies. Other paradigm shifts, having to do with such fundamental concepts as civil rights, race, nationality, patriotism, political power and financial management, have been similarly underway, though some of them are apparent so far only to those with special interests and expertise in such matters.

A common feature of all these developments—a sign of

paradigm shifting—is the disorganization and reorganization of the ways of thinking and acting in the deteriorating processes. There are fundamental changes that register on the surface as curious, arguable facts, such as (for just one example among many possible) the fact that blue collar workers seem to have lost the attitude of "industriousness," if that is the proper way to term it. An article titled, "Midwest Headache: Not Enough Workers," (Phillips, 1998) mentions that, "constant turnover has nevertheless cut worker productivity by 8% to 10% [in one plant and] . . . the turnover rate hit an astounding 60% [in another]." This casual attitude toward the job, on the part of younger blue collar workers was attributed by him to the extremely high employment field in 1998, however, this trend was well underway a decade or more before when unemployment figures were much higher. A parallel development seems to have been taking place among college students—to whom we have always looked as the hope of the future—according to Allan Bloom (1987).

In chapter six, I take Spengler's thesis—about the exhausting of fruitful derivations from a culture's basic axioms about reality—to the level of individual behavior. Viewing behavior as an active process of executing *intentions* we see why the source of behavior resides in the individual and not the environment—something that is readily apparent to most laymen and many psychotherapists, but that has been lost sight of by most traditional, academic psychologists. It will help clarify the relation between how common views of the cause of social action leads to dilemmas in confronting social turmoil and often results in succumbing to ineffective "remedies" that only further cultural decline.

In Chapter seven I continue the discussion of views of behavior in the progression of history. I offer illustrations of how many phenomena take on an entirely different appearance when viewed through the lens of a new paradigm as Kuhn

(1970) so cogently argued in The Structure of Scientific Revolutions. Just as the physics of the Greeks was not applicable for the problems solved by Newton, and the physics of Newton was not equipped to open the atomic era, so, I hope to show, many of the problems of society—which are ultimately problems of thinking about behavior—obtain new purchase when viewed in the light of behavior as the control of intentions.

Chapter eight deals with a reprise of psychological theories of development and the two-edged issue of the way many children's development currently results in both competence and incompetence. Erik Erikson's thesis—that the inherent contradictions of any culture are reflected in the types of maladjustment suffered by its members during their formative years—provides a bridge between traditional psychology of individual development and the sociology of mass behavior as seen as the sum of actions of many individuals to control their environments. I begin employing this view to revisit the idea of decline in the creation of social solutions as seen in the previously examined catalog of failures in solving major problems in society.

In chapter nine I will present a sketch of what I consider the most complete and most consistent approach to the newer feedback-control view of behavior, which has come to be called Perceptual Control Theory (PCT). We will then consider illustrations derived by the people who are developing it. I will attempt to show how a modest mastery of these ideas can prove fruitful in thinking about the historical processes we have considered previously and also in approaching the task of new solutions to the problems of individuals in a civilization in crisis.

Chapter ten examines the implication of the theory that behavior realizes intentions. It supplies a remedy for the linear logic "cause and effect" view underlying so many ineffective governmental attempts to solve social problems. One immediate consequence is that intentions are more correctly inferred from what a person accomplishes than from his or her statement of intentions, because—for one thing—we all have, and at any time are acting upon, many more intentions than one can be aware of. I intend to demonstrate the failure of the idea that external forces cause behavior, and, hence, the inadequacy of the single-variable, regimented approach to social engineering.

Chapter eleven begins with reviews of some enduring psychological "phenomena" and shows how they look when re-phrased as examples of behavior controlling perceptions, clarifying traditional psychological phenomena of self-fulfilling prophecy, self-consistency, and cognitive dissonance. They are seen as different perspectives on the same fundamental process, the process of controlling one's perceptions to realize expectations. That leads to an examination of the relation between "success" and too narrow focus of expectations—how the current psychological climate in our civilization favors the domination of certain personalities—the one-dimensional, single focus individual and the psychopathic element in political leadership, the transcendence of rules by rule-makers, and the double binds that result for common people.

Chapter twelve will look at fundamental concepts such as instinct, common sense, natural law and human nature in the light of perception-control. This examination will show how these concepts reflect tendencies toward the type of social organization that bids to achieve most satisfaction, and the inevitability of the concept of "natural law" as safety valve against control of abstract principles as objectives for their own sake.

Chapter thirteen will examine the nature of social class and social structure as control phenomena. I will review Lloyd Warner's (1941, 1953) thesis of society, as a great quasi-control system in which individuals jointly control their physical, territorial base while controlling their own affairs within personal niches in the social structure. I show how that view provides a bridge between the theory of individual control of desired living conditions and Spengler's thesis of a culture as embodying and actualizing its members basic assumptions about the nature of reality.

Warner's studies of social class reveal the stable structure of society as a hierarchy of control that fairly closely mirrors the hierarchy Powers (1973) envisioned to account for individual organization. Combining these conceptual schemes brings forward some new ways of looking at arguments like why members with the highest status in society are "to blame" for its condition while, at the same time, they have little more power than ordinary people to effect major changes. It also helps to illuminate why lack of power does not annul individual responsibility at any level in society. Society, viewed as a quasi-control system, resists disturbance in a manner parallel to that of individuals. This is really no mystery, since "society" is an abstract concept referring to functions carried out by individuals controlling perceptual variables in ever more complex human arrangements. (A perception is variable if it can occur with a range of values, like brightness, loudness, temperature, but also more abstract considerations like degree of friendliness, degree of confidence, etc. If you think about it that covers pretty much all perceptions.) Finally, the argument suggests how these phenomena create the stage against which revolutions, bloody or not, are necessary for paradigm shifts to occur, and what that means for the way that paradigm shifts do occur in the history of civilizations.

In chapter fourteen I will spell out more of the concept of reorganization of a person's hierarchy of intention-control systems. It will become apparent as another part of the process of individual survival that simultaneously produces the flow of cultural evolution.

Part IV, Chapters fifteen through the end of the book will follow this theme with further glimpses at the issues depicted in Part I, and begin to envision what it is like to break free of conventional ways of approaching these problems. I argue the power of simply changing one's thinking to affect major directions in the movement of society. Then I conclude this journey, by discussing the tendencies we all have to try to predict the future, the functioning of self-fulfilling prophecy in this process and finally, how, ultimately the policies of nations rest upon the generally held conceptions of human nature of their members.

I do not claim expertise in regard to the specific problems of overpopulation, eco-deterioration, strategies for curing environmental degradation, or political-economic reforms or, indeed, of judging which might be root problems. But, I maintain that a misunderstanding of the nature of human action is a factor in the contradictions that muddle attempts at dealing with these issues.

The educated layman is now aware of more sophisticated aids to discriminating true facts from false facts, surveys, opinion polls, investigative journalists, strategy theory, probability theory, chaos theory, decision theory, and more. As this armamentarium for separating the chaff from the grains of truth has grown, so have revelations of the misuse of such tools to give the appearance of truth for partisan purposes. There are traps posed by perspectives of bias, preconception, prejudice, predisposition, and manipulation. The net result is more skepticism and cynicism where we hoped for increasing confidence in our knowledge.

In the final analysis it doesn't matter that objective truth might prove to be as illusive as ever. We still process data in our brains using whatever tools we have the skills to apply and the experience to trust. That is, we live in a world which consists only of the totality of our perceptions and act to maintain that world, making only such modifications as become necessary when our own reality fails.

What matters most, is that all of humanity contributes actions to the onward flow of reality, for better or for worse, in accord with two sources of action: What for oneself is true; what one wants his experience to be. This is the way humans bring about change. Real revolutions in people's conception of reality, including our conception of human nature, don't come about by exhortation or mob action. They are the result of masses of individuals gradually perceiving reality in fundamentally new ways—in which, ordinarily, most are not even aware of anything different from how they have always thought. At least not until some philosopher points it out and even then he or she will only get the attention of the small minority who are interested in such specialized topics.

I do not claim to envision a particular, describable outcome to the changes currently taking place. That is the mistake that I think advocates of causes make. The goals that they urge are usually obsolete by the time they are achieved, if they ever are achieved. This is, at least in part, the effect of linear actions trying to effect phenomena that we more and more see as involving feedback/recursive systems. Real human developments take people by surprise, because they are fundamental changes in the way that we think—that will allow heretofore unimaginable solutions to emerge. The criterion for judging then also changes—from a specified process to an outcome to which one can say, "I can live with that." In regard to the warnings of the Jeremiahs and their critics—I had this fantasy vision: traveling back through time as an invisible observer on Easter Island I one day see one of the people get up in the town square and yell, "Listen to me everybody. If we keep chopping down the trees at the rate we are doing, pretty soon there won't be any more." Someone else then gets up and says, "You might be right, but I'm cold right now, and I need fire wood. If you haven't got any to give me you're no help." Playing on the physicists'[7] image of parallel universes I wonder how the different course on Easter Island could have played out, and how we will test that possibility.

---

* A note on style: I intend throughout this book to use/employ this device for concepts which can be conveyed by alternative terms, in hopes it will keep attention focused on the concept under discussion when there are various ways to phrase it, rather than on the terminology.

PART I

A Critical Juncture in History

Chapter 02

EARTH IN RUINS AND CIVILIZATION IN DECLINE?

An alternative title for this chapter might have been, "What is the Problem?" In the works that I want to consider here we shall see passionate statements that: planet earth, and by implication, humanity, is plunging headlong toward total catastrophe. That may or may not be true but the problem is the issue of determining what the real threat (if any) is and who is causing it; or again, that there is a problem but it is a struggle for (and in) the minds of humanity for the values that will dominate in the future. Or, finally, there is no problem—the intelligentsia (read, "professional critics") are doing their typical, interminable, hand wringing over the future.

I have a personal problem that logically precedes dealing with these questions. It might be your problem too. That is how to decide whom to believe. That question really carries along several others, like: how do we, as individuals, decide what is factual; how do we decide questions of the relative importance of given facts; how do we decide how much energy to apportion to our various seriously taken issues—while continuing to have any kind of meaningful, normal human life? Or, simply, What do I do about it all, if anything? The fact that we might be struggling with the question of how-to-decide how to decide is, itself, something new in the world. Formerly, people usually just decided, or weren't interested, or were at the mercy of "fate," and didn't have anything to decide. The same technological revolution that puts better prediction tools in our hands is also the one that seems to have made better prediction tools essential. Let us begin to consider the issues.

Even though the state of the earth and the state of Western Civilization are conceptually different questions we will find them mixed together many times in these first chapters. The issues have been so intertwined by many writers addressing them that it becomes artificial to separate them practically. If the earth is being devastated, Western Civilization gets the blame, because it is during its dominance that the critical limits are being exceeded, if they are. And simultaneously the leaders of the West are increasingly being challenged to lead the way toward remedy by third world spokesmen. While Western Civilization is not the only civilization/culture built on a philosophy of exploiting the earth rather than accommodating to it, the combination of western technology with the exploitative attitude has made it much more capable, than any previous culture, of devastating the world most humans knew hardly a hundred years back. That we are all in the same boat is evident like never before.[8] Just what has the Western (read, "exploitative") attitude produced?

Some people's answers to the above question can be frightening. Publications of the Worldwatch Institute (Brown, 1995, 1998) are filled with graphs of degenerating conditions heading out of bounds. In the 1995 issue of *Vital Signs*, the first point made was, "population growth rates of the sort we know today have no historical precedent."[9] World population is projected to reach about ten billion people by the year 2050, even though the rate of growth is slowing and should begin to decrease by 2025. The next arguments detail the growth of world economies, fueled by the population explosion, and their costs in environmental degradation. "A Planet in Jeopardy," by Brown, Flavin and Postel (1992) likens going on about our business under current environmental conditions to the passengers on the Titanic continuing to work on business and career plans after it had hit the iceberg, because, in each case, of inability to grasp, "an altered reality."

During my adult life projections like that started out as statistical arguments of interest mainly to specialists. Already things are different; I begin to experience what the statisticians are talking about in personal terms. A few years ago I moved from Chicago to a northern suburb that lies along the main expressway north of the city. I travelled this expressway frequently even before I moved, to visit my hometown in Wisconsin. I celebrated when it was built because it reduced my travel time from Chicago to Wisconsin from 6 hours to 4 hours. But, in the last ten or so years the population of the suburban area served by this expressway has about doubled. The consequence is tangible; at any time of day or night one can encounter a total stoppage of traffic in either the incoming or outgoing lanes. Travel times are lengthening out again.

Other consequences of the combination of population surge and current economic policies are reported in the Worldwatch volumes as evidence of global warming continues to accumulate. World wide water usage is rapidly beginning to outrun sustainable limits, as are arable land, benefit from fertilizer use, forest harvest, fishing harvest, personal debt.[10] These grim statistics continue to be updated in various publications of the U. N., of Paul and Anne Ehrlich (1990), sundry articles in *The Futurist* magazine and many other publications.[11] Even while some conditions, like air pollution, appear to be coming under control in much of the U. S. they are running out of control in most developing countries of the world. These issues, too, are no longer abstract statistics of concern mainly to specialists monitoring figures in reports. As I write this I note an article in the Wall Street Journal, "Smog Again Threatens Singapore, Sparking Fear of Foreigner Exodus."[12] The foreigners in question aren't tourists. They are the western technicians cultivated by the country to propel it into leadership in Asian economies.

Crime is another issue that has gone from a worrisome statistic to an immediate experience for many members of the previously isolated middle and upper classes of affluent societies. Witness, "An Evening at Gunpoint," (in Mexico City) by Wall Street Staff reporter John Busby.[13] He wasn't wandering around in the bad section of town. He was robbed by two gunmen who jumped into the taxi called for him by the valet of a "top rated inn .... Mine was just another robbery in a city consumed by crime. When I related my evening to some Mexican acquaintances the next day, they had much better personal stories to tell—muggings, thefts, scary moments .... The bigger problem, of course, is that the cops and the criminals are sometimes one and the same."

Busby's story also had immediate personal consequences. My wife and I had signed up for an Elderhostel course in a small Mexican town that friends said was full of old world charm. To get there, you take a taxi from the airport in Mexico City. If you can't trust a cab called by the doorman of an upscale restaurant, how much less trust one you find at the airport? As it happened, we had to cancel that trip to help care for a sick relative, but I had planned to re-schedule. Busby's article gave me pause. Never mind that there must be many people who ride cabs in Mexico City every day without being robbed. I'm sure that is what Busby thought too.

I expect that you can doubtless match my examples with your own. Instances of limitations on your range of action—resulting from out-of-control conditions at large in the world—

are becoming standard gossip in social circles. Robert Kaplan, investigative reporter and contributing editor of the Atlantic Monthly, enlarges this picture in his book, *Ends of the Earth*.[14] He investigates hot spots, from Togo to Turkmenistan, from Iran to Cambodia, beginning with his experiences in West Africa,

> In many West African urban areas, streets are unlit, police lack gas for their vehicles, and armed burglars and carjackers are increasingly numerous. In Nigeria's largest city, Lagos, armed gangs attack people caught in the nonstop traffic jams. Direct flights between the United States and the city's airport were suspended by the U. S. secretary of transportation because of violent crime at the terminal and its environs... In Abidjan, effectively the capital of the Ivory Coast, jewelry stores employ armed sentries even by day and customers often have to be "buzzed" inside (as they do on 57th Street in Manhattan)... several restaurants had hired club-and gun-wielding guardsmen, contracted by private firms... giving you an eerie taste of what American cities may someday be like.

As he progressed through the emerging third-world countries on his itinerary Kaplan observed similar conditions repeatedly, including situations that he was not sure he, himself, would survive. Kaplan's personal perspectives gain depth from Brown's (1998) *State of the World*. Chapter 1, "The Future of Growth," begins with the contrast between currently positive indicators of economic activity (but see below) and negative assessments of ecological trends. "While economic indicators such as investment, production, and trade are consistently positive, the key environmental indicators are increasingly negative. Forests are shrinking, water tables are falling, soils are eroding, wetlands are disappearing, fisheries are collapsing, rangelands are deteriorating, rivers are running dry, temperatures are rising, coral reefs are dying, and plant and animal species are disappearing... Within scarcely a generation, countries like Mauritania, Ethiopia and Haiti have been almost deforested...."

These are current examples of catastrophes in the making. The example of Easter Island, cited in chapter one, can no longer be considered some rare anomaly of past history; it is seen taking place in the countries mentioned by Brown (1998), and in other third world places like those described by Kaplan. Even those of us who are non-specialists in the fields concerned with these issues have to consider the question of how general are these phenomena of degradation. For, if they are as widespread as many environmental activists maintain, our children and grandchildren will be seriously affected, if they survive at all.

Even the positive economic developments that such a confirmed pessimist as Lester Brown concedes are not perceived as secure by all financiers, economists and big investors. There is a strident competition between those predicting continuing bull markets and those claiming that a severe "1929 type" depression is just around the corner, and the environment comes increasingly into the equation. Behind the subject of markets seemingly of interest mainly to businessmen and investors lie implications that go far beyond. For example, consider the following from an advertising come-on in a relatively calm investors' journal, TAIPAN (Bonner, 1994). Titled, "13 Trends and Events 1995-2005 That Will Rock the World," it begins with, "A Short Preview: Two Americas:"

> An unstoppable wedge is about to be driven through the heart of America. It is a wedge of technology and culture that will divide this nation

into two very different parts; the haves and have-nots....

In one part, crime will spread. Homes will be boarded up. Gangs of fatherless young men and boys will roam the streets. People will live shorter, meaner, poorer lives. Real estate prices will fall... entire areas will be abandoned....

Sounds like an inner city ghetto? Think again. This may be your street 10 years from now. Because the same plague that has destroyed the inner cities is spreading to the suburbs. There's a specific reason for this... [see next page] ... the results will be far more terrifying than anything we've experienced....

Meanwhile, just a few hours' drive from these living nightmares will be some of the finest environments ever created on the planet. These enclaves of peace and prosperity will be protected by geography and electronic fortifications....

And so on. You might write this off as typical hyperbole of an advertisement, but think about it. If, like me, you show any interest in investment news you will be flooded with declarations like this from many different sources. The point is, if so many investment-advice merchants are spending their advertising funds for flyers with this sort of message, they must think they have evidence that it speaks to readers' perceptions. There is tangible evidence that they are right. As I drive through suburbs north of Chicago I find that more and more new, up-scale housing developments are gated communities. There must be more and more people who hold views like those to which the TAIPAN advertiser wants to appeal.

The same advertisement continues by listing trends like, "The Next Plague; The Death of Public Services; War Everywhere." Then it gets better. The next trends mentioned are: "New Enclaves of Wealth and Power; Live to 120; The New Telecommunications Breakthrough; More Technologies That Will Knock Your Socks Off . . . and some more bad ones, Crime Ridden Suburbs, Hard Times Ahead for Millions and Retirement Savings Evaporate. The message is that many will succumb to these disasters, but the few can take advantage and profit from them."

Such scare tactic advertising can only secure subscriptions if it has gained some plausibility from serious economic, political and social studies of future trends. James Davidson and William Rees-Mogg (1993) in *The Great Reckoning* approach the subject of economic history and investing in what appears to be a scholarly, wide-angled historical approach, dispassionately arguing that increasing violence always accompanies the breakdown of social order, which, in turn, results from technological revolutions, especially those affecting the control of power and violence. The title of their first chapter, "The Megapolitics of Progress and Decline: Violence as a Catalyst and Consequence of Change," incorporates the circular causation paradox of feedback-control phenomena that are increasingly appearing, and that show up the inadequacy of old explanations.

Davidson and Rees-Mogg (1997) argue further that the control of violence is the ultimate source of the power to affect all other conditions, and that this is receding from national superpowers as a result of the increasing power of weapons available to smaller bases of power—what are sometimes called, "rogue nations," and private terrorists. Thus, the argument would go: hope for combatting planetary threats rests ultimately with those with economic power, which in turn, rests with possessing the control of violence. But, of course, it's hard to imagine that the agendas of most terrorists are much concerned with the condition of the environment.

Other forecasts of increasing violence do not offer

attempts to account for it but simply extrapolate trends that have been identified by specialists in sociology, law, law-enforcement, economics, history and the like. Many of the advertisements for investment newsletters, such as I mentioned above, appear to accept many of the pessimistic outcomes of the various trends averred by Brown (1998, etc.), the Ehrlichs (1991) and others (without giving them credit). But, they give the environmentalists' facts a curious twist. They foresee opportunities for making money in a deteriorating world! It leaves one wondering what foreign planet they expect to live on with their gains.

There are certainly countertrends, such as the revision of policies by the World Bank in recent years toward halting the subsidization of environment destruction, as well as instances of successful local movements to reverse destruction, such as Kaplan (op. cit.) describes in his chapter on, "Rishi Valley and Human Ingenuity." In addition there are various New Age enclaves around the world that are devoted to earth friendly ideals. But, the balance appears heavily tipped toward degradation at the moment. Constructive trends and destructive trends appear as if in a race to determine whether or not humans will have a future on earth.

Contrary Views

Not all views of the present and future state of the world are pessimistic. Robert Bailey, author of the book, *Eco Scam* (1993), writing in a 1995 *Futurist* article, "Seven Doomsday Myths about the Environment," reviews earlier prophecies about global famine, global warming, exhaustion of nonrenewable resources, skyrocketing pollution and the ozone hole—showing how current statistics refute those prophecies. The first "myth" that he takes up—global famine—predicted by Paul Ehrlich (1968) in *The Population*

Bomb, did not materialize. However, there continue to be reports of hunger, malnutrition and occasional outright starvation in many developing countries, and some signs of undernourishment in parts of the United States. My attitude about whom to believe, Bailey or Ehrlich, seems to vacillate between looking at the large scale statistics, in which on the average things have not degenerated to the extent feared by Ehrlich, or focusing on the plentiful instances of local tragedies around the globe. I can't help wondering if it is the fact that our news media now present us with bleak pictures from all over of things that might always have existed but we didn't know about them? Or, are things really getting worse as there are more and more of us demanding more and more of the same old earth?

Whether these problems are portents of worse to come, or variations resulting from wars, local population problems, and weather conditions, such as have occurred through history, are beyond my ability as a non-expert to judge. That is not a comfortable position to be in, because, if Bailey is right the question remains: Is he only right on this occasion? If he is wrong, or right in the short run but wrong in the long haul, the consequences would be magnified by the loss of time in not investing more heavily in an effort to head them off. If he is right in the long run, then no harm done in taking remedial action anyway? Not necessarily so, see Simon (1995) below.

Some of the other "myths" debunked by Bailey also have serious consequences for decision making by all of us as individuals. Should we be much more careful about getting a suntan in summer than we used to be? Reports of increases in the rate of skin cancers have so far not been debunked, as far as I know. Likewise, global warming, while still disputed, seems to be increasingly accepted as a fact, although its consequences, if any, continue to be debated. I recently read that the premier of the Seychelles Islands made a plea for it to be taken more seriously in the recent global warming conference in Japan. To him and his people it makes a big, and immediate difference. Their entire country is barely above sea level. And just the other day I saw a program on one of the news documentaries of an island off the coast of North Carolina that has been reduced to about half its size in recent decades because of rising ocean levels and increasingly furious storm erosion.

Even better known than Bailey's views are similar views of Julian Simon (1995), who sees humankind as having the capacity to overcome almost any number of undesirable conditions, created by human action or larger environmental events, through human ingenuity. In his introduction to his 1995 book, *The State of Humanity* (obviously aimed at highlighting its contrast with Lester Brown's *State of the World*), he rephrases and reverses the pessimistic quotation from page one of the 1980 Global 2000 Report to the President:

> If present trends continue, the world in 2000 will be less crowded (though more populated), less polluted, more stable ecologically, and less vulnerable to resource-supply disruption... life for most people will be less precarious economically than it is now... The years have been kind to our forecasts—or more importantly, the years have been good for humanity...."

Simon's volume consists of a series of statistical studies of the major topics of concern about the human future, Life, Death & Health; Standard of Living, Productivity and Poverty; Natural Resources; Agriculture, Food, Land, and Water; and Pollution and the Environment. Following the optimistic reports on these separate issues, in Ch. 56, "Risk Within Reason," Richard F. Zeckhauser & W. Kip Viscusi state:

> Society's system for managing risks to life and limb is deeply flawed. We overreact to some risks and virtually ignore others. Often too much weight is placed on risks of low probability but high salience [such as those posed by trace carcinogens or terrorist action]; risks of commission rather than omission; and risks, such as those associated with frontier technologies, whose magnitude is difficult to estimate. Too little effort is spent ameliorating voluntary risks, such as those involving automobiles and diet. When the bearers of risk do not share in the costs of reduction, moreover, extravagance is likely.... Part of the problem is that we rely on a mix of individual, corporate, and government decisions to respond to risk....

Zeckhauser & Viscusi discuss human fallibility in responding to risks, such as difficulties in comprehending extremely low probabilities, underestimations of higher risk phenomena—that are ignored in the media, for example, and difficulties in decision-making where a risk "does not lend itself to statistical estimation or scientific assessment."

> How should we proceed once we admit that individuals do not react to many risks "correctly"? We might ask the government to make more decisions [but] government [may not be] well equipped to compute certain risks accurately or to make sensible decisions ... Government can not act in purely rational manner; political and economic influences can and often do distort government efforts to regulate various risks. Other options, [could be] putting decision-making in the hands of experts, involving `processes enabling both agents and original principals [in making joint decisions] or improving the quality of individuals' decisions by providing them ... with

expert-certified information, much as accounting firms verify the accuracy of reported financial data.... Market outcomes provide a natural starting point for obtaining information on how risk reduction policies are valued by their beneficiaries [but] government policies are largely directed at situations in which the market is believed not to function effectively, if at all.... The policies for which no market reference is possible are the very ones in which current practice may be furthest from the optimum."

In this vein, in Ch 37, "Natural Ecology Today and in the Future: A Personal View," Kenneth Mellanby had argued that the term should be returned to use only for,

The branch of biology that deals with the interrelationships between organisms and their environment.... Unfortunately the term ecology, as used by the media and by many of the general population, including most politicians, has been greatly debased.... No ecologist would claim that every part of the earth is in perfect condition, and that serious damage may not occur from industry and the pollution industry may generate. But [the would-be doomsayer] should give us an accurate picture of the real situation . . . to rectify the situation."

Mellanby follows with examples of misinformation given by various environmental groups to foster their goals.

As an illustration of the above, in Ch. 53, "The Carcinogen or Toxin of the Week Phenomenon: The Facts Behind the Scares," Elizabeth M. Whelan tells of the February, 1989, ALAR scare, which she says came about when the National Resource Defense Council hired a public relations consultant who struck a deal with CBS whereby the network would present the results of a NRDC study (which studied mice using an excessively high dose of a by-product of ALAR that was "so high as to kill many of the mice by poisoning alone.") Whelan cites the fact that the EPA Scientific Advisory Panel had refused to ban ALAR. Dr. Richard Adamson, director of the Division of Cancer Etiology at the National Cancer Institutes and Dr. C. Everett Koop—stated that they saw no evidence that ALAR is a risk. Whelan argued further that there is no good reason to avoid use of antibiotics in raising animals, except that it could lead to bacterial strain resistance, which hasn't happened so far "in 30 years of treating livestock and poultry"[15]

The very difficulties involved in assessing dangers to the environment as a result of human population growth and consequent deleterious human activities—when compounded by inadequate or even back-firing remedial decision making—could be considered as another type of societal degeneration or environmental degradation. The whole issue of current trends and remedial attempts might some day be looked at by posterity (if any) as, itself, the decline of contemporary civilization because of its creation of conditions—the by-products of which were—beyond its capacity to handle. In other words, can we be sure that some future generation will not decide that the luddites, Amish, back-to-nature advocates were basically right? No. The question is self-answering. If the answer were to be Yes, there would likely be no one around to know it. We—world society as a whole—move ahead in our present directions on faith that we can, collectively, work it out, as Simon and his cohorts are maintaining.

Finally, in Ch. 58, "What Does the Future Hold: The Forecast in a Nutshell," Simon concludes, "The material conditions of life will continue to get better for most people, in most countries, most of the time, indefinitely.... The basis for this forecast is the set of trends contained in this volume, together with the simple economic theory stated in the Introduction.... I also speculate, however, that many people will continue to think and say that the material conditions of life are getting worse." Simon attributes this discrepancy to media practices of emphasizing the negative, to the development of higher living standards around the globe that leave people fewer challenges to which to devote creative energy, and to intergroup political struggles, "that now increasingly supplant the struggle against nature for a better material life." Why? He doesn't say, right here at least.

Simon bases his optimistic conclusions on the study of long term trends that he concentrates on in his book, admitting that there are many reversals in the short run, in all areas, but that unless individual human (reward-driven) creativity is stifled by government action, solutions are always found. "A crucial premise for using the past to forecast the future is the constancy of human nature.... The `futurists' base their predictions mainly on theories drawn from physics, biology, and social science while paying little or no attention to the long time series of history." Simon notes that human activities are seen as less predictable than phenomena in the physical and biological sciences, but argues that the truth is just the opposite. True, economists have a great deal of trouble predicting short run trends, but long-run trends "are almost a sure thing" namely: lives will get longer, families all over the world will see higher incomes and better standards of living than now; costs of natural resources will continue to decline; agricultural land will continue to become less and less important as an economic asset, relative to total value of all other economic assets.... Almost as certain is that the environment will be healthier than now [because cleanliness is a good that increased wealth makes more available.]"

Thus we find there is a running battle between various environmental groups, people like Ralph Nader, Lester Brown and Paul Ehrlich on the one hand, and various industries, seemingly so focused on the bottom line as to be unaware or indifferent to short term or long-run damage to small or large portions of the earth, on the other hand, plus the careful analysts like Simon's group and those like Brown's. Given that people are only stirred into action by dramatic and symbolic issues, reformers might have no real choice but to overdramatize their concerns. But how to explain the misuse of careful studies like those in Simon's book by corporate executives who seem truly willing (some of them) to play Russian roulette with the future of humankind? Or, on the other hand the misuse of statistics developed by researchers, such as Brown and Ehrlich, by environmental lobbies and organizations that can result in scares such as that pointed out by Whelan?

In fact, I believe there is a simple explanation that ordinary people do take into account when they can obtain sufficient background to do so. (Though that is often the most difficult consideration to realize.) That is the discount owing to self-interest. The one thing, at least, that environmentalists have in common with environmental villains, like CEO's of major polluting corporations, is the necessity to make a living from their activities. The heads of the now many environmental organizations are just as much subject to competition for patronage as are the heads of industries. Hence, it is reasonable to suspect that they will put the best possible construction on their "products," as is necessary to keep on producing.

When we look at it that way we see similarities between the opposing positions. The similarities underlie the short-term and long-term values that each are pursuing. The short term values include making a "good living" as defined by the individual. True, for the industrialist it is more likely to be making as much money as possible, while for the environmentalist it might be more like, "a comfortable living," plus a more or less conscious ambition of being remembered by future generations in an heroic light. The long run for the industrialist is the growth of the company and its bottom line (with the political power that often results) and for the environmentalist it might be more direct political power to help effect the changes in the world that he or she sees as vital. When we come to this level of analysis—where we see what is alike, rather than different—in these classes of opponents we can state the principle even more basically: all are acting to realize their highest values, as they see them. At this level, they are like me, dear reader, and you.

I can not imagine any CEO getting up in the morning and saying to himself, "Let's see, how can I help destroy the world, today," not even a head of a tobacco company. Neither can I imagine any sane environmentalist taking the route of the Unabomber to save the world by killing business executives. We sometimes hear of a business leader foregoing some profits after becoming aware of severe environmental damage that would result from a certain course of action. I also can imagine that (for example) Lester Brown might, like me, buy a redwood table for his back yard (though I don't know that as a fact). What I mean is that I think we might, almost all of us, be somewhere along the continuum toward fiddling while Rome burns, or playing cards on the Titanic, if the trends forecast by the environmental pessimists are on the verge of overwhelming humanity. Our cultural development, to this point in time, is only just at the horizon of reaching beyond our instinctual tendencies to do what past experience has led us to value, without regard for consequences beyond those we can immediately perceive.

Or, if not all of us are bogged down in living life as we are used to, the likes of Mother Theresa, Albert Schweitzer and John Muir are rare enough that the generalization still seems apt. We are locked into our historical and cultural frames to the point that most of us can only contribute what we can to the future by allotting some portion of our resources and hope that there are enough of us to make it enough. The only alternative would be a crusade. That is not unthinkable; humankind has engaged in crusades before—that is why the word has come to have a generic meaning. But, before that could happen two conditions would be essential. First, advocates like Simon (and those he exemplifies) would have to join those like Brown and Ehrlich in agreeing that the boat is sinking, or in agreeing on at least some grounds. Second, to act on their new crisis-appraisal all the rest of us would need to be "carried away" by an inspiration so strong as to render our current life style trivial. Neither of those conditions is on the horizon.

There is an urgent need for the kind of new forecasting tools that groups like the World Futurist Society are trying to develop. Tools that enable an on-going appraisal, not only of the current state and projections of trends of world hunger, air pollution and global environment degradation but continual forecasts—analogous to the on-going weather measurements used in air traffic control—along with continual refinement of the forecasting technology. If you find the opposing views of both Simon's and Brown's books (for example) persuasive, you must agree that there is a problem here, since their implications would exhort us to do quite different things. Or would they? It depends upon the level of analysis that you work on. Simon's implication seems to say, "Relax and have faith that we humans will come up with solutions to our problems before they overwhelm us." He certainly is not saying, "Go out and pollute to your hearts content." Brown, et al., on the other hand, might well recommend taking a leave from your job to get up a crowd to go picket your congressman, but I don't think they are saying, quit your job, tear down your house and go live in a tent in the woods, or whatever. So, here we have the common element. Both sides are advocating conservative action, just differing on the intensity they advise. If it were not so, Brown et al. would be trying to get their richest followers to invest in construction of a self-contained satellite at once.

The common element in the camps represented by *The State of the World* and *The State of Humanity* consist of careful collection and analysis of measurable facts. Partly, they present different facts, partly they interpret the same facts differently and partly they project different extrapolations on the basis of different overt, and hidden, attitudes and assumptions. To the extent that they both pursue the facts with the standards of modern science the findings will eventually converge. Witness the process in which astronomers and astrophysicists gradually weed out competing theories of the phenomena of galaxies and universes. The process of choosing the assumptions for extrapolating potential futures is a different one, however.

This last point is crucial in that even should there be significant convergence by the two groups as to the facts the implications for the future can not be refined as can the measurements. In this light consider the research on "Self fulfilling prophecies" by psychologist Robert Rosenthal (1976). In a series of studies on a variety of subjects he found that researchers and teachers unwittingly biased even carefully controlled objective measurement procedures so that their results tended to conform to their expectations. He proposed that this was a general feature of human perception. What we perceive as facts are determined by what we hope/expect to perceive to a greater extent than is the opposite. An optimistic attitude predisposes one to find facts that elaborate the silver lining, and vice versa. (Why this is a fundamental human characteristic is addressed in part II.)

However, it is not a hopeless situation. The very existence of modern technological civilization with its dependence on science is testimony to the fact that certain humans have learned to take the tendency to "see what one wants to see," into account and nullify it with procedures that establish hard and fast facts. This is the first step in arriving at concerted action. Only a couple of decades ago there was still a spirited dispute as to whether tobacco smoke can cause cancer in the lungs. In the interaction between researchers reporting these results and those contesting them the rules of science resulted in refinements in experimental design that gradually reduced the area of disputed facts and led to a broad range of increasingly indisputable conclusions. The same processes are currently going on concerning questions of global warming, desertification, species extinction and the like.

At this point it might seem that I should propose a solution, make my pitch, like any good advocate of a cause. However, I do not have much patience with the kind of advocacy that goes, "Let's all _____," or, "If only the _____ (government, rich people, captains of industry, terrorists, common people) would _____." That smacks too much of, "Why don't *you* do something, so that I won't have to." What I propose instead is that the procedure of competing advocacies is, itself, just one alternative for decision making—though an historically renowned one—and that a consideration of a wider range of alternatives is in order. Furthermore, I don't believe that the "Why don't we all . . ." form of advocacy ever accomplishes much beyond the occasional demonstration, or flood of letters to a mainly unresponsive political representative. What does lead to mass movements, as in the sea change regarding tobacco, is the identification of an identity of self-interests on the part of large numbers of people. In addition to the processes of refining the facts there is the process of defining and clarifying one's values. Is having a lot of stuff the chief means for happiness? Here and there are small groups testing out the proposition that smaller and simpler is pleasanter. A change in attitude or a change in paradigm can obviate the search for certain facts altogether. For example, see Thomas Kuhn's (1970) description of the loss of interest in the question of how phlogiston works, in

The Structure of Scientific Revolutions. Before considering, in Part III, what that might be in regard to the issues here, we need to examine the particular scientific revolution discussed in Part II—the on-coming revolution in our understanding of how behavior really works.

Grant that there is a race between deterioration, preservation and reversal going on in many parts of the world. This in itself raises another question, namely, how do you decide which trend will win? Is it possible to decide that? Who is in the best position to make the best judgement about it? Brown states, (also in *State of the World*, 1998), "While economists may be oblivious to the relationship between the global economy and the Earth's ecosystem, environmental scientist are not." Whether he realizes it or not, with this statement he puts his finger on another part of the major problem—the failure point of the division of labor. Laissez faire theory proposes that the end result of the competition of ideas, as well as the competition of goods, in the decision making processes of peoples, provides the best amalgam of competing points of view and the most probable resolution of outcomes. But that is, in itself, an hypothesis, a belief. It is not an immutable law of nature.

It is with us as individuals that I hope to begin the dialogue (however one-sided for now). I believe that you, like me, by being concerned about these issues at all, are hoping/betting that what you do to survive in the immediate present will coincide with, and not contradict, whatever more abstract efforts you make to contribute—and survive—in the long range. As the next step let us consider the argument that present procedures for solving problems—of many sorts—might be increasingly coming up short.

Chapter 03

FAILING SOLUTIONS?

> We seem to be rapidly getting to the point where doing nothing is always better than doing something, since anything we do makes things worse.
> Richard N. Farmer, 1977

Are traditional solutions to problems concerning environment, governance, crime, individual and social life proving inadequate? Many observers think so. Consider the "two steps forward and one step back," pace of progress on the environment. We know a lot about what some of the issues are. Take this article by John J. Fialka (1998) in the *Wall Street Journal*, "Global-Warming Debate Gets No Consensus in Industry." It acknowledges some movement toward agreement on the facts. Global warming is accepted as a fact by the advocates of opposing positions in this case. Fialka says John Brown, head of British Petroleum,

> starts this month with a plan to use his sprawling oil company as a kind of test bed for the emissions trading that the [U. N. treaty to reduce global warming] envisions . . . he thinks [his plan] will

help develop uniform ways to measure and limit emissions of carbon dioxide, which he and many scientists believe poses the planet's most pressing environmental problem .... [But] That isn't the view of Frederick Palmer ... CEO of Western Fuels Association, Inc ... [who maintains that] having more CO_2 in the atmosphere will be good, not bad ....

While there is not much scientific support for Mr. Palmer's position, he has been preaching it relentlessly...

And his what-me-worry? attitude has begun to resonate in Congress.

The article goes on to relate that Mr. Palmer, "has spent the last several years financing papers by some renegade scientists who dispute the scientific projections that underlie the global warming projections ... [and that Mr. Palmer hopes for] nothing happening on the treaty ...." Well, we know now that the U. S. has declined to join the treaty to reduce global CO_2. Mr. Palmer and his friends have had their way for the present, but some corporations are beginning to change their environmental practices on their own initiative.

On the surface this issue looks like a debate between two interpretations of the implications of increasing CO_2. But, if we look deeper, we find a broader problem. I see it as an unintended deficiency of the division of labor in society. It is our lack of the combination of expertise with political power—an inadequacy in dealing with questions affecting society as a whole. What I mean is that either scientists' opinions should have more weight than those of anyone else in cases like this—that require extremely sophisticated analyses—or the principals should be equally expert. People like Mr. Brown and Mr. Palmer should be able to agree on basic procedures for drawing out all implications of the agreed-upon facts before committing to actions that might have irreversible consequences.

Clearly everyone can't be equally expert on everything. But then shouldn't there be penalties for disregarding expert opinion when the stakes are so high? After all, we accept that principle in some areas. The food and drug administration has the authority to prevent the marketing of a substance until it meets certain tests generally accepted by the relevant scientific community. Yes, there are debates even so, but in general we condone putting a businessman in prison for marketing a drug that has not been approved, if it kills people.[16] In the case of a bad drug, a few, or a few hundred or a few thousand people might die[17], while if Mr. Palmer's way continues to dominate, and is wrong, we all die.

The president and congress do obtain guidance from expert scientific and scholarly opinion on many kinds of questions. In instances where that is the case the division of labor appears to be working as its underlying philosophy would dictate. But, when the issue is one that concerns the very survival of human life on earth, we might ask why isn't all questionable action prohibited until opposing experts achieve some basic consensus?

The obvious answer is that many other considerations besides the prospects of future damage are also taken into consideration by political leaders. Mr. Palmer, for example, would need either to go out of business, or be blessed with a hard-to-imagine solution. But, wait a minute, isn't requiring the key issue to be balanced against all the other interests, *in this kind of case*, like running into a burning building to hunt for your wallet? Acting as if the desired facts are true before the proof is in betokens a serious lapse in our communal logic. A lapse that leads some thinkers to argue that the current methods of society—for dealing with problems of monumental scope—are not up to the task.

An article, "The Real Cost of Energy," (Hubbard, 1991)

offered proposals that suffered a fate similar to that described above by Fialka. That is, they have not been implemented despite the fact that this scholarly article makes powerful points that a sensible reader should find persuasive. After drawing out many of the hidden costs (such as the expense of the Gulf War) to American taxpayers, he states, "In addition to the drag such buried costs place on the economy, they also distort the choices of both consumers and policy makers . . . ."

Among the considerations such choices must take into account are the costs of increased disease from the various types of pollution associated with fossil fuels, the cost of cleaning up spills and energy related accidents. "This question becomes even more difficult in the case of costs that are not easily quantified [as] not only building corrosion, toxic waste emissions and crop losses but also generation of greenhouse gases, destruction of natural habitats and loss of species diversity . . . and who should pay it?" (ibid.) Hubbard goes on to describe how scientists and economists quantify as many of these costs as current methods permit, and then he argues that many renewable energy processes come out as significantly cheaper when the full cost of fossil fuels are rationalized. He concludes, "the sooner that policy makers and citizens act prudently to internalize all the costs of energy (i.e. take them out of the public domain and tie them to specific "perpetrators") the better."[18]

Well, it is 11 years since that was published and have we seen policy makers and citizens act prudently? Why not? The answer seems clear: to act *prudently* would require nothing less than for all of us to begin to live a lifestyle so different from our present one that it boggles the mind how one would move over into it. Clearly, we are victims of ways of thinking the consequences of which have been brewing for generations. It doesn't seem likely that those same ways of thinking are capable of finding the way out.

Philip K. Howard (1995), focuses on illogicality, especially in the courts, in *The Death of Common Sense*. His argument deals mainly with the unintended, and often patently idiotic, consequences of mechanically enforcing rules, regulations and laws. Legalisms intended to leave no room for individual discretion by bureaucrats eventuate in outcomes that no sane person could want.[19] While it might seem a stretch to perceive disagreements such as those between messrs Brown and Palmer as similar failures of common sense, *if the issue is as critical as people like Lester Brown (1992, 1998) charge* this one is, it shows lack of common sense to act as if desired conditions are true, instead of first devoting all possible effort to find out whether, in fact, they are.[20]

Contemporary media are full of evidence in support of Howard's thesis. Popular docudramas like "60 Minutes" thrive on "ain't it awful"[21] scenarios—such as those of people having their property expropriated by outrageous interpretations of the RICO law, or of innocent persons imprisoned by narrow minded legalisms or downright unprincipled actions of prosecuting attorneys,[22] or conscientious public servants caught in the cross fire of mutually inconsistent laws, and on and on. The defensive-sounding litany, "(See) the system does work," is, itself, testimony to the suspicion of many of us that it frequently does not.[23]

If such illogicality in the face of overwhelming complexity accounts for the kinds of governmental failures that we see in approaches to chronic crises, a related category is that described by Garret Hardin (1987) as "The Tragedy of the Commons." Individuals bring about the destruction of a resource upon which all depend by acting to maximize their individual interests in it. In such cases individuals are acting with perfect logic for their private benefit but the result is the ultimate loss of the resource by everyone. Examples are battles over jobs versus ecosystems, overfishing, soil depletion, deforestation, personal convenience versus increasing garbage and pollution.

Another take on conflicts like that of Messrs Brown and Palmer is that of Hauser (1991) in Jacques Cousteau's Calypso Log[24] report on Population and Environment. It describes a situation typical of just about every effort to reverse just about any type of destructive human practice. "Commercial fishermen, asked to cut back on their catches often point to evidence of pollution with despair and ask why their livelihoods are being attacked instead of these problems." We hear similar complaints from lumberjacks, farmers, miners, oil workers, to name a few.

Still another close-to-home, developing example of a "commons tragedy," is the rapid increase of sport-utility vehicles in affluent suburbs. People buy them mainly out of the desire for personal safety on the increasingly crowded highways. In doing so they violate a common aim of reducing fuel consumption and vehicular pollution, a value that a majority of the same people hold—in principle. In the long run the accumulation of individual choices for "safer vehicles" may even turn out to be self-defeating anyway. As more and more people move to SUV's, there will be more crashes between larger and heavier vehicles, which many people currently tend to drive even faster, possibly because of the perception of enhanced security. We all—in affluent societies—live in a sea of such inconsistencies.

A further category of seemingly insoluble social issues are consequences that occur as unintended by-products of our fundamental values like private property, personal liberty and individual responsibility. Take "homelessness." It is a feature of our particular economic and social system. It is not found in so-called primitive societies, migratory societies, nor ordinarily in socialist societies like those of Scandinavia. (I wish I knew whether it was a problem in the former Soviet Union, but I don't.) It first became a noticeable problem in the U. S. during the great depression. It was easier to understand as large numbers of people were out of work.

Even so, the impression was that it involved mainly jobless men—hoboes. More people lived on farms or in small towns where garden plots could at least provide a minimum subsistence and even small communities managed to allow families to live in their homes after they lost the income to maintain them.[25] Today things are very different. A much larger portion of the population lives in large cities where basic needs can no longer be met by individual initiatives like maintaining your own garden. Individual initiatives of those at the lowest economic levels in large cities take the form of petty theft, begging, crime and welfare, all anti-social solutions.

Momentarily the current reform of welfare appears to be succeeding modestly, in large part attributable to recent gains in many types of low level employment. But, it is an act of faith that the problem will remain under control should the recent surge of unemployment continue. See discussions like, Homeless Families, (Bassuk, 1991); The White Underclass, (Whitman et al., 1994.)[26]

In what way do problems of joblessness and welfare derive as by-products of such positive values as private property, individualism and personal responsibility? The argument that advocates of shrinking government make is that people solve problems best when not made dependent by un-earned benefits and when freed of the kind of hobbling regulations discussed above. However, what happens when individuals with opposing interests have greatly disproportional wealth (and consequent political power) to implement their intentions? Consider the point as seen by liberal columnist Molly Ivins (1996), "The Issue That Dare Not Speak Its Name, to wit, the astonishing and continuing redistribution of wealth in this country, has disappeared from the campaign radar . . . 80 percent of American workers have flat or falling wages, while the richest 1 percent have amassed more wealth than the bottom ninety . . . I suspect the reason the pols are ignoring [this issue] is that none of them has any idea what to do about it." Since she wrote that the problem has only magnified.

As long as most individuals own their own homes and have an income that meets their average level of expectations it seems that we all have the same rights as regarding owning property and freedom to act for our own interests. But, the main avenue of escape from poverty—the pioneer movement, "free" land (ask any indigenous American about that!) being dependent only upon one's own hard work and personal initiative—closed around the turn of the last century. Then began the slow process to which Ivins refers, and which has only begun to loom on the horizon as a serious danger, and then mainly noticed just by liberals like Ivins. Imagine what it would be like if it continued unchecked until every last homeowner in the country found him/herself bidding against some ultra-millionaire for his own home.

Too fantastic to waste time thinking about? About 10 years ago I stopped in for a cup of coffee in downtown Santa Fe, New Mexico, and found myself talking with some angry long term residents about the fact that they saw themselves being evicted from their property—not by any illegal process, but simply because wealthy outsiders had begun paying exorbitant prices for every piece of downtown area they could lay hands upon. The resulting skyrocketing of real estate prices and taxes made it too expensive for those with modest incomes to continue living there. True, a current property owner might stand to make a good profit on selling. But, what if you didn't want to sell, because you felt you had roots there?—too bad. Further, you might not even get to enjoy much of your profit, if it were already mortgaged to pay the huge increases in taxes which had already occurred before you got around to selling. Since that time I have noted that similar things have begun happening in a few other places around the country, such as along the offshore islands on the southeast coast. A few of the displaced persons from such invasions have taken their profits and established themselves in business somewhere else. Apparently many more have sunk into poverty, lacking business skills or as a result of swindles.

We tend to write off misfortunes like these as unfortunate, isolated events resulting from peculiar local conditions, but the fact is we don't know what might prevent the gradual spread of economic domination of the many by the few without a radical restructuring of our values. And that, in turn, we would oppose. Most suggestions for such restructuring would violate our fundamental values of private property, personal freedom, and individual responsibility. I think this is the more profound issue underlying Ivins' remark, "none of them has any idea of what to do about it." Furthermore, we have good reason to be shy of some of the proffered solutions after witnessing Josef Stalin's colossal disaster based upon Lenin's mistaken conception of the nature of human nature.

But we pay a price for each moment of delay in confronting the dark side of our cherished values. Think about our increasing national frustration with our inability to make headway against various types of crime. On any day we could select news reports at random, such as this from a *60 Minutes* (December 19, 1993) story about how in Washington, D. C. jails were releasing criminals to half-way houses, because of over-crowding, and although only non-violent criminals are supposed to be sent to half-way houses, 25% at least have been convicted of violent crimes. Once there many simply walked away and were only apprehended after committing another crime, often more violent than the first. The TV program essentially suggested that the bureaucrat-administrator of this program was incompetent.

What struck me about it, however, is that it is still another demonstration of the way our society has become stuck in regard to solving such problems. I suspect that the administrator of this program was doing what he perceived as his duties, and was so busy doing them as to be oblivious to the fact that the most important considerations were being neglected. His defense (that he was forbidden by law to notify the police when his prisoners defected) was another example of the common case of an executive "going by the book," because individual discretion and common sense had been ruled out by some legalistic fine print.[27]

I have so many more clippings in the file for this chapter that it is hard to select those reflecting more basic themes from those that simply reiterate the point. I fear that I may have already pounded the theme into the ground, but let me simply list a few more headlines, as reminders of articles that you see pouring out from the media in a constant stream: "Is prison problem really solvable?" (R. Simon, 1975), pointing out the rapid increase in prison population—something that has only accelerated in the years since that was written; "Career criminals and temporary law-breakers may cross paths as teenagers," (Bower, 1993) reports a New Zealand research project on the paths to career criminality from early childhood, arguing that combinations of genetic, perinatal, and family social influences leave those least able to gain personal satisfactions through conventional means to the intellectually simpler resort to violence; "Social toxicity undermines youngsters in inner cities," (Martin and Murray, 1996), "Urban children who have little interaction with adults grow up thinking that violence and drug abuse are the norm, according to speakers" at American Psychological Association's 1996 annual convention; "Drug Abuse 1975: The "War" is Past, The Problem Is as Big as Ever," (Holden, 1975), enough said on that score, it is even worse in 2002.

What are the processes that keep these problems unsolvable? There is growing evidence that crime and unethical behavior is often rewarded rather than punished, not directly, of course, but as a by-product of some other desired goal. A newspaper article by James Warren (1996) describes Ed Rollins, "a political operative who, by his own admission lied in claiming he paid off black New Jersey clergy to keep the vote down when his candidate, Christine Todd Whitman, ran successfully for governor in 1993.... [published a book] 'Bare Knuckles and Back Rooms,' [which trashed many of his ex-clients]"... Having assured a New York publisher that he would violate a lot of confidences, he got an advance of slightly more than $1 million.... *Rather than ostracized, Rollins is embraced*.... He bemoaned 'the pollution' and 'the distortion' marking politics, the lack of talk about issues. 'We all suffer as a nation,' he said." (Italics mine, RJR.)

Furthermore, consider that there are now so many people who owe their living to crime—the criminals themselves, manufacturers of all sorts of security devices and weapons, police, private guard companies—all of whom would have their livelihoods jeopardized by a drastic reduction in crime. Our ethical mores do not permit acknowledging this fact openly. Nevertheless, an understanding of the way that abstract principles/values operate suggests that, without any awareness on their own parts, people whose livelihood would suffer from a decrease in crime could at times inadvertently act in ways that would help to perpetuate existing levels of crime.

One might wonder, along with Warren, why have so many people recently received book and movie contracts and invitations to highly paid speaking engagements after committing crimes and/or becoming notorious? Maybe the first ones in this trend were sought out by movie makers because their stories would fit the same mold of shocking, brutal, violent and sexy movies that the public seems to want on TV and in movie houses. Besides that, the curiosity of the more intellectual might include looking for clues as to how to make this kind of money. The one clear answer that is supplied by the market is: it sells. *Why* that is, is, or should be, a major research topic itself. I wonder if it indicates a general craving for excitement and stimulation? That is what it was when a teenage psychotherapy client of mine slashed her wrists, "to feel something." Is it a reaction to the deadening of feelings in an increasingly other-directed and de-sensitized population?

Or consider, *A Civil Action*, (Harr, 1995), about the lawsuit against W. R. Grace Co. and Beatrice Foods, by parents and victims of toxic wastes traced to the company. Claimed as a true account based upon direct observation, interviews and examination of depositions and notes of all the parties involved, the story draws a picture of a seeming colossal miscarriage of justice. The presiding judge comes across as either hopelessly incompetent or criminally corrupt. There is another view, however.

A sociological theory of the apparent misfeasance of the judge would be that he—being a former classmate of the leading defence attorney, and seemingly enthralled by the fact that that person was on the Harvard faculty—was predisposed to see the "logic" of his peer's arguments. Add the fact that the defence were powerful establishment corporations and the lead defence attorney was a well-known establishment representative.[28] In this context the judge, after making a small procedural error, appeared to go on bolstering the position forced by that error in a widening tide of selective perceptions and interpretations.[29]

I would speculate further that the judge, as a member of the establishment, was unconsciously guarding the establishment against what might have appeared to him as incipient anarchy. All kinds of liability cases could follow from a finding that companies with toxic waste on their property would be liable for possible harm that someone might suffer as a result of contact with it. (Note that that development has culminated anyway in recent years.) At the beginning of the trial it seemed apparent that the main defendants—if they were guilty at all—had not *intentionally* set out to harm anyone. All they were trying to do was minimize their expenses for the benefit of their stockholders and employees. All of this would be part of the "background" noise in the judge's awareness just like it would be for many of the rest of us.

A psychological theory of the judge's actions is not in contradiction to the above. Begin by conjecturing that the judge conceived of himself as a no-nonsense adherent of the letter of the law. Add the fact reported by Harr that cases of the type were new and rare and that, at the beginning of the trial, there was not yet any strong medical evidence of the disease-causing power of the toxins at issue. One can imagine, then, that the judge's conception of himself and his role might have begun with the intention of not letting a vague and questionable case overflow its boundaries. Thus, he would be alert to representations of fact that appeared to have weak foundations, especially if they also appeared to threaten to enlarge the issues into uncharted territory. This would call for a strategy of pouncing upon and uprooting such moves before they became unwieldy. That would lead the judge to experience a state of errors whenever facts began to unfold that might interfere with his existing view of the case.

At this point the judge's behavior would be in the same class as that of a number of district attorneys who have been featured in news reports as having closed minds when new facts came out in certain cases. The common inference in such cases is that they have staked their reputations and careers upon a given view, and thus perceived the threat of serious personal damage, if that view were negated.[30] If the judge determined early on not to let the boundaries of this case expand beyond what he initially considered the solid questions at issue, he would not have noticed it begin to develop more complexity than anyone could have foreseen. He would have perceived it differently. He would have perceived it as just what he was determined not to allow. The end result was possibly that—by defending certain abstract principles that most of us might support—the judge failed to perceive the deeper issue of common justice that we can see so clearly with hindsight.

The "closed mind" is not always a broad scale personality trait. A person can be ever so generous, open-minded, tolerant etc., in regard to many things and still be unable to perceive any inconsistency between his view of some aspect of reality and facts which thousands of other people might regard as irrefutable. One example would be the conflict between fundamental Christians and most other educated people about the theory of evolution. (Kuhn, 1970, is full of illustrations of this sort.)

Finally, Harr's book raises the question again as to whether "the system works," as lawyers are so fond of saying. Consider Charles Nisson, the Harvard law professor reported by Harr (1995)[31], "I used to believe in the idea that justice would prevail if you worked hard enough at it, . . . I thought if judges saw cheating right in front of them, they'd do something about it. The Woburn case gave me a depressing dose of reality." If my analysis is on the right track, the judge in the Woburn case didn't *see* any cheating going on in front of him, for the reasons I stated.

From a common-sense point of view, the intricate arguments about whether toxic wastes harm people and where they came from in this case, are much simpler than made in the trial. "The water smells and tastes bad." That was the first sign. To human beings exercising common-sense that should be enough. People should not drink water that smells and tastes bad. That is what we have sense organs for. However, these particular people owned homes from which they could not afford simply to walk away. They should then have drunk only bottled water. But, as later turned out, they were breathing toxic vapors whenever they took a shower.

This shows up the weakness of the argument that—if everyone would just be responsible for himself—things would get worked out. Part of being poor is that your ability to take care of yourself is often severely limited. The purpose of community is that people acting together can control their environment in ways that so many people acting alone can not do. The common sense of the community of Woburn was, however, overrun by a larger society in which people who did not have to drink, or shower in, Woburn water were arrogating to themselves the decisions about what the plaintiffs should be doing. In principle, yes: if they didn't like it, they should have moved. But, this principle often can not easily be followed in fact. It should not be permitted to be used as a justification for anything where it can not be implemented in fact.

The point that I have been trying to make through all the above arguments and examples is that I think there is credence in the alarms of those who charge that—as a civilization—we are failing to come up with solutions to environmental, political, and social problems on a vast enough scale or at a pace commensurate with the spread of the problems. Robert Kaplan (1996) put it this way after his tour of countries in Africa and Central Asia.

> The human race is like an awkward adolescent whose political and social mechanisms are not keeping up with his physical growth . . . many of the problems I saw around the world—poverty, the collapse of cities, porous borders, cultural and racial strife . . . are problems for Americans . . . . We can not escape from a more populous, interconnected world of crumbling borders.
>
> But I would be unfaithful to my experience if I thought we had a general solution to these problems. We are not in control.[32]

That is one take on the situation. Another comes (again) from Lester Brown, this time in an article on the way that current agricultural methods are keeping the world fed by exhausting the soil and water supplies on which agriculture depends. Updating his statistics on environmental degradation as he expects it to affect future food supplies world wide, he concludes, "if political leaders do manage to secure food supplies for the next generation, it will be because they have moved the world economy off the current path of environmental deterioration and eventual economic disruption and onto an economic and demographic path that is environmentally sustainable."[33]

What is the likelihood that they will do this? That takes us around in a circle to the issue with which we began this chapter. Don't we read over and over in our papers that year after year our government only creeps ahead, or even more often, remains deadlocked, on the major issues? One view as to why this might be increasingly the fact was offered back in 1970 by French sociologist Michael Crozier in *The Stalled Society*. His analysis deals with French society, but he states in his introduction,

> French society is not the only stalled society. Blockages seem to be an essential characteristic of modern advanced societies [because] the social tissue of each country is becoming more and more complex . . . societies are forced to look for new forms of government and administration. A slow, obscure process of social experimentation is taking place, but this alone cannot change the main forms of social regulation . . . . Even in day-to-day transactions, people are trapped in vicious circles; whatever their intentions, the logic of the system distorts their activities and forces them to collaborate in preserving the model . . . ."[34]

In a later section his comments aptly describe our present day paralysis over reforms that supposedly were "mandated by the public" in the election turnover of 1994, things such as term limits, election reform and retirement of the national debt—all things that legislators have been charged with abandoning once they were elected on promises of reforming.

> . . . a society can progress only so far as it is capable of inventing new styles of action that let it exploit the opportunities offered by general technological and economic developments . . . its success depends upon its members' ability to cooperate effectively . . . and preserve more complex organizations that will not be paralyzed by their own weight . . . .[35]

Compare Crozier's thesis from 1970 with this view by Jonathan Rauch in the Wall Street Journal in April of 1998,

> . . . a group of graybeards was discussing the reasons the revolution [of the 104th congress] had failed. For it certainly has failed . . . . When widely different reform efforts all end in defeat one begins to wonder if there is a deeper explanation than just faintness of heart, bad timing or the wrong party controlling this or that branch of the government . . . . The American government probably has evolved into about what it will remain: a sprawling, largely self-organizing structure that is 10% to 20% under the control of the politicians and voters and 80% to 90% under the control of the countless thousands of client groups.

Rauch, referring to his own 1994 book, *Demosclerosis*, argued that lobbies have come to be self-perpetuating enclaves with claims upon some portion of public funds that care more about keeping their own little piece of the pie than anyone else cares about taking it away (given the enormous cost in terms of fighting the "red alert mailings and apocalyptic TV ads" that they muster to preserve themselves). His analysis lays the blockage to problem solving in our government at a (somewhat) different door than those Crozier finds in France, but the basic mechanisms of the blockage are essentially the same.

So far it seems that the new styles of action that Crozier sees as needed are being found in multi-national corporations[36] much more than in government. That puts these corporations more nearly in competition with national governments than contributors to them, however. For example, see Davidson and Rees-Mogg (1993, 1997) who argue that civilization as a whole is undergoing a massive reorganization of the fundamental nature of power as a result of the technological revolution. Accompanying (or resulting from) this revolution they see an equally fundamental change in how people think— I would call it a paradigm revolution—about such things as nationality, patriotism, self-sacrifice and the value of governments.

If a significant number of the most powerful members of society have lost faith in the functionality of present arrangements of governance, what shall we make of the loss of faith by members at the other end of the status structure? What of the confusion of language whereby indigenous terrorists come to be called "patriot groups,"? A US NEWS (4/21/97) article, "Mainstreaming the Militia,"[37] maintains,

> Since the bombing in Oklahoma City two years ago, the popularity of militia-style groups has increased—and a vibrant industry has developed that sustains and fuels the anti-government rage.... In 1994 John Trochmann preached his militia gospel to a few hundred angry souls.... These days [he] is a

celebrity. In recent weeks the self-styled 'educational entrepreneur' has traveled to 'Preparedness Expos' [etc] in Cal., Nev., CO., and Tx . . . Since the bombing many antigovernment groups have shed their subculture status and begun attracting support from a broader range of economically struggling Americans. . . . Experts say all 50 states now harbor organized antigovernment groups. . . . These figures don't even include secessionist campaigns. . . . In part, the groups are finding a receptive audience because of the same economic challenges that confront many other Americans. . . . Terry Nichols, indicted for helping to plan the OK bombing, started his patriot career by becoming involved in groups that helped farmers hold on to their land by fighting the government and banks. . . . Part of the reason these groups seem to be gaining ground is that there are plenty of Americans who deeply distrust all forms of state power, especially the federal government. A US NEWS poll showed that 71% of men without a college education agreed that, "the US government interferes too much in people's lives.[38]

Finally, returning once more to the 1970's to pick up the thread, "Why nothing seems to work anymore," let us attempt to see where it stands today. Time Magazine carried a feature article under this title, subtitled, America the Inefficient, (March 23, 1970). The writer first lists various snafus, such as getting phone bills for calls one has not made, repairmen who fail to get the job done, then disappear, construction projects that suffer humongous cost overruns because of failure to resolve conflicting parts of the overall design before moving ahead with the work, etc. Then, moving on to government, the writer says, "followers of the Protestant Ethic who are more interested in getting work done than in obeying the rules are looked on as 'sort of scabs.'" These complaints are just as familiar, if not worse, today.

A book of the same title as the Time article, by Richard N. Farmer, 1977, argued that part of the perception of nothing working right anymore is a rising tide of expectations resulting from the tremendous advances in technology since WW II. "We also know, thanks to modern communications, what is right and good and best in any situation. We assume that if one child can read well, this becomes the norm for all children.... Our expectations really move us toward the perfect, not the average." As a consequence of such ideals, he maintained, we Americans began to demand much more from government. The process that ensued began to bring about conditions in which many things really don't work right anymore for several reasons.

First, many laws that were passed to remedy one problem or another were not examined beforehand to detect unanticipated consequences or conflicts with the aims of other laws and regulations. He continues, "Every organization has some concepts of goals and objectives.... But in this simple statement lies the seed of the major problems facing modern large organizations and their managers... A small... firm has to survive, and to survive it has to make a profit... But when a really large, multibillion-dollar company tries to do the same thing, we all get suspicious and start talking about rapacious capitalism, greed and man's inhumanity to man... [when they start] thinking about... creating more human happiness, financing educational programs, and getting ghetto dwellers out of poverty, managers run into potential goal conflicts." The specific consequences in twisting, avoiding or mindlessly heeding the law often defy common sense along the lines of points made by Howard (1995) in, *The Death of Common Sense*.

Second, Farmer argued that there has been a tendency in congress to pass "feel good" legislation aimed at high ideals but without any provision for enforcement, giving rise to a sense of frustration, suspicions of corruption and scandal among the advocates of the special interest involved. "It is surprising how many Americans believe that control costs are zero.... Our courts and jails are already overcrowded, and if anyone seriously tried to enforce even one tenth of the laws... virtually everyone would be in jail. A by-product of this neocontrol activity is increasing contempt for the law.... We are... moving into an era in which our government is for all practical purposes telling us to cheat if we want to win." (ibid.) I would say we are now well into that era.

Third, where there was continuing pressure for enforcement of these laws the cost of enforcement agencies added a serious toll on the national budget—along with the legal costs to the government of defending court challenges to the constitutionality of the laws involved. Once an agency is installed it tends to become self-perpetuating, adding an additional source of expense as well as further complexity in the administration of the country.

Viewing the situation from the focus of an economic historian Farmer described many examples of what he considers real failures at problem solving. One of the culprits he perceives is the tendency of people to view competition always in terms of zero-sum games in which either both parties will be frustrated or brutal force, of the sort that violates our civilized sensibilities, will be needed for a resolution. From the perspective of the present I believe that his observation is relevant also to understanding the increasing vehemence, intemperance, incivility and polarization of advocacy that has characterized politics and partisanship in recent decades. If you have the attitude that every gain by your opponents is your loss the pressure mounts to use increasingly forceful means to obtain your ends. The final step leads to the kind of outcome that finds pro-life advocates killing people.

It is interesting to look at the forecasts that Farmer makes implicitly and explicitly, writing in the late 1970's, from the vantage point of the late 90's. Where he saw both inflation and unemployment increasing dramatically, we now have low inflation and high employment. Nevertheless, we still find the same underlying weaknesses in our ways of attacking large-scale problems such as he described. We have not been able to get together as a nation, or in the community of nations, to address the population explosion. Experts are still debating whether it really is a problem, or what to do about it, if it is. So, it is being addressed by default—by nature if you will. In various places like central Africa people are starving. Shipments of food by the UN, governments like ours or private charities sometimes rot on the docks or are swallowed up by local criminals or tyrants without much benefit to the victims. Then some media people reveal the mismanagement, new regulations are drafted and the problem sometimes begins to get resolved for a brief period. But in the meantime people have died and/or fled to other places, adding refugee turmoil and disorganization to some new location.

It is the same with crime and violence. Local improvements, such as are reported in large U. S. cities currently, are balanced by serious outbreaks in other places. The so-called drug war has not seen any real change in decades. The contempt for the law and government that Farmer foresaw two decades ago has grown apace. Gains in environmental protection have been overbalanced by an increasing pace of degradation in other places. A quote from Adam Smith, (1981) seems appropriate, "If times have been so good, why do we feel so bad?"

Chapter 04

CONJECTURES ABOUT CAUSES

There is a picture that has haunted my memory over twenty or thirty years. I can't remember just when or where I saw it. In the foreground are a few huts made of stone. The dwellers had not quarried the stone from the earth. Behind the huts you could see, still standing, the magnificent pillars of a departed civilization from which the building materials for the huts were being hewn. That picture, worth the proverbial thousand words, has stayed with me over the years, contributing to the personal sense of apprehension culminating in the writing of this book.

This picture symbolizes what various critics of contemporary society see as the general degradation of Western Civilization. If the growth of our society's problems is truly outrunning the development of solutions, as reviewed in chapter three, it becomes imperative to understand why this is, as part of taking a stand on doing something about it.

Enough people must be worried about it that movie makers have found it profitable to produce movies, like The Postman, that depict roving bands of post-citizen savages, armed with modern weapons, but living on the edge of starvation, in the territory of the former United States. Are these movies in any sense prescient? When contemplating this scary scenario, however implausible it seems right now, one wonders, Are we lacking energy to solve problems, or have we become complacent in living with deteriorating conditions? We find proponents of both positions among the critics of contemporary life. For an example of the view that we are running out of steam, John Lukacs (1970) in, *The Passing of the Modern Age*, has this to say, "In 1903 most people were optimistic; they greeted man's self-made liberation from the laws of gravity on earth... and virtually all of the American people, thought that their civilization was triumphant. In 1969 many people, including many Americans, felt that their civilization was collapsing."[39] Or, again, "... Our civilization is in ruins because our beliefs about civilization are in ruins. We are far more beset by self-doubt than were our ancestors two or three hundred years ago. It is this self-doubt that has produced the end of empires...."[40]

Farmer (1977), in, *Why Nothing Seems to Work Anymore*, argued the other view, as noted in chapter three. His argument is that we suffer both from "a rising tide of expectations," and a new historical attitude that perfection can and is to be attained, that has resulted in tolerating a gradual disarray of problem-solving efforts as governments try to satisfy too many contradictory goals with laws and regulations that are inconsistent, self-defeating or unenforceable.

Then there are the confirmed optimists such as Julian Simon (1995a, 1995b). He envisions continual growth of wealth and prosperity world wide. While admitting to the occurrence of various temporary problems in the environment and in social conditions, his contention is that humans have always solved problems like them in the past—that the key to solutions is to liberate creative individuals to produce them and to maintain the correlation between innovation and individual rewards.

In examining these views my position is not to try for an impartial, "objective," academic analysis, aimed at concluding whose ideas are most "right," but to try to advance the integration of analysis with personal actions. As I have stated above, and will hold throughout this book, we do, as private citizens, act in our daily lives according to what we currently believe to be true and in keeping with what we consider our best interests. Our actions contain/embody our beliefs about the facts, even when we have reservations and might be convinced of a new view of the facts tomorrow. Thus, the authors I cite should be taken as examples from the marketplace of viewpoints competing to influence the thinking of those of us who concern ourselves with questions of where we are heading as a culture and civilization.

It is this combination of the acts of us billions of ordinary people on earth that constitutes the wave of the future to a degree far beyond the policies of all governments, advocate groups, movements and parties. And, in fact, that is what the policies of governments and the courses of advocacy ultimately come down to. As Richard Farmer and Julian Simon, at least, have acknowledged, scientific studies, statistical analyses and expert opinions—though they exert influence gradually—are powerless, no matter how profound, to influence individual opinions and actions, if they conflict with what the mass of people believe in the moment. The statistics and scientific arguments that make sense to us are those that confirm what we perceive on the streets, in the media, in conversation with our intimates.[41]

So, the question of whether or not Western Civilization is in decline becomes personal for each of us not only as an intellectual exercise but in terms of what difference, if any, it makes to oneself. I have already touched briefly upon those merchants of advice who see the U. S. in decline, or in a state of degeneration, which is tantamount to the same thing for many of them. Some propose moving to someplace else to preserve one's fortune or protect one's living conditions. But, if we think Western Civilization is, itself, going down the tubes, does that lead you to want to migrate to whatever second-, or third-world locale in which you think the new dominant culture will arise? Or better yet, pour as many resources as you can into a colony on Mars with like-minded settlers, hoping to leave the insoluble problems behind, as did the Puritans in 1620? Keeping these questions in mind let us look further at some of the writers who treat these issues.

Decline of the West?

So, if Western Civilization *is* in decline what exactly does that mean for ordinary people? What difference does it make in our individual lives? Then the question follows: Should the decline of Western Civilization (if a fact) be opposed to enable the development of remedies for the degradation of earth, or should it be hastened because other cultures promise to provide better solutions? These questions impinge forcefully on the debate currently going on as to whether the United States should be taking on the role of "world policeman," or dominant world political force.

We have, usually reluctantly, functioned as the instigator and chief implementer of U. N. actions to quell aggressive invasions in Kuwait, the former Jugoslavia, and civil wars in various countries around the world, and, sometimes to lead in environmental policy. More recently the previous president of the United States has stepped in to lend his authority to promote economic reforms during the crises in Asia. The current president has unilaterally taken the initiative, after 9/11, to rework a sovereign nation, albeit with modest international help. These actions have not met with wholehearted support in the United States. Some of the opposition centers on the fear that the job is too big for the U. S. Some believe that Western dominance in world affairs, underpinned by the U. S., is no longer sustainable. It might not be for want of resources, but for a lack of sharing any common value enough to commit ourselves to, as did our founding fathers in 1776. In other words, we just can't get it together.

That view seems inherent in Robert Phelps' (1965) anthology, *Twentieth-Century Culture, The Breaking Up*. It is informed by a thesis that, "Since 1900 individuals have been conscious of the passing of community." From my personal vantage point as a psychotherapist I see an underlying cause of the break-up of many marriages in the inability of the individuals involved to create community. It is typical of the thinking of many people nowadays that you must find someone who is compatible with you whereas what we discover as therapists is that many people seemingly do not have the concept that you *create* compatibility with another in the process of creating community with them. Not having the concept they have never learned the necessary skills involved.

Phelps offers other (but not incompatible) explanations about a connection between culture decline and the loss of community as he pursues his argument further,

> if we presuppose anything that our fathers did not presuppose before us, it is that every man is aware, in some unprecedented sense, of being alone. Movements, trends, groups, masses continue to flourish in our midst. We meet, march, join, and tell ourselves that we belong. But it is the loners who speak for what distinguishes our lives from those of prior centuries and the cultures of the past . . . what is happening in these decades which has not happened before . . . is the inside stories which our culture will record, and by which we shall be judged as a century in noisy decline, or baffled transition, or secret rebirth. And of these stories, there are at least three which are plain by now, which are interrelated and even overlap . . . . Since 1900—give or take a decade—

individuals have been conscious of the passing of community . . . which happened slowly but persistently, on every social and economic level, and in every form of community from the family and the church congregation to the city and the nation. The forms themselves did not vanish. Many appear to go on functioning as solidly as ever. But now they are under siege . . . .[42]

About this same time, in the earliest decades after 1900, we find a radical change transpiring in the arts . . . . Once upon a time, a poet thought of himself as an accessory to his community . . . the purpose was to please . . . .

Then for a brief time, in the nineteenth century, artists thought of themselves as pariahs . . . by 1910, and increasingly since, they have come to think of themselves as personal witnesses, bringers of revelations, self-ordained priests . . . .

"Aloneness is man's real condition," said Auden . . . And shrewd, theatrical, enigmatic Yeats . . . said: "Man can embody truth, but he cannot know it."

But that same year, 1939, an American [Agee] and little-known as Yeats was old and Irish and famous, was writing a book in which he said just the opposite: "I believe . . . that the discovery and use of 'consciousness,' which has always been and is our deadliest enemy and deceiver, is also the source and guide of all hope and cure, and the only one." Agee's [view] is presupposed in Yeats'. Indeed, it has been the rock assumption of our whole Western Civilization, ever since Socrates first said the unexamined life was not worth living. For we are conscious, are self conscious, if nothing else.

Compare this view of Phelps's—given via his interpretations of Yeats and Agee, with the hopeful conclusion of Krippner et al.'s story of the demise of Easter Island mentioned in chapter one, "But there is a crucial difference between us today and the ill-fated Easter Islanders: They had no books or histories of other doomed societies... and this information can save us." Ask yourself whether we are not glimpsing here a basic paradigm—a fundamental assumption about one of the purposes of life that Western Civilization incorporated and transformed in its exhumation of Classical Civilization during the late middle ages. From Descartes to Galileo the urge to know oneself—the examination of one's life—broadened to the curiosity to understand nature. For Descartes' great contribution was to argue that man is a part of nature (never mind that he separated out a portion as the supernatural soul, differentiating spiritual from material in keeping with the view of the church). That, in turn, resulted in the difference that Krippner et al. believe will make the crucial difference between modern society and the prior, self-unconscious, and hence, at-the-mercy-of-fate earlier cultures symbolized by Easter Island.

Accepting (for the moment) self-consciousness as a principle of Western Civilization, can it be grounds upon which we can get together to take concerted action when we (the world) need it, or is it bringing about ever increasing personal isolation and loss of any hope of consensus about the vital issues that we looked at in chapters two and three? Or, in fact, is it undergoing a paradigm revolution? Witness Richard Weaver's (1948) *Ideas Have Consequences*, and the works of Nietzsche(1883/1960;1901/1968), Ortega (1949), Bloom (1987), Bork (1996), Davidson and Rees-Mogg (1997), among others, as illustrating that thesis. As I see it, they say, Yes, Western Civilization—culminating in the United States—is coming apart at the seams. After that they diverge as to whether they find that good or bad.

Nietzsche seemed to welcome the advent of the active, self-unconscious man. His vision would seem to be, O K let civilization come unraveled; it will provide fertile ground for developing a civilization more true to the real nature of human nature. Ortega and Bloom, on the other hand, disparaged the entrance on to the human scene of the totally narcissistic individual that seems to be the present-day realization of Nietzsche's "superman." Bork agreed with the others that there has been degradation of our moral, legal and political thinking and devotes himself to fingering the guilty.[43] Finally Davidson and Rees-Mogg bring the argument full circle in true Hegelian style, finding a synthesis for the man of action with the expert in superknowledge that is made possible by the computer.

Lukacs' (1970) view, cited above, illustrating the notion that ideas have consequences[44], draws the implication that self-doubt is the agency of dissolution. A major source of self-doubt is an "awareness of complexity or ambiguity." Early in the development of a new political paradigm it is easy to be dogmatic and hold a belief in the inevitability of your insight. Later on, people become aware of the flaws, and begin to lose their sense of sureness, of the rightness of the ideals to which they are committed. He continues with a line of thought that will take on more substance when I discuss Spengler below,

> Most of the technical inventions of the twentieth century were predictable; they were the applications of ideas that existed at least one hundred years before . . . . go to a large library and look up certain European picture books of nearly a century ago—those, for example, that were written and drawn by Robida; they are all there, the pictures of skyscrapers, helicopters, elevated and underground railways, masses of people crowding brilliantly lit buildings and avenues at night . . . . What they did not see was

> the state of minds and hearts of millions of well-fed and well-clothed men and women in these air-heated and air-cooled rooms. They could not imagine how in the greatest city of the Western world millions would be living next to each other as entire strangers...."[45]

He documents this point with a description of the deplorable moral, physical and emotional condition of megalopolities like New York city. (Today one might prefer to cite Mexico city.)

And again,

> another condition that our ancestors could not foresee: that the end of our civilization is arriving with both a bang and a whimper... and we cannot speak of the waning twilight of our civilization. There is... a strange and perhaps unprecedented mixture... of the old and the new, perhaps even of good and bad. Already richness and poverty, elegance and sleaziness, sophistication and savagery live together more and more; They are next to each other not merely in the same streets but in the same minds[46].... With the democratization of war, and of violence, the symptoms of a new kind of savage life have appeared, not only on the frontiers of the Great Powers but in the hearts of their cities themselves[47]... we may be facing the coexistence of perpetual war with perpetual peace, a nomadic guerrilla existence symptomatic of the new Dark Ages, against which all of the fantastic rockets and bombs in the secret arsenals of the Superpowers will amount to nothing.... The state... is less potent than it was a hundred years ago, even as its bureaucratic intervention in the daily lives of its people is greater than ever before.

How prescient this seems thirty years later.

In his final chapter, The Consciousness of the Past, Lukacs stresses that the one most central feature of the evolution of Western culture has been the development of widened consciousness, as a result of increased ability to be interested in and recall the past and that this has led to, or has been associated with, increased self-consciousness or interiority. One gets the impression that—after frightening us thoroughly—he holds out a smidgeon of hope, along the lines of Krippner et al.'s conclusion.

Bloom (1987) and Bork (1996), writing in the two decades after Lukacs, see that self-consciousness degenerating into hedonistic narcissism. They find a loss of interest in, or reverence for, the past, and in fact an enthusiastic discard of standards in general. Though they overtly confine themselves to the narrower topics of degradation of scholarship and political principles in U. S. society, their analyses can be read to apply to the larger picture for which they have implications.[48] Namely, that intellectual laziness and indifference to quality will have serious cultural consequences down the road. One could also see their writings as documentation of the trends Lukacs (1970) was indicating, as when he talked about, "the re-emergence of savagery . . . the purposelessness of society, the fiction of prosperity, the dissolution of learning, the meaninglessness of letters, the senselessness of the arts, the destruction of nature, the decay of science, the faithlessness of religion, the mutation of morality."

Still another warning of impending decline comes from former National Security Advisor Zygmund Brzezinski. In his introduction to *Out of Control* (1993) he declares,

> My concern that global change is out of control [is that] . . . it is not possible to deal with modern global politics, . . . without taking into account the

> consequences not only of enhanced human capabilities but also of changes in the dominant content of the human spirit... our ability to understand the wider ramifications of the present... is impeded by the massive collapse, especially in the advanced parts of the world, of almost all established values... The question arises whether a global power [the U.S.] that is not guided by a globally relevant set of values can for long exercise that predominance.

Brzezinski argues that, as the leader of the western world, we in the U.S. need to "strike a balance between social need and personal gratification, global poverty and national wealth, irresponsible alteration of the physical environment as well as even of the human being and the effort to preserve both nature's patrimony and the authenticity of human identity." We need this to maintain the authority of US power to prevent the world from descending out of control into political and economic chaos.

While Brzezinski is still talking about what we need to do to preserve our leadership (and hence, Western Civilization), Davidson and Rees-Mogg in *The Sovereign Individual* (1997) appear already to have resigned themselves to the collapse.

> A sense of disquiet about the future has begun to color the optimism so characteristic of Western societies for the past 250 years. People everywhere are hesitant and worried. You see it in their faces. Hear it in their conversation. See it reflected in polls and registered in the ballot box.... One person after another, each in his own way, senses that time is running out on a dying way of life. As the decade expires, a murderous century expires with it, and also a glorious millennium of human accomplishment.... We believe that the modern phase of Western civilization will end with it.

Davidson and Rees-Mogg are members of the upper class in the U. S. and Britain, respectively. Their motives, quite transparently, are to preserve their property, wealth and position in an epoch in which the valuing of social leveling has had considerable influence. Unlike so many other upper class members they are not fighting to hold back the tides of history. They mean to float on to a new era on them. Nevertheless, they attempt to take a detached, historical perspective as they perceive the decline of contemporary society. Their views correspond on many points with history-professor Lukacs' regardless of the differences one might expect on the basis of their respective self-interests. For example:

> (D&R) "In our view you are witnessing nothing less than the waning of the Modern Age. It is a development driven by a ruthless but hidden logic . . . . We say this . . . to emphasize that the stage of history now opening will be qualitatively different from that into which you were born . . . Governments have already lost much of their power to regulate and compel."[49]

> (Lukacs) "Toward the end of an age more and more people lose faith in their institutions: and finally they abandon their belief that these institutions might still be reformed from within . . . we live in a time when both the power and the authority of the modern state are diminishing . . . . The decline of both power and authority is now involved with the decline of credibility."

An author that Davidson and Rees-Mogg cite as drawing opposite conclusions from the same phenomena is Christopher Lasch (1995). In his book, *The Revolt of the Elites*, obviously a take-off on Ortega's *Revolt of the Masses*, Lasch laments the apparent abandonment of democracy by western elites. "Once it was the 'revolt of the masses' that was held to threaten social order and the civilizing traditions of Western culture. In our time, however, the chief threat seems to come from those at the top of the social hierarchy . . . ." (In other words, people like Davidson and Rees-Mogg.)

Lasch continues,

> Violence, crime, and general disorder almost invariably strike foreign visitors as the most salient features of American life . . . . A closer look reveals only less dramatic signs of the impending collapse of social order . . . . For native as well as foreign observers, the disinclination to subordinate self-interest to the general will comes uncomfortably close to capturing the essence of Americanism as the twentieth century approaches its end. Thanks to a misplaced clemency, hard-core criminals gain premature release from prison and resume their depredations seemingly undeterred by the prospect of reincarceration . . . the most disturbing symptom of all is the recruitment of children into the culture of crime . . . . Postponement of gratification, planning for the future, accumulation of educational credits mean nothing to these prematurely hardened children . . . at some point risk becomes its own reward, an alternative to the sheer hopelessness they would otherwise be left with . . . . If the collapse of internal constraints were confined to the criminal classes, it might be possible, by means of a combination of incentives and stricter enforcement . . . to restore a sense of obligation. But the culture of shamelessness is not confined to the underclass. In their desire for immediate gratification . . . their identification of gratification

>with material acquisition, the criminal classes merely imitate their betters.

This description well depicts what strikes me as a growing psychopathic strain throughout Western culture. During the 1960s when I was a research psychologist in the U. S. Veterans Administration part of my work had to do with describing a population of men who had become dependent upon the VA for their survival and subsequently (for the most part) never returned to independent living. An earlier investigation faulted lengthy treatment processes for weakening the motive for self-sufficiency of these people, but my research found a previously unknown or overlooked factor. Most of the men in my study had in fact never been very independent. They had on-the-average not served in the military long enough to make much of a difference to anything. A great many had quickly been moved out on medical discharges. The conclusion was that they were ineffective in any military capacity because they were ineffectual in life in general.

At about the same time I happened to read Cleckley's, *The Mask of Sanity*, which was an early study of the psychopathic-, later called sociopathic personality. (At that time I did not know that Wilhelm Reich had noted many of the same features even earlier.)[50] It seemed to me that there was a substantial overlap between Cleckley's subjects and my research patients. They were mainly of the nonviolent type, as compared with the violent types of psychopaths that dominate our picture of them in the media today, but in other respects they fit the bill: Lack of foresight, evasion of responsibility, apparent lack of empathy or deep feeling of any sort, yet impulse driven as against rational control of behavior.

This led me to search the literature on this subject and, as a result, I found another characteristic implied that seemed to me to tie to many contemporary political figures: An indifference to rules, seemingly the discovery of an advantage deriving from violating any rules in any game where an opponent is attempting to retain some rule boundaries. Does any of this sound familiar? Now the next question, as relates to the subject of this chapter, is: Is this a phenomenon that might arise at any time in history, or is it one of the defining characteristics of the late stages in a cultural process?

Remember Lukacs' proposition, cited above, "Our civilization is in ruins because our beliefs about civilization are in ruins. We are far more beset by self-doubt than were our ancestors two or three hundred years ago. It is this self-doubt that has produced the end of empires . . . ." Why? And what self-doubt in particular? I think it is because many people are beginning to doubt that the mores they learned to trust as children are valid, or if still valid, are not being subscribed to by a goodly number of their fellows. I refer you back to all the failures of justice and efficiency we looked at in the previous chapter. And the self-doubt that results is a split between one's cognitive function and one's instincts—the perception that the amoral, impulse-driven appear to luck-out uncommonly often nowadays, while common-sense keeps being driven deeper into the ground.

Lasch is arguing, complaining actually, that the growth of this kind of psychopathic strain is enabled by the defection of the elite classes from contemporary society. Davidson and Rees-Mogg, as prototypical representatives of the elite that Lasch decries, acknowledge the picture he draws but see cultural chaos as inevitable and urge the rationality of their strategy of opting out. Referring to his charge that the new elites are no longer loyal to any national identity, but, " . . . are international rather than regional, national or local [and] have more in common with their counterparts in . . . [markets around the world]," Davidson and Rees-Mogg say,

> Although Lasch . . . meant his portrait of the information elite to be unflattering, his contempt for those who are liberated from the tyranny of place rests on a perception . . . of the same developments that are a focus of this book . . . When we read Lasch's critiques [and like minded critics of current trends] we see parts of our analysis confirmed . . . . Critics like Lasch and Walzer do not dispute that clearheaded cost-benefit analysis makes citizenship obsolete for persons of high skills, [they contend that] Like Pat Buchanan, the social democrats are economic nationalists who resent the triumph of markets over politics.[51]

In other words, Davidson and Rees-Mogg believe they are part of the transition to a new social order, as opposed to their critics whom they see resisting it. For them the decline of the West is taken as a fact but an irrelevant one, in the sense that they have already begun moving into the new world. In building up to their thesis they review many of the observations that can now be taken as confirmations of the trends Lukacs (1970) forecast: "In sum, the growing powerlessness of the modern state reflects the abdication, first of the convictions, then of the courage, of its erstwhile governing classes; and it is at least probable that in its wake there will follow not the blessings of increased liberty but a long transitory brutal period of insecurity and terror."

Their depiction of the (new) "sovereign individual" raises in my imagination the image of the Teutonic chieftains during the beginning of the Dark Ages who initially accepted the outward forms of Roman officials but were, in fact, essentially laws unto themselves. Over the course of time they became the dukes and barons who, alternately pillaging, and again protecting, the defenseless territories of the former Roman empire—fighting among themselves for hegemony—eventually settled down into the new feudal order. I wonder whether we are moving into an epoch marvelously parallel to those times. Present day savages coming from the underclass haunts in all the major world metropolitan regions, as well as whole portions of the populations of certain third-world countries rather than the outer forests, can be and are, described in terms similar to those employed by literate Romans about their barbarians. This image only enhances the temptation to compare our present world to Rome in the 400's, which Davidson and Rees-Mogg do.

Their views invite comparison with a book the title of which, *The Myth of Rome's Fall*, (Haywood, 1958), intrigued me many years ago. Coming across the book in my graduate student days, I naively assumed that it would turn out to be one of those maverick theses, like the denial of the holocaust. Instead it was an attack upon the tendency to look for broad patterns, or underlying principles, in history. Haywood's point was that many gradual developments, viewed from enough distance in time, can be perceived as an upheaval when they have reached sufficient differentiation from their starting points.

He cited writers of the third and fourth centuries, as well as contemporary historical researchers, in evidence of continuing scholarly and technological progress during the time when we have been accustomed to think that civilization was moving backwards. His best work, in my opinion, was to show how developments during this time were laying the foundations upon which the new practices of Western Civilization would develop, much as Davidson and Rees-Mogg are arguing that information-age technology is laying the foundations of what will be the next development in world culture.

However, Haywood unwittingly undercuts his own thesis with several observations of the sort that others (such as Lukacs), take as signs of oncoming decline. For example,

"Until about 200 B. C. the aristocracy gave Rome a good government. At about that time, however, the senators began to perceive the possibility of profiting personally from the rich overseas provinces which Rome was conquering." Change the ending to, "profiting personally from the largess of multinational corporations seeking release from responsibilities for localized consequences of their policies," and what does it remind you of?

Or, when Haywood says, "By the second century the great days of ancient science were over, after many hundreds of years of activity and some great achievement. The reason for the failure of science to continue its advances, however, was not intellectual fatigue but the law of diminishing returns in a field to which rigid limits had been set." In chapter five we will see how one might conclude that "intellectual fatigue" is a synonym for "diminishing returns." Or, again, "The Germanic raids of the third century in Gaul were the most destructive of any which Gaul Suffered. The Germans seemed to take a childish pleasure in pure destruction."

Here I would ask who nowadays is seen as taking pleasure in pure destruction? Aren't they the same as those described in other contexts as the Underclass—having no stake, because of no benefits, in present-day society? But I would go a step further. The Underclass, as a generic term for the kind of people who have destroyed large sections of a number of major cities, are not the only ones who have destroyed libraries, art treasures and scientific enclaves. This has happened many times in history when a conquering culture dramatically emphasized its negative valuing of the products of the vanquished. Kaplan (1996) cautions us to be careful about writing off any "underclass" as having no culture or no values other than pure destructiveness. Because no one has so far seen fit to look for any beginnings of a coherent set of cultural principles in such throngs—doesn't give a hint as to what might be found, if someone looked.

I could cite many more instances of Haywood's difficult struggle to argue for a gradual transition from Classic to Western Civilization, rather than a shift of cultural paradigms. I will content myself with just one more at this time—one that strikes me as unconsciously giving away the farm. "The absorption of the Germans... was nothing new... Constantine... brought in groups of Germans to farm land that had been depopulated... the danger was that *the groups of Germans were likely to live after the German way rather than take up the Roman way.*" (Italics mine RJR) He failed to go on to wonder what it meant that the Germans were likely to go on living in their own way.

What struck me forcefully as I reviewed the writers I cite in this chapter is the extent to which—writing at different times, from different political standpoints and different backgrounds—they seem to have come to similar conclusions. One must always be cautious, of course, in concluding that people with similar views have reached them completely independently. But, these writers do not cite each other, for the most part, and, since they have extensive bibliographies and appear scholarly in their approaches, they could be expected to cite each other if simply spreading the same gospel. I have some faith that they have indeed arrived at similar conclusions independently of each other, though probably not independently of the social climate of our time. That would seem more like evidence for the general view than against it.

Before drawing any conclusion about what all this might mean I need to cite two more works that contribute to the argument. The first is Arthur Herman's (1997) *The Idea of Decline in Western History*. He pointed out, to begin with, that, "the idea of progress... has served as a powerful myth in Western thought [and] Every theory of progress has also contained a theory of decline...." Furthermore, ideas about the inferiority of the present to the past go back as far as one can trace.

> Throughout both Classical and Western history ideas of progress and decline have alternately held sway among intellectuals. During the enlightenment the expectation was that Western ideas of individual freedom and scientific development would eventually spread around the world, bringing about a universal state of high civilization. Then after 1800 the tide turned and we began to have growing pessimism about the future of society. In U. S. history, John Adams's descendants became the principal carriers of this fear of "America's collective moral failure." His great, great grandsons, Henry and Brooks Adams, held that, "America's world-historical mission had been dissolved by collective unworthiness."[52]

I must skip over many interesting details in Herman's book to focus on what concerns us most here. Like Haywood he was attempting to debunk the notion of any profound underlying patterns in history—what I understand to be the position of most modern American historians—and by implication to dispute ideas of culture decline. Following this position to its conclusion leads to the idea that notions like the "fall" of a civilization are more nearly meaningless than difficult to resolve. While I agree that proposals of "laws" of history can not simply be asserted, without substantial proof, I am not satisfied merely to leave it there. After all, Babylon no longer exists. The Seleucid kingdom no longer exists. The Roman empire no longer exists. Etcetera. Something must have happened. Either it was chance, an accumulation of untoward circumstances, or the grinding out of implications/consequences of earlier decisions and developments. (I admit that the second and third alternatives might appear equivalent in certain perspectives, however, I hope to show a difference between them in the next chapter.)

The other alternative seems well developed in Samuel P. Huntington's (1996) *The Clash of Civilizations and the Remaking of World Order*. This work does speak of the Decline of the West, but argues from demographics that it is losing out to one Asian culture or another in terms of economic competition, unlike Davidson and Rees-Mogg's thesis of a new world wide paradigm. It is losing out in terms of favorable geographic factors co-incident with burgeoning population growth rates. The most important geographic factors are, especially, hitherto-unexploited natural resources for which the needs of the West will have to pay an increasing price.

However, while Huntington's argument is persuasive as far as it goes, it does not speak to why the combined military and economic power of the U. S. and Europe does not continue to dominate economic forces as did England's in the nineteenth century. I think of Winston Churchill's opposition to the surrender of India to its own people. He seemed to feel that the power that had vanquished Nazi Germany should certainly have been able to continue to enforce Western Civilization in economically and militarily weak India, as it had in prior times. But his line of thinking was no longer current among those holding office in Britain at the time. Why not? Were the new leaders really possessed of more accurate analyses and calculations of the cost-benefit contingencies; or was their thinking of a different type entirely? Had they reached a point where they drew the conclusion that their own civilized values could no longer countenance the domination of a colonial people?

That question brings us back to Lukacs's view about, "the abdication of convictions, and then courage," and the question of chapter three about whether the problems of society are outrunning solutions. So we see something of what the problem is. There can be disputes about whether or not any particular problem is or is not more severe at present than at various times in the past. There can be, and are, disputes about what the problems result from, and over how to remedy a given problem. There can be, and are, disputes about whether a given problem can be solved—with our current tools and ways of thinking. But, what seems clear is that there are many conditions of modern life that thoughtful people find unacceptable—that we are accepting anyway because, for one reason or another, they are not being sufficiently addressed. That could be, by itself, a definition of decline.

Chapter 05

SPENGLER ON THE DECLINE OF WESTERN CULTURE

In 1917 Oswald Spengler published his monumental work, *The Decline of the West*, a work that continues to hover on the edge of consciousness for anyone interested in the history of civilization. I first came across this work during my university years when fellow students were discussing the just-out *A Study of History* (Toynbee, 1947). Some of them, at least, perceived in it a revival of Spengler's idea of life span in civilizations. I looked at Spengler's work then, but was unable to form an attitude toward it at the time. However, in spite of that it persisted in my awareness throughout my career. I think it spoke to some vague question I had about where our society was going, even then. His insights had a special interest for me despite the tendency among modern historians to deprecate or dismiss historical treatises of grand scope and life span analogies. Since I am not an historian perhaps I have felt less constrained by this view.

When I returned to Spengler for the purposes of this book, I was surprised to discover that my memory had played a major trick on me. I was expecting to find in his book an effort to document and prove that Western Civilization is, in fact, in decline. Instead I discovered that he appeared to assume that view as a fact. He devotes himself to explaining his conception about *why* it is a fact. He produced an "organismic" hypothesis—that peoples/cultures have a life cycle analogous to that of persons. He offers a mound of details illustrating how forms of thought originate, work, transform, evolve, ripen and progress to their ultimate conclusion in the life of any given society—and how we can observe the process in action.

While Spengler's thesis has been a major influence in the thinking that culminated in the present book I came to realize that my goals and tasks were considerably different from his, despite a certain similarity in methods. Let me start with the latter point. Spengler, as a philosopher of history was introducing his argument in a fashion typical of German thinkers of his era—that history has broad patterns, that it "makes sense." It is not simply a chronology of events, even on a world-wide scale, that might be perceived either as simply random, or as resulting from proximal causes involving demographics, religion, economics, power, etc.

Instead, his view is that history is one of the two forms—along with science—of understanding reality. And as such, it has universally applicable principles, just as physics has universally applicable laws. They can be detected in their broad patterns, if one only takes a sufficiently grand perspective. But, the "mechanism," of history (if I may put it thus) is not physical law but destiny; that is, the playing out of consequences drawn from initial premises, as in systems of mathematics. He made it his task, then, to outline the principles underlying the "spirit" of different cultures and detail what he saw as the evidence for them.

I share, as a psychologist and psychotherapist, a method that is in some ways more congenial with that of Spengler than with that of the hard sciences. As I work, as therapist, with an individual to help him or her uncover the deeper principles beneath his/her experience of life and then, hopefully, to "take charge" of his or her fate—improve the precision of his/her control—we are interested in the sequence of events that have led to the present situation and the instances of current thinking/feeling/experiencing that derive by compelling personal logic from prior personal assumptions. What were the antecedents and consequents that preceded whatever present situation the individual is currently facing? As we hunt for these antecedents we separate out those that were merely prior—without relevance to present problems—from those that seem to lie behind the current condition. Then we explore further to distinguish what in all of this simply involved choices that incidentally produced undesirable results, and can readily be changed, from that which consists of seemingly intractable habits and hidden conflicts requiring more extensive and deep-seated reorganization.[53]

This is a method that has features in common with Spengler's view that "organisms" can best be understood as working out a destiny. Even if one remains skeptical that a culture can really be considered an organism in any significant sense, the procedure necessarily requires a from-the-inside-out focus rather than the outside-in focus of present-day natural sciences. This is true whether one is investigating individual lives or histories of social entities. In other terms: To see reality through the subject's eyes, rather than to view the subject as an object, from the outside, is to begin to understand how the present functioning of the subject (individual or society) follows a logic of its own, and what that logic is. This is the same view of science that Spengler claimed to have gotten from Goethe, in contrast to the path that Western science (including academic psychology) has actually taken (until now—?).

My interest in Spengler's thesis owes much to the parallels I have found in approaching my task as a therapist. My present task concerns what I have learned from both sources to apply as a citizen and father concerned about the destinies of his offspring. I am not in a position to confirm or disconfirm whether Western Civilization is or is not in decline, in any rigorous sense; that I leave to writers like those cited, such as Lukacs (1970), Kennedy (1987), Huntington (1996), et al. However, I do tentatively accept their conclusions as I judge that our society meets many of Spengler's criteria. It seems to me, also, that the nature—the process—of the decline, as decried by writers like, Bloom (1987), Bork (1996) and Lukacs follows, at least in a general sense, Spengler's thesis of the "wearing out" of a once highly creative set of truths about the nature of reality—by evolving beyond the bounds of common sense to their logical extremes.

Furthermore, though I am not equipped to attempt to draw predictions and prescriptions for the future of Western civilization, I hope to promote a discussion with you about personal directions for living in the present to maximize survival in a range of alternative future scenarios. That self-interested goal, that I hope you share, is subsidiary to my main goal but one which I think will interact with my primary task.

My chief task is to call your attention to a new comprehension of the nature of behavior, which I undertake in Part II, and then explore its value in understanding and furthering our common enterprises as ordinary citizens in thinking about the future of our society and our planet in the final parts of the book. However, to motivate (in the sense mathematicians use the word) that exposition I want first to point up a feature of human thinking that is seen in the evolution of thought processes both in the history of individual thinkers and in the history of societies. In Part II I propose to explain why it occurs. Before that I want to discuss how it occurs, starting with Spengler's brilliant exposition of it.

What we find most valuable in Spengler, then, is *that* in his large-scale view of the history of civilizations which is comparable to Kuhn's views of the history of science. Both of them shared the insight that systems of thought derive from basic premises which may make them incompatible with other systems of the same magnitude, and from which implications are drawn out over time in the evolution of the system in question. This view that they share, wittingly or not, will be enlightened by the discovery that human behavior is the control of perception, and what that means. But first, let us see what we gain from Spengler's thought.

Spengler's proposal that one can find in history the primitive view of reality that a horde of human beings shared as they were coming to form a common identity—in order to understand the culture they went on to develop—is a challenging and exciting proposition. This first step in formation of a culture, this sharing a common way of perceiving, he argued, was part of the process of group identity, as it developed through the members' communication with each other over the conduct of their communal life. And it came about in a perfectly understandable way—influenced by the terrain, the climate, the environment in general in which the people in question lived. Different primitive hordes that coalesced in different regions of the earth would face different coping issues and develop different outlooks because of the different landscapes that they had to perceive and the different environmental challenges they had to meet.

Chance would also be a factor, as I interpret Spengler, when he postulated that, at some given point, one member of the horde would articulate generalizations enshrouded in these shared perceptions. His (or her) formulation would then be on the way to becoming what Spengler called the spirit of that culture. Chance played a part in the sense that the particular individual who formulated the conceptions of reality that were developing would inevitably express them in light of his own personality. A different "prophet" or soothsayer might have formulated first principles somewhat differently. Nevertheless, as various members tried expressing a view of their common experience, the articulation that endured would be the one most recognized by the communal fellowship as valid for thinking and talking about their experience of reality.[54]

Spengler writes in a style that I find poetic and elegant. It provoked a caution about succumbing to the argument simply because the writing is so impressive. For example, consider this passage about how certain hordes of humankind have periodically emerged with the "goods" for forming larger, and more enduring troupes that subsequently developed into societies with distinct, distinguishable cultures.

> A boundless mass of human Being[55], flowing in a stream without banks.... Over the expanse of the water passes the endless uniform wave-train of the generations. Here and there bright shafts of light broaden out, every-where dancing flashes confuse and disturb the clear mirror, changing, sparkling, vanishing. These are what we call the clans, tribes, peoples, races which unify a series of generations within this or that limited area of the historical surface. As widely as these differ in creative power, so widely do the images that they create vary in duration and plasticity, and when the creative power dies out, the physiognomic, linguistic and spiritual identification-marks vanish also and the phenomenon subsides again into the ruck of the generations. Aryans, Mongols, Germans, Kelts, Parthians, Franks, Carthaginians, Berbers, Bantus are names [of] images of this order.
>
> But over this surface, too, the great Cultures accomplish their majestic wave-cycles. They appear suddenly, swell in splendid lines, flatten again and vanish, and the face of the waters is once more a sleeping waste.

> A Culture is born in the moment when a great soul awakens out of the proto-spirituality of ever-childish humanity.... Every Culture stands in a deeply-symbolical, almost in a mystical, relation to the Extended, the space, in which and through which it strives to actualize itself. The aim once attained—the idea, the entire content of inner possibilities, fulfilled and made externally actual—the Culture suddenly hardens, it mortifies, its blood congeals, its force break down, and it becomes Civilization.[56]

The illustrations he gives in evidence of what are the fundamental differences between the different cultures sometimes eluded me. Nevertheless certain of the general principles seemed so obvious and straightforward as to be practically self-evident. The notion of the primitive Germans, living in the deep forests of the north, where the sun had to penetrate from a great height—and drew one's attention constantly upward, seemed intuitive to me. That is exactly what I do when walking in forests like Olympic Park. It does not stretch the imagination greatly to envision that that contrast of environment with the sun baked slopes of the Greek and Roman countrysides would create significant differences in the unconscious feelings about the world in the corresponding peoples.

That something of that primitive experience would be perpetuated down through generations and make it "natural" to construct religious edifices with high vaults and huge windows, bringing in great shafts of light—to continue to draw the attention upward when in the spiritual mode—that also did not strike me as far-fetched. Even to my untutored eye the Gothic Cathedral is a fundamentally different experience from a Greek or Roman temple. Each was expressing something different about what the perceiver intended to perceive. Yes, certain engineering developments were necessary for the construction of Gothic cathedrals, but I don't find it hard to accept Spengler's argument that—given the engineering feats that were achieved by Classical Civilization—the difference would reflect more surely a difference in what they wanted than in what they could perform.

Spengler went on to argue that as modes of thinking/language coalesced around certain axiomatic principles their influence would exert itself in all areas of the society's life.

> ... in the historical as in the natural world-picture, there is found nothing, however small, that does not embody in itself the entire sum of fundamental tendencies ... between political and mathematical aspects of the same Culture, between religious and technical conceptions, between mathematics, music and sculpture, between economics and cognition-forms. Clearly and unmistakably there appear[ed] the fundamental dependence of the most modern physical and chemical theories on the mythological concepts of our Germanic ancestors ... the style-congruence of tragedy and power-technics and up-to-date finance, and the fact (bizarre at first but soon self-evident) that oil-painting perspective, printing, the credit system, long-range weapons, and contrapuntal music ... were identical expressions of one and the same spiritual principle ... [57]

Spengler then launched into his endeavor to show how from their different beginnings different cultures would follow an evolutionary course of development in which the stages would roughly follow the same order while their contents could be very different.

> There are several number-worlds as there are several Cultures. We find an Indian, an Arabian, a

Classical, a Western type of mathematical thought and, corresponding with each . . . an expression of a specific world-feeling, a symbol . . . which reflects the central essence of one and only one soul, viz., the soul of that particular Culture.

The idea of the Euclidean geometry is actualized in the earliest forms of Classical ornament, and that of the Infinitesimal Calculus in the earliest forms of Gothic architecture, centuries before the first learned mathematicians of the respective Cultures were born . . . .

The Greek mathematic, as a science of perceivable magnitudes, deliberately confines itself to facts of the comprehensibly present . . . . As compared with this impeccable consistency, the position of the Western mathematic is seen to be, practically, somewhat illogical[58], though it is only since the discovery of Non-Euclidean Geometry that the fact has been really recognized . . . our concepts are derived from vision, and the whole fabric of our logic is a light-world in the imagination . . . A mathematical . . . scientific way of thinking is right, convincing, a 'necessity of thought,' when it completely expresses the life—feeling proper to it . . . The modern mathematic, though 'true' only for the Western spirit, is undeniably a master-work of the spirit; and yet to Plato it would have seemed a ridiculous and painful aberration from the path leading to the 'true'—to wit, the Classical—mathematic. And so with ourselves. Plainly, we have almost no notion of the multitude of great ideas belonging to other Cultures that we have suffered to lapse because our thought with its limitations has not permitted us to assimilate them, or (which comes to the same thing) has led us to reject them as false, superfluous, and nonsensical.[59]

The mass of detailed illustrations that he provides in support of his assertions are often fascinating in themselves and frequently lured my attention away from his main thesis, or at least the form of it that most interests us here. That is the contention that observing, thinking, concluding, choosing and acting flow from more abstract to more concrete forms in a person, and that persons who interact intensely within a group, and in relative isolation from other such groups, will come to share these common abstractions to a large extent and hence develop culturally consonant implications and applications.

This is not a conscious process but a foundation of "common sense" or self-evident truth in the given group. Finally, this level of abstract principles comes to be refined in the interactions, cooperations, competitions of the daily life of the society/group and at the same time bounds or restricts applications to those possibilities of thinking that are implicitly "sensible" within the framework of the first principles.

That is not to say that there is no evolution of thought within society; obviously there is. But the evolution of thought through history illustrates the drawing out of implications derivable from the first principles and held within bounds of consistency with those principles. Were they to be transformed into something fundamentally different it would become a new culture. In fact, when that happens, it is because the ways of acting that are evolving are increasingly malfunctioning for the purposes of survival. And this brings about what Kuhn (1970) calls a "paradigm revolution" within the arena of history of science with which he deals, and is called "decline" of a culture in the broader tableau which Spengler attempted to explore.

I think modern historians are right: that you can not "prove" such a thesis in any scientific sense. It becomes a matter of whether or not it "feels" convincing to one's common sense, and to the extent that useful applications can be drawn from it. In that sense I subscribe to Spengler's basic thesis. I think you can find instances exemplifying it all around, if you take it in a sufficiently liberal way. Read just about any history of a movement of any sort, or biographies, or psychohistories, and you find the writer depicting the thinking of his/her subject in terms of its antecedents. The current state of a given body of ideas is often explained in terms of drawing out the implications of previously held positions. Where you have critiques of current practices (e.g. Bloom, Bork, Howard, Lasch, as a few examples) we see them denouncing the corruption of previously respectable positions by arriving at extreme—ridiculous—conclusions.

Even more specifically, some people (maybe many, if they were surveyed) are conscious of a sense of destiny in their own lives. "Destiny" meaning, in this context, the memory of having more or less grown up with a certain path or commitment to action, or to achieving a certain image in life that seemed necessitated by an inner consciousness of what their life was all about. As one example I cite, *Le Statue Intérieure*, by Nobel laureate François Jacob (1987). His inner "statue" I took as an allusion to Michelangelo's purported remark that his carving drew out the latent figure in the block of marble. Jacob pursued his course unerringly through the detours and tribulations of WW II to his stellar career in biochemistry, following an inner guiding light that he believed he sensed going back into his childhood. In his words,

> comment ne pas voir que tous ces personnages de ma vie passée ont joué le plus grand rôle, et d'autant plus grand qu'il était plus précoce, dans l'élaboration de cette image secrète qui,... dirige mes goûts, mes désirs, mes décisions. Dès notre plus jeune âge, l'imagination s'empare des gens et des choses qu'elle rencontre pour les triturer, les tansformer, en prélever

un trait ou un signe avec lesquels s'érige notre représentation idéale du monde, un schéma qui devient notre système de reférence, notre code pour déchiffrer la réalité à mesure qu'elle se présente. Je porte ainsi en moi sculptée depuis l'enfance, une sorte de statue intérieure qui donne une continuité à ma vie, qui est la charactère.[60]

This beautiful introspection of Jacob's displays a version of the fertile concept of "sense of destiny" used by biographers, psychohistorians, analytic therapists, in depicting the undeviating purpose seemingly detectable in the life course of many highly accomplished persons. The same idea is implicit in the work of historians of movements, causes, traditions and cultures. Spengler took it to a more abstract level in application to civilizations. The parallels I have found in the perhaps more prosaic self-explorations of ordinary people only reinforced my impression of the underlying personal-logicality of human thinking, from the individual to the social.

By "logicality" I am referring to an insight that impressed me, pointed out by a mathematician friend many years ago. He was trying to enlighten me about the importance of the discovery of non-euclidean geometries. He explained that although the average high-school geometry student follows the ancient Greeks in thinking that Euclid's system accurately describes reality it is not necessarily so. Other systems, starting from other first premises, reach different conclusions.

In like manner I have been struck, over and over, as a therapist, by the ways in which any and all of us are limited by our own unconscious assumptions in what we can imagine, conceive of or (as a result) do.[61] Something that seems readily apparent to one person will simply not occur to another. When pointed out it will often be strongly resisted by the other as illogical, nonsensical, unthinkable or unattainable. When exploring behind a person's inability to utilize an idea or strategy, that might already have demonstrated effectiveness in the hands of someone else, we often find either a hidden proscription, whether correctly derived or misinterpreted, from injunctions of a parent. Or we find the person's basic axioms about reality and see that they conflict with the way of perceiving that the new ideas would invoke. Sometimes this process can be traced back through a series of transformations and revisions reminiscent of what Spengler claimed to see in analyzing the history of a culture.

If I have made my case, it will not be a big jump to consider the notion—of the limiting action of first principles, or fundamental axioms of thought—at work when a person is attempting to forge a solution to a problem which he or she has not previously encountered. In such instances we all resort to whatever we have learned that might apply in the most similar conditions we can think of. But, one must then extend the familiar habit to the unfamiliar conditions. In doing so some modification or transformation is required. At this point what one can imagine is limited by one's pre-existing principles about what is possible or what is acceptable.

It can happen that one finds oneself drawing an extreme derivation from an accepted principle when the usual application fails to achieve the desired results. A seemingly silly example of this comes to mind. One time at an airport mainly closed down by a winter storm a group of us whose flight had been delayed were told, "there is a later flight getting ready to leave, but, if you get on it, you are abandoning your checked-in baggage."

On the face of it this is a ridiculous statement. The concept of abandoning—baggage or anything else—has a clear enough meaning, and one that is twisted completely out of shape by this declaration. Of course this weird wording was doubtless prompted by the airline management's desire to stay within the letter of some law or regulation that must have used that expression in a definition of conditions for which they could not be legally held liable. No one would expect that anyone could now steal the "abandoned" baggage with impunity, but that is what might be argued in a legal case, if some unimagined, freak happenstance transpired. Most of us would sympathize with the rage of a person who might accidentally be victimized as a result of this tricky use of language. Yet the complexity of modern life makes it almost inevitable that some people, sometimes, become victims of totally unforeseeable nightmarish eventualities, fostered by some such verbal contortions.

Then the next step in the social-legal process is to formulate regulations or laws to rectify or preclude such freakish occurrences. This process guaranties the further growth of inconsistent and anti-commonsensical regulations, judicial rulings, decisions and controversies in contemporary spheres of politics, business practices, and public values and aims. Consider many of the writings I cited in the previous chapters depicting what the authors found as outrageous or degenerate moral positions.[62] Farmer (1977), Bloom (1987), Budiansky, et al. (1995), Howard (1995), Bork (1996) all describe the evolution of what were once functional values into bizarre, non-functional or anti-civilized modern forms. Any of us could easily come up with recent instances where decisions of judges twisted abstract constitutional points or well-intentioned laws into inhumane outcomes contrary to the most elementary common sense simply by applying literally what they have come to mean in modern times. Just now I am merely reminding you what we looked at in previous chapters. We shall consider this further in Part III.

Now let us return to look for Spengler's candidates for those basic premises that became the fundamentals of Western thought and begin to search out how they have migrated through the paths of meaning over time. The first concept that he mentions to illustrate his contention about the differences of culture/civilizations is that of time.

> In the world of the Hellenes all experience . . . was immediately transmuted into a timeless, immobile, mythically-fashioned back-ground for the particular momentary present . . . Such a spiritual condition is practically impossible for us men of the West, with a sense of time-distances so strong that we habitually [account for events] so many years before or after Christ.[63]

He uses this distinction to compare history writing in Classical with that in Western terms. He went on to argue how that difference in starting positions led Classical society to a "negation of time [such that for them] the image [was] of a world that is not continuous but complete." Just the opposite of the views that came to inform thought in the West: Time as a factor, eventuating in the idea of "progress" (with ultimately its antithesis, "decline"); this combined with the Gothic (Faustian) concept of vision and space, into the development of astronomical observatories, clocks and ultimately the infinitesimal calculus.

> . . . finally, the whole content of Western number-thought centres itself upon the historic limit-problem of the Faustian mathematic, the key which opens the way to the Infinite . . . which is so different from the infinity of Arabian and Indian world-ideas . . . This limit is the absolute opposite of the limit which . . . figures in the Classical problem of the quadrature of the circle . . . Only in the 19th Century was this relic of Classical number-feeling finally removed . . . by the limit-idea [that] is no longer approximated to, but the approximation . . . itself . . . And so in this decisive problem . . . we . . . see how historical is the construction of the Western soul . . . .[64]

Spengler weaves this construction together with other derivatives of primitive Gothic thought, as in combination with the interest in space (as embodied in the upward-thrusting design of Gothic cathedrals), and merging with the gradual "Faustian" transformation of Christianity into the inner drives behind the colonizations of the Western powers, the conviction that such were bringing salvation and "progress" to the conquered, and the eventual Western ideas about continued market expansions.

> But whereas number, as conceived by a Pythagorean, exhibited the essence of individual and discrete data in "Nature" Descartes and his successors looked upon number as something to be conquered, something to be wrung out, an abstract relation . . . capable of holding its own against "Nature" on all occasions. The will-to-power [cf. Nietzsche, RJR] that from the earliest Gothic of the Eddas, the Cathedrals and Crusades . . . [and] Goths and Vikings, has distinguished the attitude of the Northern soul to its world . . . appears also in . . . the dynamic of Western number.[65]

Further on Spengler connects this evolving channel of thought with his assessment of Western ideas of money as they developed with the late-term process of civilization into full abstractness. "It no longer merely serves for the understanding of economic intercourse, but subjects the exchange of goods to its own evolution. It values things, no longer as between each other, but with reference to itself." Here we are reminded of *Paper Money* (Adam Smith, 1981), "faith in the system is the essential ingredient." Goodman (A.K.A. Adam Smith) goes on in his book to describe what happens when faith in the system is shattered, and that in turn, leads one to Davidson and Rees-Mogg's (1997) prophecy of the demise of societal systems as we now know them and a transformation into something completely different. But more about that later.

Next, let us look at Spengler's discussion of Destiny and Causality. "... for primitive man or for the child no comprehensive causally-ordered world exists at all as yet and ... we ourselves, though "late" men with a consciousness disciplined by powerful speech-sharpened thought, can do no more ... than assert that the causal order which we see in such a moment is continuously present in the actuality around us...." He is attempting to differentiate the Destiny idea, which he feels we have intuitively, from the idea of Causality which is an invention of the rational mind.

He continues, relating the dawning awareness of these concepts in primitive peoples to the formation of notions of space and time at the beginning of the development of a culture.

> For primitive man the word 'time' can have no meaning... He has time, but he knows nothing of it. All of us are conscious, as being aware, of space only, and not of time. Space 'is,' ... 'Time,' on the contrary, is a discovery, which is only made by thinking... only the higher Cultures, whose world-conceptions have reached the mechanical-Nature stage, are capable of deriving from their consciousness of a well-ordered measurable and comprehensible Spatial, the projected image of time....

After this he launches into a lengthy philosophical discussion to conclude (something that has emerged again as a major issue in modern physics) that we can not know anything beyond [the assertion that] Time is a "counter-conception to Space, and that all ideas (as opposed to sense-experiences) come in the form of polar opposites, the forms of which are peculiar to, and revelatory of, the separate cultures of humanity.

However, "it follows from the meaning that we have attached to the Culture as a prime phenomenon and to destiny as the organic logic of existence, that each Culture must necessarily possess its own destiny-idea...." He then spells out what this means in different cultures. From there he continues on to the primitive feeling of "Care," starting from the nurturing instinct, that in Western development progressed through the concept of mother-love, to "The Mother with the Child—the future—at her breast," to, "the paternal, and there we meet with the highest of all time symbols that have come into existence within the Culture, the State.... And here again the history of higher Cultures shows us three examples of state-formations in which the element of care is conspicuous...."

He develops this idea further, bringing in the operation of political and economic functions of the state and how these play out in a culture's development of moral and ethical ideas. "So also, the supreme ethical expression... is found in the Western Christian's idea of Grace—the grace, obtained through the sacrificial death of Jesus... is... the foundation of every confession and every autobiography; [and absent from the constitution of Classical man]...." This long exposition (though much abbreviated) of Spengler's method of tracing primitive principles through the twists and turns of implications to a final (and often degenerate) formulation is well illustrated in the modern form of the confession and autobiography as played out in television talk shows.

Spengler describes still another outcome, of a different order but similarly strangling on its own logic.

> "Free will" is an inward certitude. But whatever one
> may will or do, that which actually ensues...

> subserves a deeper necessity and . . . conforms to a major order . . . . And when the Destiny of that which was willed [has played out] we are fain to call the inscrutable `Grace.' What did Innocent III, Luther, Loyola, Calvin, Jansen, Rousseau and Marx will, and what come of [it] in the stream of Western history: Was it Grace or Fate? . . . The Predestination doctrine of Calvin and Pascal . . . dared to draw the causal connection [from Augustine]—the necessary absurdity to which the pursuit of these secrets leads . . . . The fearful soul conflicts of Pascal were the strivings of a man, at once [deeply spiritual and a mathematician], who was determined to subject the last and gravest problems of the soul both to the intuition of a grand, instinctive faith and to the abstract precision of a no less grand mathematical plan.[66]

He is saying that (unlike Luther and Thomas Aquinas) the more "upright" thinkers, by holding steadfast to the logic of the starting point, came to a conclusion that is irrational in terms of common sense, namely that a portion of humanity was foreordained to hell. Luther and Aquinas, in contrast, fudged the logic in favor of arriving at a conclusion that would have more appeal to the devout. One more example of Spengler's method, that I want to consider, is his discussion of the meaning of the concept of "will" in Western culture.

> The enigmatic something in the soul-image that is called, "will," . . . is . . . quite specially a creation of the Baroque, like the perspective of oil-painting and the force-idea of modern physics and the tone-world of instrumental music. In every case the Gothic had foreshadowed what these intellectualizing centuries brought to fullness . . . . If we can . . . state the theme of Western physics . . . to be efficient space . . . we . . .

> have defined ... the measure [of] what a man is by his activity ... and we judge all intentions, reasons, powers, convictions and habits entirely by this directedness.... The overcoming of resistances may ... be called the typical impulse of the Western soul.[67]

Spengler then proceeds to develop this idea as it progressed through politics, science and the arts. "... the heavens ... were thought of ... as a substantial quantity, like the earth [in Classical culture, but] now it was Space that ruled the universe." He goes on to connect the conception of "will" in Western experience with the concept of "freedom." "So also it was that the old Northern races ... discovered in their gray dawn the art of sailing the seas which emancipated them," He related that, in turn, with impulses for expansion of any sort, including, "The thrill of big figures," whether in astronomy or finance. Finally, he turns to the concepts of virtue and vice, which he brings together in the "phenomenon of Morale," and relates the line of thinking, above, with the course that ethics takes down through Western thought.

> Everyone [speaking of western morale] demands something of the rest. We say "thou shalt" in the conviction that so-and so will ... be arranged conformably to the order.... In the ethics of the West everything is direction, claim to power, will to affect the distant. Here Luther is completely at one with Nietzsche, Popes with Darwinians, Socialists with Jesuits.... If we allow that Socialism (in the ethical, not the economic, sense) is that world-feeling which seeks to carry out its own views on behalf of all, then we are all without exception, willingly or no, wittingly or no, Socialists.

Following his argument through the subsequent chapters we can draw parallels to glimpse how earlier common-sense perceptions of right living, "care" and "will," devolved into present-day conflicts over "entitlements," and the fight between industrialists to get regulation off their backs and ecologists to rein them in for the greater good. Likewise the principle of freedom of thought and speech has led to conflict between individual liberty and responsibility, then to unintended consequences, and the latter, in turn, into the struggle between the drive to win in politics versus the drive to protect the last shreds of ethics. The resistance against taking personal responsibility so characteristic of contemporary people is comparable to Spengler's "spiritually dead man of the autumnal cities—Hammurabi's Babylon, Ptolemaic Alexandria, Islamic Baghdad, Paris and Berlin today—only the pure intellectual, the sophist, the sensualist, the Darwinian, . . . is able to evade it by setting up a secretless 'scientific world-view' between himself and the alien."

As I have already maintained, many of the critics of contemporary society have followed Spengler's thesis, wittingly or not, in at least a broad, general way, in tracing what they see as the corruption of thought, even intelligence, if you will, from earlier simpler forms by way of increasing complexity. Davidson and Rees-Mogg (1997) in agreement with his perception of the decline of Western Civilization, focus on what seems a different dynamic,

> This is a situation with striking parallels in the past. Whenever technological change has divorced the old forms from the new moving forces of the economy, moral standards shift, and people begin to treat those in command of the old institutions with growing disdain . . . In our view you are witnessing nothing less than the waning of the Modern Age. It is a development driven by a

> ruthless but hidden logic.... We say this... to emphasize that the stage of history now opening will be qualitatively different from that into which you were born.... (p. 13.)

Their argument seems, on the surface, to diverge from Spengler's by making the engine of decline "technological change." But such change is, itself, the product of ideas. Only time will tell whether the present technology revolution was a final stage of principles inherent in the dawn of Western ideas, or a true paradigm shift in the control of information. It will eventually make the subject of a fine historical analysis. My own surmise is that there is coming about a true paradigm revolution regarding the meaning of "control," but that the present way of using this technology—by multi-national corporations, and other entities struggling to break free of old nation-state controls—reflect the latest (and perhaps last) stages in the concepts of expansion, will, and care and freedom that Spengler described.

Lukacs (1970), before Davidson and Rees-Mogg, reflected upon the decline of what had once been guiding ideas through a long period of civilization.

> Eventually the decay of Newtonianism and Cartesianism will effect the lives—and... the minds of more and more people.... The hold of old ideas is still strong. The trust in recognized experts is still strong... Americans have been... both unable and unwilling to recognize the peculiar coexistence of their, often evidently contradictory, mental categories... [accompanying this process has been] The principal characteristic of the twentieth century... inflation:inflation of money, of wealth, of production, of people, of society, of minds, of words, of communications. (p. 153)

This is a description of a collection of processes going out of bounds. This condition of processes going out of bounds is also reflected by Howard (1995) in *The Death of Common Sense*. The work of lawyers has gotten beyond the original function of law: to regulate relations between fellow citizens in terms of the rules they share by virtue of their shared national, tribal or community identity. There are no boundaries or restraints on litigants' efforts to win. (This could also include bureaucrats in governmental agencies, such as those of the IRS who recently came up for criticism in congress for brutal and unreasonable proceedings in their efforts to extract taxes.)

John Grisham's novel, *The Runaway Jury* also illustrates this picture we hold of our legal system—with its depiction of a trial in which lawyers for both sides engage in jury tampering, bribery, intimidation and extortion. Never mind that this is a novel and might draw an outrageous and distorted picture of our legal system. It complies with the perception many of us hold. The news reports of convictions of judges and politicians for taking bribes (even to free murderers) here in Chicago and elsewhere are enough to affirm that the picture Howard and Grisham draw is plausible enough to make one shudder. In the field of politics the philosophy of *Win at Any Cost*—even at the cost of doing violence to any conception of fair play, honesty or justice—seems to prevail from Watergate to Monicagate or Starrgate.

Consider whether the lack of boundaries is not another indication that we have arrived at the end of a reasoning process. I have the impression that the British upper classes at the height of England's power in the nineteenth century held to some limits—played by the rules would be another way to say it—in the rivalry between political parties, in contrast to what seems to be the case with our leaders today. That is what allowed scandal to be effective for halting a process that was getting out of bounds—something that seems no longer a factor in our current political condition. Even the sports, cricket and tennis, that that culture cultivated, continue to exhibit a "gentlemanly" kind of decorum that seems directly to descend from the rules of chivalry. In contrast we currently have a seeming epidemic of disgusting pictures of parents and coaches physically and verbally attacking referees, participants and even spectators in children's sports. This trend follows some years of seeing dirty play by athletes becoming ever more common in professional sports.

    I gained a personal perspective on the way in which the death of common sense is tied with *Win at Any Cost* (what I might call the "psychopath's law") during the free-for-all discussion at a summer workshop for professional therapists. In a community meeting we raged against a threat to ourselves and the organization from the mere suggestion that we might all become potential candidates for subpoena simply by holding an open discussion to learn what the issue was. It pertained to a case in which two members were being sued. The paranoia—whether to remain in ignorance for safety's sake, or to risk one's personal security by thinking openly—struck me as a form of fear of brutality. I was reminded of recent news reports concerning prosecutions for child—and spouse abuse. It struck me that we were fearing becoming objects of lawyer—or media abuse. Thoughts of lives "destroyed" simply by being reported on in the news or charged with crime or unethical behavior (even when later found innocent) added to the general sense of unease about holding a discussion to find out what had happened. In contrast, I had to marvel that, in the same climate others nowadays become rich by being notorious—if some publisher or moviemaker thinks he or she can profit by publishing their particular scandal.

    The idea of systems running out of control and reaching an end process in which the process itself has become an end instead of what it formerly was supposed to accomplish—is not a bad definition of degeneration or corruption when it begins to make simply living one's life an insecure matter.

It is important to note, however, that not all principles devolve into anti-social outcomes by being transformed through popular and legal thought processes. The principle of equality, expressed in the Declaration of Independence as well as in the French revolutionary motto, has gradually but inexorably fueled the arguments that lead to the gradual expansion of civil rights throughout Western society. The roots of this concept appear to derive from two ancient sources, one the Nordic Ting in which every member could speak his or her mind, and secondly, the Christian concept of *all* as the children of God. Whether this stream of thought is perceived as debased or improved seems to depend on the eye of the beholder, but, as time goes on the majority leans more and more to the latter estimation. However, the development of civil rights, too, has begun to take on forms that writers like Bork (1996) and Buckley (1968)see as degenerate, as in the growth of entitlements.

One might wonder whether Spengler's conclusion—that as the implications of a set of prime assumptions are drawn out they always degenerate—follows. Why might they not be improvements? The answer was given by Kuhn in his exposition of the nature of scientific revolutions. The implications drawn from initial premises are limited by the necessity of being consistent with them, but that ultimately leads to implications that begin to be inconsistent with each other as the whole system of thought becomes more complex. For example, take the case of modern physics, in which they have to accommodate to observations in which light is alternately viewed as traveling wave form, or as bursts of traveling particles, but not both at the same time. As implications of the basic axioms continue to multiply the ensuing confusion might ultimately force the abandonment of the whole way of understanding these phenomena, if a new, superior scheme gets conceived.

Thus, even though there have been isolated social improvements, such as civil rights gains, derivable from first principles about equality, the system as a whole becomes ever more complex and prone to unintended consequences by the very fact of the attempts to draw out ever more tenuous implications.

I hope this sketch of Spengler's thesis about the drawing out of implications of basic principles of thought in the history of any society—and the illustrations I have provided out of the many possible—serves to establish two points. First, that there is an inner orderliness—tending always toward greater complexity—in the way that thought evolves through the contentions, claims, disputes and decisions of members of a society. Second, that the causal mechanism of this process is the nature of human thought itself.

In reference to the second point I will close this chapter with a final quote about causality from Lukacs (1970), "[there is] a function of causality that is still far from being adequately understood. This is that the anticipation of something may indeed be the cause of it, whereby the mechanical relationships of causes and effects are often reversed."[68] That is what we shall consider next.

PART II

*How First Principles Evolve:
The function of Behavior*

In Part II I draw your attention to a discovery in the life sciences—called control of perception—that constitutes a paradigm revolution in the sense used by Thomas Kuhn (1970) in, *The Structure of Scientific Revolutions*. I will present enough of it, in as nearly "everyday terms," as possible, for continuing to re-examine the kinds of issues and crises pointed to in Part I.

It will not be a complete tutorial. You might well decide to master it for your own sake, and if so refer to Special Resources in Appendix 1 and Powers (1973ff). If you are already familiar with it you might well skip Chapter nine where I sketch it out in some detail. Before that I will be discussing this new way of looking at behavior in more everyday terms, but based upon seeing it as the function of hierarchies of purpose-oriented control mechanisms. I hope chapter six will provide sufficient understanding to open new insights into how this view of behavior lends more readily to understanding the process by which the phenomena described by Spengler and Kuhn come about.

The word, "control" in reference to behavior means just what we mean in everyday speech when we say things like:

> "It takes practice to learn to control your balance on a rolling ship;"

> "As alcohol concentration goes up, you begin losing control of steering your car;"
>
> "Accuracy in placing a tennis shot is a function of how precisely you can control your racket face;"
>
> "Control of literary style requires a good knowledge of grammar;"

What the word, "control" does not mean here embraces all the everyday mis-uses like:

> "Control yourself!" Usually spoken to children, where it generally means, "Inhibit your movements, or verbalizations;"
>
> "Quit trying to control me," usually meaning, "Stop trying to coerce, influence or harrass, me."

These misapplications of the word have resulted from a mistaken understanding of how control works. As you will see later the concept of one person actually controlling another—found in introductions to elementary psychology texts where psychology is defined as The Science of Prediction and Control of Behavior—is a false notion. In the first place behavior isn't what is controlled. Perception is what is controlled in behavior. Second, living organisms, functioning as control systems, resist external influences and thus are not amenable to external control efforts. Only overwhelming force can overcome resistance to external interference.

Chapter 06

The Engine of Cultural Decline

The issue that befuddled Lukacs (1970), the "function of causality that is still far from being adequately understood" was resolved in a paper published in 1960. Titled, "A general feedback theory of human behavior," (Powers, Clark and McFarland, 1960a, 1960b), it indicated that behavior is not a stimulus-response affair but a feedback control phenomenon. It was one, the most developed one, of a growing current of similar views. Feedback control is the phenomenon in which an entity (whether living organism or cybernetic machine) functions to achieve and maintain a specified state of some perceived condition, counteracting any external influence to change that state. These views reflect the beginnings of a revolution in psychology. This understanding of the nature of behavior plays a major part in the argument here.

Contrary to what scholars had believed ever since Descartes proposed a reflex type of "mechanism" of behavior in 1650 the new view is that the actions we perform bring about, and maintain, perceived states of affairs to specified conditions.[69] A common illustration is that of acting on the steering wheel of a car to keep your view (perception) of the car's front in the lane that you desire to see it in. It is now generally held that such control occurs through feedback systems in the brain.[70] The term "feedback" refers in this situation to the fact that your perception of the current state of affairs supplies the information needed to correct any deviation from the desired state of affairs. Thus, in terms of circular causality that Lukacs was concerned about: The view of the car in the road "causes" you to make the movements that you make on the wheel, and the movements you make on the wheel "causes" the view you have of the car in the road. The correct description is circular.

Feed back mechanisms were not understood in Descartes' day. As a result modern psychology developed a "split personality" (two opposing views of how behavior works) that has served to obscure our understanding of the process that Spengler examined. The task of this chapter is to pick up his argument and extend his idea about the gradual loss of power of the basic principles of a civilization by considering how that comes about through the actions of individual humans. To do that we will use the new view of how behavior works to examine the way that individual behavior creates the fundamental principles (or basic perceptions of reality) in the formative process of a society and then eventually draws out the implications of these first principles in the historical development of the ensuing civilization.

Spengler supplied the first half of this proposition, as we have seen. He outlined the way in which the members of a primitive horde might have coalesced into an emerging society. In that process some few individuals propounded ideas that came to be accepted by the mass as best expressing their shared ideas about the nature of reality. These, then, became both the creative fount and the cognitive boundaries for driving toward the destiny of that culture, and the civilization into which it developed.

But why must the first principles eventually become

Perception of Reality and the Fate of a Civilization

corrupted and result in the decline of a culture/civilization? Spengler essentially relied on the many critics of Western Civilization regarding this as a fact. Thomas Kuhn (1970) advanced our understanding of the process—though limiting himself only to the evolution of scientific thought—by showing that as scientists investigate questions about the nature of reality they are drawing out implications of the basic axioms of their science. Eventually they come upon aspects of reality that seem unable to be encompassed by any formulations that don't conflict with others already considered well established. These anomalies, as he called them, eventuate in the kind of intellectual chaos that can only be resolved in a paradigm revolution. His use of *paradigm* is closely related with the notion of first principles or basic axioms about reality as used here. In my view the process he describes applies to all human social functioning not just the scientific endeavor.

We take the argument a step further. What is it about the nature of human thinking and behavior that will produce the kind of phenomena that Spengler and then Kuhn pointed out? Implicit in the propositions of both of them is the idea that we frame our observations of reality in terms that incorporate assumptions about what could and could not be true. We then go on to generalize from those observations and derive implications which we express as special cases of the initial assumptions in concrete actions. For example start with kids on a playground. With even the simplest kind of group activities you will hear statements like, "You can't do that." "That's cheating," or the like. The observable action shows that there are constraints underlying the overt behavior. They circumscribe what the activity is and is not. As groups of people develop into communities they act in the same way. They develop rules for group action, whether expressed overtly or held unconsciously. With more complex organization, members of society agree upon certain laws to define the limits of tolerable individual behaviors. We use the same terminology to talk about (e.g.) the "laws of physics," expressing our most fundamental formulations about the nature of reality. They strictly limit the hypotheses one would entertain in looking for factual details of the various specific aspects of reality. Patent offices do not waste much time considering inventions that contain propositions inconsistent with the laws of physics. And, lawyers, politicians, etc., in their competitions to gain the right to set new rules for society, argue the consistency of their proposals with the fundamental principles enunciated in the constitution.

The psychology behind all behavior is that thinking/behaving is hierarchical and controls perceivable conditions via feedback. That is, it functions via specific execution of layers of intentions/purposes. It comes clearer when you think of thinking as a form of behavior. Go back to the example we used to illustrate the feedback nature of steering a car. It is quickly apparent that this behavior doesn't simply illustrate one feedback system. The control of your muscles in your hands and arms serves to create just the right patterns of tensions to move the wheel in such a way as to create just the right image of the front of the car where you want to see it in the road. But things don't end there. Your movements on the steering wheel serve to keep directing your car to a destination that you have in mind. Thus, beginning with why you are driving in the first place you can see a hierarchy of purposes, each determining a more concrete behavior lower down, all the way to the particular pulls of various muscle groups. If you examine the process going up the hierarchy you notice that you go from overt actions to thinking behavior. Your overall purpose resides in your thinking behavior. It only comes to light for others in the form of the overt actions that it sets in motion.

The feedback nature of behavior requires that at any level of concreteness/abstractness there is a purpose or intention that the behavioral system serves to execute. Back to the car again: It is clear that your movements on the wheel serve to keep the front end of the car in that relationship to the road that you intend to perceive. Likewise, your purpose in driving at all is to accomplish your intended reason for getting where you are going. At each level in such hierarchies some condition is being maintained (kept constant) by changes (whatever needed) in the subservient levels.[71]

In logical reasoning, scientific and mathematical thinking, legal reasoning, or everyday thinking there is the same underlying process. The first principal, or basic axiom or premise can be thought of as the highest level perception, setting the boundary upon further statements or perceptions. For example, in the familiar high school logic example, *All men are mortal, Socrates is a man, therefore . . .* , etc., we might think of the premise as the most general perception that subsequent argument is examined against. The conclusion is ruled in or ruled out depending upon whether or not it can be perceived within the boundary set by the basic premise. The process of ruling upon a subsidiary statement (it must be perceivable) can also be thought of as carrying out an intention to influence a specific judgment on the part of oneself or someone else as audience. The conclusion is the perception intended as the target of the trajectory of the logic. Thus, the original target, *Therefore, Socrates is mortal* is perceived contained within the bounds of the initial first principle.

A concrete illustration should make clearer the behavioral nature of such transactions. Assume you are engaged in an argument, whether with a spouse, a political or social opponent or some other competitor for defining the right and wrong of some situation. Your intention is to perceive (see, hear, otherwise sense) a message of some sort like, "Oh, you are right, I didn't see it that way at first." Your argument has been aiming at this outcome. Your *behavior* has been an attempt to control the interaction to achieve this outcome, that is, to produce this perception. I exclude here quarrels or emotional arguments where the objective has degenerated into an aim to hurt rather than to persuade.

I acknowledge that it might seem somewhat strange here to identify premises as perceptions. The reason I am doing it is to keep our discussion within the single framework for describing all behavior that I have been using above. The way in which you can regard the statement, *All men are mortal*, as a perception is that it represents a generalization from a group of observations (whether or not the speaker is claiming to have personally made such observations is irrelevant). Observations are perceptions; you can only make an observation if you can perceive some phenomenon. True, you can make observations within your own mind by thinking. The "man on the street" tacitly recognizes the perception in this. We sometime find it necessary to talk about viewing something "with the mind's eye" in order to convey this kind of experience to someone else.

There is nothing revolutionary in this view from a common sense viewpoint. Ordinary people commonly talk about their aims, goals, purposes, intentions. That is the same as having a perception of the desired objective in mind. It is relatively easy to see this as we look at ourselves and others doing everyday activities. We get up and eat breakfast by intending to do so. We then go to work, or engage in whatever other activities we have planned for the day, again by way of intending to do so. In each case the behavior we perform brings about the situation we would describe, if someone asked us to communicate a picture of what that action would accomplish.

The behavior of most interest here is the behavior in which people think and talk about their longer run purposes such as political, economic, religious, and social interests. Behavior in such instances does not consist of simple actions such as sitting down at the table, driving a car, hitting a baseball, etc. It is abstract and many concrete actions might be involved to implement it. For just one example take the case of someone running for political office. It involves making speeches, recruiting supporters, formulating policies, etc. Yet, for some purposes we might consider the large mass of separate acts as one complex behavior, that of "running for office." This is the sphere in which we can see how what Spengler was talking about takes place.

Every large purpose, that is, one which goes beyond the individual everyday act, is enacted within the rules of the society and rests upon its basic assumptions and perceptions about the nature of reality. Further, it also implicitly exists within the current state of these conditions, the current state of its place in time in the history of the society. Thus, to run for any political office in a given society at a given time is not exactly the same thing as it was a generation back, or a generation before that, etc. The individual who carries out any large purpose does so in a context of both cooperating with the other members of society who are acting on the same plane at the same time, but also in competition with some of them, namely those who would propose to enact a somewhat different version of that large purpose. The purpose in question is circumscribed in a sense by rules which derive from the basic perceptions about the nature of the nation or society and the nature of the reality in which it exists. It must not go out of bounds to an extent that would conform to a different type of society.

Yet the underlying principles are forced to evolve, because competitor(s)—for influencing the future history of the society—will attempt to dominate by proclaiming their proposal as more consistent with both the basic assumptions and the current desires of the relevant members of the society. Even if you claim that you are returning to the views of the founders your program can not reinstate the conditions of life that obtained for the founders. Your audience might call you conservative, but that does not mean that they think your ideas are identical with those of any previous generation.

Proposals for new rules for all the members of a society or civilization are thus formulated within a context of the previous history of that culture, the contingencies that exist because of the on-going progress of technology, the changes that population, practices and technology have imposed upon the physical environment, the restrictions imposed by the competition of other cultures/civilizations on its borders. The proposal is claimed to solve problems in all the manifold environments implied by the above. The task of gaining support against the competition of other interests must simultaneously control the perception that it is a natural derivative of the values already held by the audience and will enhance them. But, no matter how broad the purpose or abstract the intention of any new proposal for organizing the behavior of the members of society, the net result of the law, policy, public attitude, cultural belief must eventuate in concrete acts. That is where conflicts with other principles occur to create the kinds of situations that Kuhn called anomalies in the history of science, and that we might call inconsistencies or conflicts in competing attempts to control various aspects of the way the society is organized and functions.

In the evolving development (or, history) of a society an anomaly is the event that an accepted law or policy—as enacted in specific behavior—results in conflict with other formulations of the same kind. Opponents of the particular formulation might charge that it really violates the higher principles laid out in the constitution. And so on. Then the proponents either try convincing the public that the challenge is wrong, a misreading of its constitutionality or of its implications, or they have their way by exerting brute force over the opposition. In any case the accumulation of such anomalies results in the sort of chaos that Spengler and Kuhn postulated in their respective theses.

The process has gone on as individual minds have struggled to formulate proposals incorporating hierarchies of purposes, both within themselves and within the society as they perceive it. No formulation can escape the consequence that it must be executed in individual acts and that these become the grounds for inferring generalizations about the initial proposals that might have implications far from the supposed intentions of the originators. Or, might tend to bring about conditions inconsistent with the conditions that others are trying to bring about.

It must occur to you that I am not saying anything you don't already know. Everyone knows that you can't back up history. But that is exactly my point. That is why the members of any civilization who act on the level of public purpose inevitably contribute to the evolution of the moral and philosophical state of the culture. But the possible lines of cultural evolution are not unlimited. The evolution turns into degeneration when competing lines of overt actions not only tend toward different concrete conditions, but are supported with justifications that constitute wildly different versions of the society's basic premises. The fact is that the highest level concept about the nature of reality and the nature of the society—as expressed in constitution and laws—is simply an amalgam of the views shared by those members of society who deal with it. Action pertaining to it is circumscribed both by what the rules will permit (at any given time), and by the flexibility (or lack thereof) that obtains between the citizens involved with them. The rule formulating process, itself derived by individuals reaching some level of agreement, also contributes to the evolution of the rules in the way that competitors will try to claim that new proposals were already tried and failed, or are in violation of the constitution, or are really their ideas pirated by the opponents, etc. If you prevail you have automatically contributed some modification to the rules. If you fail you may still have done that, if your competitors had to make some redefinition of the rules to prevail. That is the process by which the evolution of a civilization wears out the possible rationales for the range of all public policy proposals and formulations.

Another way to look at it is that the previous generations' rules have already created the conditions you have currently and also whatever problems you now have as by-products. (Recall the critiques and complaints related in chapters three and four.) Sooner or later most of the implications of the original first principles have been exploited and it becomes apparent that there are problems that current formulations are failing to solve. Even formulations that might bring solutions are resisted by those in authority if they seem to imply different first principles than those considered acceptable in the view which those authorities are devoted to maintain (as we shall see in more detail in chapter thirteen). To give this argument some concrete substance consider how the mere claim that a proposed solution to a particular social problem would be "communistic" can result in foaming at the mouth in many of the leaders of our current society.

Let us review the way that human behavior works to produce the phenomena I have postulated above. In common parlance, it is goal oriented. In more technical terms we would say that it functions through feedback control systems of interlocking hierarchies of purpose from the most concrete to the most general or abstract. The very fact of the interlocking of systems within the context of more comprehensive systems creates the possibility of conflicts of intentions within any given person, which might lead either to paralysis of action or reorganizing of the larger system. The common expression is that a person might be "at war within himself." Similarly, individuals obviously come into conflict with each other when they are attempting to achieve purposes that would produce different states of the same condition of their common environment.

When it is a case of different individuals attempting to

define a perception of (some aspect of) reality differently each contestant will increase his or her effort to prevail. If their efforts are about equal the result will be stalemate or paralysis just as in the case within a conflicted person. If the activity in question concerns large issues pertaining to their society their struggle will resort to attempts to redefine the implications to be drawn from first principles, or finally to propose new interpretations of the first principles themselves.

Curiously enough this view of the nature of behavior constitutes a departure from many of the formulations of contemporary psychology but a return to ideas that are commonly held by ordinary people, like the ideas that behavior works to achieves goals, that it originates within the intentions of the individual, that actions can serve many combinations of purposes simultaneously, that one's actions are interconnected within larger frameworks of the mind. Current psychology has come down a path that diverged radically from the pioneering American psychologist, William James a century ago. James was moving in a direction that would have been able to handle the problem of circularity in causality as applying to the behavior of living organisms that troubled Lucaks.

In a misguided effort to make psychology more "scientific" psychologists coming after James (and Dewey) attempted to analyze behavior in terms of a linear cause-effect view, simplistically trying to ape the procedures of the physical sciences. They did this by applying what I have come to call the Cartesian paradigm (after Descartes, 1650) which views behavior as caused by external forces or stimuli acting upon the living organism to evoke behavior as reflex responses to the "stimuli." This way of looking at things "from the outside" works perfectly well when applied to physical phenomena. Physical objects do not perceive that you are examining them or trying to affect them. They do not perceive anything, in fact. They do not have intentions, and they don't resist anything you try to do to them, other than by being very solid, or very heavy, etc. And, finally, they are not trying to control any conditions to specified values.

The psychology of the "man on the street" often reflects a mish mash of the contradictory views of how behavior works. Even while he/she might talk about his intentions she will say things like, "Don't make me mad," or "I had no choice, the chocolate bar was just too tempting." The individual in this position acknowledges his or her in-dwelling intentions for actions to which he/she is willing to lay claim, and attributes to "stimuli in the environment" actions counter to his or her favored view of self. (Note that the very idea of a view of self, favored or not, suggests a highly abstract system that seems to be controlling what shall be owned and what not.)

I believe that this confusion about how behavior works might have had something to do with why even scholars interested in the history of civilizations focussed more on Spengler's probably unfortunate analogy with the life cycle of individuals rather than on his main thesis—about the process of decline in civilizations. That choice inadvertently introduced a "forces of nature" process to account for social evolution. It suggested externally acting influences upon the process of history—the very principle Spengler's detailed analysis controverts.

Notice that in the above discussion there was no place for talking about the stimuli that would cause the behavior involved in working for the large purposes in a society. That would entail a single direction of causality, but you can see that in the interplay between individuals involved in the behavior that drives the evolution of a culture there has to be a circularity. If one's intended objective is in danger of being thwarted by a contradictory intention of someone trying to influence the same cultural condition in a different direction, then one must adjust one's behavior to keep tending toward the original outcome, counteracting the disturbing effect of the other's action. The actions of the other become like crosswinds, curves etc. that interfere with one's efforts to follow the path of a road. The action to counteract disturbances is both cause and effect of what one observes as your action proceeds.

It is in these kinds of interactions that the potentialities inherent in first principles are exploited. Early on they realize new possibilities, as early Christian ideas of the worthiness of all people came ultimately to be argued to question the practice of slavery. (In Western society. Slavery is still not seen as reprehensible in certain non-western cultures.) But, as time has gone on the meaning of first principles like, "all men are equal" has become involved in dilemmas as their implications are battled out in specific debates about whether various "entitlements" are validly implied by constitutional guarantees, etc. The results have increasingly involved administrative attempts at compromise and regulations more and more of which seemingly defy common sense, as we saw in chapter four.

Since I am maintaining that the processes of behavior/thinking are most easily understood in terms of a feedback-control paradigm for understanding behavior it will be useful to flesh out a few more aspects of this view for the discussion of the next two chapters. After that, in Part III I will present in more detail the most comprehensive and explicit version of this paradigm. It will provide a fuller background for the discussions of the following chapters.[72] This version is being developed by a growing number of life scientists who have come to title the collection of their various separate investigations, *Perceptual Control Theory* (PCT).

As we saw in the example of driving a car, the process can be understood as using feedback in controlling action toward achieving the desired state of affairs. Control is pretty much seen in the same way already used by the "man on the street" in describing efforts to control one's game, one's performance, one's job and all the other things to which the term is applied. What hasn't been widely recognized so far is the way feedback functions in control processes. To attempt to control something, whether the temperature of a building, the sighting of a target, or the impression you want to make on a new acquaintance, it is necessary to have a perception of the current condition of the situation of interest, plus a conception of the desired condition and finally, some means of bringing the existing to match the desired. The desired state is identified with the intention of the actor, and behavior is seen as the entire process of realizing an intention by causing the observed condition to match the intention.

There are technical terms for these concepts which we will consider in chapter nine, but it is not necessary to master them at this point. Some more features of this overall scheme are important to bring out now, however. Besides the idea of hierarchies of control it only becomes apparent when actually working your way through these ideas that we automatically resist any external influences that would interfere with the continued control of a state of affairs at its desired value. We saw that in the discussions about competition between opponents trying to affect the values of various conditions in the physical or social milieu. Let us take these ideas to a further look at Spengler's view of the trajectory of a civilization's destiny, even at the risk of repeating some of the previous discussion.

Chapter 07

History and the Control of Perception

Spengler saw history as the working out of the destiny of any given society by the development of implications from the initial conception of reality—the basic axioms held in common by the members. He called the mature stage of that process civilization. The process continues until the creative potential of the first principles is exhausted. In his view the decline of the West exemplifies that process at work. I have attempted to extend his contribution, proposing a mechanism of how that process works in terms of individuals' behavior. From that point of view, the process is the same for any social unit—individual, family, tribe, society. It originates in the behavior of human beings in living, achieving control over vital perceptual variables of their environment. In that perspective a culture/civilization is the collection of high level perceptions, controlled individually, but functioning jointly through the overlapping interaction of the members of society. The members develop mutual interests in controlling their conceptions of reality and desirable values in congenial patterns; that is what holds them together as a society. Certain of the earliest formulations become adopted by the original group and form what Spengler called the original axioms or basic forms of thought of that culture.

Let us examine Spengler's view of how those axioms develop. I have pieced together his answer from various points distributed throughout the two volumes of his work. He goes back in every case to surmise what might be the circumstances in which a primitive horde of people take the first steps toward developing a culture. He draws upon the evidence of the earliest writers he can find in each of the cultures he considers, plus what the existing archeological evidence indicates, and reports from outside observers of the culture, if any. Then he finally draws his conception of what the basic nature of Nature is like for the culture in question.

His conjectures embrace what can be inferred about the physical milieu in which the people in question were living, what social pressures they might have been under, and how the combination of these would constitute the challenges they would face, individually and as a group. Each member of that primal horde would be coping with the tasks of development and survival, using methods derived from the instinctual cache of human nature enhanced with the techniques each developed and shared among his or her fellows. The techniques they learned were then retained via their communicative interactions. In time some of them would be communicating about their communications—forming concepts. As we know, concepts are schema that incorporate the common elements from a collection of perceptions.

As we translate Spengler's thesis into terms of behavior we see more clearly the relationship between the acquisition of individual competences and the development of the culture. Each developing individual is observing, and being trained in, techniques/actions/ behaviors of the other members of his/her society and simultaneously organizing her/his own hierarchy of purposes with peculiarities unique to himself or herself. The general schema all hold in common are being assimilated through the interactions that each has with the other members of the community during his own development.

Both discrete experiences, and chance, enter into the development of the hierarchy of control systems that any one individual develops. Spengler's insight was to see the underlying patterns of behavior that one shares with the others in terms of the patterns which come to comprise the culture. As the language of the primitive horde begins to embrace not just momentary commands and expostulations but concepts—what hold experiences together through time—some particular person's way of expressing his or her view of the nature of reality is taken over by the others as the best way of expressing it. Thus, chance also plays a part in the development of the culture resulting from *which* particular individual's way is commonly accepted. As these events proliferate they eventually become the axioms with which the members apprehend reality. The members progress from horde-with-habits to society with culture.

Spengler outlined the different conceptual foundations of the various cultures that he studied by filling in many lacunæ with surmises drawn from overlaying the outlines of all the civilizations for which he had evidence so as to infer the unique form taken in a given culture by the general pattern. In doing so he admittedly risked making errors. His procedure was no different from what archaeologists do in collecting some bones and/or shards from one dig, others from other digs, deducing what would be necessary to fill in the gaps, in deriving a whole picture of the species or society under investigation. Regarding his work in terms of individual behavior we can both comprehend what he depicts and speculate about the mechanisms via which behavior works in the development of the conceptual foundations.

He asserted that as cultures/civilizations[73] evolve over time a penetrating analysis will show that the original axioms or first principles of that culture continue to underlie the patterns of thinking and invention that transpire within its members. In fact the development of the culture consists of drawing out implications—and hence, applications—until the original trove of potentialities starts to become exhausted. We are reminded here of Lukacs (1970), "Most of the technical inventions of the twentieth century were predictable; they were the applications of ideas that existed at least one hundred years before . . . ."[74] Kuhn's (1970) parallel insight in the history of science shows repeated instances of this phenomenon of drawing out implications of initial axioms until their creative potential is exhausted. Then occurs what he termed paradigm revolutions. He called the period of drawing out applications of basic axioms, after a paradigm revolution "normal science."

Both Kuhn and Lukacs (among others) described, to some extent, how given individuals modified and synthesized their intellectual inheritances from earlier compeers to come up with new applications of the basic paradigms.[75] Sometimes, in the process of doing this, a person would discover that there was no way the accepted paradigm could be milked to produce an answer for a problem he or she perceived. At such points s/he would be forced either to give up and go on to some other task, or when "lucky" reorganize in a way that produced an entirely new paradigm. Thus we can see the interplay between the dilemmas of individuals and the crises of cultures. A culture crisis occurs when many of its members incur similar dilemmas, in either their practical or spiritual lives, or both. We will examine the theory of behavioral reorganization in chapter nine and further in fourteen. Suffice it for now to accept that there is a need for a concept like reorganizing to account for how human competence grows—and by extension how culture grows as a function of how individual experiences grow. In the previous chapter I drew a parallel between individual and cultural developments as they progress into the period of decline when useful innovations from the implications of first principles begin to dry up. There are some studies of human aging that suggest that individuals face depression and despair when their ability to reorganize to meet new challenges declines. Perhaps that is a crude parallel to the presumed demoralization of a culture in a state of decline. Perhaps it is the very process, writ large on the societal level.

Spengler's view, that civilizations degenerate as the potential of their initial axioms becomes exhausted, looks at human behavior from the outside in. It tacitly assumes some kind of historical forces or underlying principles. Behavioral theory, in contrast, points up the possibility that there are no such things as historical or social forces; instead, the idea of an historical "force" expresses an individual's description of the sum of actions of a mass of humans. It looks like some kind of natural force in history because of viewing it from an external point of view.

The current behavioral theory has been based upon building and testing models of the phenomena of interest. As such it requires that we look at behavior from an internal point of view. We ask, What is the nature of an intended perception that an individual seeks to control, that when viewed externally, looks like that person is an implement of some large "social force"? Take for example, the point of view reflected in complaints about the "death of common sense," or "why nothing works anymore," in our culture by the critics we examined in chapter four. It's not hard to infer that the subjects of such complaints are in distress. Their attempts to control some given conditions ended up in failure either through conflict with other goals of their own, or because of interference from the actions of others. Whatever habits for coping with everyday life, the person learned while growing up, proved to be inadequate for the challenges he or she currently faced. When this happens to isolated individuals we lay it up to bad luck, incompetence or an unfavorable environment. When it involves large numbers of people we grudgingly begin to suspect that their normal coping habits are no longer well suited to newly developing conditions of life in that society. AND that no one else in the society has culled a solution from the intellectual resources of their culture.

Erik Erikson (1950) has contributed to this picture putting forward a thesis that the kinds of developmental malfunctions that may occur in children in a given society reflect the moral dilemmas of their culture. He states, "we would in principle like to believe that with therapeutic investigations into a segment of one child's history we help a whole family to accept a crisis in their midst as a crisis in the family history."[76] He then extended his description of family crisis to that of the community, and then the society. He saw the nature of such crises, in general, as caused by attempts to satisfy contradictory goals or values, with the consequence that individual behavior oscillates ineffectually or hangs up.

In part II of his book Erikson provides detailed accounts of the way in which such conflict develops as individuals try to cope with societal contradictions, how it impacts the development of children and how, as the disarray progresses, it constitutes moral dilemmas for the society as a whole.

He begins his analysis with a study of modern Sioux culture as it has been impacted by its history with the United States. "Only the most stubborn of romantics will expect to find on a reservation of today anything resembling the image of the old Dakotas who were once the embodiment of the `real indian' .... But this once proud people has been beset by an apocalyptic sequence of catastrophes, as if nature and history had united for a total war on their too manly offspring."[77]

He relates that the Sioux had, themselves, only relatively recently moved to the high plains to organize their lives around hunting buffalo. Then white settlers moving west had "playfully, stupidly" decimated the buffalo. Further,

> In search for gold they stampeded into the Black Hills, the Sioux' holy mountains, game reservoir and winter refuge. The Sioux tried to discuss this violation of their early treaties with United States generals, warrior to warrior, but found that the frontier knew neither federal nor Indian law.[78]

The consequence was the sporadic warfare that finally was resolved by the Wounded Knee massacre when the Indians were outnumbered by U. S. troops four to one, and were forced on to a reservation (of the poorest land). Erikson mentions that even some U. S. generals were shamed and embarrassed by the patent disregard of treaty after treaty that the country had signed with the Indians. Here we observe conflict within individuals deriving from basic principles that could not be wholly reconciled. Throughout its history the expression "We are a nation devoted to the rule of law," has reflected a basic principle of U. S. culture. However, at least two other Principles were also at work in the individuals involved in the history that Erikson cites. They were those of individual freedom and the idea of private property.

The principle of individual freedom would seem to have evolved over the course of time into the view that the individual, himself, determines what is and is not permitted. The way in which people generally determine this in our society is by acting on one's own impulses and retreating in the face of legitimized opposition. By legitimized opposition I mean everything from appeals to conscience, community pressure, public opinion, and ultimately law enforcement. In our present day society it is common for a person to discover "what the law really intends," by testing the limits and then backing off when threatened or confronted with arrest, or lawsuit.

Our law does not seem to have much moral force in the absence of the machinery to enforce it. Erikson saw it that way in regard to the Indian treaties, and it is only more evident today with traffic moving through a stop light. Or in such common occurrences as police officers telling a person fearing violence, "We can't do anything until he breaks the law." Law abiding citizens often feel like sitting ducks under threat by a predator, as is periodically portrayed by programs like "60 Minutes." Erikson indicates this condition was already in evidence a century ago in his statement about the lawlessness of the frontier. Many people permitted themselves to do whatever they were not restrained from by direct police action. At the frontier U. S. law was effectively suspended.

The sanctity of private property shows up as an even more poignant issue in the case of Indian lands. Let alone the fact of race and ethnic prejudice—in which the laws clearly did not apply equally to second class citizens—the Indians' more collective view of ownership would not have disposed them to move quickly to obtain Philadelphia lawyers to secure their property rights after the negotiation of a peace treaty. It wouldn't have occurred to them as something any one would need to do. It wouldn't have occurred to them that there were laws to regulate such matters, even if they had been able to read English, because the idea was so foreign to their own cultural paradigms about land tenure.

Thus, we see that the potential for inconsistency in application of the basic principles in the American version of Western culture disposed both the perception by the Indians that Americans lacked morality and the experience of internal conflict by various members of American culture themselves. As Erikson said, some invaders among the pioneer types were people with whom the Sioux could identify cultural values of their own, such as trappers, soldiers and even Quakers and early missionaries whom the spiritual Sioux could respect for their "consecrated belief in man." However, he continued, the Sioux found least acceptable the class of white man who was destined to teach them the blessings of civilization—namely the government employee.

The young and seething American democracy lost the peace with the Indian when it failed to arrive at a clear design of either conquering or colonizing, converting or liberating, and instead left the making of history to an arbitrary succession of representatives who had one or another of these objectives in mind—thus demonstrating an inconsistency which the Indians interpreted as insecurity and bad conscience. Red tape is no substitute for policy; and nowhere is the discrepancy between democratic ideology and practice more obvious than in the hierarchy of a centralized bureaucracy.[79]

One might well consider that there is a warning here about the potential for violent conflict between ourselves and large sections of the third world in present day affairs. However, I have cited the above materials for a different purpose than to advocate how we should conduct our international relations. Because Erikson is looking at a broad panorama of intercultural relations, our attention is drawn to the generalities that can be derived from the actions of large numbers of individuals. It becomes easy to disparage the decisions of particular secretaries of Indian affairs and particular Indian agents in regard to particular issues—to disparage them as corrupt, mindless and heartless, if we are liberal, or as fostering irresponsibility and dependency, if we are conservative.

In any case it is all too easy to concentrate on the consequences from an outside point of view without ever putting oneself in the shoes of the individual making the decision. We easily forget that—as an hierarchical control system—any of us, in any social role, is keeping a great number of perceivable variables matching our own intentional settings, all at the same time. Whether Indian agent, farmer, social worker, social commentator, social critic, banker, soldier, politician, policeman or cleric we must first of all continually insure that our actions will result in putting food on the table on a regular basis. In addition to that, unless you are your own boss, it is necessary to have an acceptable relationships with one's superior(s). Besides that is the maintenance of familial and social relationships. And—for some if not most of us under a sufficiently broad definition—all of this is subsumable under the requirements of maintaining one's whole-System concept, embracing one's conception of reality and principles like sense of justice, higher purpose and spiritual affinity, and self image.

The daily-activity counterpart of normal science is to be found in the habits that any individual caries out routinely in going about his or her daily affairs. These habits simultaneously take care of providing the requirements for food and shelter, the routines of daily living and the conduct of normal social relations—all within the limits of one's highest order of personal assumptions and values. One's self concept embodies one's image or idea of oneself, nested in one's socially learned and experience-tailored interpretation of the basic system of his society and its view of the nature of reality.

Thus, when trying to imagine our way into the thinking of an Indian agent (to keep with Erikson's example), we start with what we see him actually do. It is the best indication of his most abstract conceptions. He is aware of the decisions he has to make in his daily routine. He is probably not aware of the highest principles to which those decisions must conform. But, in the background of the Indian Agent's daily activities are "rules" like the need for understanding what his supervisors and their supervisors require—all the way to the U. S. congress—e.g., that lands which are attractive to voting citizens moving west must be kept available. Then opposing claims of local Native Americans must—*somehow*—be perceived to be invalid.

This brings up a situation in which two control systems (at least) attempt to control the same perceptual variable (like the disposability of some area of land) to different values. The Indians' chief value would be to secure the historical situation, the Indian agent's would have to approach a redefinition of the situation. In such a case the possibilities are:

1) One party resets their priorities to approach the value setting of the other party—(surrender);
2) Both parties re-set their basic intentions to the same value; (compromise)
3) One party employs overwhelming force to control the situation in question, acting as if the opposing party does not exist. (Conquest, or suppression.)

In human affairs throughout history the third option has been most frequently employed whenever there was a large disparity of power between the contending parties. This was the case in most dealings between government agents and American Indians. But there had to be further consequences within the individuals involved. The Indians would refer to agreements previously made, would take actions believing in their validity, would employ such force as they could, when other options failed to achieve control over the conditions they were perceiving.

The Indian agent, on the other hand, would have to deal with them in a way that did not violate the higher injunction that the Indians must give way to the invading people. He could offer such compensation as he personally commanded, he could make promises, threats, appeal to "reason," (I. e. "It's beyond my control, you must give in or be wiped out.") If the value at which he controlled his perception of this issue were disturbed by some actions of the Indians he would automatically begin acting to correct it. (And likely assign malevolent intentions to the Indians.)

Lower level systems would be constrained to "make sense," staying within bounds of the highest level commands. For example, "the Indians are savages, you can't reason with them, they don't respect laws about property or refraining from violence." Action to correct disturbances to a high-level perception does not take place in isolation in a person. Our Indian agent presumably also had principles such as sense of fairness, humaneness, loyalty, responsibility and the like. Any and all of these were likely to become affected by outputs correcting the initial disturbance. If his principles could be maintained by adjustments that would not result in conflict with other intentions, they would adjust without even coming into awareness.[80] This is the mechanism of the process called, "rationalization." On the other hand, if action to correct some perceived error state results in an increased sense of error for some other intention, that comes into conscious awareness. Consciousness, while still a rather mysterious phenomenon, apparently is a good indicator of where error is mounting in a human control hierarchy.[81] With the Indian agent having a strong sense of fairness or abhorrence of inconsistency between the words of treaties and his perceptions of the immediate situation, there would be a strong possibility of bad conscience and accompanying anxiety. How he would resolve this would depend, of course, on how the rest of his behavior controls were organized.

If the agent had strong values pertaining to the Christian principle that all humans are equal in the eyes of God, his sense of justice would likely become affected. Then he would have to take some corrective action. It probably sometimes happened that a particular individual would resign his job in protest against the conflict imposed by the overreaching external requirement—just as we see in our present-day papers, with whistle blowers, and corporate or government officials taking stands of conscience. In other cases the individual would, gradually or radically, revise some values in order to harmonize them with others, giving rise to what was perceived as a new insight, by the subject, but as corruption by an opposing observer.

Thinking within this framework points up the perspicacity of maxims like, "consider the source," in understanding any person's stated position. It also highlights the need for sufficient and specific details for constructing one's model of the person behind the actions, if you are trying to analyze his/her actions. In drawing up such a model one must also be aware of one's own purpose for it.

Erikson illustrates the job of eliciting and then harmonizing details of this type in the case histories he supplies in his book. His purpose was the practical one of facilitating a more constructive approach to life on the part of the patients he described. In another context, some modern businessmen do something vaguely comparable in attempting to facilitate more creative interactions with subordinates and peers. In each instance it requires an understanding of the subject's views of self and reality. A different application, in the late 1960's[82], was JFKs consultation with a panel of psychologists, psychiatrists and psychoanalysts to learn from their analysis how Nikita Krushchev most likely viewed reality and thus how best to relate to him in the tense confrontations they had in the cold war.

In each of these instances the person in question attempts to construct a model that would allow her to envision her subject of interest from the inside out, an essentially empathic point of view. This approach requires evaluating all the possible interacting motives in the subject and attempting to see how they would balance out in action in specific situations. Although earlier attempts at such modeling were not constructed with the new view of feedback-control in behavior, I mention them here as possible adumbration of that approach to understanding personality in action. Without an hierarchical model, however, assigning priorities among the various motives interacting within an individual would be a matter of considerable guesswork.

Spengler did not concentrate upon the task of the individual facing his or her specific challenges, as Erikson did, of course. His interest was in identifying the process by which the structure of a civilization deteriorates. In a certain sense their tasks were mirror images. Where the latter focused upon how individuals could be strapped by inconsistent demands from societal rules, the other looked at the way in which societal rules become transformed in application by numbers of individuals. The common point between them, is that the thinking and action of any individual, even in the most practical matters, is ultimately limited by his basic axioms about reality. For example consider this excerpt from Spengler

> Aristarchus of Samos, who in 288-277 [b.c.] belonged to a circle of astronomers at Alexandria . . . projected the elements of a heliocentric world-system. Rediscovered by Copernicus, it was to shake the metaphysical passions of the West to their foundations . . . . But the world of Aristarchus received his work with entire indifference [because it] had no spiritual appeal to the Classical Culture [even though] it was differentiated from the Copernican . . . by . . . the assumption that the cosmos is contained in a materially finite and optically appreciable hollow sphere, in the middle of which the planetary system, arranged as such on Copernican lines, moved . . . by this device of a celestial sphere the principle of infinity which would have endangered the sensuous-Classical notion of bounds was smothered.[83]

The thing to note in the above is Spengler's contention that even though Aristarchus faced the same problem that Copernicus did, and arrived at a similar solution, it was circumscribed by something that had to be kept even more true in his culturally prescribed way of thinking: that reality consists of bounded objects. Hence space, and therefore infinity, would be nonsensical concepts and no intellectual crisis was then perceived by his audience. As time went on and Classical science developed further it reached the stage where what Kuhn (1970) called *anomalies* piled up to the point that various individuals were beginning to experience the discomfort of sensing their basic paradigms falling apart. That was what Kuhn called a scientific crisis—in terms of the scholars concerned. It didn't occur in astronomy until the relevant axioms of Western thought were being spelled out in Renaissance science. The paradigm revolution that eventually followed would be a result—in personal terms—of what we could regard as reorganization. It would involve the highest perceptual level—the basic nature of reality as a system of the whole.

Returning now to the more individualized, personal, developmental crises that interested Erikson (1950) (he and Spengler do use the same word, *crises*) let us draw this idea out a bit further. We consider the hypothesis that "disturbed" behavior of a child reflects chronic attempts at re-organizing on the part of the developing organism. This happens when a given course of action fails to achieve the realization of a desired condition and the consequences begin to affect the balance of the intrinsic system. (The same sentence in everyday terms would be: The individual's capacity for rationalization begins to break down.) The particular case studies Erikson dealt with certainly demonstrate chronic reorganization attempts. His subjects were continually failing because the intellectual and emotional climate (of the child's household and community) would not support the kind of control efforts the early reorganizations prompted. For example, consider the first case in the book.

He tells us about a small boy, Sam, whose mother was

disturbed by strange noises from his room one night and, upon entering, saw him in a state that appeared to her like the heart attack "from which his grandmother had died five days earlier." Subsequent attacks were followed by a medical diagnosis of epilepsy, with amended diagnosis of "precipitating factor: psychic stimulus." The amendment acknowledged the fact that the subsequent attacks had followed finding a dead animal in the yard, and next, accidentally crushing a butterfly in his hand. Whether there might have been some mild, indeterminate cerebral dysfunction is questionable. The boy was in good health and there was no history of any pathology. Erikson surmised that the idea of death was the "psychic stimulus." His further details show the boy as bright, energetic and aggressive but with his aggressiveness mainly sublimated as teasing because of pressure from his parents to be a "nice little boy" in a new neighborhood where his parents were concerned about acceptance. In his old neighborhood, "he must have received at an early age the impression that it was good to hit first, just in case." Erikson adds more details about the boy's "low tolerance for aggression [that] was lowered further by the over-all connotation of violence in his family."

He traces the issue further back in terms of the boy, "being caught in this, his parents' conflict with their ancestors and with their neighbors, at the worst possible time for him" in the sense that the parents felt vulnerable as the only Jews in a gentile community and with a history as, "erstwhile fugitives from ghettos and pogroms." His estimation of "The worst possible time" was in reference to the fact that the boy was going through the maturational stage characterized by intolerance of restraint and the sadistic kind of infantile maleness commonly occurring between the ages of three and four.

Let us go back and pick up the evidence Erikson gives that is suggestive of on-going reorganizations. First, he recounted that a month after witnessing his grandmother's heart attack (from which she died after five days) the boy found a dead mole in the yard and became agitated over it, asking his mother many shrewd questions as to what death is all about. He ended up unsatisfied, finally commenting that she did not seem to know either. That night he "cried out, vomited and began to twitch around the eyes and mouth." I would see this as an indication of something interfering with the systems we consider the physiological realm. The boy had been rather forcefully and abruptly confronted with the phenomenon of death for which he apparently had had no previous preparation. And that in the context of his own ambivalence about his aggressive impulses. Erikson also reported instances of Sam throwing objects that hit him and the boy's mother, and the boy's signs of guilt and fears of reprisal. In these circumstances the boy was faced with controlling a new set of perceptions, that is, attempting to get them to values that would conduce to acceptable overt behavior. In other words to reorganize so that impulses connected with these perceptions would be subject to his developing sense of rules and principles of conduct.

What do I mean about needing to achieve control over a new set of perceptions? First, let me remind you of the temperature control system of a building upon which to build an analogy. You control the ambient temperature by setting the thermostat. That provides the perceptual condition to be maintained. The word, "control" is ambiguous here unless you conceive of the temperature control system as an extension of yourself. It is, in the sense that by the act of setting it you signal to it your intention about temperature. It is thus a lower order system controlling more directly the condition of your comfort zone regarding temperature.

In an analogous fashion, Erikson's patient, Sam, was faced with the task of finding a way to think about the phenomenon of death that he had just experienced so dramatically and apparently for the first time. We make that latter inference from Erikson's report that at first the parents had told Sam his grandmother had gone away on a trip, but he kept asking questions that showed that he found lacunæ in their stories. By saying he had to find a way to think about it I mean that he needed a category to hold the whole array of details he had concerning something in common about his never-again-seen grandmother and the unmoving mole and butterfly.

How is that like controlling the temperature in a building? Clearly temperature is something that is experienced by the body in a number of ways. Right now as I write this it feels hot in my study. I sense this in my body but I could not tell you just which sense receptors are at work. They might all be skin heat sensors, or there might be internal detectors transducing other signals as well. It has been in the 80's outdoors today and my reading of the thermometer downstairs coincides with my subjective sensations. I am aware through memory that this medley of sensations is experienced by me as a single variable—the perception of how hot/warm/comfortable/cool/chilly/cold I can feel at various times. Right now my subjective awareness is equivalent to a particular value. That awareness is in some sense prior to, or more primitive, cognitively, than my activity of classifying it as a type of experience, namely as that particular perceptual variable that we name, *temperature*.[84]

That is what I mean if I say that developing a category is a form of behavior that classifies my physical experience. My body controls the variable to which that verbal category refers, by opening (or closing) pores and permitting increase of sweating, and whatever other physical measures that physiology has discerned. A higher level intention extends this activity of my body by making movements for the purpose of opening a window and/or administering the temperature control system. (This is still something my body is doing, even though we say "I" am doing it at this level, instead of "my body is doing it"). But if I want to think about, or talk about this to someone as I am now to you, I need to control a different type of phenomenon—that of categories of thought, and words to express them, that we must both have learned through cultural training.

So, if little Sam did not yet have a category for thinking about—containing—the phenomena involved in his encounters with death they, the phenomena, would reside for him in the realm of pure, overexcited emotions. Let us return to Erikson's description of how the boy began to extend his control in this area. (I omit his explanation of how the child had connected his worries about death with his own aggressive impulses.)

> One afternoon soon after the episode in which I was struck in the face, our little patient came upon his mother, who lay resting on a couch. He put his hand on her chest and said, "Only a bad boy would like to jump on his mommy and step on her . . . isn't that so, Mommy?" [She acknowledged that maybe he was having such an impulse and tried to reassure him that even a good boy might sometimes feel like doing that.] "Yes," he said, "but I won't do it." Then he added, "Mr. E. always asks me why I throw things. He spoils everything."[85]

What might that last sentence mean? I think he means that Mr. E's question elicits anxiety. It confronts Sam with the need for a concept that he doesn't yet have. At the same time it furnishes the challenge that requires reorganization to resolve: To become aware of the constellation of observations and feelings—and then to recognize that they pertain to words he has heard grownups use, such as *injury*, *sickness*, *death*. That is reorganizing his "cognitive structure," in the conventional psychological terminology, or as I prefer to say it, "reorganizing his hierarchy of behavioral control systems." Sam's dilemma comes in part from the confusion resulting from his parents' ambivalence about sharing their honest perceptions of the phenomena he needed to assimilate, and their ambivalence comes, in turn, from their conflicted perceptions of the societal rules their family should uphold.

Now to relate this discussion back to Spengler's contribution with which we began this chapter. You might already be convinced that the formative principles of Western Civilization have become corrupted, as Spengler claimed, whether or not you subscribe to his thesis that that is an inevitable result in the evolution of any culture over time. If you do, it might well be from making similar interpretations of the evidence described, and decried, by the various writers mentioned in chapters three and four. But, as I keep repeating, the job is not yet done until we have a better sense of knowing how it works. And knowing how it works is essential, I believe, for working with it—increasing one's own effectiveness in doing something about it. Something that makes a significant difference.

Besides the cognitive framework of the view of behavior I am using, which I trust you are beginning to absorb, our tools will be the concepts of Kuhn (1970) and Erikson (1950) already discussed. There might well be others who have supplied equivalent tools, but these will suffice. I have already stated that Kuhn's concept of paradigms and paradigm revolution is not limited simply to understanding the history of science. Those concepts can equally well be used to think about the history of cultures/civilizations. They are both the creative frame for understanding reality and the limiting bounds that prevent certain potential restructurings of it. They preclude some possible reformulations because they simply would not make sense with what members of the culture already hold as self-evident.

Paradigm revolutions occur, according to Kuhn, as the

useful implications of the basic ideas are developed through more and more applications. As that process continues and begins to accumulate anomalies, they might at first be set aside as imprecision in measurement, or some such incidental effect. When they become sufficient irritants to existing "truths" the ground is set for a paradigm revolution. One such example given by Kuhn, is

> The technical problems to which a relativistic philosophy of space was ultimately to be related began to enter normal science with the acceptance of the wave theory of light.... If light is wave motion propagated in a mechanical ether governed by Newton's Laws, then both celestial observation and terrestrial experiment become potentially capable of detecting drift through the ether.... Much special equipment was built to [detect] it. That equipment, however, detected no observable drift.... [But theoreticians came up with plausible explanations for that.] The situation changed again only with the acceptance of Maxwell's electromagnetic theory.... Maxwell himself was a Newtonian [and] still believed... his electromagnetic theory compatible with some articulation of the Newtonian... view. In practice, however... the required articulation proved immensely difficult to produce [creating] a crisis for... the paradigm from which it [Maxwell's theory] had sprung.[86]

Placing ourselves in the position of Maxwell, or any of the other scientists Kuhn talks about, it is not hard to imagine that their sense of confusion, discomfort or puzzlement in the face of the information they were attempting to assimilate into a coherent framework makes them different from Erikson's Sam only in terms of the degree of abstractness of the issues they were encountering. In the case of the generation following Maxwell, as people began to tease out the implications of electromagnetic theory the most recent derivations of the current paradigm for space were becoming corrupt in that the newest facts, as they were discovered, did not allow of sensible interpretations within the existing paradigm. With a little stretching of our thinking we could see the parallel in Sam's case as his concepts regarding the reliability of the picture of grandmother, initially supplied by his parents, was becoming corrupt as he tried to reconcile it with the other facts he had in awareness.

Apply this same way of thinking to the broader issues of the evolution of cultures. In this case not all the facts are discovered as they are in science; besides scientific and philosophical discoveries, other facts are created by political, judicial and business decisions. For one example, consider Marxist theory, at least as articulated by Lenin. It turned out to be incompatible with so many paradigms of Western culture that some people reacted violently against it upon first contact. It postulated that the state, not the individual, is the most real social entity; it predicted that individuals could come to give higher priority to common rather than individual needs; it assumed a teleological principle of economic development whereby capitalism would inevitably migrate into worker ownership. It even affected to discern that genetic evolution included a kind of Larmarkian factor—mutability through conditioning—as it eventuated in Lysenko-ism.

The onward flow of history appears to have revealed quick corruption of the implications drawn from Marx, if you accept the criticisms some thinkers have made, that his theory has never been purely applied in any human society. In that view communist countries, as we look back on them currently, could be thought of as having evolved corrupt derivations of Marx's ideas rapidly—in effect a short term, mini-culture that shot through its history in a few generations. On the other hand, if you view Marx's theory as a derivation of Judeo-Christian principles, turning some on their head by taking them to the extreme—like holding early Christian congregations as a model for society—it would seem to be an offshoot of Western paradigms. I'm not sure that Spengler would not now take that view and see it as another evidence of the degeneration of Western paradigms.

As to how such processes go forward, individual by individual, we can observe them all around. Step back, mentally, while arguing some serious issue with a friend, and try to see the axioms in terms of which your arguments are framed. For example, when Sam threw a doll and hit Erikson in the face, and he asked, "Why did you do that?" and if Sam had said, "because I wanted to," Erikson could have then asked, "What is it like to want to do that?" or, "How do you feel about that?" or, "Do you know why you wanted to do that?" If Sam had a pertinent answer his consciousness would have moved up a level. He would have been speaking from the aspect of the level that "ordered/commanded" the action. The part of self that ordered the action would be perceiving the level that executed the action.

This description has so far been confined to increasingly abstract functions in oneself. In a philosophical role you could look for the cultural mold within which your own higher level perceptions were framed. And in the role of philosopher of history, that Spengler was taking, he traced the evolution or devolution of major cultural values or principles back to their roots in the formulations of the culture-forming period. For one example, again, accepting his notion that the primitive Germans brought to their Roman conquests the very different notion about space than that of Classical civilization, he would conjure the track of the spiritual impulse associated with that perception all the way from the building of the Gothic cathedral to our present day fascination with space travel.

But all these processes are taking place in, and only in,

the brains of individual human beings. Human beings, acting to control the myriad variables of daily living from the most prosaic to the most abstract (for the given person), do things. Each and every one of those doings is simultaneously controlling many levels of perceptual variables, each within the constraints of his or her highest level. If one asks either the three year old or the sociopath, "Why did you smash the window," and the answer is, "Because it felt good [to do]," they are very likely exposing the highest level perceptions they were controlling thereby. If, on the other hand, you ask the soldier, "Why did you fall on the grenade?" he might say, "Because it was necessary." Superficially that would seem not much different from the others' answers. But, underlying the necessity would be the much more abstract principle: To make his biggest possible contribution toward the preservation of "his way of life" in that moment.

Actions in the social sphere, defined large to include the political life of a nation, are taken by human beings, individually or in concert only as a result of interaction between immediate goals and the more basic axioms within which they are constrained. The judge in Illinois who has been pointed out as making decisions that have totally devastated the lives of several children was acting in each case to maintain principles of law that had come down through the twists and turns of successive legislation and prior judicial decisions. He must have held honoring the law as an abstract value, over and above whatever consequences it had in particular instances. At least there is no evidence that anyone bribed him to make these unpopular decisions.

Stepping back from the process to ask how a current exigency of law could result in such inhuman outcomes, we have what Spengler meant by saying that the basic principles of a civilization eventually degenerate through being drawn out to their logical extremes. And we have what Kuhn in his more restricted sphere called the anomalies that eventually produce an intellectual crisis. And we have the inconsistencies observed by social critics that lead them to perceive our society as morally bankrupt. And, at the base we have the personal confusions—the experiential aspect of control systems locked up in internal conflict—that is seen from an external point of view as corruption or political apathy. All that gives rise to the conditions for cognitive reorganization, which can lead to many different outcomes in different persons, from the highly creative paradigm revolution to the "every man for himself" narcissism of the sinking ship.

Chapter 08

HIERARCHY OF PERCEPTIONS AND EVOLUTION OF IDEAS

The title of this chapter refers to something two seemingly unrelated processes have in common: The way in which the hierarchy of behavioral systems develops in a human being and the way in which ideas evolve within a culture. Within a human organism, as well as within the quasi-organism of a society, the process begins with certain givens. In the case of a human being it begins with a genetically supplied set of intrinsic control systems that keep the infant organism functioning and set the stage for the further development of the learned-behavior hierarchy. Within the horde of primitive humans on the verge of coalescing into a society it begins with the body of instinctual human tendencies which the interaction of the members will modify as they develop their particular culture.

It was Freud who noted that the behavioral habits an individual develops to survive in her/his initial physical and social environment serve both to satisfy the demands of the intrinsic/instinctual/genetic givens and the demands of his or her social milieu. He observed further, that whatever these initial habits happen to be, they exert a profound influence on subsequent development.[87] That this really is a fact is frequently confirmed in the experience of clinicians, but is no great news to the "man in the street" either. Adages like, "you can't teach an old dog new tricks," or "A leopard can't change his spots," also reflect this insight to some extent.[88]

Freud built his therapeutic approach on his observation about the persistence of the earliest behavior patterns in personality development. However, his theory about *why* that is really amounts to a circular thesis that it is so because that is what we observe. The newer behavioral theory has taken us a step further. Tentatively accepting the notion of successive reorganizations of the learned behavior hierarchy, we have the implication that when reorganization occurs the new pattern thereafter controls the perception of subsequent sensory signals. Subsequent signal patterns will either be consistent with the new organization of behavior—the current experience is *familiar* and the organism keeps on with "business as usual,"—or in the case where incoming signals do not match the expected signal of some control system they might either not be perceived, or perceived but no control action taken.

If the continuing sensations—in the modality in question—are not brought into harmony with the expected pattern by the control effort it can eventuate in triggering reorganization. Only then does the "paradigm" formed from the initial experience get overturned. This leads to two important implications. Existing control systems resist disturbances to the perceptual variables that they control, whether such disturbances originate from the environment or as a result of reorganization elsewhere in the organism. The corollary is that people resist changing unless reorganization breaks down existing control systems. In short, we don't change unless we have to.

This abstract account of early development as a series of successive reorganizations is readily illustrated with a concrete instance. The psychoanalyst child researcher, Rene Spitz, published a fascinating little experiment many years ago, applying some early techniques in ethology. He investigated the question of what perceptual pattern really evoked the first smiles of the (about 3 months old) infant. He cut out several circles of cardboard and attached them on sticks, much like the simple fans people used to use in un-air-conditioned rooms. He created several different versions of simplified features of the human face. On one he drew two round circles in the position of eyes. In another he drew a vertical line perpendicular to a horizontal one in the position of the nose and mouth. He also drew the other obvious combinations. What he found was that the drawing with the two eyes was sufficient to evoke the smile. This was at that time called the "gas smile" according to an earlier belief about its nature. It has by now been established as a true controlled perception.

You might wonder why I called it a controlled perception instead of a controlled behavior. The visual sensation the child receives creates an error in a—genetically set—intrinsic/instinctual control system. The intrinsic system would call for perceiving a second configuration, this time of a certain pattern of muscle tensions in the muscles of the cheeks: A smile, from the external point of view. Think about it. The infant can not see himself in the Spitz experiments, so he is not imitating a visual image. Yet he produces a set of cheek muscle signals that creates the image of a smile for the observer. He doesn't produce this pattern all of the time—he doesn't smile continuously—only when the two-eye pattern is present. So, there must be a genetically determined control system "waiting" for this incoming pattern, to produce the outgoing pattern. The outgoing pattern does not consist of a fixed pattern of nerve impulses to the muscles but a stored intentional pattern. An "intention" that must be matched by the proper configuration of kinesthetic signals from cheek muscles.[89]

This line of theorizing requires us to assume that this

particular intrinsic system was "waiting" for a two-eye pattern in some fashion like that in imprinting. When it is perceived (at the ready-moment) an error occurs in the genetically given system which it corrects with an output that matches a built-in value for the configuration of facial muscles that we call a smile. As I said, the child can not see himself and as far as we now think he can not consciously determine to smile. If you grant that for a moment we turn to what kind of system would go into action given the sensations occurring in the child. What we have to work with is Spitz's evidence that the simple "two eye" pattern is enough "stimulus." I prefer, "environmental signal," at the price of being a bit awkward, in order not to mix theoretical paradigms. The child's smile is the organism-end of the transaction.[90]

The smile seems to be *evoked* by the visual input. But to say it is evoked is simply to say that it happens in the specified circumstance. To search for a mechanism of how that would work we utilized the newer view of behavior that I have drawn upon in this work. The fact that this is only a speculation has been dealt with above, but I will reiterate here—because this way of thinking does require some on-going reorganization on your part—that that is the first step in the type of model-building whereby any behavior mechanism has any hope of being elucidated.

This fairly long excursion upon a seemingly small point was necessary to help us focus on the level of detail that we need to continue the elaboration of how behavior grows, step by step, upon the foundation of what has already been brought under control. So now we have the young infant producing the smile to sets of eyes moving slowly from side to side in front of him. (Check this out by watching relatives doing their part to get an infant to smile.) At the same time the baby is simultaneously registering other sensations. Parents regularly coo in concert with the eye movement. Gradually the whole constellation shows that it has become a unified pattern for the child, because we see the cause-effect pattern sometimes reversed. The child now smiles spontaneously at times but does not continue, if it doesn't soon perceive the pattern the relatives must supply. The further development in this thread eventuates at about eight months when the child shows discrimination not only for two eyes but for the whole facial pattern of the mother, and maybe a couple other regularly seen relatives. He or she shows distress at other faces—what is technically termed, "stranger anxiety."

The single important fact for our purpose in all this is the evidence that a certain template has come momentarily to match the expected-perception of what a face should look like, and any other pattern of signals is treated as erroneous. I am referring to the fact that the child is now controlling a perceptual variable—image—of "what a face should look like." Faces that do not match the now-established expectation are met with built-in defense mechanisms. At least that is what we infer from the child's retreat from unfamiliar faces at this age. As time goes on there are many reorganizations in this and all the other developmental threads, as shown by the Plooij's (1996) work as well as the earlier work of Piaget. We must remember however, that overall development is creating a hierarchy in which control systems at each more abstract level resist inputs arising from reorganization in lower levels that trigger errors in what already exists. Sometimes that reorganization persists to effect the higher levels as well. Otherwise, it seems that some new pattern developing in a lower level persists, because it is in some essential way syntonic with systems of the level above. This is a crude picture of what it means, functionally, to argue how early development exerts influence on subsequent development.

Now consider that I have implied that the mechanism of what in traditional psychology are called "the cognitive" systems is not fundamentally different from what have been known as "motor" systems. In everyday terms, thinking works the same way as (bodily) action. The thinking abilities of the organism work in a more distant, but still ultimately direct way, to accomplish what spooning the porridge to the mouth accomplishes. This is apparent in the hierarchical view we have been using, but in traditional psychology the notion of hierarchical organization of the cognitive systems has not been much developed. Different individuals have control levels of approximately the same type—in terms of levels of abstraction. But, the systems on each level may vary greatly from one person to another, depending upon the kind of environment the individual needed to control during development plus differences in genetic predispositions, plus the effects brought about by the random element in reorganization.

Some control was always going on from the beginning of life. Hence, all development takes place within the context of what is already controlled. Thus, the point with which we started: That early development persists as a fundament, underlying and constraining subsequent development, as so neatly expressed by Jacob (1987),[91] "how could I fail to observe that all the "selfs" of my past have played a major role—the earlier the more so—in the construction of that inner model that dictates my tastes, desires and decisions."

Jacob is a good subject with which to take the argument from the individual to the cultural plane. As a Nobel winner he does indeed manifest how working to realize/perpetuate his essential self in on-going reorganizations also shows up in his conception of reality. It should, since for him as a scientist, discovering reality was both a personal and occupational goal. He produced observations and ideas that served to correct gaps in his own reality-system-concept and simultaneously contributed to others focused on the same issues. There is no required social force or mysterious leap between individuals solving problems and the growth of their culture. Any peer group—scientists, artists, legal scholars, journalists, etc., working at a given point in history and interacting, cooperating, competing, communicating—forms a community. The peer community, by coming jointly to accept certain fundamentals, continually align and re-align their individual system concepts. The result is what we perceive as a shared culture, when we take the outside/in view of it. Whatever conflicts occur as they compete with each other occur within the limitations created by the fundamentals that they jointly accept. That shared culture also migrates conceptually over time as the members contend with each other for qualities such as dominance by drawing ever new interpretations from their shared basics. And also by the efforts they make to keep attracting, or enlightening, their target audience.

You could go back and take another look at Kuhn's (1970) book as a set of case studies of exactly that. In other areas of culture we have comparable expositions, biographic histories and the like. What we see as culture is the collection of customs, rules, habits, conceptions and mores as seen from an external point of view. All of us hold an internal view, sharing large aspects with each other, and our actions to control the perceptions of our social environment create the phenomena of culture that we observe when we switch to take the external view. The development of competence in a given individual interplays with that individual's moving into a position or role in society. The cohort of individuals moving into complementary roles in society, repeating generation after generation, creates and continues the evolution of the culture of that society.

As an individual continues reorganizing his or her hierarchy of control systems during the early years of life, he/she does so in the context of social relations. They form a matrix within which many of a person's behaviors are under control without being disturbed, either by the actions of others or by large changes in the physical environment. Other conditions are controlled jointly as when two people lift a box that neither could lift alone. At still other times the control action of one individual disturbs the on-going control of a perception that is important to another, as when I set the thermostat down and my wife complains of feeling cold. Then several possibilities come into play. The persons in conflict might spontaneously (even unconsciously) modify their objectives to reduce the disturbance experienced by one or both. Or, one might do that, changing his or her own expectation in a way that reduces disturbance to the variable as perceived by the other. They might communicate and agree to such an adjustment. They might negotiate to test relative power in a determination of whether one or the other might simply continue controlling at his own value, compelling the less powerful one to give way. They might physically fight with one leaving the field. They might communicate in a fashion that is a symbolic version of a physical fight, but just as effective, given cultural "rules of the game," that might apply.

This list does not exhaust the possibilities but it will suffice to indicate how thousands of such interactions, taking place on a daily basis in a society, will eventuate in shaping and gradually transmuting unwritten rules, or mores, as the society evolves. Eventually someone (or several) will articulate them into formal myths, constitutions, legislation, and manners that constitute the culture. What occurs in this process became the chief focus of Spengler's interest in the history of civilizations. We find a sketch of a mechanism by which such cultural principles migrate in meaning and ultimately devolve upon final forms in an article, "On Degrees of Freedom in Social Interactions," by William Powers (1989).

> although the degrees of freedom in the physical environment might be inexhaustible, by banding together in civilization and pooling our efforts we create a shared reality in which the size of the universe

in which we actually live is bounded by the goals and actions recognized as means in our system. The more of us there are, and the more closely-knit the society we perceive and accept, the fewer become the unused degrees of freedom.

What is the relation between individual actions and the degrees of freedom in society?

When it is said that we are not free to shout, "Fire!" in a crowded theater, there is an unspoken assumption in the background. We are not free to do this if we are aware of and reject the alternatives: causing a fatal panic or going to jail. Of course if we are willing to accept the consequences, or are unaware of any, we are perfectly free to shout what we like where we like. It is not any law of nature that limits our freedom in such circumstances; the only limit is imposed by the organization of the person in question ... limitation of freedom is imposed by the fact that doing certain acts that satisfy one set of goals or purposes ... can cause other controlled perceptions to depart from their reference levels....

Suppose that someone possesses n independent control systems at some level in his hierarchy. This means ... this person could set independent reference levels for each of the n perceptions in any way he liked. But now suppose that he has ... already specified n-1 reference[92] levels ... there is only one value that can [still] be specified ... that will not create direct conflict [which] will destroy the ability to control ... [in] an hierarchical control organization. The higher level systems set lower-level references as their means of control; if the lower systems come into conflict [there] will be an impairment of higher-order

> control processes ... [this is] a purely *mathematical* limitation on the freedom of the whole system ... The principles ... apply ... to a social organization, because ... [that] as a collection of control systems ... must work in harmony in order for the whole to function properly ... [so there is a parallel with] a collection of individuals, each of whom acts as a control system in any given circumstance, and all of whom must learn to live in harmony to avoid the dangers of social conflict.

If you find some of the more technical terminology in this piece difficult to follow, come back to it after chapter nine, where the background of this way of thinking is spelled out in some detail. Powers continued on with this analysis of how the degrees of freedom actually become circumscribed as the systems become more complex. This applies in the analysis of the quasi hierarchical-control-system that is a society, because that quasi-system exists as the joint perceptions of its members. It suggests how the continued increase in complexity of the hierarchy of an individual, or a society, can result for a time in increasing competence and then begin to turn around and begin to go in reverse. Powers spells that out in relation to our society,

> We live in a society in which competition is praised as a spur to greater efforts and a higher quality of production. The free enterprise system in principle permits each person to look after his own interest, advancing himself relative to others by increasing the value of his work to others. Again in principle this process should lead to the state in which each person has found a niche which maximizes the benefit to himself while at the same time maximizing his contribution to the well-being of all other persons. Our educational

procedures... nurture this competitive concept of social evolution.

When sufficient degrees of freedom exist, this design for a social system would seem quite feasible. It is, in fact, a heuristic that leads to the minimization rather than the emphasis of interpersonal conflict [because if it worked as imagined, each instance of] conflict would result in a winner and a loser, and the loser would turn to some other endeavor. Eventually each person would find a [niche]....

There are least two important factors which prevent this system from operating to reach a low level of conflict. The first is the fact that a person in a society can interact with the society only as he understands it, not as it actually is. It is not generally understood that [the outcome of] free competition ought to be a minimization of competition. Instead, the way we train ourselves . . . has resulted in a glorification of conflict itself... The achievement of such rewards and such prestige becomes a goal accepted as important by large numbers of people, even though few of them have any realistic hope of joining the small circle of winners.... In a society that accepts conflicts as something to be sought, little value is placed on the cleverness with which we find social solutions that avoid direct conflict. *Each person's understanding of the nature of his society ... organizes all his lower-level purposes. If those purposes do not [minimize] direct conflict, it becomes unlikely that we will find a peaceable solution to our social problems.*[93]

[The second factor is that] Whatever theoretical notions a person may have about his society, he is not going to continue entering conflicts deliberately if the result is consistently against his interests.... One can not take care of himself or his family if the major part of effort is cancelled out by the efforts of others. . . . Sooner or later one looks for the path of least, not most, resistance. Then the question becomes: does such a path exist? The answer depends upon degrees of freedom.... [the] perceptual model within which we find our goals... is almost entirely a manufactured world... [made smaller by the extent that] The more of us there are, and the more closely-knit the society we perceive and accept, the fewer become the unused degrees of freedom... the final result can only be a society in which for each person there is one and only one conflict-free set of goals possible, at every level of his organization . . . . The more standardized a society becomes, the fewer become the individual goals and the means for achieving them . . . . Long before actual exhaustion of degrees of freedom occurs, the level of conflict within a growing and increasingly standardized society must begin a rapid ascent... an increasing amount of difficulty [is] experienced by everyone in going about his affairs.[94]

This theoretical analysis gains support from experimental studies of the effects of overcrowding in animals.[95] Freedman (1975), after reviewing the range of studies available at the time, and describing the kinds of behavior pathology that they found, and the theories that had been advanced to account for the findings, drew the conclusion that, "Although each of the explanations discussed previously has something to offer, it does not seem . . . totally adequate . . . . Something more is needed. I would propose that the effects are due at least in part to problems involved in the social interactions of the animals . . . . The more there are the more frequent and intense the social interactions." The actual mechanism, then, would appear to involve the problem of degrees of freedom among the potential intentions which an individual can attempt to realize.

The analysis in terms of degrees of freedom also provides another way of thinking about how principles begin to conflict as social systems undergo increasing complexity. It is obvious that thought evolves within an individual. We change our minds, we learn more, we grow in skill. When we say that our thought is *evolving*, however, we imply that the change is going in some direction—it is not merely random. This is probably most easy to see in the life of mathematicians, as any mathematician's thinking progresses through solutions of more complex problems within a given area. But, we find indications of it in anyone who *thinks*. There seems to be a general tendency for more people to become politically more conservative as they age, than the other way around. This might be explained in terms of increasing awareness that many youthful enthusiasms—while noble in aspiration—turn out to be too difficult to achieve, or to have previously unnoticed undesirable consequences. The observation that many beautiful ideals prove impossible to realize in a given cultural milieu does not necessarily mean that they could never be realized in any milieu. It could be that the degrees of freedom has already been co-opted by different values for the perceptions that would be required in that society.

In adulthood, the perceptual variables that one controls tend to undergo less change unless and until a crisis occurs. And crises occur less frequently as a person acquires greater competence. Competence *means* making fewer errors, having fewer crises, controlling finer details in one's work. But increasing competence also brings one eventually to a new horizon, where crisis again becomes more likely. Everyone gets promoted to his level of incompetence; I think that was a "Peter Principle."

The crisis is often one in which some important aspect of one's physical and/or social environment has changed, either for external reasons or because the individual him—or herself has achieved greater status and thus a new social horizon. The individual lacks the ability to control some perceptual condition that is vital to him as a system. Getting fired from a job might well disturb the control of many variables, but among the most important would be control over resources like food and shelter. The extent to which reorganization, rather than simple error correction, would be needed would depend upon the structure of the person's self system.

Conventionally we have been used to differentiating the development of skills from the development of cognitive abilities. The former generally involve physical actions of some sort that can be readily observed by others. The latter need to be inferred from more abstract performances. Hence we might more readily talk about *competencies*. Increasing one's competence at some job, whether carpentry, bulldozer operation, basketball or investing, consists of improving the control of all the variables that make for the most desirable results in each respective endeavor. The work of the scientist, lawyer or clergyman can be thought of also in terms of competence. In order to do that you must have a picture, image or model, of what would be the most desirable results of those endeavors. They can in principle be broken down into finer details just like the more externally observable handwork skills.

A trial lawyer, for example, in practicing his craft in his most critical arena would be trying to control the perceptual condition, "jury decision." It can be thought of as a variable, with at least two-values, "guilty-innocent." In many cases it has a greater range of values, though still as a discrete variable, such as *Innocent, Manslaughter, Negligent homicide, Murder*. He can not control the variable of jury-decision directly however, because there is no firm linkage between his action and this result as there is in the action of moving the steering wheel and the path of the car. What he does control is his choice of words, his tone and loudness of voice, his gestural signals, facial expressions etc. He is not conscious of this level of doing. He is more likely to be conscious of his strategy. All the bodily expressions are operating to carry out the verbal and visual image that his choice of strategy implies. It, in turn, will, he hopes, evoke[96] a course of reasoning in his hearers that should tend toward the result that he desires.

People with relevant experience have little doubt that they can differentiate lawyers with greater trial competence from those with less, just as sports audiences judge the abilities of athletes, teachers judge the abilities of students and so on. Ordinarily we have objective measures, like cases won or scores made, that harmonize with other judgments about relative competence. Given this obvious point, it follows easily that we can also make judgments about increasing or decreasing competence in a given performer in a given arena over time. Where competence increases—what we call maturing or seasoning—it is found that it consists of greater control over more detailed aspects of overall performance. The result is better and more consistent "scores" of whatever is the measure of performance.

Since individual competence does not develop in isolation, occurring, rather, in a social context in which peers are both cooperating and competing in controlling the same types of perceptual variables, the communal refining of the art becomes a function of the number of separate niches, or specialties of competence, that can be found. The practitioners observe, copy and modify their own productions as they learn from each other. If the creation of new kinds of work—new areas requiring new kinds of competence—does not keep pace with the niches that different individuals acquire, eventually some individuals will come into conflict.

This is how competence evolves in a given field while the practitioners in that field are developing individually. But, the degrees of freedom to reorganize into unique niches becomes a limiting condition for the development of competence in the sense noted by Powers. Here I return to Kuhn (1970) for some of the best illustrations of all three of the features Spengler discerned in the progress of thought in a culture. Kuhn provides many illustrations of how a given line of thought would gradually develop and point by point result in an increase of power of some scientific pursuit. At the same time, such lines of thought continued to be constrained within the paradigm currently accepted as basic by all the players in the field. Finally, he argued, the kinds of anomalies that accumulated would result in so much personal discomfort (because of apparent contradictions or violations of parsimony) that some individual would undergo a reorganization in which he would perceive/create new fundamental axioms for conceiving of the phenomena in question.

Extend Kuhn's concept of anomalies both to other aspects of culture besides science, and to the lives of individuals. It can be most readily observed (and is often most dramatic) in outstanding individuals when their intellectual competence meets defeat. If the person's decisions begin to fail to secure desired results and he keeps trying—keeps reorganizing—he might make a great discovery. He might also keep going around the same track until in frustration or desperation he attempts something that is not new but is out of bounds. It could be out of bounds because it violates some basic premise of his culture—as in Spengler's example in the previous chapter about Aristarchus anticipating Copernicus's solar model almost a thousand years earlier, only to find no-one was interested in it. (It didn't fit with the system-concept of reality of classic civilization. It was, in other words, a "bizarre idea.")

Another way to go out of bounds is to attempt to control an uncontrolled variable with an act that is criminal within one's own culture. Basically this is not different from the other way of going out of bounds. At the deeper level the society members' overlapping versions of system-concepts concerning the fundamental nature of reality would result in a sense of error in the members when perceiving the out of bounds behavior. What they would do to correct it is mainly a function of whether anyone defines it as falling under an established rubric like the law. Then the correction takes whatever form the law prescribes. If it can not be identified under any existing form of sanctions, it is ignored. In fact, it is cognitively invisible; people who hear it spoken about don't hear it, as happened with Aristarchus.

I can illustrate that with my favorite funny-but-true stories about perceptual-set in language recognition. On two different occasions my wife and I were in Helsinki, Finland, as tourists. On the first occasion we had just purchased tour-bus tickets in a little boutique at the back end of what appeared to be a private walk between stores on a business street. It had taken us some exploring to find the boutique in its improbable—to us—location. As we were waiting at the curb for the bus I overheard two other Americans puzzling over the same problem. I walked up to them and said, "The place you're looking for is down that little walk," pointing to it at the same time. They both looked at me with totally blank expressions. Then the wife turned to the husband and said, "See if you can find somebody that speaks English around here." Another version of the same phenomenon occurred on the second occasion, years later. In this case we were standing in the square in front of the Helsinki train station when we heard a fellow American loudly and agitatedly exclaiming, "Doesn't any one speak English around here?" My wife, who is bi-lingual, walked up to him, and said, "Can I help you, Sir?" He looked at her and then said in an angry tone, "I don't speak Finnish," and stalked off. This was an example of psychological "set." The predisposition (desired or Reference value) to perceive a certain percept corrects an unexpected percept, making it agree with the predisposition.

It is likely that Aristarchus was simply not heard by his fellow citizens; what he was telling them was so foreign to the world view they "knew" to be true that it didn't register. What he had to declare was nonsense in their view of reality, but secondly, they must have had no occasion to experience any anomaly that his theory would repair. Their world was working all right. Aristarchus must have been on a private quest without fellow scientists sharing his experience of anomaly that would require personal reorganization. It was quite different at Copernicus's time. Because of an accumulation of other scientific discoveries he was member of a peer culture where others were beginning to share a sense of something wrong with existing celestial concepts. In his time the existing paradigm was degenerating, becoming corrupt, ripe for a new paradigm.

Summary of the argument

Let me summarize the argument here at the end of Part II. I have proposed that the feedback-control explanation of behavior provides a theoretical base for explaining the common theme which I find in both Kuhn and Spengler. I have maintained that Kuhn's concept of the development of scientific ideas—from initial paradigm to normal science, to accumulation of anomalies, to crisis, to paradigm revolution traces a pattern in the history of the sciences similar to that which Spengler claimed to detect in the history of civilizations. I have argued, further, that the drawing out of theoretical implications and practical applications in the phase Kuhn calls normal science corresponds to what Spengler called the achievement phase of a culture. And what Kuhn saw as the growth of anomalies within a given scientific paradigm corresponds to what Spengler described as the phase of degeneration of the practices devolving from the formative axioms of the culture—leading to the decline of that civilization. What Kuhn termed crisis and paradigm revolution compares at least roughly to what Spengler saw as the demise and overthrow of one civilization by the culture that will next become dominant. I have attempted further to show the mechanism of these processes in the behavior of individuals making up these social entities.

I used this argument to refer back to the dismal picture of our world and our own civilization that has been drawn by so many modern writers, reported on in Part I, and to point out that those writers who see conditions getting worse and attempted solutions getting nowhere are illustrating the deterioration and exhaustion of the potential of the founding ideas. I went on to propose that a paradigm revolution that is just beginning in the life sciences can suggest how the degeneration of a set of basic themes/ideas/schemas/paradigms comes about in the life histories of members of the culture. The principles which the members of the culture grew up believing, have begun failing to provide solutions to practical problems in everyday life. That is, simultaneously, the deterioration of the culture. But then, just as some paradigm revolutions result eventually in new societies so the new theory of behavior might be a useful tool both for a better understanding of these historical processes—by the interested scholar—and for navigating the tortuous course through a world in chaos, by the concerned layman. That is because the new theory's more adequate understanding of the nature of behavior yields implications that broaden the range in which a person can look for new solutions to old problems of his or her self or of his or her society.

Behavior is determined by the organism, not by forces in the environment. The role of the environment is that it is the territory in which the conditions the organism controls exist. Furthermore, it follows that what we call, *intentions*, goals or purposes in everyday parlance conform to the technical concept of specification of the controlled variable. When we perceive the environment as exerting influence on behavior, it is because it is comprised of the conditions that must be controlled to survive but also—since many of them are continually changing, like temperature—such changes continually disturb the steady state of perceptual variables thus making continuing control adjustments necessary.[97]

In practical terms this means that behavior is the observable aspect of achieving/maintaining one's purposes/goals/intentions. It also means that you can only affect someone else's behavior by aiding or disturbing his or her control. If you aid it, the result will be relaxation of the aided party's efforts, unless he or she changes her expected intention. If you disturb his controlled perception the other party increases his or her effort to keep the condition at his or her intended value, with interpersonal conflict the eventual result. (To get a concrete sense of both of these eventualities refer to the experiments and demonstrations cited in the resources noted in Appendix A.)

Behavior is the final, externally seen result of the functioning of a hierarchy of control systems of which a person is comprised. Disturbing a condition controlled at some level in a person's hierarchy will eventually involve the whole person, if the particularly concerned control system does not immediately neutralize the disturbing influence. This feature can be seen to account for concepts like "self consistency" or "tendency to reduce cognitive dissonance," which have been postulated by traditional psychologists.[98] And the postulate that organisms act to realize their intentions/purposes can be seen to account for the "Pygmalion Effect," the findings of a series of investigations by psychologist Robert Rosenthal (1976, 1977, 1978) to the effect that people in various circumstances were found to bring about consequences that conformed to their expectations even when they were consciously exerting no influence on the outcomes. (I will mention these phenomena again in chapter ten where they can be ilucidated further with the material to be presented in chapter nine.)

Finally, there is the implication that the formative development of a person consists of periodic reorganizations of the brain circuitry in the construction of a hierarchy of control systems, in which the highest levels control very abstract perceptual variables such as "Who I am," "government," "the nation", "science," etc. Further, these abstract variables—in order to be implemented in a widening arena of life as a person's social world expands in adulthood—incur reorganizations that broaden the programmatic and strategic systems that comprise what we ordinarily label as the competence of the person. As a person's competence grows he or she finds fewer instances of crisis or challenge, so long as the physical and social environment *does not undergo great changes*, and therefore reorganizes less frequently. But that entails that changes in environment will be met with greater resistance—to maintain control (at existing values), if they do occur. Again in everyday terms, this last point restates the old saw about the "hardening of categories" with age, not simply as an observation, but as to why it works that way.

Finally we must consider that internally caused crises in a civilization happen in a context of the society brushing up against other societies—people who do not hold all the same truths as self-evident and who have other shared concepts of the basic nature of nature. They therefore present challenges on a society-to-society level in the form of individual confrontations between leaders, businessmen, tourists, terrorists, and others. The attempts to control their own fates, on the part of alien people, can be seen to constitute disturbances to control of various values by the society in question. That, in turn, creates the conditions under which control intensity is raised by the members of the culture (through the influence of leaders, of course), which results in what historically we see as treaties, culture clash, conflict, war and/or conquest. Whenever any of those measures is successful the control of abstract perceptual variables continues to be maintained. When it is unsuccessful it begins to create the conditions under which the random reorganizations of individuals produce what we see externally as proposals by would-be new leaders of measures to solve the growing problems. If these proposals begin to go out of the bounds of the most sacredly held values in that society, you again have what Spengler was describing as crisis and degeneration of the civilization.

The most original, creative, members of society are the ones that keep finding new implications of the basic themes to meet the new challenges that keep erupting as time goes on. However, there does not seem to be an infinite number of implications that can be drawn from a set of basic postulates. The fountain of really new ideas begins to taper off, even as the challenges from outside grow more pressing. Powers's analysis of the degrees-of-freedom problem has shown how this works in the interplay between reorganization within individuals and their ability to contribute solutions to problems within their society.

PART III

Open Loop and Closed Loop Systems

Western Civilization developed ideas of the importance of the individual and the reality of space in ways that led to powerful applications in the manipulation of physical reality, including the virtue of exploration, the infinitesimal calculus, and the mass production assembly line (among other things). All these implications of first principles employed an analytic approach, linear logic and the role of subject in relation to the object of manipulation—nature thus perceived as inert and passive.

That development succeeded in the the conquest of space and the production of *stuff* far beyond that of any other civilization. But, now we have reached an impasse. As material problems have increasingly been solved the successful approach that worked with them is seen to be failing when applied to human problems. Human beings (as all living organisms) are closed loop, feedback control systems. That means that we automatically and inevitably resist externally applied influences upon our behavior. Only internally instigated reorganization results in fundamental changes in behavior.

Chapter 09

A More Technical Exposition of Feedback Control Systems

As I reported in chapter six there have been an increasing number of psychologists and life scientists who have noted how behavior is a feedback-control process. Among these Powers in particular has developed this view in the most consistent, plausible and detailed fashion—beyond that of other authors in this field starting with his 1973 book. The basic idea—that behavior functions to control perception—was the beginning of a development that has been growing ever since. It will be useful to take the trouble to acquire some more technical grasp of his ideas. I will show in subsequent chapters how certain difficult or confused psychological concepts become much clearer when illuminated by this view. I present the rudiments and hope you will grasp it for its own sake before beginning to look for implications, applications or flaws. Powers's work came eventually to be called *Perceptual Control Theory* (PCT) as the scientists attracted to his idea wanted to distinguish it from control-systems theory in engineering fields.

The discovery Powers made was that—contrary to what scholars had believed ever since Descartes' proposed "mechanism" in 1650—behavior "works" to achieve/maintain/ realize a perceptual state or condition. It also *works by* doing that. The actions we perform bring about, or maintain, perceivable[99] states of affairs in specified conditions. Our example of acting on the steering wheel of a car to keep your view (perception) of the front end in the lane that you desire to see it in works via a "feedback mechanism," as I have been saying earlier.[100] Let's define that more precisely now. A Feedback mechanism is one in which the continuing flow of perceived results of action is "fed back" into a component that compares results with some specification, often technically called the reference value. By "specification" I mean the result-that-should-be-perceived when the action is occurring. Thus, the on-going action is continually being modified so as to keep the perceived result closely matching the should-be-perceived result. Certainly there has to be an incoming flow of sensory signals in perception; that is only part of a control loop, in which specification and action are additional components. The complete control loop is seen as "closed" through the environment. That is, the results of control action/output upon the environment affects the continually changing perception we have of the environment.

Anyone can easily repeat Powers's discovery. In fact, we all do it all the time, although so unconsciously that we fail to see it. Close your eyes and fasten or unfasten some item of clothing, or pick any other of thousands of such "behaviors." How do you do it? By the feel of it. How do you *know* you are doing it? *By* paying attention to *how* it feels. The all-important ingredient, always previously left out of the analysis and description, is that you must already know *what feeling you need* to be feeling. The sensations that accompany your current movements have to match that expected feeling. We do it the same way with our eyes or ears, but I gave the eyes-closed example because it more readily draws your attention to what you must do to accomplish the task.

In any case we need sense perception of some type to be able to perform an action. And it is the sense-perceived *result* of action that we ordinarily call "behavior." Simultaneously, it is with that same sense perception that we know we are performing the action. Which comes first? Do we do something by sensing it, or do we sense something by doing it? It has to be both; that is the riddle of circular causation which bothered Lukacs.

This concept needs careful spelling out to avoid many misconceptions inherent in most peoples' notions about systems and environments. First, of all, the concepts of system, environment and control are interlocking concepts, defined in relation to each other. A system is a group of interconnected components so interdependent that removal or change of any one might result in it becoming either a different system, or a non-system. Yet many systems also have redundant properties such that removal or alteration of one or more components may have no detectable consequences at all. Both of these seemingly contradictory properties must be retained in the broadest definition of system.

Powers worked out the following model of a generic perception control system. Control systems are comprised of:

Input—any form of sensing the controlled condition

Reference—a specification for the controlled condition

Comparator—a component that compares the Input with the Reference, reflecting any mismatch

Error signal—magnitude of the mismatch between Input and Reference value. It is fed to the

Output—or source of action that can affect the sensed Input (via effects of our action on the environment we are perceiving).

The most obvious controlled conditions are aspects of the environment that we perceive as we go about our business. For example, in driving, as described above, the steering wheel and other appurtenances of the car are objects outside one's body; the road, roadside scenery, etc., can also be thought of as objects. But we consider all of it as "the environment" here. In this example, the controlled condition is the relationship that you maintain between your view out the windshield and your expected sight of the road. But, consider: that relationship is neither object nor environment. It is a perception in your head. It is, however, what you control; whatever effect you have on the objects in the environment comes as a by-product of controlling perceptions.

But, "What about the situation where you have incoming sensations and you are not doing anything, aren't you perceiving then?" you might be asking. It is a question of definition to be able to conclude that there is ever a case when a living organism is not doing anything. I personally doubt it. But, even assuming such a situation there is a question of what function a set of sensory signals can have when there is no template in the organism's memory against which to match them. I recall a report of an anthropologist who had made a movie of a primitive tribe and then showed it to them. He was startled to find that they thought it had some interesting light patterns, but they didn't see any people or village scenes. They seemed to have been lacking the templates for matching their incoming sensations to familiar patterns.[101]

Human groups, communities or societies have also been described as control-systems, or quasi-control systems, controlling the group environment. Environment in the sense used here has a double, and potentially confusing meaning. Its first meaning—similar to 20th century common sense use—is the entire physical surround outside the skin (or boundary) of the organism relative to which it is defined. This can also include other systems. They sometimes are sources of disturbance to the physical environment variables that one is attempting to control. They can also be sources of variables in a social environment which an individual is also attempting to control. But, as you will see below, the "environment" of a control system consisting of a neural network in a human body can be other control systems—those that the higher level system controls.

The term 'control' can also have different meanings that lead to confusion. To say that an organism "controls its environment" means that it is constructed to work upon the environment so as to keep its own perceptual variables (which derive from energies of the environment) equal to its own Reference values.* In this process the environment might itself be changed. But this is always as a by-product of the actions of a control system.

If the above picture has begun to seem overly complex and confusing as we add details, it can be greatly simplified by reorienting our view to within the system, instead of from the outside in. From the internal point of view, a control system exerts whatever action necessary—within its capacity—to maintain the reading/value of its perceived variable at its Reference value. For example, if you are carrying a basket and want to keep it at waist level, and I pile an armful of books or rocks in it, your muscles tighten enough to keep it where it was. If none of a control system's actions achieves control, it continues to increase output until it breaks down, or internal mechanisms shift the Reference values to feasible ones, or it reorganizes into a different system, or it settles upon an asymptotic output characterized by some amount of chronic error.

---

* The terms, "Reference," "Principle," "Program," "Sequence," and "Category," are capitalized when used in the sense of technical terms in the theory.

Everyone controls his/her "environment." But, environment is different from person to person; one's environment is what one "must" control—"must" in that everyone's intrinsic functioning is maintained by one's unique hierarchy of interlocking control systems. That is how one's oxygen level, electrolyte balance, etc. are ultimately related to one's self-concept and one's theory of reality.

Next consider the relationship of consciousness and purpose. The old view held that consciousness and will were different entities, and that "the will" could have only one purpose at a time—and that defined consciousness. A new view of consciousness—as the perception of a variable currently being brought to its intended value—would suggest that some one of the many purposes in a system comes into focus of consciousness during error correction. For example, think of how you can be walking along completely unconscious of how you are walking until you slip on a banana peel (or whatever). Further, the fact that the systems of our bodies (and minds) are controlling so many conditions at once suggests the potential for developing conflict, since many purposes might simultaneously give different orders to the same lower systems, (as output mechanisms of the higher systems). And further, that the organism might be unconscious of such conflict whenever its attention (consciousness) is directed to a still different perceptual variable. This conception, along with the conception of a hierarchy of levels in a complex control system, produce implications that result in unifying many concepts introduced by writers on human nature in recent generations. This will be presented in further detail, with examples, below.

Enough Technical Stuff for Now?

You might skip on to the heading *Time In* if you feel you have enough grasp of the nature of control systems in behavior to understand applications in subsequent chapters. What follows here will provide a more technical outline of the model of behavior for the reader who is interested in mastering it for its own sake. I feel, in a way, that it is a shame to be covering the same ground here that is so beautifully covered in all the various readings and demonstrations presented by, and following from, Powers's original work. However, despite the high quality of this growing body of work, it is not yet as widely known as I think it deserves. I present what I hope will be enough of the basic ideas here. It might well improve the reexamination of the serious issues of modern life in subsequent chapters.

The main reason that this work is gaining ground so gradually is that everyone already "knows" that behavior is *determined* by perceptions. That is, if (e.g.) someone sweeps his hand rapidly toward your eyes, you blink. Or, if you hear a loud sound, you turn in that direction, etc. That view has descended from Descartes' (1637/1972), assertion that human action results when impulses coming into the body from external objects serve to trigger various reactions—what subsequently came to be called, "reflexes." Howard Rachlin (1976), a modern psychologist, proposed that Descartes probably got his idea by observing the kinds of clockwork figures that were being developed at the time. They moved mechanically when set off by triggers of various sorts. Looked at in this way, it was a small step to declare that the environment supplies the triggers/causes of action. Theory building often begins with reasoning from analogies in that way.

Descartes' explanation satisfied the thinkers of the immediate time—as they were following his lead in seeking to study living organisms in mechanical terms of the newly developing sciences of physics and chemistry, replacing the former theological explanations. It continued down into modern psychology through Pavlov's (1937) "conditioning," further extended by B. F. Skinner (1938), the father of behavior modification. The "Cartesian" explanation of behavior continued to be taken for granted for so long because no one came up with anything better until our current era.

The Cartesian way of understanding behavior is now built into our language, our way of thinking about everyday affairs. We say, "What is your *re*-action to that?", or, "Look what you made me do," as if behavior is caused by forces coming into a person from the outside. By now so many behavioral scientists have devoted so much energy to looking for these environmental "causes" of behavior that they are stuck with this way of looking at it. It is very much like the situation when Galileo was forced to take back his claim that the earth goes around the sun, because the authorities of his day were stuck with the older view.

Powers was not the first to realize that human behavior shows the characteristics that mechanical control systems are built to imitate. Ashby (1952), Walter (1953) and Norbert Wiener (1948) had recognized that feedback-based machines were reminiscent of human action in respect to their ability to resist external influences upon conditions they were maintaining.

What Powers *was* the first to realize was that you can't really explain feedback mechanisms in terms of stimulus and response. That way of explaining behavior assumes "linear causation;" it goes in one direction, whereas feedback mechanisms always involve circular causation. Even before Wiener and Ashby, Claude Bernard had described how the circulation of the blood involves mechanisms that maintain blood pressure relatively constant in the face of varying demands. I believe it was Walter Cannon who coined the term, "homeostasis" for that function of maintaining a steady state in spite of changes in the environment of the system. Bernard's and Cannon's "explanation" of their findings consisted of presenting their observations in all the detail possible. That illustrated homeostasis, but was not an explanation of *how* it worked.

Powers applied the developing theory of control systems (feedback mechanisms) to account for this feature—of maintaining constancy[102] against external disturbances—that is the prime characteristic of behavior. He succeeded in doing so by analyzing the feedback function into a pair of simultaneous equations that allowed for modeling the circular-causation effect. He tested the analysis by building computer models that embodied the equations and they worked as expected.

He also built a solid, mechanical model, showing that it wasn't just some sort of computer programming trick. The latter, which I have personally experienced, was a shaft—on which he attached a silhouette of an arm—which was controlled by a feedback system working a motor such that, if you pressed upon it, it would resist your effort to displace it. This gadget felt like it was alive. It worked just as your arm would, if I asked you to hold it out and keep it level and then I pressed down on it. Your muscles would immediately tighten, there might be a tiny bounce, then your arm would stiffen and remain just where it was as long as you decided to keep it there. The "arm" could also move to a different position, as your arm does when you decide to move it. To do that there was a dial with which you could change the location-specification. The gadget encompasses all the components of a feedback-based control system. (All real control systems are feedback mechanisms, so I will drop the redundant terminology from now on.)

Perceived relationships in the environment, are not the only kind of perceptions that we control. It also happens within the realm of thinking. It is possible to perceive a relationship between relationships. We call that noticing a correlation. Does that involve controlling anything? Yes, you can think about it as regulating the comparison of two relationships for the purpose of noting a more abstract phenomenon lying behind them.

The nervous system structures that perform these functions are currently being uncovered, although you often wouldn't know that without a good knowledge of PCT, because current discoveries by most researchers in biology and medicine are still usually reported in stimulus-response language.

The controlled (to-be-maintained) condition exists in the environment of the system. Strictly speaking only the lowest order of human control systems are in contact with the environment outside one's body. Some aspect of its condition, that can be sensed by some form of sensory receptor, constitutes the Input, and that same condition must be able to be affected by the Output. The Input keeps sensing its state even as the Output is affecting the condition that the Input senses. Thus the Input reflects the effects of the Output, as it is affecting the external condition, whether or not there are also other influences affecting one's perception of it.

In practical terms, control—in the above example of keeping the car in its lane on the road—consists of counteracting the continuing flow of disturbances such as curves, side winds, bumps, etc., that would distort one's perception of the controlled condition (by distorting the actual position of the car if uncorrected). Your eyes provide the Input, your intention supplies the Reference. The Error signal keeps being continually computed in your brain, and the signals to muscles of your hands on the steering wheel constitute the Output, which—by combatting/minimizing the Error—keeps the controlled condition at/near the Reference state. The most immediate to-be-controlled condition is your view of the car in the road.

That, in turn, serves more complex controlled conditions, like your intention to get where you are going. The simpler controlled condition serves the more complex one in a hierarchical fashion in which the Outputs of higher-order control systems *constitute* the Reference settings of the systems immediately serving them. Notice that this analysis shows that behavior works in just the opposite way of what earlier writers had thought. The truth is: *behavior* is the entire process of action controlling perception. Your actions keep what-you-are-perceiving matching what-you-intend-to-be-perceiving. That, as Marken pointed out, would be a profound discovery, even if Powers's theory of how it works had proven incorrect.

As Powers began working out the theory that expressed his insight he worked back and forth between deriving implications from the developing theory and observing real human behavior to discern what the theory must account for, and to see whether or not observations confirmed the apparent implications of the theory as it was being developed. In the process he worked out a model of a hierarchy of control systems that might in principle be applied to any behavior.[103] The following demonstration derives from his observations of real behavior in that work.

Hold your arm out firmly, palm down, and then ask someone to push it down quickly by giving a firm poke to the back of your hand. Do this a few times until you both notice and feel how it automatically bounces back to where it was. It does that because its position is under feedback control. You can change its position by giving it a new setting (just *decide* to hold it somewhere else, like two inches higher or lower). Notice that as long as you don't change its setting (by wanting to move it) it will bounce back to its original position whenever disturbed. This control of bodily conditions requires a system of several interlocking levels of feedback systems. Let us identify some of the several levels of feedback control in this "simple" behavior.

Start with what you would call the behavior of "holding out your arm." You create this event by first bringing the arm up to the desired position, then maintaining it there. To get it to the desired position several muscles must be coordinated in changing tensions—moving the arm. Then the pattern of tensions at the final position must be stabilized to keep it there. There have to be specifications of a different kind for coordinating such tension changes than the specification for the position to-be-attained. The system for maintaining a fixed pattern of tensions is controlled by a system for changing the tensions that are "perceived" moment to moment, and that in turn is controlled by a system that controls the rate of change of the changes. If that seems hard to believe, run the "little man" computer model that you find on the CSG website mentioned in the Special Resource List, Appendix A. You don't need any expertise at all. Anyone can run it.

This can be pursued further. Think of the still more abstract specifications involved in deciding to do this little experiment in the first place. Think of them as also conditions that you control by your action. That is, it results ultimately in your action, but above that you are controlling intentions—whether conscious or unconscious—that devolve upon that action. In this case "action" isn't only the movement; it includes the decision that resulted in the movement. That might be why people have developed that vague, catch-all word, "behavior," to refer to any or all aspects of these phenomena.

A specification for a highly abstract type of condition/variable[104] must serve to satisfy the specification of a control system of such complexity that it "contains" all the simpler control systems as components. If such a system exists, what would you name it? I suggest you could name it your "Self" system. You might envision how that would not be a bad name for referring to all the controlled perceptions involved in reading this material right now, your choosing to try the experiment, what it implies about who you are that you made these decisions, and all the other conditions that you keep making true in order to keep being the person you perceive yourself to be.

To continue with the experiment: Have you partner hold his other index finger out a couple of feet away from your extended arm, and extend your index finger in a pointing posture. This time when he/she taps upon the back of your hand, have the intention of immediately matching your finger tip to his other index finger. That is, swing over to match his other finger when you feel the tap on the back of your hand. If you are trying this experiment now, try it before reading what I say next. Try it a few times, making sure to prevent that initial bounce from the first push.

All right, if you've now done it, you might well have discovered what most people do at this stage of this experiment. You have discovered that you can't prevent that initial bounce.[105] That happens because the partner's push simultaneously creates an error signal in the system for the position you are holding and an error signal in the system for occupying the new position, because the position-maintaining system is part of the position-taking system. The "lower order" or simpler system is thus already correcting the disturbance resulting from the partner's push when the (same) sensory signal serves to indicate "time to change position," in the superordinate system. Only then does the superordinate system incur the error signal that activates resetting the Reference for the position-maintaining system. This demonstration experiment was an early attestation to the plausibility of the hierarchical control systems idea.

There are more steps to this and other demonstrations, but for that I refer you to The Special Resource List. It is sufficient here to grasp that behavior, in general, can be conceived of in terms of more and more complex behavior as the control of perceptual variables that constitute—on each level—the components of the level above. We are not particularly interested here in the control mechanisms of bodily actions. I am interested in having you conceive of how the same theoretical scheme can account for behavior as the control of perceptual variables of more and more abstract types such as those with which we control our social, economic, political and communal lives. Here is the set of tentative labels that Powers gave to the higher levels that he discerned, in ascending order:

Relationships—the perception of event-happenings that occur together regularly.

Categories—the control of perceptions of groupings of relationships.

Sequences—of categories of movements/actions/thoughts as the step by step movements/actions that are the components of Programs for accomplishing large scale intentions like—doing your work; shopping; playing (a) game(s); planning an(y) activity; worshipping; forming an opinion; communicating a (particular) message; etc.

Programs—like those described above that command and strategically employ sequences of actions—as components, or in this instance, better-named instrumentalities, for attaining and maintaining your Principles/ values/standards like—*good parenthood*; *good citizenship*; *honesty*; *effectiveness*; *respectability*; etc. (Your own formulations of these Principles.)

Principles—in turn being collectively controlled at settings/ values necessary to satisfy your Whole system concepts like—

System Concept—(Self-image you hold of who you are—as one example.)

Readers familiar with these ideas might skip the next section where I enumerate a variety of further examples to help readers unacquainted with feedback system thinking about behavior get more of a "feel" for it. If you are familiar with them go to Time In.

Time Out for More Examples

Since the dawn of time we humans have searched for, and invented, labor saving devices. The most powerful such are control-system machines. They imitate the (simplest) control systems in human behavior in many respects since first coming on the scene about the time of World War II. The cruise control in your car is one. Auto pilots in planes and boats are another class of them. The temperature control system in the home is another. Note, I didn't say, "the thermostat." People, taking short cuts, sometimes say that the thermostat keeps the house warm or cool. It does not. It is the combined Input, Reference and Comparator components of a temperature-control system consisting of a temperature-sensing part, a comparing part, electric wires and an Output mechanism-furnace and/or air conditioner. You supply the Reference by setting the dial to a given value. It takes all these components to make the control system.

Without any one of those components a control system does not work. But, notice what all these various control systems do. They do what a person would otherwise have to do: steer, keep pressing the gas pedal, shovel coal or turn the gas or oil valve on and off, etc. These and other control systems are but crude imitations of those operating in a human (or animal) body.

Biologists had already been busy finding such systems in the body. As mentioned above, Claude Bernard had begun these observations with the fact of blood pressure being controlled, but it took until our present era to realize that the sense organs of the body supply Input, comparators exist in various brain Centers and the muscles and glands provide the Outputs that can affect the environment that the sense organs sense. In other words, the components of control systems are all there in the body. The fact that body temperature is ordinarily maintained at 98.6 degrees fahrenheit, is another example of control. But here the biologists fell prey to the old way of talking. They called 98.6 a "set point" (instead of a Reference *setting or value*) to indicate the existence of a system that was normally set to that temperature—like a thermostat in a house being set to one reading and never moved again. This little difference in terminology constituted a fatal error in theorizing, in a certain way. It occurred because of thinking about the system in stimulus-response terms. The body's temperature-control system is not so simple that it always keeps one temperature. Let germs invade your body and the Reference value gets set to a higher degree. We call it having a fever. There is no little man in the body to change that setting, so how is it done? The body is not a chaotic mass of independently acting systems; it is apparently a pyramid of control systems in which a "supervisory" system can change the "set point" or Reference value of systems under its control. On to still more illustrations.

If you did the arm position-maintaining experiment, imagine how doing that resulted from commands from a much higher-level control system in yourself: a system controlling an image—a self-perception—as a curious, learning, growing person. Call it a Self or ego. It sent a Reference signal to systems just below, the Principles/values level. At that level the Reference to-be-matched would be an intention valuing something like, "gaining new information." To satisfy that Reference envision a command to the next lower order, Programs, something like, "cooperating," to see what would happen if you followed the instructions.

The meaning of "cooperation" in your own self image is what set various sequences of your action in motion. That is, how you would read, interpret and carry out the instructions. To do that, the Program-level system chose a position to which to move your hand and thus set the "goal" or Reference signal for the Sequence systems below it to maintain the position of your arm relative to your body (Relationship-level). The systems below that are the ones we refer to as "physiological" or bodily action systems. Once your arm reached the new position your position-control—Configuration-system maintained it automatically by keeping the arm muscles fixed at the appropriate tension levels. control of bodily movement levels (lower order systems) won't concern us in detail here.

It takes a bit of effort to envision what it is like to "control" abstract types of variables, because, in fact, even if you are sophisticated in modern psychology, behavior is not really explained there. It is taken for granted. That is, if I say (for example), "Close your eyes," and you do, anyone observing that, including you and me, might call that your behavior—of that moment. In typical psychological studies, behavior is postulated to be whatever it is described as. All right, but that doesn't explain how it works. True, there are physiological psychologists who study how nerve signals reach the muscles, others who study what part of the brain "lights up" when different thoughts or actions occur, but there are gaps between "facts" like that and thoughts and intentions. It is just assumed that phenomena like thoughts and intentions are somehow the epiphenomena of presumed "stimuli" that elicit the actions in question.[106] As a result we get in the habit of not wondering further about how it all really works. Another consequence is that we often fail to see anything wrong with statements like, "He drove into the ditch because he was drunk." What does "because" mean there? Already infected with the Cartesian view of behavior, people will often offer the explanation that being drunk is what "made him" drive into the ditch. What a difference it makes to re-view the episode in terms that alcohol damages the control system for driving so that control over maintaining position-on-the-road was lost. The mechanism in that can be (and in fact has been) demonstrated in research. But, there is no research that demonstrates how inanimate objects or environmental conditions can "make" a living being do anything. There is no such research because, if there were, it would assign purpose to inanimate objects. That idea died in Western Civilization when the Romans finally threw down their stone gods.

"Wait," you might say, "What about the example of the person's hand sweeping toward your eyes. That is what made them blink, isn't it?" How would you imagine that to work? Does the sweeping hand push on the eyelids without touching them? That would be action at a distance, but that idea—as in gravity—was finally abandoned when Einstein's alternative proposal eliminated the need for that kind of magical force.

As a different option try this: imagine the control of eyelid position being subject to a genetically set Reference of "not-too-fast" for increasing size of the central image on the retina.[107] This is of course only a vague scheme for how it might work, but one that in principle can be investigated—in terms of rate of increase of nerve signaling from the retina, and so forth. In other words, what we have are two proposals about the mechanism of the eyeblink in that example, only the latter of which postulates a feedback system that could be subjected to study with our current physiological methods.

Time In

Here is a powerful illustration showing the superiority of the hierarchical control system scheme over the older theory of reflexes. I once was told how a certain lady got a couple black eyes, flattened nose and bruises over her face and upper body. She had slipped going down a stairs. Because she was carrying her baby, she didn't put out her arms to catch herself, she raised the baby instead. Putting out your arms to catch yourself in a fall is supposed to be a "reflex," and reflexes, by definition, are supposed to be automatic and invariable. So how can it be that, under certain extraordinary conditions, a reflex can be nullified? Current day psychology has no explanation for how that might work. With the hierarchical scheme one can deduce that a higher level system—in this case the level labeled, "Principles"—reset (a cascade of) Reference signals culminating in the one for arm-position, overruling the reflex. The exact route of the descending signal through the intervening control systems all the way to the arm muscles is admittedly still subject to speculation. My point is that it is a type of speculation containing at least the outline of a mechanism, whereas the older psychology comes up blank with such questions.

When Powers realized that complex control operations would have to be performed by mechanisms in the body that could set the Reference values of other systems he deduced that one way that could be done would be for the Reference of a "lower order" system to be determined by the Output of a higher order system. That inference has now proven correct in computer modeling of behavior simulations, and what we now know of brain anatomy reveals arrangements that appear to conform to the models. He proposed (tentatively) eleven levels, starting at the bottom with the simplest—intensity, or magnitude of a signal, and going up to the most abstract-system concept. The lowest five levels refer to phenomena of physical sorts, so are not germane to our discussion here. We reviewed the higher levels in the discussion above.

How do Reference-values/perception-specifications originate? Powers theorized, as a logical necessity, that they must initially be perceptions of the consequences of random action that become "stamped in" in memory. First, why random action? Because any movement would only be random if there were not already a Reference value in memory for it to match/realize. In other words, random action only occurs when you do not already have a control system for regulating the particular state sensed in the perceptual-display in question. If you did have such a Reference value—and it was being matched by the perceptual display—then the action would not be random; it would be controlled. How do the original movements occur for their signal patterns to become stored in memory so as to be available as future References?

How such random action occurs constituted another logical gap that would need to be filled if the theory were to be comprehensive. To meet it he proposed another feature of a human (or animal) nervous system that must be involved in the organizing and developing of the postulated hierarchy of control systems. He labeled it the "Intrinsic system." It is comprised of the various life-support control systems that biologists have been uncovering in the older subcortical portions of the brain—the portions we inherit through genes and share with other animals. Error states in this intrinsic system give rise to a flow of excitation (read: random signalling) through the rest of the brain.[108] The result is random movements. If, in the course of such random movements intrinsic error begins to subside, the current perceptual signals would be stored in memory. They would thus be available for future requisition—to reproduce the original pattern of movement—as Reference signals. This constitutes reorganization of the learned hierarchy, what we otherwise call developmental learning. In the case of a newborn you might rather call it organization instead of reorganization.

So far this is a hypothetical solution for the logical gap noted above. I don't know of any alternative explanations. However, there are some heretofore unexplained phenomena for which this tentative model immediately suggests explanations. The first is something any one can observe in infants. How much of their action appears to be random motion. But, if it is, what is its source and what results from it? I don't know of any research as to its source.[100] As to what results, several studies of human development have begun to spell out the fine detail about the evolution of vague, uncoordinated movements into more and more control.

For instance, if a tiny baby waving her arms and legs around randomly in her crib accidentally touches a little bell or toy hanging overhead and it rings, you will notice her perk up and pretty soon do it again. After a few times you will notice that she can move her arm directly to it. She doesn't have to wait to touch it accidentally anymore to hear it ring. She now can hear the bell ring when she wants to. That looks like an instance of developing a new control circuit for increasing control over the environment, doesn't it?

Other studies, especially in the wake of Piaget's work, have shown how an infant will at first set eyes—apparently by accident—upon a person entering near the crib. Then a short time (in days) later he will turn the eyes to glance again and again at the new image. A few more days later the infant shows the ability to turn repeatedly to look for an image that is not presently there. These studies indicate increasing fineness of control becoming organized out of previously random movements. And then, finally, Franz and Hetty Plooij (1996, & F. X. Plooij, 1987) have demonstrated the development of successive levels of control, consistent with Powers's hierarchical scheme, in their researches on chimpanzee and human infant development. In another study (1989) they showed a relationship between vulnerability to falling ill at modal times associated with typical stage-periods of reorganization in child development.

Another application derivable from PCT, concerning intrinsic-system driven reorganization of the learned control hierarchy, yields a plausible explanation for the differences in outcomes that can occur when a person who does not know how to swim is pushed into deep water. What usually happens is that the person flails wildly around and winds up having to be fished out by someone else. But, I have heard of instances where a person has apparently learned to swim under these circumstances. What would account for these very different outcomes? If the hypothesis about reorganizing is on the mark, the first thing to consider is that the brain centers where oxygen level, CO_2 level, and so on, are monitored would begin to diverge from their Reference values. The resulting intrinsic-system error signals would instigate random movement—flailing around. If it is truly random, then by definition, the right movements constituting swimming would occur sooner or later, sooner in some cases, later in others, too late in most.

Further implications derivable from the theory provide suggestive insights into still other aspects of human behavior, even if they have not yet led to confirmatory observations such as in the Plooijs' work. For example, the kind of practical advice that psychotherapists have come upon through experience—when uncertain what to do in an unfamiliar situation, do something "to see what happens"—often spurs new learning. In other words, by simply relaxing and not immobilizing oneself through "holding oneself tense," the reorganizing system impels random actions from which creative solutions have the opportunity to emerge. I have found that simply giving this hypothesis to a person has often been useful in providing a rationale for trusting a hunch that he or she was timidly considering.

Another very powerful application of the reorganization theory was discovered about 20 years ago, by one of my early students of PCT. She was also serving a practicum in a psychological rehabilitation center at the time. One of her favorite patients began seemingly to go into reverse after making a lot of progress. One day when that patient was complaining, "I feel so confused, nothing seems right to me any more..." my student suddenly had a great insight. She said, "Wait a minute, that means you have begun to change. You are thinking in new, unfamiliar ways. The ways of thinking that got you here don't feel right to you anymore. That is just what you want to happen." This was followed by a very positive outcome. I have since used this simple explanation to help others recast how they perceive their discomfort, and hence to see it through, while undergoing reorganization.

As for why reorganizing can be so uncomfortable that one would try to abort it, by regressing to familiar behavior patterns, think about the implication of random activation in the nervous system. When it gets sufficiently extensive that would mean that all kinds of functioning control systems in the body get disrupted by the spreading neural activation. People experiencing this describe it variously as anxiety or stress. The combination of physical and mental aspects can increase in intensity until some new action results in "solving the problem" via doing something that particular person has never done before. Then the discomfort subsides. The other alternative is to abort reorganization by regressing to simpler, older and more secure habits, often however, at the price of sacrificing more adequate coping.

One more implication of this theory—that everyone knows but can lose sight of when emotions are aroused—is that *because* we are all constructed as hierarchical perceptual control systems—*in principle* any of us might behave as any one else. While that is true in principle, it is not true in reality. How to explain that? If we can do so, it would illuminate why only some people engage in such undesirable behavior as crime and violence (for instance). Liberal social thinkers correctly point out that individuals who develop socially undesirable behavior do so more frequently in stressful physical and social environments. Conservative social thinkers correctly criticize this thinking as flawed by pointing out numerous-enough instances of very creative people coming from such backgrounds.

The likely explanation seems very simple. "Bad" environments surely trigger reorganization often and intensely. But if reorganization functions by promoting random actions, then a great range of developmental outcomes become probable, AND whatever the growing individual is doing—when intrinsic satisfaction occurs—lays the foundation for subsequent habits. Thus the expression, "There but for the Grace of God go I," gains down-to-earth meaning. It suggests that we can better understand behavior that repulses us by trying to imagine how "I could have done that," than by perceiving the other as too alien to understand. It simultaneously provides a suggestion about how "hardy" or adaptable children can emerge from the same environments as those from which delinquents come.

Such a shift in perspective is not limited to questions of "empathy." All research in PCT involves a shift in perspective. It proceeds by the creation of true models of behavior, which necessarily call for examining behavior from the inside, rather than viewing human subjects as objects as in stimulus-response research.

By this time you are probably getting comfortable with the equivalence of the terms, *intention* and *reference signal*. It is the to-be-met condition toward which action works, essentially instantaneously, in the case of simple systems, with longer and longer operating times for more complex systems. As you think about that, though, it might also strike you that here our language is not quite up to the task of communication. In psychology, up until now, when we used the words intention or purpose, we unconsciously assumed that we were talking about what is in conscious awareness. But, in a hierarchy of control systems many purposes are being carried out at any given time without awareness. For just one example, the purpose a spinal center gives to a lower center to institute the new set of References that will result in moving an arm or a leg. Thus we had the inference that some intentions are unconsciousness in the earlier discussion.

I have some concern that you might focus on the fact that many of the explanations above are provisional upon further research. If you focus solely on their tentative nature, you might overlook that the hypothesized explanations concern phenomena that have heretofore been merely accepted as facts without any explanation as to how they might work. Obviously there is a rich vein of material for biological and psychological research here; much is already going on.

What I hope you do keep focus on is the fact that many of these ideas never even occur to one to think about until you begin thinking about human behavior as a perception control process. The scheme, itself, provides suggestive insights for thinking about the issues I pointed to in parts I and II. We shall apply them in the social, not the biological realms, although you might find it encouraging, as I have, to consider that the same explanatory scheme applies equally well whether we are talking about biological or social phenomena.

Chapter 10

Inadequacy of Linear Logic

As far back in history as one can trace humans have perceived their own experience as resulting from the impingement of outside causes. It was a natural conclusion from people's observations about how things happened. A rock rolled down a hill, hitting another rock, and it moved. Icy sleet blowing into your face "caused" your eyes to close. A dead branch fell in the forest and you dodged to avoid injury. Effects followed observable causes. In a superficial view all these events appear similar. Behavior was just another type of effect from a cause. Even when the cause was a human action, such as throwing a spear, the effect—that it hit something—adhered to the general notion of cause and effect, in which the causal source was external to the object or organism affected.

The same principle was preserved at a more abstract level when primitive peoples attributed events happening in their environments to actions of spirits, demons and other nonmaterial entities. Eventually they personalized these "forces," identifying them as gods whose actions, often completely arbitrary from the human point of view, created disturbances to the environments in which people lived.

People also came to believe that one could sometimes acquire causal powers, and the concept of magic was born, giving rise to a tug of war between supernatural forces of various sorts and human actions to submit to them, or outwit them, appease them and survive them. But, in each instance humans perceived their actions in terms of re-acting to outside forces. With the concept of destiny, as in the Greek tragedians, you had a full-fledged view of behavior as caused by abstract forces outside the individual. Thus, Descartes was not completely original in developing the stimulus-response view of the nature of behavior. He simply demystified it, taking it out of the realm of the supernatural and putting it down to natural causes.

Whether viewing living individuals, natural conditions or supernatural beings as the causative agent for a particular event—from an external point of view—the event seemed to be the effect of a causal agent. This is a linear or cause-effect logic. People regarded behavior the same way that the early Greek scientists understood causality in inanimate nature. You put a lever over a fulcrum, bore down on the long end and you could move a heavy object on the other end. To see behavior in a comparable way was not surprising. We humans typically use analogies drawn from what seems understood to explain what we have not previously understood.

Nevertheless, another stream of thinking about behavior was developing simultaneously. As self-consciousness became a focus of attention for some people it led to the realization that there was an aspect of behavior for which the term, *intention*, was needed. Some thinkers, at least, recognized that their actions were preceded by an imagined scenario of the consequence or desired outcome toward which action was directed. People also attributed intentions or goals to others, as in, "You are smiling at me, so you must want me to be friendly." There is a hidden assumption indicating that the two ways of looking at behavior came to be merged in one's thinking. The person on the receiving end conceived of the intention of the other as something like a lever to move something in himself. It took Machiavelli to point out—to would-be princes, not ostensibly to everyone—that the intention underlying an overt act might have any one of several different goals, some of them quite at odds with the seeming tenor of the manifest behavior. It required several more centuries to realize that that, itself, invalidates the assumption of linear cause-effect in explanations of behavior.[110]

Meanwhile the application of authority to influence behavior careens along as it has for the last thousands of years, resting on the implicit assumption that effects result from applying force, of one sort or another, to an object. Parents, teachers, bosses, policemen, mayors, governors, legislators, presidents, promulgate prescriptions and proscriptions aimed at controlling various states of affairs. Rules and laws consist mainly of specifications of actions that should be performed. Stop for the red light, Pay tax by April 15th, etc. The implicit assumption is that the embodied command will act like a lever to move the actions of the targeted subjects toward the desired result. The promulgator of the commands is external to the subject of the commands just as English syntax divides subject and object.[111] His intention, or desired outcome, is more often assumed than explicit in spelling out the required action.

The logic used in such lawmaking is linear. It attempts to equate behavioral events with the cause-effect flow of physical events. And it frequently fails in its objective because the behavior of organisms is not accurately encompassed by this scheme. For an example consider a "60 Minutes" story about the failure of the assault-gun ban in a previous crime bill.[112] The law had spelled out specific names and descriptions of the forbidden guns. In anticipation of the ban a flood of purchasers rushed to buy them. And manufacturers simply made new versions with different names and/or fittings. According to the broadcast, the result of the assault-gun ban law was to increase rather than decrease the supply of assault guns.

This was an example of linear thinking—trying to control the behavioral action rather than the desired result. You might wonder why the congress made the law so vulnerable to evasion in the first place by enumerating each and every existing model. The answer was given by writers like Chase (1963), Farmer (1977), and Howard (1995).[113] Essentially the answer is that many earlier attempts at controlling social phenomena, by *not* spelling out the minutest details, were open to endless court challenges on the meaning of the laws or regulations, and/or judicial rebuffs on the grounds of vagueness. So there you have it. Previous attempts at solving unanticipated consequences of linear-logic approaches to problems resulted in more linear efforts, which had further unanticipated consequences.

Without a consensus between those legislating and those governed, laws promulgated under linear cause-effect thinking regularly are met by efforts to thwart them. Anyone who perceives him—or herself adversely affected tends to minimize the error state created by the new rule. He/she will be inclined to produce a variety of nullifying actions. That is often followed by another attempted remedy which will be more of the same—another single-effect trial to hem in the behavior of the governed—answered with further efforts at maintaining whatever state of affairs the recipients were originally controlling. It would seem that the only alternative to such proceedings is the application of overwhelming force by authorities. This might well be an explanation as to why peoples sometimes welcome dictatorships when democratic processes grind to a halt under endless conflicts between opposing interests. Howard's and Farmer's books provide a veritable deluge of examples of these interminable deadlocks.

The problems are beyond the scope of previous ways of understanding behavior, as Newtonian physics was not capable of carrying science into the nuclear age. People whose intentions are thwarted or disturbed by external sources continue attempting to control their perceptions at their intended value-settings, just as one controls the path of one's car on the road despite the effects of external disturbances. When the source of disturbance is another hierarchical control system, rather than inanimate natural forces, the likelihood of loss of control increases greatly. If neither of the two systems in conflict have the needed higher order systems for strategies like negotiation or compromise, the situation will rapidly deteriorate to the use of raw force. If one adversary possesses overwhelmingly superior power, his or her control is maintained as if the other party's output did not exist.

Social phenomena of all sorts are comprised of the interactions of living control systems. Linear-logic efforts to influence them are nullified like we counter the effect of the wind when driving a car. Often one corrects without even being aware of the disturbance. Only when repeated corrections are called for does attention shift down to the source(s) of the disturbance.[114] It is true that any given living hierarchical control system—i.e. human being—might have higher level systems controlling principles like, "honor the law," or, "be fair to others." Controlling abstract perceptual variables (Pvs)[115] of that sort can, result in resetting goals in such a way as to lead an external observer to think the person's behavior was "caused" by an exoteric influence like a law. When it happens that a higher control system, like that of a "self concept" resets the value of a Principle and it changes the action strategy to satisfy a value like honoring the law it might mean that the individual momentarily sacrifices a personal advantage for the higher goal. But, this has limitations, as in a situation where a person is faced with choosing to obey a law or starving.

In many normal situations a person might unilaterally avoid, or retire from, a conflict, not because of being externally forced, but by maintaining control of a superordinate value as just noted. Further examples: In some circumstances a person in a hurry might choose to continue driving at a lawful speed even if he owned a radar detector. A factory owner might decide to stop pouring mercury laced sludge into the sewer at night, even at an increase in overhead costs. In all such instances behavior that might look like a "response" to a linear-logic mechanism, such as a law, can be understood in terms of resetting a desired perception by a higher order value (for example: I'm a responsible citizen) in the person's control-system hierarchy.

This gives a better scheme for understanding phenomena of the type studied by social researchers interested in compliance with law or the lack of it. It suggests that we should examine the higher order systems—the principles and self concepts—of subjects, rather than pursue some ultimate refinement of linear logic in a hopeless quest for compliance with externally imposed regulations. This highlights another hidden assumption of linear-logic attempts at solving social problems. It is the assumption that everyone will be influenced in the same way by a mandate, if only it is formulated with sufficient stringency. When we look at it this way we see how linear solutions inevitably fail to take into account that all the individuals potentially affected are controlling perceptual variables relevant to themselves, often differing greatly from person to person.

Any major issue can be examined for the shortcoming of linear-logic solutions. You only need to read the daily paper to see that proposals for solving large scale problems are almost invariably framed in terms of prescribing single-variable actions—what we should do, instead of what condition, or state of affairs, we want to see resulting. If you run the simple demonstrations of PCT, like tracking a randomly moving target on a computer screen, and then study the theoretical analysis of how control works in that task, you see that there is no way to program in advance what you are going to do. You can't allow for future disturbances of the controlled variable because you can't know what they will be until the situation is current. Control works by immediately countering real time disturbances as they occur. The appropriate actions can not be effectively anticipated. Laws and regulations can simply not be programmed to anticipate every confounding action against disturbances to variables controlled by those they impact. The fact that they do not control in real time—like keeping a car on track—has led to a mistaken judgment that they involve fundamentally different phenomena. They do not.

The reason is that no one can know in advance what will be the countering efforts of people who perceive themselves adversely impacted by legal injunctions. Even those who are affected can not know in advance what their actions will be. The countering actions of affected individuals constitute disturbances to the control efforts of those making regulations and laws. It becomes a real-time control situation when(ever) the affected person—by knowing the law and thinking about it—experiences it as disturbance to control of some perceptual variable important to him. He then ponders what actions to nullify the disturbance to his own control efforts. That is what makes adapting to legal regulation essentially comparable with a simple tracking performance. Keep that point in mind in going over the critiques of failed attempts at solutions of social problems described by writers like Chase (1963), Farmer (1977) and Howard (1995). Invariably we find that the proposed "solutions" have been proposals to do something, in the future, to control conditions that the framers envisioned as likely to obtain, based upon their understanding of those that obtained in the past.

Think of all the different individual and joint actions that nullify decisions and decrees which want to have the force of law. Consider the continuing failure of efforts to remedy major chronic issues—the UN's inability to stop wars, famine, terrorism, anarchy in 3rd world countries, or problems of our own society. A typical example is the World Bank contributing to destruction of the ecosystem in Brazil by lending money for the "good" purpose of helping small farmers to get a start in farming. But they were destroying the rain forest in the process. It is a one-variable-at-a-time cause-effect remedial flop.

When Individuals Confront Chronic Social Issues

Let us examine more deeply some perennial social issues, comparing linear cause-effect problem solutions with those that a control-theory approach would entail. Chapters two and three described the social problems and futile attempts at solutions decried by various writers. Since then we have begun digging into the questions about why. We have seen that the word, intention, is synonymous with "controlling a perceived condition to a Reference specification." *Behavior*, not a precise term in theory, generally refers both to the action one can see a person exerting and the consequence that it achieves. Thus, to swing and miss a pitched baseball, and to swing and hit it, are both instances of behavior. In the former instance the higher order control-system that has the intention, or purpose, for swinging the bat would suffer an error. Which subservient system would be reset to correct the error would depend upon the organization of that particular control hierarchy in that person.

At a still more abstract level the perceptual variable involved in, say, perceiving oneself as "successful" would require bringing a sum of perceptions to appropriate Reference values—a perception of one's image in the eyes of others to a positive reading, for example. Plus perceiving one's income as bountiful, one's assessment of having fulfillment of earlier ambitions, etc. Likewise, if your intention is to perceive your society as, say, "humane" or "advanced," it would involve subsidiary intentions to perceive certain kinds of verbalizations and abstract actions by a majority of people as showing empathy for others, concern for the welfare of those less fortunate and things like that. The common control-theory element in these, and any other potential examples, is that people act to establish internally supplied Reference signals (read: intention/purpose/goal). That calls for (neurological signals representing) particular values of the variables controlled by subservient systems which produce whatever action necessary to realize those intentions. This is accomplished in every case by actions of speaking and doing in real-time. It is hypothesized that these higher-order Reference signals might be assembled by accessing, and manipulating imaginatively, stored recordings of previous perceptions.

An everyday way of saying this is straightforward and easy to state: We act to bring about (or maintain) *what we want*. So the first practical step in applied control theory is knowing what you want—explicit specification—NOT what moves should be done. That is, what should be perceived as the action takes place. Error leads automatically to corrective action. That does not contradict the aphorism that practice makes perfect, but it suggests that what practice consists of, in detail, is assembling and refining (often completely unconsciously) the myriad lower order systems necessary for adequate functioning of the system of interest. Thus, the sense of error in swinging and missing the pitched ball could be understood as matching the most recent (relevant) sensory input with prior recordings of successful control. Error signals in the subordinate systems would be reduced through resetting the Reference signals down the line to their subordinates. That suggests why one would like another pitched ball immediately after swinging and missing. Or, why members of a political party defeated in an election would like another election as soon as possible so they could use what they learned from the last one.

Where do all the wants come from? As we examine the behavior of living organisms we encounter a major question not faced by engineering control theorists.[116] That was the question of how the original Reference signals come about. It won't hurt to review the formal answer from chapter nine in the practical contexts we are looking at here. The reason engineering control theory does not deal with the origin of Reference signals is because the engineer knows what he wants a control system to do when he builds it. He (or his boss) supplies the to-be-achieved signal, and the system is built incorporating it. This might also explain why engineering control theorists failed to grasp that control systems work by controlling their perceptions. They didn't need to know that in order to apply feedback signals to a system's output so as to maintain the built-in (and often invisible) Reference value. A living organism, however, does not have an external engineer to stick a screwdriver into its head to adjust its intentions. We get by in the first few minutes of life with built-in genetic systems, that regulate basic life functions, but if they were all that we had, all our behavior would be completely instinctual. It would be so rigid that the concept of reflex would be good enough to explain it (though still technically incorrect).

However, higher organisms develop controls over time that were not there in the first place. If built-in controls would be too inflexible to allow the adaptability we see in human action there is only one other possible explanation. There must be some biological mechanism whereby new control systems come into existence in the developing organism. Perceptions of random actions must sometimes be recorded and converted into Reference signals for subsequent use. Powers suggested an intrinsic system—a system that turns on random signals throughout the brain when genetically set life maintenance values are violated, something like the "check engine" warning signal in modern cars. In practical terms this can produce the kind of struggling that we see in a person whose air supply is interfered with. Random action that is followed by return of intrinsic values to safe readings involves reorganization of the hard wiring of the central nervous system, producing new abilities.

The practical implications of this insight are simple and straightforward: 1) We only change when we have to, that is, when intrinsic errors are accumulating. The first actions in such circumstances must be random, for if the person already had the ability to control his life-support situation, it would already be controlling and the crisis would not be occurring. 2) Significant new learning involves taking chances (whether willful or at levels below consciousness). 3) You can't know whether something you've never done before will be fortunate, unfortunate or neutral until you actually do it and experience the result.

It is important to keep in mind while examining serious, chronic issues in our society that—in contrast to the external attitude of linear cause-effect thinking—we view behavior from the point of view of the behaving organism rather than the outside observer. This point is deceptively more profound than appears at first glance. It means that understanding behavior doesn't consist of finding some external co-variate and postulating that it is "causing" the behavior, it means understanding what perceptual variable the subject(s) is(are) actually controlling.

That objective calls for either of two approaches for discovering what perceptual-variable the subject is intending to control—to what Reference value. Either you ask the person, and he tells you his intention honestly, or you perform the test for the controlled variable. Each strategy has different strengths and weaknesses. It is more often the case than we could wish, that a person will verbalize one thing as his goal and another system within himself is intending something quite different. This is what is crudely called deception or self deception. I say, "crudely called," because the words, "self deception" imply that there is another little person inside his head that intends for him or her to think she has one aim, when in fact she has another. While something like that might sometimes occur, what is more likely is that a person—any of us—has many control systems that have never been put-into-words/made conscious to oneself. That is real unconsciousness.[117] These systems can be running merrily along while other systems are busy "explaining" to oneself, as well as others, what we are doing. Findings of some previous social psychology researches suggest that such "explanations" are often formulated in terms of trendy fashions about what is good to be doing, and don't always give useful information about the variables one is really controlling.

When we confront someone whose stated aims do not seem to coincide with what we perceive his actual behavior is achieving it is common to assume some sort of malevolence on the part of the other person. We get angry, thinking he or she is trying to mislead or defraud us, unless we see that he or she is suffering some disadvantage herself. Then we call it self-deception. Looking at the same situation in control-system terms we do better to test for the controlled variable. The Test, remember, consists of finding a way to disturb what you suspect is under control. It can be as simple as giving a luke warm cup of coffee to someone who has just declared he likes his coffee hot. If the person acts to re-establish the pre-disturbance condition, let's say, by putting it in the micro wave, that suggests he or she really was controlling that variable. If no corrective action is taken, our hypothesis was wrong. It can take considerable creativity at times to come up with worthwhile hypotheses to test, as well as to find effective ways to disturb the hypothesized perceptual variable. But, when it works you are relieved from having to wonder whether or not the person is doing what he or she says. It may often also show that what seemed like the other person's attempt to cozen us was far from his intended goal—so far, in fact, that he probably was hardly aware of us at all.

A corollary is that the surest way to understand a person's intentions is to observe what results from his actions. But, it is often not quite that simple. As I said previously, we can think of ourselves as a mass of control systems operating at the same time. It is not surprising then, that sometimes one can be working at cross purposes with oneself, or with someone else with whom one is trying to cooperate. I have often had therapy clients suffering great frustration over the fact that some highly valued goal keeps getting sabotaged by other of their actions that nullify it. I experience the same thing with myself.

It can take a long time to change a Reference signal for desired body weight, for example, or for learning any new skill, or developing new habits where there are prior bad habits, or for gaining perspective into an undesired aspect of one's public image, etc. The solution, when one gets there, seems to require discovering the highest level intention affecting the situation. Resetting that might result in the automatic readjusting of all the subsidiary systems, but not always. Resetting of lower order References may result in new conflicts between systems along the way. That is one of the reasons that remedial programs take so much time. I don't mean this is something we do consciously. You must consciously formulate the desired goal, but after that much of the work consists in trying to become conscious of all the variables involved in the chain of command that now interfere with each other. The resulting cacophony of error signals is then experienced as anxiety. That might then dominate consciousness. It can include systems you never realized were even involved.

It is the same with participating in social action. If you are wondering why I have been discussing the practical aspects of control in individual organisms when I started to examine how PCT applies to thinking about major issues in society, the point is that we all participate in what becomes social action by controlling variables that pertain to our own individual structure. We perceive such variables in whatever terms we have personally formulated them,[118] and social action is the joint result of many individuals controlling closely similar perceptual variables to more or less similar values. Just the fact that all of us, whether common citizens or leaders, are always controlling many different variables at the same time should serve as a reminder that action-specifications that are aimed at one goal at a time, and require specific actions, are likely to omit consideration of why or how they might be nullified.

Any problem one would attempt to solve, in your own life, or when enlisting in any social effort, entails trial and error, testing for (what is/are) the variable(s) of concern, and then attempting to control them to desired results. If there is no existing control system that can control the variable(s) of interest, reorganization is required. Analogies to previously controlled phenomena might provide suggestions for efforts to try, but analogy is not an adequate basis on which to build solutions to unsolved problems. Much of what goes into the effort to assert control over variables in nature or society is entailed in identifying the real hierarchy of systems involved. Let us consider some concrete examples.

Problems Concerning Child Rearing in Our Society

There are several reasons for beginning our search with the question of child-rearing. It is clearly the process whereby culture is carried on and evolves. Parents try to teach their children the skills they have mastered as a foundation upon which the children should develop further. The understandings, and maybe even more the misunderstandings that children get from their parents' teachings play a major role in the derivation and extension of applications from the basic axioms of a culture. Erikson's hypothesis—that difficulties children encounter during their development reflect the unresolved dilemmas of their culture—brings Spengler's thesis about cultural degeneration down to the level of individuals. The current stress that politicians put on family and child concerns suggests that there are issues of general concern here.

A 1974 Esquire magazine cover headline shouts, Do Americans suddenly hate kids? The associated articles presented statistics purporting to show recent declines in fertility rate, number of children desired by prospective young mothers, increased use of contraception and abortion, decreased adoptions; a new trend toward apartment developments "catering to the unencumbered set;" a trend among young adults to have fewer, or no children, so as to be able to devote more time to self-gratification. But, the writers declared in mock puzzlement, their exemplary couple "are open, friendly, and giving—oddly altruistic in their preaching of egotism." As exemplars they, "have joined a set of coreligionists [i.e. those fleeing the "seductions of commitment or reliance on the 'the system' (any system)" who] . . . are brief forerunners of a mood noticed everywhere on campuses—the tentative approach to everything, the withdrawal into privacy, the distrust of social pressure . . . . Communes have given way to hermit cells; and hermits have no children."

The writers went on to describe a visit to a commune only four years earlier where children, typically, were parented by everyone and no-one in particular, and where, "Children, of whatever age, must be or become allies; since adults . . . are immature, sexually experimental, infantile in their material demands, while the kids discover fidelity and responsibility . . . ." The overall message was that there was beginning to be an anti-children attitude among young adults in the middle 70s and beyond, and that it grew out of the self-centeredness of their hippie parents that left them to fend for themselves when the communes broke up. I can't help but reflect on the fact that these attitudes were followed by those of the next college generation that Bloom (1987) perceived in *The Closing of the American mind*.

Another article in the same issue comments on advice to young parents by Dr. Bruno Bettlheim (guru of child rearing in those years), which starts, "Examine your goals . . . arrive at a master plan. Then you have to make up your mind whether to get the child you have in mind won't entail sacrifices . . . Then you have to settle whether it's worth making such a sacrifice to get the child you want to have." The writer comments on this advice, "Inherent in this is what may be termed the 'product fallacy,' making possible the easy substitution of such words as 'car,' 'house,' or 'color TV' for the word 'child' in the above passage."

Still another series of articles report cases in which judges have done utterly horrible things to children, like returning them to parents who had already brutalized them, finally to be killed by them. In another case a judge took an orphaned child away from loving foster parents who had begun to bond with him and gave him to a pair of ex-convicts who had no relation to him except that the female had been a presumed friend of the mother. They later abandoned him and he became a delinquent. In still another case a judge took a child who had been abandoned by his parents from a set of foster parents ready to adopt him and returned that child to the biological father who was said to want the child as evidence of his virility. He later moved out of the house.

These instances seem to me to show an attitude toward the children as objects, as was imputed to Dr. Bettlheim's use of words in the article cited previously.[119] It is not too hard to conjure up a view of how the judges made these decisions. One does not have to see them as some sort of monster seeking to create as much damage as possible (although in some instances that is an appealing hypothesis). They were acting consistently with common practice in our society to control the letter of the law at higher priority than its consequence in any specific case. Once more a one-idea-at-a-time, cause/effect approach like those reported by Howard in *The Death of Common Sense*.

Do these various reports from decades ago up to the present pertain to the issues that plague us today? Politicians have been campaigning on the need to strengthen "family values." Killings of children by parents and of parents by children are continuing to be reported in the media, bitter controversies rage over the lack of values inculcated in schools or the lack of values held by children as they arrive in school. Upper middle class children are said to be under immense pressure to achieve, in sports and academically, while lower class children are stressed from overwhelmed and demoralized parents, abandonment, and abuse. Despite all this, efforts—to protect children from physical and sexual abuse, gain medical care for all children, strive to equalize quality of education throughout the country, protect inner city children from community violence—continue to languish in state legislatures and congress.

Typically, efforts to remedy one problem or another are met with fierce opposition from opponents who perceive them in terms of particular by-products that they fear will be injurious to themselves. That focus gains higher priority than the whole-picture approach because that is too hard to calculate in terms of personal gain and loss. The narrowly limited proposed remedies tend to be perceived as wasteful boondoggles, or unrealistic, or whatever. That is not surprising. Attempts at remedy are typically framed in terms of specifying narrowly defined action. Their goals are frequently nullified by efforts of a host of people controlling other variables that interfere with those of child welfare. If, we as a nation don't hate our children, it might still be argued that many of them experience precious little love.

Example. When it was found that many children coming to school in poorer neighborhoods around the country were under nourished, laws were passed to supply funding for a standard level of nourishment to be provided in school lunch rooms. But this had to be done very carefully. Purveyors competed to be the suppliers, while teachers and cafeteria staffs complained about uncompensated extra work. Questions were raised as to why adequate meals were not provided at home, given food stamps and all. As is so frequently the case, attempts to survey the results after a few months, or a few years, generally found some children better nourished, many unchanged. The attempts at remedy were framed in the usual cause-effect, linear logic way that took an abstract variable like "level of nourishment" and addressed it with an abstract program of action. The children almost drop out of the picture of the bureaucratic process in large scale remedial efforts. The law does not allow any discretion to a person being responsible for the outcome rather than the process.

Admittedly it would not be easy to change such approaches. It would demand an examination of the web of controlled variables involved in such a situation, although it is done here and there in small scale efforts, such as Kaplan (1996) describes in his chapter, "Rishi Valley and Human Ingenuity." (But that isn't in the U. S. either.) A control-system approach would need to begin with the undernourished children. It would need to find out how they view their eating behavior, where they look to get food, what they view as proper food, from whom they will and will not accept it, when and where. Then the problems of coordinating those controlled variables with those relating to the practicalities of supply would need to be faced. The self-interests of politicians supplying the funds, and purveyors supplying the goods are legitimate concerns because they are being controlled in ways that will disturb the functioning of the delivery process, if not taken into account. All that must be hierarchically subservient to the highest goal—health of the children.

When attempting to control a perceived condition the control system established to do it must be capable of countering disturbances or control does not exist. To move from the way things are done now, (I should have said, "attempted now"), requires thinking in terms specifying goals first, then experimenting with as many programmatic variations as are necessary to achieve them. That is contrary to the way most people think about remediation currently. True reform will only come about as more and more of us begin thinking in terms of controlling for results rather than actions. Beginning with running our own lives in a new way, we will gradually enlarge our individual scope to thinking in similar ways about cooperating with each other to solve our mutual problems in society.

A comparable issue concerns the apparently deteriorating levels of educational achievement in many schools in our country. A recent article reported a move on the part of universities to absolve themselves from teaching new admittees to read! The recommendation was for this function to be delegated to junior colleges. Two trends in primary education had converged to create this problem. One was the linear-logic idea that a "best" teaching technique was to be found by research and then prescribed to all teachers as a manual to follow. This had the effect of pressuring the teacher to control her perception of faithfully following the manual at a higher priority than focusing on the goal for any particular child. Doing what the manual said became a higher level goal than her perception of what a student was actually doing. The second defect was similar in nature, but as relating to the child; it implicitly viewed all children as standardized objects that could be given the same treatment. Behind the controversy over whether the whole-word, or phrase—or phonics-strategy is best is a fact that some people learned to read by each of these methods, or by combinations or variants presented by parents and/or teachers. The mistake then was for an authority to decide that the one he/she perceived to be best must be best for everyone.

This tendency to prize standardization seems to have continuously gained momentum in Western civilization ever since the industrial revolution. No one can dispute its effectiveness in the mass production of objects. But objects are not control systems. They don't counter efforts to standardize them with objectives of their own. I believe the greatest remedy to functional illiteracy that plagues our educational establishment today would be for teachers once more to be allowed to focus their attention on each child's performance, and for the children to be encouraged to state and pursue their own goals for achievement, certainly, in negotiation with the teacher's wider knowledge of the world.

A complementary solution might be for the President of the United States to call a conference of English teachers, encyclopedists, dictionary publishers and media leaders to reconstruct our English orthography to create an alphabet with single sound values for letters and spelling reformation in which words are spelled as they are pronounced, as in German or Finnish. Many more children would be able to master such a system by themselves with less help from overworked teachers than is now the case in especially inner city classrooms.

Returning once more to the common element in the Esquire articles, we can look to them to help understand conflicting perceptual variables that take energy away from solutions like those described above. What was behind that headline question, Do Americans Suddenly Hate Kids? Following the statistics, the next article described a young woman writer advocating childlessness as a constructive life style, "attacking the maternal syndrome as a way to narrow human love, not extend it." This was just a few years after the 60's theme of civil rights activism, anti-war love-ins, communes, where loving all children was perceived as better than focusing on one's own and excluding the rest of the world. It was held to be irresponsible to contribute to the population explosion, and irresponsible to have a child if you were going to be involved in the many causes that had come out of the foregoing era. Add to that the new attitudes about developing one's own potential to the fullest (sensitivity training and human growth training were all the rage), plus the rationalizing of emotional values, as indicated in the critique of Dr. Bettlheim's lecture, and the question about a changed attitude toward kids and you have the kind of question that attracts journalists for short-term sensationalism.

While it is doubtful that the Esquire authors meant their headline question literally—Americans hating their (our) kids is too vague and general in the first place—the linear logic employed in the articles suggests that an effect the writers were hoping to cause in their readers might have been shock, perhaps with an admixture of curiosity and concern. What perceptions of their own would they be trying to control? Imagine yourself publishing this headline and these articles. Shocking headlines continue to be a typical communication style to focus attention on phenomena that media publishers are defining in the process of putting out their material. If we consider the writers in terms of controlling a whole hierarchy of perceptual variables, we note that the magazine needs first of all to make a profit to stay in business. Therefore, the selection of articles, as well as the viewpoints expressed must be such as to attract the attention of its presumed readership. In addition, the writers would likely also be controlling their own self-images as open-minded, enquiring, alert and knowledgeable viewers of general trends and themes. They would also see themselves as potential contributors to the remedy of undesirable conditions by virtue of exposing them. But it makes a huge difference which variable is controlled at the highest level. All other purposes must be adapted to the requirement of keeping the higher level perception on target.

Since the best guess about what a control system is controlling is to see what state of affairs remains constant you can use that observation to guess what the publisher might be controlling for. Besides the circulation statistics, one of the most constant features of almost any periodical publication is the letters to the editor section. Why is that so ubiquitous a feature? What does it accomplish for the publisher? Obviously it provides some chance to sample the attitudes of his most involved audience toward his offerings. But, that just gives him information about how he is doing. Considering it as a kind of perceptual variable we ought to be able to make some inferences about what Reference level of this variable he is trying to meet with his effort. Following the rule of thumb I suggested above, a good candidate might be: letters to the editor in the next issue on the order of, "You really woke me up to a serious national crisis there." Or, "what you say is so clearly true," etc. That would be the kind of perceptual outcome a publisher would be trying to control. It would be potentially reassuring that the circulation statistic was under control. And the projection of shock would be one method for inviting such heightened involvement.

It is hard to tell whether the treatment of children is in any way affected by media outpourings like that, or whether they will have served a simpler purpose in creating a moment of emotional charge, from which the reader goes on to other concerns. The atmosphere of linear thinking in which we conduct our lives so much of the time fosters perceiving one dimension at a time. Despite all the talk about the need for holistic thinking, that is still in very rudimentary form in our national dialogue. I find it disheartening that the institutions of our society are so poorly integrated that an expanding readership and good advertising revenue might be the highest PVs a publisher might be controlling.

Political leaders' and lawmakers' decisions probably don't give high priority to the welfare of all U. S. children. Not that they aren't caring parents and grandparents, for the most part, to their own children or grandchildren, or even the neighbors down the street. But they are controlling many more immediately urgent variables. If the message of movies and TV documentaries about alienation of kids and high achieving fathers is to be believed, not all decision makers even put their own children high on the priority list.

Failure to Deal with Issues in General

To enlarge the discussion to the whole category of linear, cause-effect thinking let us return once more to *The Death of Common Sense* (Howard, 1994). In a section titled, "How Law Replaced Humanity," he contrasts the U. S. constitution, a "model of flexible law," with "ironclad rules that seek to predetermine results." The purpose of flexibility in the constitution was to rest upon the use of judgment and discretion by human beings, whereas ironclad rules are intended to obviate exactly that. Think about applying ironclad rules to an activity like driving your car to work tomorrow morning. Beginning with yourself in the driver's seat imagine programming: "turn steering wheel clockwise such that center bar is 3 degrees from horizontal, move gearshift to reverse and apply 2 foot pounds of pressure to accelerator pedal for thirteen seconds. Then turn steering wheel 27 degrees counterclockwise etc. Ridiculous, you say. Of course. Where would those numbers come from in the first place? Suppose you had machinery that recorded them on the previous day's trip to the office. Would the exact same movements accomplish your goal today? You can't know what the conditions of the environment, traffic, weather and so on will be until you are actually performing today's task. Yet this kind of precise specification of what shall be done in the future is exactly what Howard documents in case after case of regulatory horror stories.

Is it a fair analogy? I say it is. Remember Howard's (1994) case of the failure of the Nuns of the Missionaries of Charity to succeed in converting an abandoned building into a homeless shelter. How could that happen? It involved a loss of common sense, but how did that work? Who was in charge there? Clearly not the mayor or any of the authorities who had welcomed the plan. No, it was an abstract principle: all buildings of the type must have elevators when remodeled. The law allowed no room for exceptions, no mitigating circumstances, no discretion by even the highest of authorities. The bureaucrat who pointed to it ended up being the person really controlling the situation. As he controlled it the words in the lawbook had higher priority than the intent behind the body of law in general.

The arguments in favor of making laws impervious to adjustments came from values controlled at high Reference levels—values to which all of us, more or less, subscribe. We like to say we are a nation of laws, not men. What we mean by this is that we have gotten sick and tired of certain people putting themselves above the law whether through status, legitimate power or corruption. So "society" tried to insure that there can be no exceptions to the written word. The unanticipated consequence has been, over and over, a death of common sense. In Howard's examples we note that the laws and regulations he cites do not begin with a statement of the desired consequences to be looked for. Even less would you expect to find them written in a contingent manner—to say that if, by a certain time, the desired consequences were not obtained, the law would be revoked, or would transform to Plan B, or would be assigned to a czar (like the current drug czar) to be revised and reworked until the desired consequences are perceived. Further, current lawmaking does not ordinarily carry any definition and resources for a means to detect whether or not the desired consequences are forthcoming.

This state of affairs has not come about because the leaders of Western civilization have been infiltrated by alien beings endeavoring to paralyze our social system. It has descended from competition in applying the fundamental principles upon which our civilization has been based—being drawn out to the extreme, as Spengler contended. How that occurred is plainly and simply a function of the way that behavior works. We control our perceptions of who we are, as individuals and as members of a community, nation, civilization, in terms of the identities we acquire during our development, accommodating our unique, peculiar self images with societally given templates. We (automatically and mainly unconsciously) set Reference values for the principles comprising our sense of our world. When these fundamental principles collide in our individual lives, different individuals resolve the inconsistencies in different ways according to the structure of the rest of their control hierarchies. The principle that all are created equal collides for some with the principle that people should prosper according to their efforts. In competing for advantages with fellow members of our species we keep stretching the boundaries of these principles, trying to keep as many true as we can but ultimately, to preserve our own survival. A widely found derivative of some fundamental Western principles seems to be that separating tasks into small and interchangeable parts is an efficient way to accomplish tasks. It has certainly worked out in mass production of goods, but is failing miserably as a way of solving problems of human behavior.

Here is a final example of the way one-dimension-at-a-time control of a self-image, instead of control of one's life, can be idiotic. It is an instance where control of the self-image to a particular value resulted in destruction of the physical organism supporting that image. The Japanese movie, Kagemusha is the story of a warlord family of the 1500's that ended with a vast army lying dead on a field in front of an opposing army upon which they never laid a finger. The defeated army was led by the son of a warlord who had been mortally wounded in a previous battle. Otherwise the son would not have been in command, as the father had already passed him over to designate a grandson as his heir. Before the battle the prince's generals argued for holding off, that they were at a disadvantage, but the leader ordered the attack anyway. The generals said farewell to each other. The scene showed to the audience that the leader could clearly see a line of riflemen, posted behind a picket fence toward which his troops would have to advance. His troops did not have rifles. They were mowed down before their weapons could ever be brought into play.

From the point of human drama, the story is one of enormous hubris. Or incompetence, or stupidity. But, it is certainly a realistic scenario. Such things have happened repeatedly in human history. If the prince were ready to sacrifice his whole army it must have been that he was controlling a higher priority perception than that to win the battle. We immediately think of some facts we know about Japanese culture. There are some eventualities worse than death—for example, losing face. However, losing face is defined by oneself, in terms consistent with what is held among one's peers. As I contemplated this idea I recalled that in 6th or 7th grade I was regularly beaten up by a bigger and older kid. Why wouldn't I surrender? I remembered why. It was more intolerable to be regarded as a sissy than to suffer the beatings. In my adult life I have sometimes been complimented by peers for perseverance. Looking back on my childhood discomfiture I can't help but regard it as drawing out a valuable principle to a nonsensical extreme, controlling the variable, self-image, at an anti-organismic setting.

In the next chapter I want to go on to argue how the Cartesian paradigm has spread through all aspects of life in our civilization, in large part because of the way in which we have come to psychologize our approach to thinking about life. Western psychology, in attempting to follow the lead of the physical sciences has concentrated on viewing behavior as the function of external "forces" on the individual. Thereby have we lost the chance to understand behavior as a function of self regulation, and have gained many consequences that equate human beings with the objects on mass production lines.

Chapter 11

ROLE OF CONTEMPORARY PSYCHOLOGY IN THE LOSS OF ACCOUNTABILITY

The field of psychology has gradually acquired a catalog of relatively reliable observations of various sorts. Taken together they might justifiably be called a body of knowledge. When I say reliable observations I mean that different people have described similar observations in comparable circumstances on more than one occasion. Various of them have been collected and named by someone and subsequently come to be called "the theory of _____." If one accepted physical science criteria, it would be difficult to call any of such collections of observations a theory because they lack any mechanism explaining how the purported phenomenon works—what underlying processes produce it. However, they exist currently as probably the best of contemporary psychology, because you can extrapolate that—in similar circumstances—you are likely to make more observations of the same type. That is potentially more useful than much of the rest of what currently passes for psychological research—reports of experiments in which some correlation between two purported phenomena is made once and then never heard from again.

Several of these reliable phenomena have been defined by the work of certain noted psychologists. I made reference to some of them in chapter eight. The "discoverers" often treated their observations as independent facts of human behavior. They did so, I believe, because they, like almost all psychologists, were thinking within the linear-logic mold that I have been calling the Cartesian paradigm.[120] It was natural for them to see the behavior in which they were interested as separate phenomena—which is how it appears when you look at it from an observer's viewpoint. As we view it in terms of perceptual control theory, however, each of the following phenomena can be understood as a different, special case of the same underlying process. Each is a separate perspective on the behavior of people controlling high level (abstract) perceptual variables. The given circumstances, externally defined, account for different names applied to the "different" phenomena. One is called the phenomenon of "self-consistency," another is, "Cognitive Dissonance," still another is "Self-fulfilling prophecy." The underlying commonality is that they are all instances of maintaining some aspect of self perception relatively constant.

The theme of self-consistency was first (to my knowledge) proposed, in a book of that name, by Prescott Lecky early in the century. Using an essentially anecdotal approach he described many examples showing that individuals pretty typically act to preserve or increase the match between different instances of one's image of self, or to enhance consistency between different instances of one's statements or actions. Some decades later Leon Festinger (1954, 1957, 1959) seemed to discover essentially the same thing.[121] He called it a tendency to reduce cognitive dissonance, or the Theory of Cognitive Dissonance. Cognitive dissonance was defined as an uncomfortable feeling one gets on becoming aware of inconsistency between one's statements or between one's words and actions.

A closely related phenomenon is what Robert Rosenthal (1976, 1977, 1978) called the self-fulfilling prophecy. He first became interested in this phenomenon when he found students unwittingly influencing the results of experiments involving learning in laboratory rats. He then carried out a series of ingenious studies, the most famous, and probably most practical, of which was *Pygmalion in the Classroom*. In this work he showed that when children were falsely identified as potentially high, or low, achievers to teachers at the beginning of a school year, they tended to conform to those predictions in tests at the end of the year. This was so even though only the teachers, not the children, knew of the predictions and in spite of the fact that the predictions were randomly assigned and not based upon any real tests of potential.

All three of these "phenomena" are fundamentally alike. They show examples of control systems bringing observed variables to some particular value and maintaining them there in the face of disturbing influences. Or, more prosaically, they are formalized versions of the folk wisdom that people "see what one wants to see, and hears what one wants to hear." These three "phenomena" then, are not separate phenomena of human behavior. They come from different ways of naming the results of keeping certain types of perceptions at chosen values.

It might be a little more difficult to see the underlying similarity between self-fulfilling prophecy research and the other two "phenomena," so permit me to spell it out. In self-consistency and cognitive dissonance research the results generally confirm that a person becoming aware of mis-match between different of his statements, or different self-descriptions or self-attributions, or between his/her words and actions, will do something that reduces the perceived mis-match. That is straightforward correcting of error in one's self system. You have to make the assumption that most (if not all) of us have a system-concept-level system controlling the image of ourselves that we desire to project in the world. I have gathered some experimental evidence seeming to confirm this notion.[122]

Correcting self-image mismatch requires resetting the Reference values of certain lower order control systems to enact concrete actions that effectuate the desired image of self. Example: Mother says, "Good little girls are nice to their little brothers." Little sister then lets go of the toy she was yanking out of brother's hand. This doesn't always happen. When it does we are justified in inferring that sister is controlling a self-image of "nice little girl." It, in turn, governs Principles concerned with what "nice" is and that, in turn, governs what the child does and doesn't do. When little sister doesn't let go we can conclude either that she is too young to have a strongly developed self-system, or that, if she does, it isn't currently controlling a Principle like a desire to be seen as "being nice."

Here is another example, this one a true story. I was having an argument with my boss in a job I had many years ago. He was relaying to me his boss's dissatisfaction with something I had done, but wasn't engaging in the type of give-and-take about it that I was used to with him. Instead he was being hard-nosed, laying down the law without permitting any response. Becoming frustrated I blurted out, "You aren't the Joe Smith I know, today." He paused, looked a bit sheepish, and relented, carrying on a meaningful exchange of views after that. Wouldn't you say that qualifies as an instance of correcting a self-image mis-match? Or, in the other framework it would be called reduction of cognitive dissonance.

Now as to the underlying commonality with the self-fulfilling prophecy findings, the superficial difference is that—instead of self-image—we are looking at behavior relating to what the subject believes or expects to observe. Rosenthal did some nice work trying to identify just how the rats in his earlier experiments could have performed differentially in just the ways that they did. As I recall, what he thought he found was that various of his student lab assistants were developing attitudes toward some of the rats like toward pets. They would thereupon pet them (which might have had a relaxing effect-?), and sometimes give their performance the benefit of the doubt in borderline measurements, etc. In other words, the rats were being encouraged, even assisted maybe, to live out their keepers' expectations. The lab assistants couldn't control the rats directly, of course. What they were controlling were their own handling of the rats, and the concrete actions they performed in doing so influenced the measurement of results in various ways, such that "my pet obviously is one of the smart ones," or things to that effect.

Rosenthal surmised that in his Pygmalion in the Classroom study something comparable was being done by teachers in facilitating their expectations that students would perform according to the "predictions" made at the beginning. There is reason to believe that these lab assistants and these teachers would justifiably be indignant if charged with tampering with the research. What they were consciously aware of, almost surely, was the protocol of impartiality in research. But they also had expectations as to the outcomes. In the lab study the expectations seemed to derive from whatever feelings of fondness they developed toward particular rats. In the classroom study the expectations were expressly inculcated by the phoney assessments of potential. The more mundane behaviors, carried out with lower order systems involved in talking, walking, keeping notes, making measurements, etc., do not operate independently. They exist within a control hierarchy in which they are constantly adjusted to keep minimizing error in higher orders—like the concepts involved in expectations—even while satisfying the concrete targets of immediate behavior.

All these studies have had interesting and sometimes even counter-intuitive, findings. I am not meaning to denigrate their contributions to the collections of reliable observations that psychologists have been accumulating. My point is to draw your attention to the way they are expressed—as curious features of behavior, as if behavior is somehow a phenomenon in its own right instead of a noun that we use to refer to the fact that people do things. It is another example of regarding perceptions as something "out there," shaped by abstract forces, that impinge upon a person to cause behavior. Just about all contemporary psychology is formulated in that way. It fosters looking at humans from an external point of view rather than to understand from the internal point of view how an organism would have to function in order to produce the phenomena that we observe. It also has the consequence of isolating behaviors, making them look like independently functioning processes. Although social scientists keep talking about the integration of behaviors in people, the paradigm in which their science has developed is not conducive to thinking in such terms.

A further feature of this paradigm that you can see when you look for the common structure of psychological experiments is the implicit assumption that all the subjects of an experiment are equivalent in regard to the characteristics of interest. That way the results should show the effect of applying an external force/influence to them in the experiment. Think about it. This procedure requires you to regard the human subjects in an experiment as equivalent objects like those of a mass-production assembly line. It is no accident that this field has developed in that way. The discovery or invention of mass-production arose from the same underlying, analytic paradigm that also informed the genesis of interest in studying behavior scientifically. The manner in which the analytic method evolved in Western civilization permitted an individual, though himself an hierarchical control system, to forget that he is dealing with organisms like himself when he functions as a psychological investigator. In that role he comes to regard other individuals as open loop, linear systems controlled by outside influences. Descartes' great contribution to liberating the development of western science from church dogma backfired when the empirical method was transferred all too mechanically, from the natural sciences to the social sciences.

The gradual spread of this way of thinking throughout our culture has fed into several forms of mischief, as regards behavior, even as it has triumphed in the manufacture of stuff. For one it results in "the devil made me do it" defense in all manner of crimes. It is a perfectly logical conclusion. If behavior is the result of external influences, then undesirable, anti-social behavior is the consequence of bad influences, leading to the abrogation of individual responsibility of which so many social critics complain. Another consequence is the failure of responsibility for taking positive actions. One example (among hundreds possible) was provided by Buckley (1968) in his faulting of modern liberalism for a loss of commitment to any firm values by recent generations of students in the major universities.

> Higher education today emphasizes the development of the critical faculties—though to what purpose is not clear; and that it is not clear is the central revelation of the contemporary critique of higher education.... Princeton... [inter alia] would never be caught corporately urging a dedication of the intellectual faculties to the service of a particular world view. Such a thing being, in an age of relativism, unmodish, and in any case, proscribed by the rites of academic freedom. But, what strikes one most... is... the related feeling of personal powerlessness, projected at every level...."What can I do about the march of

history? another student asks rhetorically. He can do nothing, he means us to understand that no one can. The great events of the modern world are shaped by forces that individual human beings cannot influence. Great events are for great bureaucracies, and sociologists, to deal with. Political tidal waves are not deflected by the exertion of individual wills.... Man's destiny is wrought on a billion roof gardens; that is why personal states-craft is boring, and mechanized.[123]

Up to the last sentence he bears witness to that tendency of feeling powerless that was also remarked by the other writers I cited in earlier chapters. But, I found the last sentence curious. To me it contradicts the foregoing, although it obviously does not for Buckley. I, too, believe that "man's destiny is wrought on a billion roof gardens," but what I mean by that is that all of us humans, controlling whatever perceptions we individually do, are having effects upon the environment (both physical and social) which average out to what look like, "forces that individual human beings cannot influence," when viewed from the point of view of a disembodied, uninvolved observer. But, in fact, there are no such observers except when we personally adopt such a pose. That view is a concept that comes from subscribing to the mythology of "forces" that shape history. Indeed, most of us, most of the time, control many of our higher order—abstract—perceptions at values similar to those we perceive our peers are doing. We are social animals after all. We have thousands of generations of traditions of acting in concert. Only when I want something different from what most others are wanting at the moment, do I perceive what looks like evidence that I am being swept along by "forces" that are beyond my control. The frequency with which that happens—that any of us is likely to find ourselves on the outside of the majority attitude—increases as the population of the perceived reference group increases, for reasons put forth by Powers (1989) in his discussion of degrees of freedom.

But that is only tangential to what Buckley was aiming at in the excerpt quoted. He was registering his disgust that the crop of undergraduates about whom he was speaking seemed to have given up the practice of taking firm public stands on political issues. He blamed that on their acceptance of their professors' views that education should consist in the ability to make even-handed, dispassionate, intellectually neutral examinations of all the philosophical positions they examined.

Returning to how this applies to my own argument, Buckley, and earlier Weaver (1948), and then later, Bloom (1987), and Bork (1996), all roughly in the same tradition, criticize what they see as the degeneration of 19th century liberalism into, (Buckley again), "the prevailing view of things in the average college [is that] We don't feel deeply because there are no fixed, acknowledged norms by which . . . we grasp and then insist upon the need for reform. What norms there are, are merely conventional. They are not rooted in the natural order."

If that criticism has merit, and I think it does, up to a point, how did this condition come about? Bloom and Bork lay some of its development at the door of liberals after John Stuart Mill.

> Liberalism without natural rights, the kind that we knew from John Stuart Mill and John Dewey, taught us that the only danger confronting us is being closed to the emergent, the new, the manifestations of progress. No attention had to be paid to the fundamental principles or the moral virtues that inclined men to live according to them . . . this turn in liberalism is what prepared us for cultural relativism and the fact-value distinction . . . . [124]

Weaver traced the theme to even deeper roots.

> For four centuries every man has been not only his own priest but his own professor of ethics, and the consequence is an anarchy which threatens even that minimum consensus of value necessary to the political state . . . we look about us to see hecatombs of slaughter; we behold entire nations desolated by war . . . . Everywhere there occur symptoms of mass psychosis. Most portentous of all, there appear diverging bases of value, so that our single planetary globe is mocked by worlds of different understanding [which arouses] fear [that] leads to desperate unilateral efforts toward survival . . . .
>
> Like Macbeth, Western man made an evil decision, which . . . occurred in the late fourteenth century [which] was that man could realize himself more fully if he would only abandon his belief in the existence of transcendentals.[125]

If Spengler were still with us, I suspect he would trace the theme to even earlier roots, possibly as with St. Paul's teachings figuratively laying the hand of Christ on the German savages to tell them that all men are God's children, and hence we must all find a place here. How that devolved into the modern ethic, that everyone's truth is worthy of equal respect, is the story of a long line of rationalization (in both its positive and negative connotations) that occurs as humans argue with each other, resorting to higher principles that each presumably holds, when attempting to control concrete, everyday-life circumstances, each to his own desired setting. A powerful example is found in Brown versus Board of Education where even the southern judge was compelled, via the strain to self-consistency, to recognize the evidence showing that "separate but equal" was only separate, and had never been equal, and thus violated, "We hold these truths to be self-evident, that all men are created equal...."

In such debating, however, the basic paradigm gets stretched in the manner that produces what Kuhn called, "anomalies." Because people—all people—control for immediate, specific perceptions in their everyday dealings, the negotiations involved in attempts at conflict resolution, resort to the authority of the basic principles, trying to arouse sufficient cognitive dissonance in opponents to secure their capitulation. But this requires arguments framed in newer interpretations of the principles. You can't resort to interpretations that have already been countered by previous interpretations, especially of the sort made by the Supreme Court. That is the essential process by which the evolution of thought, that Spengler described, occurs. As interpretations close to the common sense of ordinary people in a culture get "used up" in the march of arguments, newer interpretations are forced to migrate ever further from their original positions.

Over and over in history one can see how the only way around debating the relevance of higher principles to resolve conflicts in immediate circumstances is the tyrant's route of overwhelming force in which the implications of higher principles are simply ignored. But this method is, itself, such a corruption of the way in which human thinking controls the derivation of implications and the subsequent reconciliation of contradictions that it reveals most tyrants as basically psychopaths, with no abiding higher principles, and therefore, no lasting impression upon history once their application of force is lifted.

It is common among people under the thumb of a tyrant to become apathetic about asserting any appeal to rights, whether universal or not, and to concentrate upon controlling immediate, day to day survival conditions. (With the occasional outbreaks of rebellion by those so circumstantially depressed that they no longer have much of anything to lose.) Such behavior seems to me completely rational. But how does it relate to the seemingly comparable apathy that Buckley, and later Bloom, claimed to detect in students in the leading institutions in the country, who are not under the stultifying atmosphere of a tyrant? As I have previously suggested, the Cartesian paradigm is so prevalent in the psychology of our culture that it provides the rationale by which people justify/explain to themselves why it is useless to attempt to assert control over the kind of perceptual variables Buckley et. al. were discussing.

However, I don't think the concept of external forces obviating individual choices is enough by itself to account for all of what we see. Young people might be accurately perceiving that many of the perceptual variables proffered by various sources in contemporary culture are illusory. When that is the case people soon discover that attempts to control these variables are fruitless. In such situations it makes sense to turn one's efforts to variables which one can control. Perhaps that accounts for the relative decline in student passion for world-saving that was characteristic of the post World War II students and the turn to making money instead.

There is, in fact, another kind of tyranny in effect right now in certain areas of modern life. But it is a tyranny in which decision-making has effectively moved from the people, via their elected representatives, to those special interest groups who have become more truly the constituents. They more truly are, by virtue of providing the funds that get the politician elected. That development has, itself, resulted from another devolution of guiding concepts to their ultimate limits. I am referring to the legal interpretations, a few centuries back, that permitted the recognition of business corporations to be treated as individuals. At that time the concept seems to have been a wholly positive one for it provided a means for individuals to pool their resources to set up businesses which then could own property in the guise of a quasi-person. By now that idea has come down to a condition in which it seems that almost the only significant "persons" on the political scene are those corporate entities—businesses or their advocacy-group antagonists.

Like any other logical process this migration of a once-beneficial idea to something many now regard as corruption occurred one decision at a time. But I believe its particular trajectory is peculiar to our culture; it wouldn't follow that course in every civilization. The other underlying concept that helped it go this route is, in my opinion, once more the external point of view, linear logic kind of thought that legal reasoning shares with mass production organization and Cartesian psychology. It is the thinking that helps to confine decision makers to one dimension at a time and the sense of helplessness in taking action regarding the whole picture.

The most pernicious applications of this kind of thinking are coming to be seen in the fields of advertising and publicity. These applied psychologies have reached the point where the control of a single perceptual variable—the volume of sales, or the percentage of desired poll responses—comes to be pursued in a fashion that ends up tolerating what would in other contexts be clearly recognized as fraud, deception, hoax, swindle, calumny, or libel. Thus another one of our sacred principles—"freedom of speech"—gets corrupted to safeguard such proceedings.

That situation has produced some horrendous ironies. A few years ago a radio or television reporter did a program maintaining that some tobacco companies promoted advertising that was enticing children to smoke at an early age. They sued him and won. Years later evidence has been produced from their own records that appears to support his original charge. In the field of journalism such revelation would call for a retraction. A common sense view might see an appropriate analogy by which the winners of the libel suit would have to give back the money. No such thing happens, of course. The ruling legal fiction there is that whatever is found to be the truth by a jury remains truth even when it turns out to be a lie.

In order for legal and commercial processes to work within the framework of Western thought, as it has now developed, such fictions are necessary in all kinds of situations. They are part of the processes Howard decries in *The Death of Common Sense*. If you experience cognitive dissonance in trying to digest such fictions, as I believe more and more people are coming to do, the immediate effect might be frustration and indignation. The longer range effect is often a desire to withdraw from the arena, if possible. It calls to mind a personal experience in which I withdrew from a situation, that I perceived as a no-win encounter with a managed care enterprise. It originated with a public relations newsletter, conveying a cheery, friendly tone, purporting to give useful information to "providers." (Why *providers* instead of therapists or professionals? But let that go.)

Proclaiming that providers and care managers are partners for quality care of patients, it listed several "issues" that affect quality, ending with, "In each of these issues, the care manager-provider partnership can make an important contribution toward producing the optimal outcome for the patient." Now what is wrong with this statement? It is a typical managed care administrator's PR statement aiming at convincing therapists to regard case managers as collaborators rather than opponents in the work. As such there seems nothing wrong with it. If a therapist signs on as a "provider" for a company, he/she knows his or her work will be reviewed and often curtailed by a care manager. Better then to try for a cooperative rather than an adversarial relationship.

Nevertheless, I perceived the message as an appeal to submit to a fraud. I have worked with several partners/

collaborators, at times in my career. I know what a partner is. This public relations message was asking me to subscribe to a definition of that word which would warp it entirely out of any intelligible shape anent my experience. I already had sufficient personal experience inclining me to reject the notion that I could be in partnership with any care manager that I had met so far: Someone I had never met personally, who would never encounter any of my clients/patients, about whose training, if any, I had no knowledge, and who, in fact, might be a set of entirely different human beings at different times on the other end of my phone. Defined as *my partner?* No thank you. And further, somebody who, in one of his/her incarnations, had said to me, "We do not support personality reorganization, we are only interested in symptom relief." I perceived the newsletter message as fraud—of the innocent sort, maybe—commonly found in advertising and public relations pronouncements.

I call it "innocent fraud" in that I did not perceive the writer to be addressing me personally with malevolent intent like a con man trying to steal my money. Nonetheless it constituted a seduction to substitute an externally defined perception for my own immediate experience. If you have been open to this revision of how we think about the nature of behavior, you might well agree that there is no way that a person can substitute a set of words for one's own experience. The most we can do is simulate that, if we have good reason to do so.

In some conditions I might have decided to humor the fiction and deal with what I perceived as the main perceptual variable the writer was trying to control—i. e. namely, not to give his care managers too hard a time. It doubtless derived from the writer's desire for me to be willing to compromise and remember that they are most of all controlling the variable called *cost*. If I had felt my career would be seriously eroded by rejecting the request to cooperate, I might have held my nose and knuckled under. But I wasn't in that position. What I perceived instead, was that to knuckle under would violate an aspect of my self image—as someone allergic to fraud. So, I quit.

There is another, even more perfidious, aspect to this practice of all-too-blithely creating fictions to smuggle in an idea in the shape of a human being, like with the body-snatching parasites in science fiction movies. That is the organization of all kinds of work with the tacit assumption that human beings can be substituted mechanically for one another like objects in the mass production assembly line. This fiction has indeed made possible the writing of standardized duties-manuals and job descriptions to which each human operator fits him—or herself to produce a more or less uniform output. In the manufacture of things this practice of forcing humans to adapt to machines has resulted in great increases in productive efficiency and perhaps at not too great a human cost other than boredom.

However, as that idea has spread to viewing human beings as standardized objects for standardized treatments, the picture becomes more complicated. Right now our nation is deeply mired in the debate, and in the experiment, over whether such a development is going to work in fields like medicine and psychotherapy. The logical conclusion of present trends would be for practice to be done by the manual, as with dishwasher repair. The already established practice of labeling practitioners as providers and client/patients as consumers is a step in that direction, but premature in my opinion. It is perhaps too inadvertently accurate in reflecting that the highest priority variable under control is the transfer of money. But, I think it is premature in that it conveys the unconscious message that a standardized product is being transmitted. While it is true that humans are constructed basically in the same way, and that designated illnesses function in about the same way in people, it is still the case that much in medical, and even more in psychological, treatment is strategic and only the separate elements of the practitioner's strategy are routines.

What I mean by "strategic" is more aptly characterized as "programmatic." One hierarchical control system negotiating with another hierarchical control system can not rely upon the assumption that any given control action will be successful. This is true even with cooperative patients. Let me illustrate with the presumably more difficult instance of the uncooperative patient. Years ago when I was employed as a psychologist in a rehabilitation hospital a frequent task was to find out why a physician's treatment was not working out as well with this patient as it had with that patient.

Sometimes these questions resolve into what we call "personality differences." But that is not an explanation. It is simply another way of naming the fact that the treatment is not progressing, and nothing seems to account for it, and the staff are thinking they perceive malevolence of some sort in the "uncooperative patient." Yes, there might be qualities that justify the term. After frustrations begin to mount perceptions of disaffection begin to be realistic. Sometimes in those cases my careful questioning would reveal that patient and doctor didn't particularly like each other, but was that cause or effect? When the reason was mysterious, we psychologists assigned it to what we in our more Freudian days called a transference reaction. Other times it became clear that one or the other (but usually the patient, because that was the angle from which I was paid to regard the situation), was controlling some perceptual variable that the doctor's treatment effort was disturbing. The patient's output to maintain the variable at his preferred Reference value then constituted a disturbance to what the doctor was trying to control.

Sometimes it had nothing directly to do with the interaction of doctor and patient. We had a certain number of charity cases in which it came out that the patient was enjoying a more agreeable life style in the hospital than he had previously had. In such a case he would be controlling his continued stay with us at a higher priority than "getting well." Ordinarily it would be impossible to discern whether he was aware of this attitude. Since it would be a morally reprehensible motive, only the most naive person would admit to it to others. Often I found reasons to believe that his conscious focus was on something for which continued stay would be a by-product, like demanding more perfection of his recovery before risking behavior that could lead to a setback.

Now the question that should arise here is why a specialist should be required to learn these facts, and then act as intermediary between the principals to try to find a ground on which they could meet. If the physician could perceive the patient in terms of controlling a hierarchy of variables, and refer to his own hierarchy to intuit or empathize what variables the patient was controlling, why couldn't they have worked this out themselves? The answer is that physicians, patients and psychologists are ordinary members of our culture in this respect. As members of our culture, none of us has been predisposed by our upbringing and education to see others as living control systems controlling a hierarchy of perceptual variables, or to think that we can understand others by looking inward at ourselves. The more highly trained we are the more *objective* we are.[126] And that means focusing on our own intentions and expecting patients to be patient, i. e. to hold still and not interfere with what we are trying to do. I often think that the least educated of us does best at practicing empathy, for reasons I will take up further in the next chapter.

Chapter 12

BIOLOGICAL BASE AND CULTURE PARADIGMS

When I was in graduate school "nurture" was given the dominant role in the "nature/nurture" debate. Now the times have come full circle and nature is given greater weight. This has happened partly because of the many new discoveries made in biological disciplines, from brain anatomy, ethology, genetics, to psycho-biology. Others have seen it gaining greater prominence for political reasons. Conservative political attitudes are often associated with the view that human nature is not as malleable as liberals would have it. There is a limit to the extent that we should expect education, therapy and social engineering to result in great changes in social phenomena. Biological approaches to the treatment of psychological dysfunction are seen as more solid (and cheaper too) by the people who hold power today.

Whatever the source the increased importance of ideas about our inherent qualities has meant that inquiry into basic human nature has again become more fashionable. In terms of perceptual control theory the issue is one of learning what are the genetically given control systems, and what are their parameters? Then, how are they involved with the development of the learned hierarchy in the "higher" brain, and how do these systems interact? Answers to those questions will have a significant bearing upon our thinking about the limits of control. That is, what phenomena—environmental variables—can humans come to control, and to what extent? As a rough example, consider the failures of planning in the Soviet economy as an example of attempting to defy the nature of human nature. A line of Soviet leaders, from Lenin on, acted as if they had been assuming that ordinary people would accept (momentarily, according to the theory) surrendering their private efforts at controlling such things as their food supply. They were supposed to submit to the state plan as the "bigger picture" in the belief that it would result in the greatest good for all. It didn't work because individuals continued to function as individual control systems, controlling such variables as they could to their individual Reference settings, rather than to the "rationalized" intentions that central planners tried to force upon them.

The thinking behind this experiment was not pure fantasy. It derived, not only from Marx's belief that he had perceived a rational "force" in history, but also from Pavlov's application of the Cartesian paradigm that he called, *conditioning*. Not that Soviet leaders relied much upon psychological factors for social engineering. But, as Pavlov's findings were rather dramatic and, as classic examples of external-focus, linear logic psychology, they could be perceived as support for the idea of applying external pressure in controlling human behavior.

The failure of the Soviet system adds one more consideration to those already accumulating in support of the contrary conclusion: That the psychological paradigm of *Behaviorism*, with its implicit assumption of almost unlimited possibilities for changing behavior through conditioning, is proven wrong. Human beings can control an astounding variety of environmental variables—physical variables as in the continuing improvements of Olympic performances, for example, or social variables via our increasingly complex organizations. Finally, however, we come up against the limitations imposed by the intrinsic system. The concept of *instinct*, which was practically ruled out as an important factor in human behavior a couple generations ago, is back with regained importance. Several different findings and lines of investigation led to this result, such as that of instinctual drift, ethology and sociobiology.

Desmond Morris among other ethologists, has presented thought-provoking observations of animal behavior in natural settings that suggest parallels with various aspects of human behavior. Morris, in his introduction to *The Human Zoo (1969)*, says,

> Under normal conditions, in their natural habitats, wild animals do not mutilate themselves, masturbate, attack their offspring, develop stomach ulcers, become fetishists, suffer from obesity, form homosexual pair-bonds, or commit murder. Among human city-dwellers, needless to say, all of these things occur.

While some of what might be called "deviant behavior" has now been found in the wild, the general tenor of Morris's remarks still holds. Deviancy is found in animals under stress, as in animals in zoos, or in animals whose territorial ranges are under attack by human settlement or other sources of disturbance such as droughts, floods or loss of natural prey and predator balance. Calhoun's (1962) studies of animal crowding showed many of the pathologies that Morris described, as crowding intensified, and Freedman's (1975) hypothesis about the cause—interference with the ability to carry out instinctual patterns of action—is readily understandable in terms of control theory. Konrad Lorenz

(1952) also noted that various animals will destroy their own young when their nests or nesting patterns have been disturbed.

The common thread in these studies is that behavior which appears analogous to deviancy in humans ordinarily occurs only when instinctive or preprogrammed control systems suffer error states beyond the organism's capacity to correct. Though we still lack a great deal of understanding of the detailed function of many control systems for instinctual behavior, the evidence we have suggests that Reference signals of "pre-programmed" or instinctual control systems are determined by genes. "What we inherit [genetically] are neurobiological traits that cause us to perceive the world in a particular way and to learn certain behaviors in preference to other behaviors," (Wilson, 1998). Just *how* failure to satisfy genetically given Reference values results in the malfunctioning that Morris noted, will need continuing detailed studies to identify the controlled variables that are in error states when instincts go awry. In the most general sense, the variety of behavior extremes that we find in "behavioral sinks" (Calhoun, 1962) is just what one would predict on the basis of Power's theory of reorganization under error states in the *intrinsic system*.

While the applications of ethology and sociobiology have brought many more positive traits into focus as showing strong genetic predispositions even in humans, it is malfunction that gets our attention most directly because that is where our communal attempts at correction have been aimed, and so far, are seen so regularly to fail. Is it going too far to argue that, just as the Breland's (1961) found animal behavior to degenerate from trained patterns and migrate back toward instinctual patterns, so might there be limits to the extent to which human behavior can be modified in contradiction to our basic nature? The fact that human nature is far more plastic than that of any other animals does not mean that there are no limitations on it, as seemed to be implied at the height of Behaviorism.

The perennial interest in the nature of human nature has been greatly energized in recent decades by studies in sociobiology. Its interest for us here is in its implications for the question of what happens when cultural forms depart too radically from "instinctive"[127] human behavior. This line of thought adds another dimension to Spengler's definition of cultural degeneration. Rules, regulations and laws that attempt to require behavior that goes against "what comes naturally" to people will lead to breakdown of behavior. As the derivations of basic cultural premises become more extreme and impractical, individual reorganizations produce more desperate attempts to reduce threats to individuals' survival.

This leads to the question of the affinity between three areas of thought: The idea of common sense, what E. O. Wilson (1998) calls the *epigenetic rules*, and the older idea of natural law. The *Encyclopedia Britannica*[128] describes natural law as, "a term used, not always in the same sense, to denote a system of right or justice held to be common to all mankind and so independent of positive law." According to EB Aristotle was a major contributor to the tradition that, revived and built upon in the Middle Ages, led to modern philosophical views such as that stated in the Declaration of Independence, regarding "self-evident, inalienable rights." Aristotle held, "that there was a natural justice valid everywhere with the same force." St. Thomas picked up his views and modified them to conform with his developing Christian thought. EB continues

> The next ethical topic that Thomas had to handle was the meaning of natural law. Three definitions of it had descended to him: [Ulpian considered it] . . . what nature taught all animals; Isadore (after Gaius and Justinian) . . . what was common to all societies of

men; Gratian [defined it as] what was taught in the Old and New Testaments, such as the Golden Rule.... Thomas broke away from the tradition to define it... [as a] natural light in men's minds enabling them to tell good from bad.[129]

There was an increasing emphasis on the ethical aspect of the concept of natural law so long as most thinkers were approaching the question in religious terms. That was until the 17th century when Hugo Grotius, "saw the whole universe as dominated by a rational law of nature.... For man the law of nature is the collection of those rules which follow inevitably from his essential nature." (Ibid.)

These ideas, developed through Hobbes, Locke, Montescuieu, Hume, Kant, Spinoza and others in more secular terms, implicitly expressed the notion that human qualities necessary for survival precede and form the basis for formal laws. The emphases varied as the writer interested himself more in finding a source for morality or in the idea that human beings have a built-in set of perceptions regarding conditions one needs in order to be optimally human. As "Montescuieu... argued... natural laws were presocial and were superior to those of religion and of the state."[130]

My point in reviewing this history of the concept of natural law is to show that early, pre-scientific views of it were attempts by thoughtful observers to conceptualize intuitive perceptions of that which Wilson (1998) came to call "epigenetic rules." His concept, in turn, overlaps, if not parallels, Powers's (1973, 1978) idea of "the intrinsic system." Wilson has contributed considerable detail about what these "rules" or instinctual/genetic Reference signals are, and Powers has postulated the mechanism of reorganization by which they contribute to the development of the learned hierarchy of adult control systems. That, in turn, eventuates in the development of culture, as discussed in chapters five and eight. The force of this concept has gradually grown from instances like the Declaration of Independence to the Nurenberg trials in the sense that there are basic human qualities—pertaining to the requirements of survival—that people grasp intuitively. They underlie the laws, customs and regulations that we call civilization and take precedence over them when doubt arises as to what being human entails.

Admittedly, one might argue that postulation of certain essential human qualities is contaminated in instances where political rationalizations are involved. However, the underlying assumptions have continued to grow in force gradually in regard to issues of human rights in recent decades. The sponsorship of more and more military actions under UN authorization pays at least lip service to the universality of basic human needs and rights. This is something new in human history. Although it would be ingenuous to presume that such actions were basically altruistic in nature, without political considerations playing a part, it is still true that they indicate further development of the evolving idea of civilization. They contrast strongly with instances of genocide and other massacres that were perpetrated in the past without any effective protest by the rest of the world. The immediacy of the news certainly has been a factor in this development, but by itself would not generate the sense of revulsion at such scenes without the existence of human capacities such as altruism, empathy and identification.

Little by little the same notion has spread to judgments about the brutalization of peoples within a country by their own leaders. And finally, the same social atmosphere, if not the same line of thought, can be seen in those cases where disenchanted Americans have come to see their own government as corrupt because of laws and regulatory interpretations that have had disastrous effects upon their, or others' personal lives.

Wilson (1998) raised the question, "What is human

nature?" He answered, "It is not the genes [but] something else for which we have only begun to find expression . . . the epigenetic rules, the hereditary regularities of mental development that bias cultural evolution in one direction as opposed to another." With this definition, he connects the genes to culture. His numerous concrete illustrations begin to give us some inkling of the intrinsic system and hence the base of inferences as to when reorganizations are likely to be triggered. Besides the physiological variables that are controlled by the circuitry of the intrinsic system, he would add the genetic underpinnings—whatever they might eventually turn out to be—of such fundamental "instincts" as *Kin selection, Parental investment, Mating strategy, Status, Territorial expansion and defense and Contractual agreement*. He sees them as functioning in the coevolution of genetic endowment and human culture. It is interesting and probably more than coincidence that as our scientific knowledge of human nature (and that there is such a thing as human nature) has expanded, so has the list of basic "needs" subject to appeals regarding rights and entitlements.

Another trait that might bear some semblance to an intrinsic variable is a "need" for excitement, stimulation, exploration. It might turn out to be simply a particular way of perceiving random behavior in reorganization of higher level systems or it might be energized by particular epigenetic rules that produce the kinds of action that go by the various names above. However that might be, there are many situations, starting in early childhood, where—instead of purposeful behavior—we see what looks like the pursuit of an intention to seek out environmental challenges. This trait, if it is one, would be among the Reference values that make sex and violence subjects of such great interest in the movies, television, theater and political competitions. Its opposite condition, boredom, is often cited as one of the major curses of both work and education in modern society. Sex and violence are the two easiest and cheapest ways to provide that surge of excitement for which many people appear to feel a need.

This presumed trait might well help to understand the appeal of the kind of television talk shows where dysfunctional people display their pathology to the world. The contrast with the routine lives that many viewers lead might supply, vicariously, an ingredient of a kind of satisfaction akin to the fascination many people experience when encountering new and strange customs and scenes. That would be in addition to the obvious incentive of observing self-images to which the viewers can feel superior. But, there is still a further ingredient in the excitement and titillation of public scandal, true confessions and the periodic attractiveness of antisocial behavior. That is an unconscious "research" if you will, into the nature of human nature. We expand our conception of human potentials as much by learning about actions of which we would not have thought humans capable, as by our fascination with the lives and actions of the exceptionally talented, celebrated or notorious.

Most of the epigenetic Reference signals involved in these fascinations are difficult to discern for other reasons besides the fact that the science involved is still at a rudimentary level. It is hazardous to one's public image to admit to fascination with proscribed activities. So we deny and repress excitement of this sort. Thus we get situations — often labelled *hypocritical*—where conflicting Principles result in oscillation of the Programs with which we implement our curiosity. The error signal in one Principle increases with action taken to satisfy the other and vice versa. In such instances both sides of the person's conflict might be unavailable to awareness as consciousness is occupied by the lower orders' display of first one then the other type of concrete perception—creating a form of obsessive-compulsive ritual.

When phenomena of intrigue with sanctioned behavior become wide-spread we get the kind of cultural dilemmas which Erikson faulted for the confusion suffered by children during development. And as more and more individuals become affected and go into reorganization we see shifts in cultural ideals—paradigm revolutions. Chronic conflict within higher orders can not go on indefinitely in an hierarchical system without eventually affecting systems that immediately service intrinsic system functioning. Then basic functions reassert themselves. Proto-cultural motives or epigenetic rules—more fundamental than traditional cultural strictures—are acted upon. Normally law-abiding people act in defiance of laws in such instances. Carl Sagan's (1977) book, *The Dragons of Eden*, contains speculations about this process. Reviewing the "ontogeny recapitulates phylogeny" argument he pointed out how the human brain essentially comprises three versions, from reptilian, through mammalian to human.

> MacLean has developed a captivating model of brain structure and evolution that . . . 'amounts to three interconnected biological computers,' . . . . Each brain corresponds to a separate major evolutionary step . . . distinguished neuroanatomically and functionally . . . if the triune is an accurate model of how human beings function, it does no good whatever to ignore the reptilian component of human nature, particularly our ritualistic and hierarchical behavior.[131]

I can't help wondering whether we were viewing such a phenomenon of behavior governed mainly by subcortical mechanisms in December of 1998 when purportedly a large majority of U. S. citizens were apparently opposed to the sanctioning of an impeached president for alleged violation of law. The simple minded analysis implicit in the pronouncements of some critics—that the "American people

Perception of Reality and the Fate of a Civilization

admit he did wrong but they don't care," seems to me not an explanation. It might be true for some truly apathetic individuals but one ought to expect them to choose the "no comment" category when questioned in a poll. Instead there was a great deal of interest by the populace at large. An alternate explanation was that most people didn't want to risk their perceived economic condition in exchange for sanctions that they believe would not improve their material condition. If a fact, that interpretation could be understood in either of two ways. One interpretation would be that the majority of the people are concrete thinkers mainly focused on what they perceive as their selfish interests and indifferent to higher moral principles. The other interpretation—and the one to which I subscribe—would be that "something *feels* wrong" in the issue as it was currently being played out. If that turned out to be the case (and it may take a long time to determine, if ever) I would call it an instance of the expropriation of cognition by deeper (more primal) control systems, comprising an epigenetic rule.

I will even go out on a limb to offer a candidate for what that epigenetic rule might be. I drew it very tentatively from an analogue with wolves, lions and gorillas: *Alpha males do have more privileges and they have more responsibility for the welfare of the pack.* I am aware that that surmise might strike you as pretty much "off the wall" and I am not heavily invested in arguing for it. I am interested in explanations that look for controlled variables underlying what we actually observe instead of bemoaning the behavior in question as "irrational." I came upon this speculation from attempting an application of perceptual control theory, starting with the proposition that *that which remains constant* in the face of changing environmental conditions indicates the variable(s) that are under control. Second, that which is really under control may or may not coincide with the avowed intentions of the controller(s). Third, control of higher-order/abstract variables deteriorates when intrinsic system error activates the reorganizing system. Thus, I looked for a case where behavior like that actually is found, as an alternative to calling it "irrational,"[132] and came up with the Alpha male. Understand, I'm not saying that people *think* this way. Behavior at the level of instincts is unconscious.

I admit that resorting to an analogy with animals would seem to weaken my case, but in fact much of the hunt for epigenetic rules that Wilson offers for investigation started with animal analogies. The main point of my argument here is that—when behavior on a large scale seems not to make sense—the weakness must be in the examining lens, unless you take the position that the devil is causing it. My final point is that "instinctual" behavior is deeper, more profound, more powerful than learned formulations. It takes precedence for the layman over culturally prescribed propositions put forward by opposing political camps. By "culturally prescribed propositions" I refer to arguments involving (e.g.) interpretations of the constitution, and the demands of various would-be leaders of thought that people *see* a certain conclusion as compelling.

Higher order control systems are there to support the life of the organism not the other way round. Hence, as Sagan argued in the piece quoted above, qualities of the more primitive brain, the intrinsic system/epigenetic rules, continue to assert themselves through the behavior controlled at higher levels of the brain. Perhaps another way to say it, in reference to the curious attitudes toward the impeachment issue, is that the great mass of ordinary people might have little stake in the niceties of the competition between politicians, to control system-concepts like "the constitution," or "rule of law." Instead they rely on *feelings* about what those concepts are intended to achieve in the broadest, commonsensical terms.

I happened to chance on what seems to me a similar point of view in a news article while thinking about this point. The writer, Wendy Shallit (1998), reporting on a furor among some black parents about the assignment of a book called, *Nappy Hair*, in a Brooklyn elementary school, disagreed with a New York Times editorial supporting the position of the school officials. The experts had praised the book and the parents were criticized (by implication) as ignorant. But, Shallit counters,

> "But what if the parents were right? . . . what if their anger was justified? . . . . When the . . . parents protested they didn't know the book was written by [an African-American author] . . . . Chancellor Crew gathered from this that the parents were uninformed . . . an equally logical and less condescending conclusion is that it doesn't matter who wrote the book. These parents reacted viscerally and indignantly: Why in the world is my child learning that combing her hair 'sounds like crunching through deep snow . . . instead of learning how to spell? Why isn't the teacher encouraging her to take pride in something within her control . . . for example, doing well on an arithmetic exam?

I think that Shallit grasped that sometimes when a "visceral reaction" dominates cognitive behavior, it could be the visceral reaction that is right. Right in the sense that the more instinctual perceptual variable *makes a more important difference* in the lives of the persons in question than does controlling the intellectual variable. The intellectual percept might be more important to the experts and authorities, but that is Shallit's point: Whose education are we judging here and who should be judging it?

Public policy evolves from whatever are the current intuitions of human "needs," wherever government is responsive. And conversely, in a democracy, the responsiveness of the government is assessed by citizens in terms of their perceptions of the correspondence between public policy and their sense of well-being. That is equally valid whether we are talking about immediate local issues, or about the relationship between the philosophy of government enacted by legislators and how that spells out as ordinary people perceive it in terms of their general conditions of life.

When the mass of ordinary people begin to perceive incongruity between the forms and the substance of their social organization the ground is set for resistance and potential collapse or revolution with possible shifting of social paradigms. As Spengler argued, not only does the collapse occur when the potential in the first principles of a culture has become corrupted, but, he also argued, the cultural development that replaces it gains its energy from primal roots in basic biological, environmental and spiritual sources of the primitive people who will form the next civilization. In other words, a people is more energized the closer the individual members remain to their biological core.

A patient/client of mine, a tradesman employed in a transportation system, was filled with indignation on a particular occasion, over the mistreatment of laboring people. Petty bosses routinely blamed him (and his peers) when equipment failed and would tell them that how to solve it was their problem. Innocent people got scapegoated, often, it seemed just as a way for the bosses to exert their authority. In the course of getting him to be specific and to focus on his own emotional reactions he began to tell me about efforts he was making to get his co-workers organized to get justice about such things. I was struck by the way that he first needed to vent his emotions and then got to thinking and planning how he was going to attack the problem. I pointed this out to him and he agreed. He then asked if I could help him find a "cathartic group," like Synanon (in which he had participated many years before). His idea was that he freed up his creative energy by first releasing his emotional tensions.

That led me to think about how we know what really helps people. From there I jumped the track to my familiar belief that what we do "naturally" (like scapegoating) tells us about our instinctual mechanisms or epigenetic rules. For example, we see behavior like scapegoating, or prejudice (we clinicians might call it transference), when people are threatened or frustrated. Overt aggression like beating, browbeating, etc, is typically employed by the more primitive members of society—yet most professionals seem not to draw the conclusion that these ARE what people do "naturally" to work out frustration, and attempt to control their environments. These forms of behavior are more "primitive" because they are more physical. Presumably they indicate a poverty of options in higher order control systems, but they also illustrate a basic or biological quality that we all show as children and can easily relapse into, even as sophisticated adults, under stressful conditions.

Chapter 13

SOCIETY AS QUASI-CONTROL SYSTEM

Social anthropologist, Lloyd Warner, who studied social class phenomena in the 1940s and 1950s, propounded a view of society as a broad scale system having among its functions control of the social and physical environment of the members.

> All societies are essentially adaptive orders where accumulated human learning experience is organized, contained, and directed in symbol systems which adjust human biological groups with varying degrees of success to their several environments. Although human adaptation *seems* largely social, there can be little doubt that its core continues to be species behavior... From the larger point of view, all human society which is not species behavior is symbolic... . Human society is composed of symbolic processes, in the sense that what we are to ourselves, what others are to us, what we are to them and they to themselves, consist outwardly of words and acts which inwardly are beliefs to which we attach values . . . [Our] technology . . . consists partly of knowledge, which

> directs, organizes and adjusts our control over the
> natural environment. (Warner, 1953, pp. 42-44.)

Although Warner worked prior to the introduction of PCT his approach was highly compatible with the view of a society as a quasi-control system comprised of highly similar System-concepts shared by the members of the society. The sharing of System-concepts regarding the nature and identity of the society imparts to the communal life of the members qualities that make it resemble a living system in some ways. " . . . the several varieties of communities and local groups . . . although they vary widely . . . from the very simple to the very complex . . . are essentially the same in kind. They all are located in a given territory, which they partly transform for purposes of maintaining the life of the group." (Ibid. p. 41)

Warner described society as hierarchically organized in three social classes, which he later elaborated into nine by dividing lower, middle and upper classes each into three further subclasses. His major work, the "Yankee City" series, beginning with *The Social Life of a Modern Community*[133] details the functions of the different social classes in carrying out the workings of society as an integrated system, with members of the upper class controlling more abstract measures and the lower classes carrying out the concrete details in a manner that corresponds well with the view of descending specifications from abstract to concrete perceptual variables in Powers's scheme. Warner's examination of details in the different areas of life depict the many ways that individuals contribute to the life of the community. From our present point of view we can see it as a quasi-organism in which individuals control the variables pertaining to their personal lives and simultaneously maintain the shared Systems-concept of their society and culture and the necessary Principles serving it.

As a concrete illustration consider the tasks of a mayor of a city. He has a nominal responsibility that garbage be collected regularly, snow plowed, streets repaired, schools maintained and so on. Yet, when he first enters into his job upon election these functions are already organized and workers are already controlling their own perceptions relating to what it means to do those jobs. Only if there should be a serious deficit in the performance of one of these functions would the mayor direct his attention to it in detail. And even then, the nature of his action would involve control of his perceptions about what the commissioner should be doing, or has been doing, to bring the variables from error states back to their reference values. Implicit in this are conceptions of *roles*, the role of mayor, the role of commissioner, the role of equipment operator—which roles are understood automatically. They are part of each one's conception of the roles maintained within the society. In carrying out their respective roles each member acts in a certain way as a single control system for a specific kind of variable pertinent to the community or society as an hierarchical quasi-control system, even as he or she is simultaneously acting as a true hierarchical control system to provide for his own daily bread and other social and biological needs.

Warner's analyses of the public rituals of national holidays show in detail how members of the local community and by extension, the nation-society, create and maintain common Systems-concepts through communicating around symbolic events that serve as focal points to demonstrate their unity in diversity. One of his examples—the Memorial Day ceremonies—illustrates how diverse efforts flow from planning meetings by separate local organizations into the parade ending at the cemetery where all levels and segments of the community coalesce in paying tribute to the heroes of the past who have sacrificed their lives for the continuance of the whole. He documents the way in which social class is a major dimension of the organization of control of the variables essential to the existence of the society. Higher status members of the community initiate and organize the ceremonies, but all levels participate in the final demonstrations, and all share in the symbolism defining the nature of the community and society.

Warner's depiction of the different types of tasks performed in public arenas from local to national government, by the members of the different classes, accords well with the type of variable associated with each level in Powers's hierarchy of generic human control systems. For example, the most sacred scriptures of the United States, the Declaration of Independence and the Constitution, spell out a Systems concept—defining what this entity—*The United States of America*—is, its organization and how it should be preserved. The intimate connection between the founding fathers' construction of this collection of perceptual variables and their *de facto* emergence as what Warner called the Upper upper class of the ensuing society demonstrates the link between the status which a person holds in society and the level of abstraction of the types of variables which he controls when acting in his "official" role. By "official" I mean any job which a person performs that embodies a role in maintaining the society, as distinct from those maintaining one's personal existence. For some that means filling various roles in government. For more ordinary citizens that might mean voicing opinions about civic matters, expressing patriotic values and sentiments, participating in civic actions and ceremonies, voting and the like.

The President, leading members of congress, the CEO's and directors of the largest banks and corporations in the country, as well as the leading clergy, presidents and some faculty of the leading universities, the scions of "old families," constitute the upper classes of society. Much of their official activities typically involve controlling perceptual variables that have to do with defining and protecting the conception of the society as a system—the system consisting of both the symbolic organization and the structure of the members' relations with each other and with the physical environment. Other of their duties involve formulating Principles—policies and projected images about various aspects of the physical and social environment—that the work of others will implement. Those members of the upper class who are in government have this as their prime duty while those in other positions at the top of society act from time to time to influence the control of the image of the country.

They do that through their influence on members of the government. They do it in formal settings such as party conventions and informal settings, on the golf course, casual conversations at dinners and parties, through their lobbyists and the various other ways that they use. Likewise, the on-going, day to day passage of laws, judicial decisions interpreting the laws, formulation of regulations in government agencies and in corporations, churches, schools, local communities—embody the control of Principles which are measured in terms of their consistency with the Systems concept of the nation. They specify the goals that are to be achieved by the specific action programs that executives of agencies, institutions and corporations direct.

Examine the organs by which the upper class members document the day to day expression of the Principles which should be implemented by those charged with administrating the institutions of society—such media as the editorial pages and letters to the editor of the Wall Street Journal and other leading news/opinion instruments. Consider the interplay between the policy makers' control of perceptions important to themselves and the simultaneous control of their shared perceptions of the national identity. Even as they compete with each other for improved control of their own situations and for their share of influence in society, that which they hold in common provides the broad outlines of values that they pursue jointly for the preservation of their society.

The public dialogue concerning impeaching President Clinton was particularly rich in examples of individuals controlling various Principles so as to reduce errors in their personal Systems-concept of the nation. Statements like, "We are a nation of laws," express the conception of the speaker, and set reference signals to Principle level systems like, "We must follow the constitution." For the President's opponents to satisfy that Principle it led to controlling Program settings to correct their error concerning the violation of law, specifically the impeachment process. There clearly were conflicts between Principles controlled by different persons as to the remedies they sought, and there was also evidence of conflict within individuals oscillating between different Principles within themselves. Their tendency to act in one way created errors in Principles set to act in opposite ways.

I also observed that different actors appeared to be controlling at different levels of "gain," that is, different intensities. Some seemed to have unconflicted Systems-concepts activating Principles like, "He must leave office." For others the *problem was* to reorganize enough to clarify their concept of the essence of the national spirit. And for still others it seemed clear that they were operating on lower control levels. It suggested that their Systems-concept was defined or specified by others. They accepted what they perceived as the modal definition of whatever reference group to which they adhered. This raises an interesting thought about the disparity that observers sometimes perceive between the formal or inherited status of an individual and the level on which he or she operates in relation to the preservation of the society.

That helps to explain why some candidates for high office are never taken seriously by the mass of ordinary citizens even though they seem to have as many formal assets as those really in contention. When you are familiar with thinking in control terms it seems natural to focus upon what variables one can actually see under control by different individuals. It becomes less important to determine what they are conscious of. Ofttimes an instinctual component appears as a significant factor, maybe even more so than the intellectual, as I suggested in the previous chapter. What also resulted from the turmoil is that inevitably the concept of The United States—as a system—was being forced to evolve in this process.

Returning now to the discussion of the connection between different individual's controlled perceptions regarding their personal life and their controlled perceptions of the roles they fill in society, we humans organize ourselves into social structures according to the level of variables that each one controls in concordance with social status because we are organized *internally* that way. We look out upon our social-physical environment and perceive it with those same systems with which we personally control concepts (partly consciously and partly unconsciously) of *"who I am."* We develop Principles that serve to maintain that concept—within terms of the folkways and mores of our own society and doing that simultaneously controls Pvs involved in maintaining the folkways and mores. Whether the society is a dictatorship, in which the Systems-concept of the nation is defined and maintained by the edicts of the dictator, and may only exist in his head, or a primitive society, where elders express the idea of who they are as-a-people, my reading of the field work on individual societies suggests that Warner's and Power's complementary concepts provide parallel approaches for understanding how we humans organize ourselves socially in controlling our shared environment.

I defer to the specialists in social class phenomena to spell out the details of the mechanisms of social control, social status, class interactions and the like. I introduced Warner's views here and paralleled them with Powers's to suggest an idea of the process comprising the "mechanism" of the class phenomena that Warner details. This was in pursuit of my two interrelated goals—to suggest the process whereby social systems gradually degenerate, and to examine specific examples of how the process works in the practical actions of individual people. In keeping with those aims I want next to discuss a series of contemporary aspects of status in our society.

Why Status-striving is functional

When I was growing up, in a fundamentalist, conservative Lutheran synod, I was well-imbued with the spiritual value of *humility*. I cite Garrison Keilor in his Lake Woebegone spoofs as my authority that this is a Principle level Pv for many Lutherans. Thus, it came as a great shock to me when I encountered the wider world, as a newly discharged WWII serviceman and college entrant, to find many people actively pursuing enhancement of their social status. I felt embarrassed for them, and I can remember being somewhat puzzled that they didn't seem particularly embarrassed, themselves, about the aggressive ways in which they pursued social mobility. (It never dawned on me at the time that I might be valuing the same goals but repressing awareness of it because of the conflict with my Principle valuing humility.) I was not completely off the mark, however, as I have since observed that nowadays many people are more ill at ease about discussing their status ambitions openly than they are about discussing sex openly. While it is not too hard to see people frankly pursuing higher social status we tend to shade it with euphemisms like, "keeping up with the Joneses" rather than the cruder terms, like "status striving." And, after all, we do have an (ambiguous) national Principle stating that "all men are born equal."

But what motivates this human tendency? Let us separate the mechanism by which it works from the utility it might have in practice. The mechanism is simply the fact that we are organized along hierarchical control system lines. Well into adult life most of us keep reorganizing our mental apparatus into increasingly complex control systems. More complex control ability automatically results in extending the range of one's influence, which is one definition of higher status. Thus, increased status in a community might be viewed as an epiphenomenon resulting from a natural tendency that we all possess to increase personal control over the perceived environment. Of course there are many reasons why some individuals achieve greater status than others. Not everyone can occupy the "king of the hill" position at the same time. In simpler societies physical strength, energy, raw intelligence (assuming there is such a thing) and chance all must be factors in the contest. But, the sharing of Systems-concepts must soon also enter into it. Early religious prophecies in many places seem to have been concerned with indicating first *whose* enunciations of the Systems-concepts should be honored. Otherwise, why would so many people all around the world have been persuaded that some of their fellow members were already designated by fate, heredity, the gods, or God to formulate more "true" Principles for the community?

Once society became more complex and some members acquired skill in recognizing abstract perceptual variables, a new factor entered the picture. There came to be individuals who could consciously perceive that a social role that involved stating the shared image of "Who we are and what we are about" would give one personal competitive advantages as by-products of such a role. This made it possible to begin valuing high status as an end in itself, with all the consequences that have constituted the main material of historians.

Status Mobility and Class

The personal side of the story concerns the results of all the different reorganizations that various individuals undergo. Technological improvements in warfare and resources, more effective religious and political ideas, science—all are results of reorganizations that different individuals undergo. Of course people vary as to the extent to which they keep reorganizing. I drew the corollary earlier that we only reorganize when we have to, that is, when environmental variables of some sort fail to be controlled by existing systems to the extent that life support is challenged. This results in *stress*, which might be another term for the internally experienced aspect of the initiation of reorganization. But, that refers to another dimension on which people vary considerably.

When I said, "we keep reorganizing," I was taking a shortcut, referring to a generic tendency that works out differently in different persons, no doubt due to particular immediate conditions. One individual might be undergoing stress while another in seemingly identical conditions is not, according to whether the one and not the other has intractable error within his or her hierarchy. One individual might develop under coddled conditions in an affluent home and never experience many error states of the sort that would lead to developing a Principle valuing the acquisition of increased recognition and influence—status striving, in other words. Another individual might grow up in a lower lower class environment with just sufficient nourishment and other basic requirements to survive. He also might not incur enough error states to reorganize very frequently. His Systems-concept would contain a "low horizon," he might not have sufficient opportunities to perceive that he or she has other options. Other individuals in either of these circumstances might reorganize frequently. The difference would come from greater challenges in the specific features of one's social, and/or physical environment, such things as whether or not one's parents or peers enunciated values for enhancing one's influence or against it, as in "not getting uppity."

For the person who does incur the conditions that result in frequent reorganization she or he will probably sooner or later observe that many variables come automatically under control when one acquires higher status. He/she notices that other people perceive—and are organized to enact—Programs that result in implementing Principles relating to the survival of the community or society as a whole. Thus, the connection between status and the functioning of the community as a superindividual or quasi-control system is seen in the role of an individual who strives to control perceptual variables relevant to the common condition. His/her function in such a role corresponds to the higher level systems of a true hierarchical control system. Control may be exerted simply via a statement of opinion by a high status person, as when a whole generation of Russian art lurched in a new direction when Josef Stalin went to an exhibition and said he didn't like it. Our American assumption is that they feared for their lives, but that might be our outsiders' projection. They—dictator and artists—were organized in a society that functioned in that way. The reaction might have been so automatic that the artists (many of them at least) didn't feel anything more than that they had a new direction.

One can see the process by which people organize these hierarchies already taking place on school playgrounds. The kid who yells, "Let's shoot baskets," (e.g.) and other kids immediately take up this activity, is a living demonstration of how enunciating a Principle—jointly valued in a particular social group—can result in many variables being brought to the leader's reference settings by others. "Here, Johnny, you're not good at this, hold my coat and I'll show you how," could be how someone stumbles on the discovery that formulating Principles can give the illusion of controlling others.

Thousands of personal observations might go into the formation of insights like this. The brew of traits that underlie differences in personal power are hard to articulate, but we usually have little difficulty intuitively grasping them when making observations in real circumstances. People wearing clothes identified with the working class generally step back when getting on and off elevators in favor of people dressed more formally. Certain member's opinions get heard at community meetings more readily than other's—often independently of merit—but in association with apparel, manner of speaking, diction, vocabulary, amount of public recognition or celebrity, etc. As individuals perceive others around themselves controlling variables of similar levels they begin to identify them as more like themselves as compared to others, who are likely to be physically farther removed much of the time, as well as controlling variables of different levels. This is the "mechanism" by which complex societies organize social classes.

Anthropologists and sociologists who study these phenomena in detail document the consequences of striving for and holding higher status along many different dimensions. Here I confine all those to the single dimension of controlling perceptual variables. Just as the higher levels within an individual's hierarchy sets the Reference values for lower levels, the individuals with higher status in the quasi control hierarchy of a social system set Reference values for variables that will be controlled by the immediate actions of those lower in the system. Those individuals whose personal hierarchies are so organized that they notice this, whether consciously or not, will act in ways that elevate their personal status while simultaneously keeping communal variables under control, because realizing their personal ideals harmonizes with the society's systems-concepts. To the extent that one prefers the intellectual work of controlling Principles and Programs over the physical work of controlling Relationships and Events (as in running machines, serving meals, waiting on trade, etc.) it becomes apparent that increasing status brings tangible personal rewards even as it involves perpetuating the shared variables of the social structure. One could argue that a society such as ours benefits as a system from the close tie-in between social status and societal functioning, as compared with other societies where the link is less firm. Our national image contains a fairly high value on Principles that promote the recognition of individual creativity. It also provides more immediate feedback from the correction of error states in variables pertaining to the survival of the society than happens in many other societies.

This is a predominant feature of U. S. society, as pointed out by social science researchers, in comparison with many European societies where status position tends to be more nearly fixed. It has both assets and liabilities in terms of the functioning of the society. In the U. S. competition for the accoutrements of elevated status—income, address, celebrity, name, honor, etc.—insures the continual pressure to differentiate individuals on as many dimensions as possible and stretch out the scales, such as income differentials between executives and workers. This has probably been a factor in the dominance of U. S. bred executives in many fields. On the other hand it also results in more stress, more reorganization, more casualties. It might also have dire consequences for the society as a whole if the infrastructure deteriorates because everyone starts wanting to be a stockbroker or celebrity.

Another serious consequence, that creates a never-ending tension between the classes in any society, is the circumscription of control over personal environment on the part of individuals whose References are set largely by others. This results in the kind of anomalies that we see when people on welfare, for example, prove resistant to moving off into jobs that would pay slightly more than they get on the dole. Such behavior is usually judged negatively from an external frame of reference by other members of society. But, from the point of view of the individual, his or her control over what meager resources he has might well be greater when not having a major part of his time and initiative occupied by working for someone else at low pay. Various observers, from Christian defenders of the poor to Marx, have viewed the people with higher status, who set the references for those of lower status, as everything from "their brothers' keepers" to "heartless exploiters of the poor." But these assessments are all made from an external point of view. They attribute moral defects to people whose control of perceptual variables important to themselves results in influencing and dominating others. They seem to forget that we are all built this way—to control our environment as fully as we can.

Counter to them are people for whom Ayn Rand is often seen as spokes-person. They hold that it is natural for some people to rise to positions of influence and power over others. They are by and large more creative and more risk taking than those whom they come to dominate. In this view those who derive the greatest benefits from a society are those who give most to it. We remember that everyone shares with everyone else the feature of controlling PVs to one's own Reference values. Consequences for other people are mostly by-products of one's own control efforts, not the result of direct intentions. That is except for people whose jobs specifically consist in governing. The functioning of a society as a whole comprises the combination—in each member—of control over purely personal variables with perceptions contributing, one way or the other, to the control of the whole-system environment.

This picture has become more complicated as civilization has evolved. More and more subtle forms of deceit have been developed to short cut the processes both of negotiation and brute force in achieving common systems concepts. Industries such as advertising and public relations specialize in combining various forms of deceit with pure information dispensing. They keep varying the mix in the pursuit of most effectively influencing target audiences to accept exoteric Reference values. That has created the ground for still other professions to arise to counter their influence, such as print and television journalists who specialize in exposing the artificers of subterfuge. While such developments provide interesting exercises in the study of social complexity for historians and social scientists, the immediate, concrete effects upon the lives of many ordinary people are anything but mere intellectual games. The principle of *caveat emptor* is expanded to apply not only to making purchases from unknown merchants, but to the intake of all sorts of information, the evaluation of properties and commodities, the judging of political appeals, and on and on. A secondary result has been that the mastery of the skill of image-creation—by definition that of manipulation and deception—has begun to rival the skill of acquiring and wielding economic and political power as a means of gaining status.

I fear that that development might be another form of the kind of degeneration that Spengler saw in the decline of our civilization. The skills involved in exercising economic power presumably relate to the control of materials pertinent to the basics of life. The skills involved in political power concern the control of order in a society. Both of these skills have to do with variables that can contribute to the quality of life, for better or worse. Granted that the ones who exercise the most control over such variables benefit the most from them, but they do involve useful applications of the division of labor. I'm not so sure that holds true for the skills of manipulating people's view of reality. It remains true, however, that, despite the drawbacks inherent in more and more people focusing on single-minded goals of status striving, those who succeed at it are most nearly insulated from the deleterious effects of destructive cultural developments.

Class Warfare and Communal Control of the Environment

Given that status striving is a more prevalent phenomenon in our society than in many others most of us sooner or later settle down in whatever cultural niche we have gained by a certain point in adulthood and begin to concentrate on increasing control of other variables. Or, at least we decrease the energy devoted to that one goal. We accept the various pressures to modify Reference settings to values more or less matching what others are controlling for. Implicit in that is submission to values determined in large part by others. At the same time many of us attempt to identify consciously with those whose interests we think nearest to our own. There are various reference groups that one might identify with. A common one entails identifying with the values of a given social class. One thinks in terms of general contingencies applicable to the class and assumes they provide a best estimate of one's own contingencies. Since it is difficult to detect the most likely effect of large scale policies on one's personal life, the best estimate is often to judge how they might effect the class with which you identify. Hence one assesses the blandishments of political candidates in terms of their expected consequences for the group with whom you identify. Take, for example, the frequent analysis in the papers of proposed tax laws in terms of which social class (read "economic level") would stand to gain or lose.

Conflicts of Principles can easily occur, however, between those relating to personal values and others pertaining to class values. For example, in one of the recent national elections, my reading of various polls and election results led me to surmise that a large group of citizens, family farm owners, seemed overwhelmingly to prefer candidates of a political party whose stated platform proposed policies that would lead to the extinction of family farms. In the years after the election I observed statistics that seemed to confirm this with an increasing rate of foreclosures of family farms. Assuming, for the sake of illustration, some validity in these hypotheses, the question is why did these people, on average, act against their own self interests? Were they simply unaware of the implications of the announced platforms? Or, did they (possibly correctly) assume that party platforms mean little in the way of concrete implications? Certainly one could argue, as a number of economists have, that no political initiatives could sufficiently counter economic forces that were at work. But that would be a digression in the sense that, whether or not the economic conditions were insuperable, different policies of government might still either facilitate or retard the rate and intensity of the effects.

A different type of explanation may apply. Simply put, when controlling one type of variable it will be impossible to control, simultaneously, another variable that utilizes the same output. Or in everyday terms: you have to keep your eye on the doughnut or the hole; you can't do both at the same time. In the case of the family farmers in the election in question I surmised that many of them perceived the party that ultimately bit them (if you see it that way) as the more prestigious one. They thus would have felt more personal honor to identify with it. My evidence for that is admittedly not strong, it is based upon remarks made by a few members of that group. But it fits with my general impression that status identification is a sufficiently powerful motive for many Americans that it might take priority over "bread and butter" values in some circumstances.

However, after the consequences of both economics and policies began to take their toll there was a reaction against the bankers who held the mortgages—the most immediate cause of distress. This trend escalated to include "the government" in the minds of some people, especially in the west, supposedly contributing to the growth of the anti-government militia movement there. This is one example, though somewhat disjointed, of class warfare. Some observers have considered its injurious effects as one of the factors leading to the Oklahoma City bombing. It has been a long time in the West since the "classical" days of class warfare with their bloody strikes, government suppression of laborers and the like. The new version is mainly carried out with lawsuits, competition for political influence and negotiation, underpinned with cost-benefit analyses of the different courses of action. The lower order variables controlled in these new ways of proceeding are different, but the higher order variables which they subserve are little changed.

Since it appears that all societies serve the function of unifying (to greater or lesser extent) the common control over the shared environment, and do so by organizing in some sort of hierarchical fashion, and then gel into classes of individuals who identify more with each other than with members of other classes and finally that that results in group attitudes and tensions that have often been termed class warfare by sociologists, it seems reasonable to conclude that the process relates to a basic feature of human nature. It has both instinctual and intellectual components. The instinctual we can guess from the observations of social structures among other primates. The cognitive features derive from the parallel control of similarly perceived variables by groups of individuals sharing the common environment. The question then arises as to whether it is inevitable that classes develop and incur the tensions that can result in class warfare—and what that spells for the society. In my reading of anthropology and history there do not seem to be any classless societies of long duration. I have already argued that the processes of controlling one's own PVs to one's preferred settings—what we all do—results simultaneously in the phenomena of hierarchical organization. When members of the lower classes in a society complain that they are worked beyond their limit or are deprived of the resources to live in the fashion that they deem appropriate that is comparable to a control system being called upon to act beyond its ability. The breakdown of services could lead to reorganizing of the larger system. In this sense, class conflict in a society might be a factor in the society remaining adapted to an historically and physically changing environment. Let us examine some journalistic reports of class and status conflict in American society from the point of view of what they tell us about the functioning of our society as a system.

Michael Lind (1995) published an article in *Harpers* on "The American Class War," pointing to all of the different oppositions in contemporary society: "Conservatives at war with liberals; Christian fundamentalists at odds with liberal Jews; blacks at war with whites," etc. He argued that today the upper class in America has put everyone else into an underclass, heightening their competition for the same benefits.

> Judging by the headlines that have been leading the news for the last several years, public debate in the United States ... has become a war of words among the disaffected minorities that so often appear on the never ending talk show[s].... The noise is deceptive. Off-camera, beyond the blazing lights, past the ropy tangle of black cords and down the hall, in the corner offices ... people in expensive suits quietly continue to go about the work of shifting the center of gravity of wealth and power in the United States from the discontented many to the privileged few.

An article titled, "Look Who's Cashing in on Congress" (Dowd, 1997) takes a similar approach, essentially arguing that our cherished ideal of equality is being violated by the very officials in charge of maintaining that perception under control. In her article, from *Money* Magazine no less, she reports a discouraging list of correlations between subsidies, tax breaks and grants to large corporations and their campaign contributions to the legislators dealing out those bounties. One of her charges struck me as even more ominous than the usual legal "graft" by which taxpayers are chronically abused. That was, "The recent horror stories about Fen Phen . . . which caused heart abnormalities in at least 100 people . . . is an example of the danger of using drugs [for non-approved uses]. Now there is a move in Congress to prohibit the FDA from requiring medical-device manufacturers [to ensure that] off-label use of their products are safe . . . ."

Another kind of benefit for high status is reflected in a *Wall Street Journal* feature story (Lublin, 1998), titled, "Pay for No Performance." In it the author quotes Carol Bowie, "research director of Executive Compensation Advisory Services, 'You are definitely losing the linkage between pay and performance.'" Ordinary employees in most companies are fired if they don't perform their duties according to expectations. Why should it be the opposite with CEOs who, by definition, are presumed to get high pay because they are at high risk? Some of the answers were suggested in a three-way interview between the Journal writer, a CEO and a professor of Human-Resources-Management at Stanford. "In principle, the more reciprocity there is between the board and the CEO, the harder it is to monitor pay." A more thorough answer came, I believe, from the research of an economist, Bill Williams, who did a study of the boards of a large number of major corporations.[134] He found a large overlap between board members of different companies. The implication of his study for the question raised in Lublin's articles would seem to be: Boards approve high incomes for CEOs because they are essentially giving them to each other.[135]

Lloyd Warner's depiction of the social class hierarchy of our nation showed it as a broad based pyramid with a considerably condensed population at the top. One of the advantages a small group has in exercising domination over a much larger number of underlings is that of increased ease of personal communication. It is easier to determine where you have consensus with others in personal interactions as compared with having to make inferences from mass meetings, printed reports, media claims and the like. The level of personal acquaintance between the members of the "ruling class" predisposes their pulling away from the larger society especially under conditions like those we have currently— where the nation seems to be becoming increasingly dysfunctional as an effective quasi-control system. The view of a legislator as a representative of the people has become corrupted by the necessity of pandering to those rich enough to support the horrendous costs of getting elected.

They are the very ones who are beginning to identify their common class interests as separate from, and possibly more important than, their citizenship, if you believe the charges of writers like Lasch (1995) or the assertion—almost a boast—of the same point by Davidson and Rees-Mogg (1997). From one point of view this is an example of the widening gap of privileges between the different classes of society. But, from a longer, historical perspective it is illustrative of the degeneration of our national Systems-concept of national identity.

That view ties in with Davidson's and Rees-Mogg's (1993)argument in *The Great Reckoning.* There they maintained both that the world was on the verge of another great economic retrenchment and that it would be accompanied by dissolution of great nation states because they can not reorganize sufficiently to conform to the structures required by the new technological developments in the world. They state that it was common opinion in the Enlightenment that faltering empires suffer moral breakdown, lose their civic spirit, and divert ever more of their energies to nonproductive pursuits. They cite Adam Ferguson, "Writing 'Of the Decline of Nations,' where he said, 'Whole bodies of men are sometimes infected with an epidemical weakness of the head, or corruption of heart, by which they become unfit for the stations they occupy, and threaten the states they compose, however flourishing, with a prospect of decay, and of ruin.' In 1766, when Ferguson wrote, there was no Congress of the United States. Long before *The Bonfire of the Vanities* Ferguson described the moral atmosphere of a society heading for a fall:

> 'the individual considers his community so far only as it can be rendered subservient to his personal advancement or profit: he states himself in competition with his fellow-creatures; and, urged by the passions of emulation, of fear and jealousy, of envy and malice, he follows the maxims of an animal destined to preserve his separate existence, and to indulge his caprice or his appetite, at the expense of his species.'"[136]

This disturbing observation reflects a view that I have gotten from other sources too. It provokes one to wonder what the psychology is of this. It brings up the interesting question of whether the elite of society desert it because it is coming apart at the seams, or whether, as Christopher Lasch maintained, that the dissolution is the *result* of the desertion of the elite. Ferguson's view strikes me as consistent with the notion that individual human beings are the prime entities. Societies and cultures exist or become reorganized in terms of the net result of what individuals are controlling *en masse* at any period. The bottom line would seem to be that individuals adhere to a given society to the extent that they perceive it as functioning successfully as a quasi-control system over the physical and social environment in which they are struggling to survive. When that perception falters members of the society turn to whatever private strategies they can muster.

A related question about social status and social cohesion concerns the extent to which those with highest status have reason to be community-centered versus self-centered. The tendency to identify with one's own class can reach such extremes that the members begin to perceive those of the other classes as not part of humanity. Then the way is open for the incredible cruelties by members of one class toward fellow society members of their own society. It usually begins with the upper class perceiving overtures from below for redistribution of wealth and/or decision making power as attacks upon the System-concept of the current society, and hence upon themselves as its chief guardians. History is full of instances of power elites lashing out violently to suppress increasingly loud and extreme complaints and actions by lower class citizens. Looking back on a given instance we can perceive it as "visceral reaction" in which people are described as "out of control." There is some question as to whether this is really so, however, because the lower order control systems—those using muscles in the actual breaking of heads—remained under perfect control. In highly developed societies, instances of leaders "losing it" and ordering such savageries have almost invariably been followed by at least small steps toward reform. The reforms obtained followed from error signals in the picture of the society as a unified cultural fabric.

Such reforms, however, often turn out to be too little and too late and when the revolution finally comes, as in France, 1789, the members of the middle and lower classes show themselves as no less capable of the same cruelties. In a healthy society the members of the upper classes hold Systems-concepts that are realistic enough that there is little discrepancy between their personal Systems-concepts and those with which they perceive the whole society as a system. When that picture begins to deteriorate it results in the kind of degeneration that so many writers have decried.

Perhaps there is also a positive side in the dissolution. Individual reorganizations can result in tolerating perceptions of how things could be that would be too radical in more stable times. Such new, unimaginable views have at times affected a whole civilization's concepts of the nature of the world, and of humanity, like Jesus's view of the significance of the individual person—still driving the course of Western Civilization today.

Chapter 14

REORGANIZATION: INDIVIDUAL AND SOCIETAL

We reify institutions, organizations and societies, talking about what *it* does, what *it* wants or believes, partly because societies are in fact in some ways like living organisms. Our linguistic habits have unconsciously incorporated that sense, and besides that, we tend to identify society with anyone who speaks for the whole in a given instance. We tend to organize ourselves in groups as hierarchical systems, as I argued in the previous chapter. A society/nation/group functions as a quasi-control system in ways such that—as individuals control their particular PVs within their status roles in society—the whole seems to be controlling the many aspects of its environment via the collective actions of the members.

Take for example, a baseball team in action as an illustration of a working quasi-control system. The environment of any individual player includes both the physical environs, and the appearance and movements of one's own and the opposing team. His understanding of the game is comprised of the PVs he can control. That is, at some particular moment player n is more likely to perceive Tommy

Jones—whom he knows well enough as the kid from across the street—more as *the opposing pitcher* than as Tommy Jones. He has a Reference value for perceiving a ball coming toward him from the pitcher as he stands in the batter's box, and his Program of action at bat is at higher gain than any other of his Programs for interacting with Tommy Jones. At the same time *n* is perceiving *teams*, his and the other, within his *playing baseball* Program. His team-oriented Principle *win-the-game* is integrated specifically at this moment with his personal Principle *hit-the-ball—hard-as-possible*.

I hope that small example was sufficient to convey what I mean about the quasi-control system of a human group (of any kind) being comprised of overlapping and similar Pvs of the members that make the group into the sort of entity that it is. This way of viewing things sets up the next point—that if one or more members of a group incurs a reorganization within his own hierarchy, involving his perception of the nature of the group, that will be the first step in what could become the historical evolution of the group-entity. Before that can actually happen other members must either undergo comparable reorganizations themselves, or else buy into the image the first person creates. For example, consider an established leader having the insight, "my rule is authorized by God; I rule by divine right." This might be a new concept to the other members of the entity, but if it somehow "makes sense" to them the nature of their social entity evolves into a new form.

We, as individuals, can incur internal conflicts between the values at which we would control various Pvs when acting purely out of self interest, and the values to which we would control the same Pvs when acting in a social role. We humans, *en masse*, have tried out probably every conceivable way of organizing ourselves to ameliorate these conflicts. History is mainly concerned with the political organizations (of every sort between anarchy and totalitarianism) and war, the major engine of it all, as attempts to structure ourselves as quasi-control systems over the physical and social environment. Though we have never previously had the concept of society as quasi-control system that is now still another way to perceive it. Every way of organizing our joint efforts has some drawbacks. Ultimately they produce the need for reorganizing to cure the ills that accumulate as a previous form degenerates in its capacity to meet the majority of basic needs.

At least since Thomas Hobbes the idea of the social contract has come to be widely considered the most reasonable basis of governance, the best compromise, in Western thinking anyway. His view—that a citizen has the right to abandon a ruler who could no longer protect him—has underlain political thinking of many stripes in the Western democracies. It embodies the notion of exchanging an individual allegiance for the sovereign's contribution—protection (broadly defined). And it implicitly recognizes the inherent controlled perception even though the traditional way of describing behavior lacked the means to express it overtly. The desired state is fairly well defined from both sides in vehicles such as constitutions and patriotic declarations. When it fails of realization the result is an automatic increase of the gain/effort of control. When that fails it provokes the tendency to reorganization.

The issue of incipient reorganization has come out in the open in our country in recent decades as many people began to question whether the state is failing to fulfill its part of the bargain. Both in the secessionist movements of disaffected citizens, such as the civil militias, and the advocates of individual sovereignty such as Davidson and Rees-Mogg (1997) the overt or covert message more and more stridently proclaims that the state—the U. S. government—is guilty of fraud. It is not hard to make the case that our government is failing to protect life and property adequately, if you read the daily papers or follow the various TV expose programs.

Topics such as crime, the drug war or conflict between government and private owners of property fill the media every day. There are frequent and powerful disturbances continually affecting everyone's control of his or her immediate environments. This suggests that we are all frequently precipitated into reorganization. That, in turn, implies a high level of personal stress as the common condition.

Looked at in terms of any given individual, reorganization might simply constitute psychological growth or development. In terms of the effects in society, reorganizations in individuals who influence followers provide the stream of social experiments that are the overtures toward solving problems. But here we come up against the phenomena that Spengler postulated. Some experiments—that might be viewed as highly promising by an impartial observer—will fail of serious consideration, if they fall outside of accepted principles of the society. The corollary is that the only "experiments" left to try in a creativity-exhausted political culture will essentially repeat previous efforts. Real innovations must wait for dissolution of the current state.

Suro (1999) details a case like that in an article, "Gore presents anti-drug plan." He reported that the former vice president, "who released the Clinton administration's annual drug-control strategy Monday, called drug abuse a 'spiritual problem' and said that young people beset with feelings of emptiness and alienation are more likely to succumb to 'messages that are part of a larger entity of evil.'" The reporter continued that the vice president then called for greater efforts to improve schools and more economic opportunities for, especially, minority and low income youth. To implement these goals the administration would allocate about two thirds of the $18 billion budget allotment to law enforcement, interdiction and other efforts to attack the supply of drugs, with the other third to go to efforts to reduce the demand.

However, the reporter continued, this strategy "drew criticism from advocates of greater spending on programs meant to reduce the appetite for illegal drugs. The Drug Policy Foundation . . . said . . . that [what is needed is] to shift from a criminal justice-based drug policy to a public health-based policy." Finally, the "centerpiece of the administration's prevention strategy" is to be an advertising campaign to alert adolescents to the dangers of drugs.

I don't see how that relates to the vice president's "view of attending to the broad underlying causes of drug abuse." That is the very issue we should consider here. I don't mean the issue of the broad underlying causes—although that would be a worthy project, in my opinion—but the issue that, if the vice president really meant what he said, there was no apparent connection between where his money and his mouth were. I have read Albert Gore's book on the care of the earth, and I take him to be a sincere and highly intelligent man, one who can probably be very effective when he might have the power to execute practical programs. But, both the administration's strategy and the presumably competing one proposed by the Drug Policy Foundation struck me as *more of the same*. For years already, the government has implemented programs to arrest drug dealers and users, to attempt to prevent the importation of drugs, and to exhort young people to find something better to do with their time. There doesn't seem to be much evidence that any of it has brought any long term changes so far. However, the proposed plans, the real ones, the one's upon which money is to be spent, are pretty familiar. We can debate the details, the proportions of resources to be allotted to this or that emphasis, but the general idea is in line with what we, as a people, do.

Looking at this situation from the perspective we take here many considerations come into focus that are not accounted for in the current approach. First, start with the presumption that we—all, vice president, citizen and drug user alike as living control systems—control our perceived environmental situations to our own specifications (to the extent within one's power). We do so in terms of the priorities in our personal control hierarchy. That reminds us to look first at what this means specifically, from the highest level down to that of practical execution, in the particular individual or individuals in whose behavior we are interested. In this case that means the vice president as the one to whom the term "administration" referred in the article. We can readily guess that he was controlling above all for a certain state of one or more systems-concepts. We ordinary citizens don't know what they are exactly, so we make our best inferences. A sincere vice president (as I take Mr. Gore to be) would, in my opinion, have been first of all controlling for a systems-concept defined as "the nation," because his official role requires his devotion to its preservation above all other priorities. The perceptions that must be kept constant at this level would, by definition, have priority over any other considerations; all lesser goals must avoid causing an error state in maintaining that purpose.

That brings us back to our general awareness of the familiar what-we-do. That is, what conforms to our common notions of "the American way" and what does not. To see that, take a contrasting view. Imagine what we would do differently, if we were a different nation. The example I propose is one I hope we might actually be evolving toward. We begin by defining the to-be-controlled condition. Who should define that? Theoretically it should be all of us since we profess to be a democracy. What might come closest might be a national poll, securely arranged that no one could vote twice. In principle legislators have more reasoned judgment, because they are supposed to have no other job than to know and weigh all the contingencies involved in carrying out the functions of government. The ordinary citizen, by contrast is at risk of being superficial if for no other reason than that he or she can't give the matter her/his undivided attention. However, many of us have begun to have misgivings about the devotion of many of our legislators to that singular goal.

Continuing to try to envision a plan that rests upon democracy but contrasts with our current way of doing things, imagine confining decision making to *electors*, whom we will presume to have a larger stake in having informed opinions about serious national issues because they put their lives on line for the nation. That is, we define an elector only as one who is, or has been, in the military, somewhat as in the Swiss tradition.[137] Then let legislators and administration members propose solutions like competitive bids for commercial business and let the electors select the winner via the type of secure poll mentioned above. Finally, we arrive at the formulation of the to-be-controlled condition. Let us imagine it phrased like:

> A. It is our intention that our society is one that is free of addicts to (drugs x, y, z).

Keeping in mind the definition of a control loop we realize that the above statement only specifies the Reference signal, the desired end state. What remains is to construct/identify the perceptual signal—the means by which the existing state of affairs is to be measured for comparison with the desired state of affairs. Thus, A-1 might be a continual epidemiological survey in which all hospital admissions, plus all arrests, plus all voluntary applications for admissions to rehab facilities, plus all complaints by parents and other concerned citizens—are accumulated in a central agency that eliminates duplications and produces monthly, weekly or daily statistics showing the real time condition of the controlled variable. It would be something like the real time computations of all the stock trades registered on a given day, a technologically feasible application.

Note that the real variable here, like the real variable controlled by any real control system, exists in the environment. This requires a look at the subjects, and that is a whole separate issue, which I will take up after discussing the output. The precision of control by the system is dependent upon two variables: The accuracy of the measure comprising the perceptual variable, and the Gain of the system—the amount of effort available to counter the Error signal. The Gain is the system's ability to counter any increase in the gap between the value of the Reference signal and the perceived value of the controlled variable (the current statistic of drug usage).

That finally brings up the output mechanism of the system. In a real hierarchical control system, like a human being, the output mechanism is the effector structure of the organism—the muscles and glands—that can make things happen in the environment of the organism. In the quasi-control system of a society the closest analogy is the service and enforcement arms of the society—police, doctors, counsellors, clergy (in one of their roles), relatives (also only in certain of their roles), teachers (ditto). Their procedures would need to be spelled out and authorized by a defined authority, established by a process similar to the one we posit for defining the goal. They would have to function freely of anything that might paralyze their effective operation. And—and this is the most important departure from our current way of organizing things—the procedures must function in such a way as to affect the measured variable in a perceptible manner. In everyday terms that means that, if the Error signal—the gap between the desired and the measured statistic—is not being reduced (in time periods also specified in advance) the output mechanism is altered, and re-altered until it is effective. It is not allowed to go on indefinitely wasting resources, as often happens in our current situation.

When I proposed the collection of electors as a meaningful

representation of "the nation" and their collective decision as the output for that one aspect of our collective self-image, that output could be considered a Principle or priority in common terms. In order to be implemented that Principle would need to be executed with a more specific goal like (this is only an example, remember):

> addicts to drugs, x, y, z shall decrease in number by (say) 10% per year until an asymptote (plateau) is reached where no further reduction occurs after 5 years.

This would be the reference value for a Program geared to bring that condition about. It would need to specify goals for prevention and also add a further specification, call it B.:

> that current addicts be provided rehabilitation to achieve surcease of craving.

To achieve this sub-goal another detailed effector mechanism would have to be spelled out, again, having all the elements of a control loop and continually tested for effective operation.

This is what we already have, at least as far as the general goal and the social roles of the people involved in it. But, what is lacking in our present system is that it is not a control-system; the links between the Reference state, the perceived state and the output mechanism are missing. Furthermore, other aspects of the systems-concept of the nation bear upon the extent or intensity to which each individual identifies with his societal role as against acting as a wholly independent individual. That is also not taken into account in our current way of organizing our national energies. The result is the frequent state of impasse in moving toward goals that most of us seem to share. What one wants regarding one desire causes error states in others, reducing movement toward the former, and vice versa. This is where intractable errors in the systems of individuals and of society eventually force the reorganizations that might be constructive for the society but destructive for the individual, or vice versa. This brings me to the issue I had to leave dangling above, the issue of the subjects of the highest level intention.

Drug addicts, as well as individuals who are lured but not yet addicted, are also members of society. They are unless we define them out of it, as some so-called "right wing fundamentalists" would seem to do with homosexuals. If the electors in our hypothetical, reorganized society, are also controlling for other Principles—like equal justice, free speech, due process—they will experience personal conflict in attempting to keep their perceptions of society consistent when some members (the addicts) challenge who should determine what substances who will ingest. Specifically the current conflict on this issue is between the conservative position, that certain behavior must be judged in terms of its consequences, and forbidden if deemed bad, and the "Libertarian" position—that only oneself can control what one does with one's body. Then, if the Principle is not changed, and if some people act counter to the majority intentions either the Principle will be violated or coercion will be introduced. That brings us back to what we have currently. To continue with the attempt to describe an alternate organization of society, suppose the Principle at issue is reformulated like this:

> It is our intention that we are a drug free society and we will use all forms of persuasion that we can command to induce all our members to subscribe to this majority value. Anyone who does not so subscribe will not be coerced, so long as he or she does not bother anyone else, providing also that they will sign

> a contract not to apply for welfare should they become indigent, and that they understand that they will not be taken to a hospital should they suffer physical debilitation from using drugs.

Further amendments would soon be needed, such as what to do about minors who get caught in the cracks of such a policy. It is readily apparent that the amount of individual reorganizations needed to produce a societal reorganization in this direction would be so enormous as to be unthinkable in any period of time short of decades if not centuries.

In attempting to build a control system that would really affect the to-be-controlled variable we might be forced to consider even more extreme measures. When current effort to bring a perceived variable to a desired state proves more difficult than can be achieved with available resources, either you must keep increasing the resources (the gain) or you must abandon the goal, or you must re-formulate it. One of the currently most decried consequences of drug addiction is that addicts tend to lose their normal concern for others and prey on the rest of society to sustain their habit. This fact could well defeat many initial attempts to achieve the goal, resulting in many people losing patience with the project. Thus, the logic of the above approach might bring a society eventually to consider an even more extreme position like:

> If he or she does bother anyone else they will be deemed an enemy of society and immediately killed.

That would imply reorganization way beyond any possible image of ourselves as a nation as we currently exist. Still other versions could be formulated. I deliberately proposed one that would be extreme in our society, but not unimaginable in the sense that extreme measures already exist in other societies. Each could be viewed as the result of one kind of social reorganization coming from a consensus that must have been achieved by individual reorganizations in many members of that society. We realize that any formulation would have specific consequences in how it would be implemented by control systems down the line. Remember that the story with which we began, Suro's article, indicates no attempt to institute a control system for addressing the desired goal. Yes, there are individuals whose behavior controls their own related perceptual variables, like the policeman enforcing the law as he defines it, and the teacher advocating "moral behavior" as she defines it, and the physician curing people of any and all illnesses that she can. Their actions doubtless make a difference in individual lives. But, as best we can tell without a clearly stated national Principle and a definite instrumentality for achieving results, we have only our impressions of the phenomenon at the broadest level. My impression is that the phenomenon is not controlled. Or, it might be a controlled variable, all right, but if so, it is controlled to a relatively invariable compromise value by the joint interactions of drug dealers, drug users, and drug enforcers. Their actions are essentially in balance and nothing changes.

There is some evidence that some behavioral phenomena are currently crudely and unconsciously controlled in that way. The current state of affairs remains at a more or less constant level and shows corrections of deviations from that level. Some years ago, in a college course on PCT one of the students, a probation officer, grasped the concept that when a phenomenon is under control nothing changes even when external force is applied to effect change. With some surprise he said he could document that concept in his work, "Whenever things get too quiet in my district the cops get uneasy and they go and hassle the gang kids until we start to get some action again." This does not mean that you could honestly accuse the police of inciting crime. It does mean that individuals can inadvertently affect their own Pvs in what seems a counter productive direction simply by controlling their highest order perceptions, unconscious of how that sets the References for lower orders.

Returning to the details of the current real situation of the "drug problem," there are really two entirely different kinds of "demand" that any real campaign would need to confront. The first, and most paradoxical, is the stake that large numbers of people now have in the various aspects of the so-called drug war. Our typical way of talking and thinking about social problems casts a veil over any hint that honest people benefit from activity that is either criminal or immoral. We build in a layer of hypocrisy in any curative program because of the profound implication that no "decent" person would have any reason to hinder the success of the program just because it would mean losing his livelihood.[138] However, just because certain personal Principles are kept out of sight they do not lose their influence. They may neutralize the efforts of other control systems to achieve the publicly endorsed goals. I wonder sometimes how our society would be different if we were to own up to our selfish interests when in conflict with endorsed public objectives.

Take the example of tobacco farmers in today's struggle to reduce this source of lung cancer. What would it be like for anti-tobacco lobbyists and legislators to admit, "Yes, we intend that you give up your current means of livelihood." I for one would propose that it might be in the interest of all of us to compensate their cost of going over to another means of making a living. That is the only realistic way to reduce their need to oppose the reforms most of us might want.

The problem resides deep in our traditional way of thinking about behavior, the one I keep challenging throughout this work. With the linear logic that we are used to applying it is virtually impossible to get a set of interacting efforts that succeed in avoiding tangles of conflicting tendencies. That problem is automatically solved in an hierarchical control system as each level keeps resetting Reference values down the line to "hunt" for reduction in its own error state.

You might at this point note a seeming inconsistency between my claim that Spengler's thesis conforms to a picture of society as a quasi-control system, just as Warner's does, and my claim here that in our governmental actions we operate as a linear-logic open ended system. It is not a contradiction. Society operates, roughly, and awkwardly maybe, as a quasi-control system but we *think* about behavior in the Cartesian, linear-logic, way. The more conscious and deliberate our formulations, the more they diverge from what actually happens. Let us finally come back to the rest of Suro's (1999) article with that in mind.

I want to argue that Albert Gore's statement about the spiritual aspect of the "drug problem," while seemingly unconnected to the practical plan that he described, suggests an unconscious perception that the observable behavior is somehow controlled by higher level systems in the individuals involved. I can't fault him too much for not knowing that a control-system perspective could bridge the gap between what he intuited and the habits of thought that he worked with. Nobody can know everything, especially in a society as complex and with as diversified division of labor as ours. Some day behavior, as the control of perception, will be common knowledge, just as today reward and punishment are "known" to be the means of influencing behavior.

We already know that conversion to a spiritual group or religion has been the most effective means for many individuals to change their Reference settings for drugs. Synanon, The Black Muslims, strict Islam, born-again Christianity—and other such commitments have been frequently identified as the most powerful sources for giving up addictions and dysfunctional habits. Gore could consider this information as support for his thesis. But, how could he have made practical use of it in his role in government? Each individual who changes his lifestyle from that of drug user to follower of a strong religion must have undergone a significant reorganization of his highest level systems—involving his self concept and concept of the nature of reality.

It is hard to see initially how any government program that fails to address the individual on this level could have similar results. What we can do, and what government can do, officially, is check out what we know about the attraction of drugs in the first place. I think it is generally held that the main attraction of drugs is that they make one "feel good." This picture has been further enlarged by sociologists' research findings that, in general, people who want to feel better are often those whose life conditions are routinely miserable. For them the illegal drug is not materially different from the Novocaine that most of us are happy to take when visiting the dentist. The theoretical answer would then be that when people have more pleasure to lose than to gain from drugs their attraction would begin rapidly to diminish.

But that is not the whole picture. Just yesterday, again, I read somewhere (I hope in a reliable source) that 70% of illegal drug usage in the U. S. is by upper middle class and upper class yuppies. If that is so it shows up our preliminary hypothesis as either wrong or indicative of only one among several motives. Could that reflect a more profound, underlying common ground? I think so. I have also read recently about the profound boredom that some people find in their high paying jobs. They do not feel, for the most part, that they can afford to leave them. But, they feel in need of some further challenge or stimulation. This state of affairs can ultimately become almost as uncomfortable as the state that people experience in extreme poverty. (Almost, certainly not the same.) So, if Al Gore surmised that many individuals feel a need for more spiritual involvement, more excitement, more important goals to which to devote their lives, he might well have had a point.

Are there any other ways of gaining such a sense, for those to whom a fundamentalistic religion does not seem to have the answer? I think yes. I think that many Jewish Americans have found such a mission in devoting themselves to the survival of Israel. I think that many Islamic young people have found an exciting challenge in blending their traditional values with the technological developments that have grown up in the West. (But that might take a quite different course in non-Western societies.) As for the rest of us, we had a taste of what such a future direction could be in the space explorations of the 1960s. There was a time when many young people chose to turn to the TV channels that were then occupied with the space race, instead of the excitement of the traditional modes of sex and violence. There is a limit, however, to the length of time that one can stay involved vicariously. How might a large number of people involve themselves actively in an enterprise that carries them beyond themselves, say into the exploration of space? It would take a major reorganization of the higher orders in a large number of people. Were that to happen it would constitute a major reorganization in the way we think of ourselves as a society. It would (will?) provide young persons with something larger than themselves to which to devote their energies.

I like to think Albert Gore sensed that in his statement quoted by Suro (1999). However, it is not surprising that Gore seemed to jump from a broad scale, profound look at the problem to the shallow, unpromising program that he then outlined. In his role as number two executive in the country he had to keep many other systems-level variables in their steady state. In the background of our national attitude about the drugs that have been declared illegal (as against the many that might be equally harmful but bring large profits to drug companies) is a moral judgment that the users are *choosing* an evil course. As yet we do not tend to put ourselves in the position of those we are judging, in order to understand what variables are being controlled by their actions. Instead we tend to take the external attitude—from our own standpoint—and perceive their action as hostile to ourselves, to our belief that we know right from wrong and good from bad. Thus, whatever he may know about the deeper issues involved, Gore, to maintain his position as a national representative, had to control values that would not depart greatly from what the majority of us find familiar. Only when a great many of us personally reorganize will that change.

I believe that you could review many of the issues in which our society seems currently to be going around in circles—those Howard identifies with the loss of common sense—and find a lack of any clear reference values and defined perceptual variables to compare them with. The problem is that the entire *system* involved has not been identified. A lame, truncated description has been substituted for it. Think about it as operating in the same way as if someone kept yanking on the steering wheel of your car without your realizing it, while you were driving in traffic. In general the omitted source(s) of disturbance are members of society who are treated as if they didn't exist in the current formulation of a problem. In the case of illegal drug use the portion of our population who either don't want their behavior regulated, or who don't want their taxes wasted on programs that don't work, might well be a significant majority. Imagine so large a number of individual reorganizations—like that of the sexual revolution—that drug users and drug opponents were holding dialogues to search for a common Principle as a starting point to change the current situation.

This is not unthinkable. I have heard of small scale, beginning dialogues between proponents and opponents of abortion looking for a common ground. Likewise, I can't imagine wealthy yuppies all showing indifference if asked whether they really don't care how many little old ladies get their face bashed in by muggers desperate for the price of a fix. But, nobody has asked them. In our present linear-logic situation we have just the opposite condition. People with broad views of things do not easily come to wield power at high levels. It takes extreme single mindedness to master a system concept that will control all the variables involved in simply gaining the power of a CEO, let alone try to keep in mind how one's actions will affect the world as a whole when you get there. While reading an *Amicus Brief* from the Natural Resources Defense Council about their fights with polluters I wondered: Does any polluter really believe that the warnings about disaster looming ahead are false? My guess is that they are often kept too busy to think about it seriously at all. Or, when they are brought face to face with such an issue they have good grounds to suspect that at least many of their opponents' contentions are overblown. They know how they, themselves, manipulate concepts to influence those they need to influence. Furthermore, if they are familiar, even at third party acquaintance with studies like those of Julian Simon they have the reassurance that we, as a whole, will find ways to change bad, general conditions by reorganizing our individual approaches.

Julian Simon's views might be considered specific instances of Adam Smith's *invisible hand* in regard to the relationship between people's economic behavior and all our other values. However, the element of *time* is not accounted for in their analyses as far as I can see. Given enough time many negative trends do get reversed as more and more people begin to suffer more disadvantages than advantages. However, races between destruction and renovation, corruption and reform are not always won by the good guys. New concepts such as Catastrophe Theory have begun to clarify when conditions can reach boundary states where reversal is no longer possible. Biologists now study how species become destined for extinction even when some number of the members still remain. Some of this work needs to be factored into the predictions of optimists like Simon.

Still another point that should be considered as we contemplate the connection between reorganizations within individual control hierarchies and the way that societies evolve is the postulate that reorganization is, by definition, subject to randomness. That means that—given the same personal experience of crisis—different individuals will come out with different "solutions." Likewise, a given individual can arrive, time after time, upon an apparent solution that falls through for any of various reasons as he or she begins to implement it. Recall the US NEWS (4/21/97) article we considered in Chapter three

> Since the bombing in Oklahoma City two years ago, the popularity of militia-style groups has increased—and a vibrant industry has developed that sustains and fuels the anti-government rage.... In 1994 John Trochmann preached his militia gospel to a few hundred angry souls.... These days [he] is a celebrity.... Experts say all 50 states now harbor organized antigovernment groups.... the groups are finding a receptive audience because of the same economic challenges that confront many other Americans....

At first glance it struck me with horror that Americans could, in some number, perceive the Oklahoma city bombing in such a way as to turn against their fellow citizens. But, I have to admit that my attitude was an outside view. It failed to take into account the variables that the people in question were trying to control. One thing that is apparent is that an event like losing the family farm is a severe crisis and the perception that this has been going on for a long time with no likelihood of being reversed is a stress leading to reorganization which, in the case described above, could hardly be described as a successful reorganization, a non-solution as far as curing the economic problems of the participants.

I expect many more individual reorganizations of people's attitudes about governance as the various social crises of our times mount up. They, in turn, will eventually cause reorganization of many people's systems-concepts of what a nation is, what a government is, what the nature of life is really about. These will force various proposals for solutions many of which will turn out to conflict with others or to be faulty because of leaving important considerations uncontrolled. We can speculate about some of the directions that such processes might take in the near future, based simply upon the dissatisfactions that people express in surveys, polls, everyday conversation and TV talk shows.

For example, a chronic issue that I keep hearing about is the cost of law enforcement and the failure of coverage because of a shortfall of funds. One day I heard someone, I can't remember where, say that law breakers ought to pay the added cost of policing made necessary by their contempt of the law. I had thought of the same thing while grumpy about healthy people using up all the spaces for handicapped people in various places.[139] It seems such a violation of common decency.

Now and then TV stations or a newspaper will run an indignant story on this item and the local police usually respond by complaining that they have only limited resources to meet all the requirements placed on them. I ruled out as impractical the idea of lawbreakers of this sort paying for the additional cost of enforcement. Some time later it occurred to me that while this idea would have been totally impractical a generation ago, modern technology has begun to change that situation.

Here is how it might work. Say that a given community takes its current police budget as a baseline. Then it obtains estimates of how many traffic violators, confidence games, fraud schemes, building code violations, health code violations—the kinds of crimes and misdemeanors that the law attempts to discourage with fines—go undeterred because of lack of police power. Then, using modern computer methods they calculate how much additional it would cost to employ temporary police to patrol these venues until a significant reduction is achieved. Finally, they calculate the average cost that baseline fines would have to be raised to pay for the additional coverage and add a surcharge based upon this figure to the fines that the increased number of caught perpetrators would pay. There are many services supplying temporary workers—nurses, guards, engineers, even physicians, lawyers and police, so that that idea is not totally unrealistic.

I did not intend in the above to ignore the hierarchical nature of society as discussed in the previous chapter. I set it aside to discuss the interactions between individual experiences of error and how they ultimately result in societal reorganization. Sometimes the lag time is extremely long. A major source of that is the fact that the more powerful members of society often do not experience the error states of those on the bottom. That is what makes social status a prize in itself in societies that have open mobility.

Sometimes reorganization in those with the greatest error states—especially in regard to basic life essentials—produces what the higher status members define as crime, justifying their use of coercion. That then becomes another source of delay in addressing what might eventually prove to be a dysfunction in the society as a whole. A frequent concomitant of low status is deficient education. The people in question do not achieve sufficient skill to grasp the implications of the (unconscious) systems-concepts that they themselves might hold—the unrealistic conceptions that keep them from perceiving workable solutions to their problems. Sometimes the *cognitive dissonance* between higher level controlled variables only gradually creates error in those members of society "above" the problem. Think of how long it took to achieve Rowe versus Board of Education, yet the essential Principle was already there in 1776.

Kafka-esque true stories are beginning to abound in the U. S. media about different branches of government in conflict with each other, trapping individuals in "catch 22" situations. Several times in recent years *60 Minutes* has featured stories of foreign nationals being thrown into prison on various charges despite being vouched for by U. S. agencies that had brought them here. They had actually been opposing their own tyrannical governments in alliance with U. S. governmental agencies. This gives a picture of agencies at war with each other, without any higher authority coordinating their functioning. This kind of chaos also occurred during the collapse of the Roman Empire. It provides a perspective for understanding how during the *Dark Ages* as central power declined rival baronies and dukedoms competed with each other for power over local fiefs. This picture seems to confirm the views of (already reorganized) Davidson and Rees-Mogg (1997) whose "sovereign individuals" look remarkably like those barons of the dark ages.

PART IV

*Virtual Pioneers:
Ordinary People in
Times of Crisis*

Chapter 15

INDIVIDUALS AND CIVILIZATIONS

I wonder whether it isn't more than simple coincidence that we find a paradigm revolution concerning how behavior works occurring during an apparent revolution in civilization. I think that as Western Civilization has become more chaotic, more tangled by inconsistent implications of basic principles, it has provoked reorganization in many individuals' most abstract perceptions of reality. That might well have inspired renewed interest in how behavior really works as well as in one's conception of social reality. Consider George Soros's (1998), *The Crisis of Global Capitalism*. According to a review in the *Wall Street Journal* (Wolf, 1998) this capitalist *par excellence*, ponders, "the unredeemable awfulness of capitalism." This just when capitalism, as an economic philosophy, has seemingly won out over all other economic approaches on the world stage. Why? In this chapter I continue the discussion of how one's view of *how behavior works* is a factor in how one conducts any activity, and particularly including societal governance in a capitalistic world.

It probably happens fairly often that people undergo reorganizations of their world outlooks, if lesser measures fail to recoup a sense of mastery over one's fate. A new concept that an individual might then announce would likely attract the attention of individuals who are, themselves, experiencing some amount of crisis. Thus, Powers's views spoke to persons who were coming to question the traditional view of the nature of behavior, and Soros's might well speak to the various people who believe they see shortcomings in the current functioning of capitalism despite its many apparent achievements.

These two ostensibly unrelated developments have at least this much in common: They happened at a time when many writers are seeing large cracks in the social fabric, as we considered in Part I. They both relate to broad issues concerning how individuals and societies really function. It has simply become more and more difficult to think straight about one's personal understanding of what our world is. That makes it harder to develop for oneself a consistent strategy of survival. I don't mean just basic survival, although that is a growing issue for an increasing number of people in the under classes of the Western countries as well as in the third world. I mean survival in the sense of controlling the lifestyle of one's position in the social structure to your Reference value. Thinking straight about it requires that daily activities—the Programs one implements in one's social role—are governed by consistent Principles. The actions produced by those Programs should confirm one's Systems-concepts about reality, including the nature of one's society while simultaneously achieving mundane satisfactions.

If the conceptions of reality one shares with peers begin to fall apart the Principles that mediate between them and practical actions lose their anchors. The field of who is a peer might begin to shrink. In really egalitarian societies members of different status levels can still perceive each other as peers in regard to broad concepts like "citizenship." When society becomes more complex, or the mutual interests of some social classes become more concentrated and more distant from those of the society as a whole, as we considered in chapter 13, the result can be a loosening of the sense of nationhood. The society may be in incipient dissolution unless it achieves a reorganization that once again articulates a broad base of common interests. Davidson and Rees-Mogg (1997) see the present as a case of irreversible dissolution, but they also think they foresee much about the new forms of culture that will arise from the ashes of the present one. Let me review the quote from chapter four.

> A sense of disquiet about the future has begun to color the optimism so characteristic of Western societies for the past 250 years. People everywhere are hesitant and worried .... Just as an invisible, physical change ... in the atmosphere signals that a thunderstorm is ... imminent, so now, in the twilight of the millennium, premonitions of change are in the air. One person after another, each in his own way, senses that time is running out on a dying way of life .... the modern phase of Western civilization will end .... This is a situation with striking parallels in the past. Whenever technological change has divorced the old forms from the new moving forces of the economy, moral standards shift, and people begin to treat those in command of the old institutions with growing disdain .... Governments have already lost much of their power to regulate and compel ....[140]

Computers, the internet and the overcoming of the advantage of large weapons of offense by the small weapons of defense are, together, the engine of this revolution as they see it. From our point of view here each of these developments represents multiple reorganizations in many individuals coming together in a ground swell of cultural upheaval in civilization. "In our view [this is] the waning of the Modern Age. It is a development driven by a ruthless but hidden logic . . . . We say this . . . to emphasize that the stage of history now opening will be qualitatively different from that into which you were born . . . ."(Ibid.)

I agree with them in a general way and make the task of the remaining chapters to examine the situation of individuals in this "new stage of history" and try to explore the potential of the PCT view of behavior in thinking about the perils and opportunities it presents. What can we infer about the state of American and Western principles in current affairs? When I began writing this chapter the President of the United States was facing charges of having violated his constitutional trust. I am mindful that his two immediate predecessors were also accused of lying under oath and subverting the intentions of the U. S. congress—and calls for their impeachment were also heard. What does this mean about "the rules of the game?" What it suggests to me is that the rules concerning politicians' discipline—the limits of tolerable political behavior—have been breached. We should perhaps all be wondering how three national leaders in a row came to the point of being charged with transgressing limits that we used to think were firmly established. There are many social commentators now claiming that these events illustrate the loss of morality in society, the deterioration of political integrity, and the degeneration of the principles upon which Western society has thrived for the last thousand years.

The case of President Clinton strikes me as a good place to begin our examination of what perceptual variables one might have been giving highest priority (when theoretically we all should have been operating on the highest plane of our constitutional principles). It might help our understanding of the stage of history in which we, ordinary people, have to survive. My own process of coming to a position on the whole affair was rather surprising and more than a bit disconcerting.

I think it illustrates nicely the kind of individual crisis and reorganization about which I have been talking.

I experienced the events of the "impeachment debacle" in a personal way that resolved upon tolerating a mass of inconsistencies and logical contradictions. That left me feeling quite unlike myself. If many of us found ourselves in that position,[141] that alone might be taken as evidence of the decadence of our culture by some of the prophets of doom whose views we considered in earlier chapters. What strikes me as an individual, an ordinary person in these times, is that—while I became clear in my mind about the outcome I desired—I could not derive a consistent rationale to justify it.

That is not like *me*, the self-image I hold. I found myself in strong agreement with the so-called "conservative" view, that honesty under oath is a requisite for any credible system of justice; likewise, I regard semantic creativity with common-usage words as detrimental to reliable standards of communication. Furthermore, I value the American principle that everyone should be equal before the law (though I don't believe it obtains in fact); I also believe that prominent figures are perceived as role models by many young people. I hold with the notion that people generally observe what prominent figures do, as portrayed on the screen or in the news, for current information about "what people do," in much the same way that I watch other cars and try to blend into the average rate of travel in traffic rather than adhering strictly to the speed signs.

I think that doing in Rome what the Romans do is a reasonably good strategy for setting reference values to control many phenomena of everyday living. In fact, I think the statement I often heard as a child, "Just because Johnny does xxxx doesn't mean you can do it," to be one of the most foolish admonitions in the child-rearing repertoire. In actual practice it exhorts the child to allow the unscrupulous all the advantages in the competitions of life. A good case can be made for the argument that society is best coordinated when people share similar standards for behaving and for evaluating the behavior of others. Any other position sooner or later devolves into distinctions of privilege and exploitation. But, back to the question at hand.

At the same time that I found myself in sympathy with all those ideals stated above I also never wavered in my opinion that there was something distorted in the political process concerning the judgment of the president's conduct. I surmised that the enemies of the president had started with a Principle that *he had to be removed* and pursued any plausible means to accomplish that aim, never mind how tortured the rationale that had to be found for it. In other words, I saw the whole process as a transparent, normal instance of behavior aiming to control a pre-ordained goal.[142] That perception by itself might well have left me feeling on the sidelines, and impotent, as I have felt when learning of the multitude of cases where innocent individuals have been framed and railroaded into prison, sometimes death row, by police and district attorneys working to reach preconceived perceptions in spite of apparently contradictory evidence.

Pause a moment to examine how behavior works in such cases. Back in chapter eleven I showed how such "phenomena" as self-fulfilling prophecy, experimenter bias, and so on, are simply special cases of the fact that behavior consists of controlling perceptions to desired/expected values. Our actions keep true the expectations that we bring to perceiving the world. Thus, when police and prosecutors decide, from whatever initial perceptions, that they have a guilty party it is only human if they subsequently seem immune to evidence that they have been wrong.

Once you perceive a "fact," any further observations conform as necessary to keep that "fact" inviolate. *That is why* an important aspect of the training of professionals like scientists, physicians, lawyers, police and others, is, and needs to be, focused upon this potentially dangerous derivative of the way we are built. Special training is needed to alert us to, and inculcate safeguards against, misperceptions of this type. Even so, the closed mind set is an all too common occurrence. It is seen most readily when a professional person is acting, even innocently, unaware of this universal tendency for predispositions to guide perception. Add to that the factor that often there are personal advantages at risk, if one admits to being wrong, though there may be no penalty for being wrong if you don't admit it. Thus, you have the ingredients for a fulminating brew of corruption such as has been exposed here in Illinois and elsewhere in the press in recent years.

Since I was aware of how this kind of process works, I was predisposed to look for signs of it in the early stages of "the impeachment debacle." My judgment was affected by other considerations as well. I did what I could to ascertain who, exactly, were driving the process. There I had to rely upon the public media as I don't have insider information on Washington. So, yes, if the media really have a liberal bias, as some have claimed, I was getting a slanted picture. But, what does one do when you sense that as a possibility? What I do, and I'll bet you do too, is an informal consistency analysis. I read the reports that the attacks were being financed by extremely rich people who also seemed, among other things, opposed to certain instances of free speech, environmental protection, etc. That came down to a judgment that if those most opposed to the continued tenure of the president were to have their way, it might not be good for ordinary people like me.

Why do I say that? Remember back in chapter three when I talked about ordinary people in Santa Fe being "thrown out" of homes they had lived in all their lives because other people with hugely greater resources were invading them—and that there have been reports of similar things happening in many places? Well, rightly or wrongly I perceived the president as offering some bulwark for retarding developments like that—and those most eager to get rid of him as striving to increase the discrepancy of wealth and power between people in our country. Let me rephrase that last point. I don't think their *intention* is to increase the discrepancy. I think it is a side effect of maximizing the variables they control, just as we all do.

So, whether or not my motives were really in harmony with the supposed two thirds of the country opposing impeachment, my desired end point was the same. Other considerations—personal and emotional—were also in play, as they always are in cases like this. I remembered that Hunt, the Texas oil millionaire, was reported one time to have said, "I can buy Ph. D.s a dime a dozen." I shuddered when I heard that, and I still do. I perceive it as an implicit threat. If enough people like him gained enough influence, people like me could end up feeling like slaves. OK, that is hyperbole, but it accurately conveys my emotional response to the kind of ignorant arrogance I read into that statement. What I mean is that I don't believe that making a lot of money automatically insures that one is wise. In fact, the time and energy spent making a lot of money might often detract from learning other things, like the things that make one wise. Therefore, I have severe misgivings about people making decisions that can affect the lives of all the rest of us simply because of their economic power. (Even though I know that that is unavoidable to some extent.)

So this was the thought process of which I was aware. If there was a deeper, more instinctual process beneath the cognitive level—of the sort I speculated upon in chapter 12—by definition any influence from such a source would have been unconscious. This then has been a sample of the background of my perception of the beginning phase. Starting from my Principle: I don't think I trust the kind of people behind this process to be interested in the welfare of people like me—I began to look for the implications that followed. The first was my emotional reaction, described above. Then I perceived other aspects. There were the media reports about various people in the pack attacking the president being "guilty" of the same things. (I put *guilty* in quotes to honor the contention that a good portion of what was being charged against any of the principle figures was admittedly not against the law.) Then I noticed other things: the imbalance between the supposed perjury that was to be prosecuted and that of the two predecessors that was not prosecuted; the apparent divergence of the independent counsel's quest from what was announced as his initial mission.

It boiled down for me to an assessment that the appeal to noble principles to which I heartily subscribe, was somehow perverted even though I could not exactly arrive at a satisfactory analysis of what was really going on. I chose in the end to honor my visceral feeling that a major revolution in the government status quo should be avoided because there was something questionable in the process driving it. Apparently many of our fellow citizens were having comparable visceral reactions.

My understanding of perceptual control theory influenced my judgments about these events in several ways. I firmly think that the "me"—of before becoming acquainted with PCT—would have felt compelled to abandon my visceral reaction in favor of what logic seemed to demand. As it was, I freely accepted that I was choosing to be inconsistent, in spite of my theoretical and constitutional diffidence about that. My Systems-concept of reality has grown over the years to encompass that many basic propositions are inconsistent with each other, like quantum theory and Special Relativity, or wave and corpuscle theories of light. During the same time I have come to trust my visceral reactions to events when feeling cognitive dissonance between how I want things to be and how I reason about the alleged facts. When faced with a complex field of contingencies I often judge my visceral reaction as my best computation of what they all boil down to. I know that a purely emotional reaction can often arise from a miscategorization of superficial features, so I have developed a strategy of not acting on my visceral reactions—if I can possibly help it—until I have done as much of a systems-analysis as possible on what I perceive.

Furthermore, my conception of the control system hierarchy leads me to look always for the highest controlled perception that I can find, in myself and others. I identify it with the test for the controlled variable: to look for what resists change even when affected by would-be disturbances. So when I noted the lurch in direction of the independent counsel's inquiry I began immediately to wonder what higher level reference was driving his action. Since I couldn't read his mind I had to infer it from what information I had, like who had proposed him for the office, who was championing him, what else he was doing. Finally, my attention focused on what outcome I desired, and arrived at the analysis that I described above. Yes, I concede that it might include a healthy dose of resisting disturbance to the status quo—a case of preferring to "bear those ills we have rather than flying to those we know not of." I have not found that to be a bad strategy in many instances.

Reorganizations within the control system hierarchies of individuals may take many different forms. I hope to achieve a greater integration of my view of reality and the Principles I intend to control in regard to my political thinking than I have so far. I am still currently feeling as if there has been an assault on them in my experience of the great impeachment debacle. Since my mind keeps coming back to my analysis and I keep looking for evidence for and against the outcome I hoped for, I know that I am undergoing reorganization of some part of my highest levels. I am curious about where it will come out. It is possible that I will come to see things in a light that will mean more approval of those I now suspect and more disapproval of those I now support, or the opposite. One other outcome of my personal analysis of these events has been somewhat surprising and a little disconcerting to the *self* I used to be. That was becoming aware that I more unabashedly direct my decisions in terms of what I judge as most likely best for myself and my kin. I "knew" how I was supposed to be judging. "Supposed to be," in the sense that I perceived the eye rolling and head shaking of the various public figures who have since been implying—or saying outright—that ordinary people were by and large choosing selfish personal ends over higher values, like the constitution and the survival of the United States. It's possible we were, but I came up with another view of it.

The need for new ways to understand reality arises from the kind of cognitive dissonance (conflict of same-level control systems) that I described. Other present day sources of such dissonance stem from the interaction of now obsolete (though often unrealized) ways of doing things with the very technological revolutions that have helped to call old understandings into question. The result, in some individuals, involves paradigm shifts, the most useful of which can become paradigm revolutions. If Davidson and Rees-Mogg, Lasch, Ortega, and the other writers—who claim that Western civilization is coming apart or undergoing shifts that will change its essence—are right, then the reorganizations occurring in individuals feeling their survival shaky in present circumstances will coalesce into reorganization of the culture as a whole. It would happen when enough ordinary people endure similar-enough reorganizations of their way of experiencing reality.

This is beginning to happen in palpable ways already. I have been curious about a supposed new phenomenon called "jury nullification" reported in the media recently. It is described as a process where jurors are thought to disregard clear evidence in order to arrive at a verdict they *want* to produce instead of the one that logic says they *should* produce. In writing about my approach to the impeachment issue above, it occurred to me that one could make a fairly good case that that is exactly what the outcome of the great impeachment debacle amounted to: jury nullification by the U. S. senate.

I hadn't made that connection until the very moment of writing the paragraphs above, but I had been interested in the phenomenon when I first heard about it. I don't know where the term, "jury nullification" came from. What I have read about it is that some juries with predominantly African American members have found black defendants "not guilty" in the face of strong evidence to the contrary. It seems clear that some other Principle than "follow the law" was being set as the Program reference by the highest order systems in a majority of the jurors. (I could understand some liberal letting out a scream of indignation here as to why a couple hundred years of normal practice in dealing with African Americans by juries in the south was never perceived as perverted, but let that go for now.)

The point is, that for such a practice to arise is evidence of some degree of cultural disintegration. The individuals in those juries, by not controlling for Pvs that you would expect, are reshaping their culture—tacitly commenting that they don't fully share in the majority scheme of things. This is not new, of course, it came to a head as a result of inconsistency between two of our basic national Principles in our two civil wars, of the 1860s and the 1960s, and resulted in reorganizations of our culture, though short of overturning the whole civilization. The jurors in the current cases controlled some other Principle at a higher priority than that of the conventional way of making legal judgments. Their actions clearly were following precedents set by others in the past to opt out of the "system."

It represented an assertion, through action rather than

words, of what writers like Boot (1998), Harr (1995) and Howard (1995) have suggested—that our legal system is already seriously corrupt. In such instances it is easy to develop the principle of *everyman for himself (group for itself)*. In fact such action by an Afro-American jury could be said to follow the precedent set by white juries in the South during the Jim Crow era. It gives rise to a thought that the members were controlling variables for asserting and maintaining their group power at higher value than maintaining the Nation concept, or higher priority than abstract concepts like justice. Perhaps also they were signalling that ethnic identity might be coming to outweigh national identity in some instances. If that were true, one can immediately wonder whether we aren't seeing something similar going on all around the earth right now in various ethnic "cleansings."

I have still another interpretation, not necessarily inconsistent with the above. The perceptions the individuals in the "jury nullification" cases might have been controlling seem basically the same as that in James Davidson's description of his decision to migrate to Bermuda, despite his proud Jamestown heritage. He depicted it as a form of opting out of a system he perceives as inimical to his personal interests. We might say the same of the various anti-government groups now roaming around the country. Of course, other variables are under control with the same actions. Variables like group identity, sense of belonging, "racial purity" and the like. In fact, I see the senate vote on impeachment, jury nullification, the history of white juries' typical handling of black defendants in the old South and wealthy people moving out of the U. S. as all having one common element. That is the exercise of choices that conflict with abstract principles to which the individual otherwise subscribes. It creates the necessity to contain the kind of cognitive dissonance that I identified in myself as tolerance for inconsistency regarding the impeachment issue. The common element is setting a Principle of self-or group-interest at higher gain than some other Principle like "the sanctity of the law" or "The U. S. is the greatest country in the world."

The fact of a concrete Principle like self-interest superseding an abstract Principle like "putting the law above personal interest" I take to be a symptom. British and American history is full of homilies about the nobility of putting principle above personal interest. If that value has come into disrepute one explanation would seem to be a lowering of the position of those abstractions in many people's Systems-concepts of reality. When formal law is seen as breaking down it leaves one with one's own sense of natural law, which I have maintained arises finally in our instincts. The reorganizations in individuals that are involved in that will invariably modify the nature of our civilization, if in fact, they don't change it radically.

In this context recall Haywood's (1958) *The Myth of Rome's Fall* where he said, "It is surprising to find out how many things remained the same in the West, even after the control of the Imperial government had been relaxed and the Germans ruled undisputed." What he is saying here, as in his thesis in general, is that ordinary people did not experience any drastic changes in their lives even while the events were taking place that were later to be called the *fall* of Rome. Individuals' control hierarchies might undergo drastic reorganization in severe crises like that of being caught in a war, famine, natural catastrophe or having one's career skills become obsolete. But, things like political turnovers only force major reorganization in the fervent partisans. Ordinary people linked to a particular spot on earth and a concrete way of sustaining themselves fall back on just keeping on living, if major political events do not immerse them in catastrophe. Yet political turnovers or technological revolutions can contribute to cultural revolutions and gradually change the living conditions of everyone. People will earn their living in ways that only a pioneering few can even dimly grasp at present. And with that will come types of lifestyles that would amaze most present-day citizens, even though we could guess that future scholars will look back and trace the roots of these changes in events and fashions that we currently live in the midst of without seeing their future implications. But for most people the transition will be gradual and conditions of living will continue to seem normal.

The revolution in civilization that is already underway has some disturbing parallels to events that occurred in the downward spiral of the Roman Empire, like the fact of large numbers of people seemingly having nothing useful to do with a significant part of their time. I am thinking here of the apparent shallowness and homogenization of ways of killing time—the increasingly large amounts of time devoted to spectator sports and endlessly repeated crime dramas on television. It seems reminiscent of the bread and circus that occupied the Roman underclass during the waning days of the empire. These people had lost their lands and their means of making a living through their own efforts and needed to be kept entertained so as not to become a threat to public order. The comparison is not perfect. Most people have a job today, but those jobs seem increasingly dependent upon a never ending need to consume the stuff that mass production continuously spouts. Much of it nobody really needs. People seem constantly on the lookout for ever more sensational experiences, such as even the entertainment-like quality of the docudramas in the great impeachment debacle or the real wars displayed on CNN. As technology keeps displacing people from meaningful activities more and more time is consumed in activities that don't make much difference to anything, or in other parts of the world, in war.

Another new development, as far as I can tell, is the role that crime and corruption play in the achievement of status mobility by way of celebrity or notoriety (which are becoming increasingly indistinguishable). And as the multinational companies that dominate many aspects of world affairs today more and more resemble the feudal baronies and dukedoms that arose during the political anarchy at the end of the Roman time local drug lords and terror chieftains began building regional centers of power. In the feudal system that developed in the Dark Age gang leaders—warriors—became important figures through their prowess in applying brute force to maintain physical control of their regions. The nobility of the subsequent ages were descendants of persons who would be considered thugs or hoodlums in more stable times. One wonders what parallels are beginning to arise in the present.

This type of process is going on in modern society. The social status gained by the descendants of gangsters bears testimony that control of concrete variables pertaining to material matters can be realistic and practical in comparison to valuing abstract variables in times of relative anarchy. Especially so when important abstract principles are in conflict or become drawn to extreme interpretations that begin to defy common sense. Crimes, themselves, might eventually undergo re-definitions as more people understand how control works. Many different types of examples could illustrate this point. I will use the example of our current muddle over how to use the power of the state—or any other power center for that matter—in the deterrence of crime.

The common sense view about major crimes, as I see it, requires the satisfaction of two basic human attitudes regarding what should be the consequences of committing a crime. One is that future incidents of a like type should occur less often, preferably not at all. The other is probably a more intuitive or even instinctive sense—that of re-establishing a balance or securing restitution. Social science provides examples of many human societies where some form of restitution is thought to be the proper resolution for even such acts as murder. The restitution might take very different forms, however. In some societies a money payment is the accepted answer while in others the balance is evened by the death of the perpetrator or one of his kin.

We have both of these resolutions, but in a muddled sense. The state now has the function formerly performed by a tribal council or king. But because the modern state is composed of a heterogeneous mix of peoples with different traditions our laws have come to incorporate compromises that entail inconsistencies. For example, we add considerations of intention and responsibility. We hold intention to be important because it has long been recognized that there can be accidents that have the same result as intentional acts. For example, I might jerk my arm back to avoid some injury and hit you with my elbow. Or I might decide to hit you with my elbow and do so. The action is the same in both cases, but should you retaliate, if I didn't know you were there? We in the West have long tended to think, no. On the other hand if I want to hit you with my elbow, but don't want to be held responsible, I will claim afterwards that I didn't know you were there. Only a mind reader could definitely distinguish which explanation was genuine and our science does not endorse the idea that mind readers exist.

This dilemma would never have arisen in a society committed to restitution of damage regardless of how its occurrence is explained. In our society we make this distinction but we can not honestly do justice to it because of our lack of mind reading capacities. So we resort to substitutes, like the judgments of a jury. The pooled guesses of a panel of ordinary people probably does better than chance on the average, but they can go badly wrong in particular instances as we have seen in recent TV stories. Our legal reasoning can also go badly wrong in my opinion in the opposite direction where we impute lessened responsibility to someone laboring under the "handicap" of being drunk or psychotic. In both of those cases the thinking implicitly rests upon the Cartesian view of behavior as the result of outside "forces" impinging on the individual. Although both intoxication and psychosis are internal to the subject they are viewed as independent of the subject's "will." In that sense they are external forces. As a result someone who kills someone else with a car while intoxicated will go to prison for only a couple of years, or not at all, while a person who kills someone else with a gun will usually be sent to prison for anywhere from twice as long to ten times as long, or even in some states to the death penalty.

From the point of view that behavior is not a response to external forces, but the means of bringing a perceived variable to its desired state, we ask what is the desired state for the person in process of becoming intoxicated? It is the amalgam of experiences that obtain for him/her when intoxicated. That is undoubtedly different for different people but there are common elements such as the state of lessened awareness of emotional pain, slowed reaction times, reduced clarity of vision and deficient foresight. How is the desired state accomplished? By the actions of drinking alcohol. That is the result of intentional behavior which originates within the individual. At the point of beginning to drink any individual who lives a normal life in our society knows these by-products of intoxication and thus is implicitly choosing to accept them. If the person's normal activities include any amount of watching television or reading the newspaper, he or she also knows that a frequent by-product of drunk driving is accidents in which other people are often maimed or killed. Hence, he or she is choosing to accept this set of probabilities.

Curiously enough our legal thinking has evolved in such a way that we often hold non-living entities like corporations liable for damages to individuals more strictly than drivers who intend to become intoxicated. We say it—the corporation—was negligent, it "should have known better." Obviously other considerations are at work, like the likelihood of the plaintiff attorney to make a large profit even if merely as a source of nuisance to a wealthy corporation. But, why is it so hard to see that that, in itself, results in the kinds of conflicted judgments about our values that contribute to the degeneration of common sense in our society?

The question of culpability when the perpetrator of a heinous act is judged to be "insane" is another issue where we fall into the error of imaginative mind-reading. Here the test for the controlled variable shows a way around the impossible task of looking into the mind of the person. If the perpetrator attempts to escape being caught, that, plainly and simply suggests that he or she knew what he or she was doing at least to the extent of knowing that the act is unacceptable to the members of society. Yet, I have not seen this argument used as an alternative to dubious psychiatric opinions as to the individual's state of mind at the time of the act. I believe that I know why: because our dominant theory for thinking about behavior is the Cartesian paradigm of stimulus-response. It leads us to focus attention on what influences might have "affected" the person rather than on the fact that *by attempting to avoid capture* the individual is clearly demonstrating his knowledge of how others view his actions. The idea that people act by setting references, internally, rather than being "conditioned" by events external to them—will surely lead to changes in many types of plans for influencing wide scale behavior. In time I think we will give up the procedures of making believe that we can accurately determine what is the state of another person's "mind" and go on to concentrate on the outcomes that we collectively desire, prevention and restitution, somewhat along the lines that we might take in regard to the question of drug use.

Still one more challenge, one for our civilization as a whole, is to rectify the injurious consequences of the industrial and technological revolutions. Within the short space of the last two centuries the people of the earth have created a condition that humankind have never faced before. When populations were relatively stable and in harmony with environment the materials that people used came from the environment and the waste products, being natural in the first place, generally did not do undo harm even when thrown into rivers and streams around which people lived. In addition the amounts were such that they could be "digested." Now, for the first time in history we have unnatural substances, substances made by chemistry that the ecology has never yet become able to assimilate. Additionally the amounts of waste are much greater than could be assimilated even with waste matter that would be bio-degradable. Yet most people's habits continue in the old ways, unless through education or personal experience they come to see the need to change their habits.

Problems of this sort impact ordinary people first and most. Those of higher social status insulate themselves to some extent by utilizing all the refinements of modern technology, such as buying bottled spring water, making sure not to live in areas of high toxicity, and the like. Society's leaders—legislators and executives—are usually among the last to promote reforms, for the reasons we have seen above. They too are members of the insulated classes, but even more important, in their roles as *governors* they are the ones who monitor the highest level Systems-concepts of the country. Monitoring that level *means* controlling against disturbances—against change. Thus, rulers by the very nature of their jobs, tend to preserve the *status quo*. Rulers who contradict this pattern, like Czar Peter the Great, are rare enough to be seen as great just because of diverging from the usual pattern.

This introduces still another factor in the evolution of societal solutions to chronic problems. That is the competition between different civilizations along their boundaries. Western Civilization, as epitomized by that of the U. S. is at present clearly in competition with Islamic civilization in many parts of Africa and the new states of the former Soviet union.

Both, in turn, are potentially challenged by the new patterns that may be emerging in the far east. In many regions that have long been Islamic in tradition and religion the forms of economic and social patterns of capitalist democracies are not being welcomed even while western technology is. The reorganizations of Systems-concepts in individuals throughout these areas will constitute the major forces in this competition. We don't know yet whose ideas will prove most utility for the people of a region to meet their survival needs and pursue meaningful lives.

The range of different alternatives evolving within the Islamic and Eastern worlds seems to be a much broader range than we see in the West. What will these different peoples with their very different outlooks on many aspects of life make of the potentialities of computers and the internet? It seems to me naive to suppose that they will just fall into the Western pattern of thought because of their contact with the information technology revolution. Likewise I wonder what will be the effect of gaining the insight that behavior is comprised of feedback phenomena, controlling one's perceptions. The most important aspect of that insight for ordinary people will be the conviction that will come about slowly through actual demonstration—that coercion inevitably invokes resistance to which the only final resolution comes about through cooperation or brute force. And the outcome of the use of brute force is devastation of the land and the waste of natural resources upon which people must live.

When I say that I believe PCT to be one of the revolutionary developments I don't mean to say that I can predict how people will be different as a result of it. But, certain implications are quite apparent. People will more and more demand clear definitions of the perceptible variable and its desired condition before endorsing social programs and governmental initiatives of all types. This will come to include programs both for improving things like education, and reducing undesirable social developments like crime. This new approach is already being tested out by Edward Ford (1989, 1994), an early applier of PCT in the fields of education and relationship counseling. He developed a system of organizing learning in elementary schools that helps to eliminate many of the conflicts between teachers and students that plague other systems. He trains teachers to understand that children, like themselves, are already controlling certain Pvs—for *purposes* important to themselves—that they are intent upon realizing when they enter the school door. Their purposes can't be identical to the purposes their teachers have for them because they don't initially know what school is supposed to accomplish, or what their teachers intend. They might very well have fantasies derived from things parents have told them. But, whatever the fantasies are, the child will experience them in relation to his or her own purpose. Some or many actions of the teacher will be disturbances to the child's control of his Pvs. Ford trains both teachers and students how they can establish effective working conditions instead of a clash of purposes by identifying the relevant Pv and re-orienting the task to sustain rather than oppose it.

Some observers will see this as something that really good teachers have been doing informally since time immemorial. That is true. But those who have been so effective have usually been exceptional in tolerating inconsistencies between what actually worked and the so-called "theories" of instruction to which they were required officially to subscribe. The official theories are supposed to be based upon current psychologies of learning which regularly incorporate, consciously or unconsciously, the Cartesian fallacy about behavior. Their rigid application frequently results in extreme cases of brute force on the part or teachers, students or both. From time to time we see examples of intuitive grasp of these factors as in movies about exceptional teachers, like "To Sir, With Love," (starring Sidney Poitier), or in books like those of John Holt and Jonathan Kozoll. All of them illustrate the idea that you get marvelous involvements with children when you contact them where they live. However, the writers of these insights arrived at them empirically. They had to ignore the accepted wisdom about how education should be done. I believe that is why we have never seen any generalization of their insights. Ford is the first to supply a theoretical basis for the competency shown in the movies and authors noted above.[143]

Ford's work might serve also as a good illustration of the way that personal reorganizations eventually bring about revolutions in practices. His approach grew out of his search as a social worker looking for more effective ways to help people solve their personal problems. He realized that one of the biggest deterrents to the acceptance of good intentions (like those of physicians, teachers and reformers) is the "objective" point of view by which the practitioner conceives of the need to do something *to* others, as *objects*. Even when the recipient believes in the good intentions of the person trying to act upon him or her, he/she can not simply suspend control of the Pvs which she is currently controlling. In the most ideal conditions the patient, student, citizen suspended judgment, that is, made himself passive as a result of faith in the knowledge and good intentions of the other party. Now, with the widening gaps between the social classes, with increasingly diverse cultural contacts, with television and news stories filled with episodes warning not to trust strangers, the treating individual is on probation from the start. If he or she fails to find the point of common interest he or she will fail to elicit cooperation and compliance.

The change is coming about in many other areas of living as well as education. Recall the reports about employers frustrated by employees who no longer subscribe to the old values of industriousness and financial rewards, that could be taken for granted with earlier generations. Studies are beginning to show that many workers are not willing to give up purposes of their own where they don't mesh with those of the workplace. A not insignificant number of people are opting for alternative lifestyles that don't sustain the old values. R.C. Longworth (1996), a Chicago Tribune staff writer, in an article on "The Painful cost of economic revolution," quotes French president J. Chirac, "'Globalization has come hand in hand with rising joblessness, job insecurity and poverty.'" He continues that the global economy, "being global, has escaped the control of national governments . . . . 'In the U.S. the responsibility of the CEO is to deliver shareholder value. Period.' (quote of Albert Dunlap, CEO of Sunbeam Corp)." But, in Japan there is a contrasting attitude, "We are part of a social system, with a responsibility not to create unemployment. So we have a wider role, involving workers and other stakeholders." (Yoshihiko Miyauchi, CEO of Orix Corporation.) And in Europe, "all stakeholders: employees, customers, community & country must be taken into account." David Marquand, professor of politics at Britain's Sheffield U. sees a moral failing in the way that U. S. & British execs have grabbed an unfair share of the productivity gains created by modern technology because they are under no obligation to respect the claims of others with stakes in the organizations that they govern.

Each of these different attitudes represents a competitive bid, if you will, for the patronage of ordinary people around the world. While the single minded American view of the most efficient production at the smallest price seems to promise the world the most *stuff* it is not certain yet that that value will win out over all others, such as greater stability of expectations, that might result from less economically efficient production systems. Consider this observation by Paul Kennedy (1987) concerning the difference of cultural paradigms, "To readers brought up to respect 'western science,' the most striking feature of Chinese civilization [13th to 15th centuries] must be its technological precocity . . . [with the] evidence of cultural and technological advance it is . . . not surprising . . . that the Chinese had turned to overseas exploration and trade. [But, then it was totally abandoned, as] a key element in China's retreat was the sheer conservatism of the Confucian bureaucracy."

We have a counterpart of that kind of stalemate resulting in failure to come up with what to most observers would be an effective solution to the problems of mass transportation in our country. I found an example in a recent article about how the transportation problem in the Chicago area might best be solved by a TGV train web of Detroit, Minneapolis, St. Louis with Chicago as a hub. Among other things that would make Milwaukee's Mitchell field 35 minutes from the Chicago loop and thus it could become the third Chicago regional airport and solve the huge expense of a Peotone airport, which all major airlines have already said they won't use. But, it occurred to me that for that solution to have a real chance there would have to be someone in power in the entire region—whose interest would have to be for the welfare of the whole region, rather than the competitive interests of smaller local regions like we have now. But the politicians in power in Illinois already have friends who have bought up land around Peotone and are waiting to make their profit. They would lose it if a TGV train hub were put in place instead. The politicians have little to gain in a tangible way from an improvement in regional transportation and the support of these friends to lose, if they were to take a broader view of what is best for the region as a whole.

That would suggest that if a party in power in congress succeeded in re-empowering the individual states at the expense of centralization the result might be an increase of narrow chauvinist competitiveness—which in turn could result in enough chaos to bring a majority of the people to yearn for an increase again in centralization. That thought, in turn, leads one to think about the historical development from republic to empire as Rome grew—that has been repeated in many places in the past. It seems to me that the more central the leader, the less provincial will be his scope, if he is a good one. If that is true, then the attitudes of more and more individuals would lead inexorably to favor centralization as the solution to wasteful local competition in a quasi-control system, like a country. (Along the lines that reorganization leads to higher level systems in living control systems). In the final analysis a successful reorganization lasts only as long as it succeeds in creating control systems that satisfy the survival needs of the organism. That is true whether limited to an individual or in the case where some individual's highest order Pvs are adopted as in the quasi-control system of a whole group, be it family, community, society or civilization.[144]

Different civilizations settle upon different Systems-concepts through the kind of cultural process that Spengler postulated. Once the initial group of people begins to coalesce into a new society, the normal process of controlling new perceptions tends to circumscribe which further innovations will be adopted into the growing culture. There is a nice illustration of this in a museum in Peubla, Mexico. On one wall in a long hall in the museum was a mural or multigraph of six different cultural and geographical areas between the years of 2700 BC and 1500 AD. It showed the comparative development of Meso-America, Europe, Oceania, the Near East, North Africa and the Far East. On this panoply Meso-America was shown to have been among the earliest to develop the art of pyramids and temples. But, then there was no further development in architectural and engineering skills. Instead the peoples of this region developed a high order of religious ceremony connected with a florescence in the plastic arts. They knew the wheel, but never used it for any practical applications. They continued to use only human hand work for all their practical endeavors. Their civilization persisted in that form until conquered by Cortes with his technological superiority in weapons.

Chapter 16

THE POWER OF ORDINARY PEOPLE

When a culture becomes unwieldy or disintegrates, whether it be the culture of a neighborhood, community, or whole society, established roles or niches in the social structure no longer serve as effective frameworks for living. We do not ordinarily think of the abilities of daily living as trained behavior—outside of university social and behavioral science departments—but they are. The term "social role" refers technically to the development and maintenance of the many control systems whose functions continually produce the actions that maintain one's normal existence. They serve this function by causing variables perceived by the senses to match reference values established in prior experiences. When the familiar environment undergoes change it results in disturbance to many separate controlled variables—the routines of everyday existence to which we ordinarily don't consciously attend. Then the individual's capacity for reorganizing becomes the chief factor in survival. I recommend Kaplan's (1996) *Ends of the Earth* for its illustrations of this. It is replete with examples of the creative ways that ordinary people have found to survive in places where traditional ways have been falling completely apart.

Just as there have now developed hitherto unknown types of environmental crises we are beginning to see new types of remedies. New types of interest groups deliberately pursue objectives like protecting the earth—groups like the 100 year old Sierra Club. They employ the same techniques of research and development that enabled the technological revolution which has been a source of many of the problems. Additionally, some well-educated people, especially in first world countries, are applying their understanding of the critical issues in increasing personal commitments. Some opt out of traditional lifestyles and habits—that they perceive as destructive to the natural environment—adopting alternative life styles such as homesteading ruined farms, organic farming and the like combining scientific study and personal convictions. But they are still a small minority whose experiments are further complicated by tax laws that force unrealistic evaluations of their real estate, valuing their land as comparable with the factory farms that some experts fear are ecologically unsound. Their innovative experiments in combining new and old adaptations are in a sort of race with the destructive processes.

We, in the social and life sciences, do not yet understand what makes the difference as to why one person rather than another has the insight that constitutes a great advance in civilization—whether on the level of an ordinary person's private outlook or that of a universal insight.[145] We tend to think of great insights as the necessary ingredients for improved survival or improved standards of living. Yet, in catastrophic situations just to survive can be the key challenge and many individuals can develop abilities they would never have imagined possible, because of the random element in personal reorganizations.

Many writers have an elitist view of human problem solving and progress. Thinkers like novelist Ayn Rand hold that rare and exceptional individuals have produced the great ideas and inventions. In many cases the "great person" started out as an ordinary person with what only in retrospect appears to have been vastly superior thinking ability—like Isaac Newton or Albert Einstein. Their kinds of insights require a combination of logical and intuitive ability plus the inspired use of the mathematic tool—a cultural product of many contributors. Great insights appear to result from a combination of knowledge of the tools, exceptional personal discipline and possibly some third, element, x, that we, rightly or not, think of as special intelligence. The truth is, we don't at present know whether any of these great people had extraordinary *brains* or whether the randomness of the reorganization process must be given a lot of the credit for the fact they, and not someone else, made the great contribution.

However, if Spengler was right ur-concepts are the production of savages. Highly trained people often are good at drawing unforeseen implications of a culture's axiomatic principles, but are too well organized to incur enough intrinsic error to reorganize fundamentally. My guess is that Einstein was an exceptional person by virtue of having it both ways. Ordinary people express the implications of the culture's first principles by functioning in social roles of their status in society and then either have normal lives or meet up with the pitfalls and disasters that come when conditions change drastically and their current skills fail to meet the new exigencies. Many succumb to one or another type of personal disaster in this process but statistically speaking ordinary people go on surviving hardship and desolation. While many succumb, here and there some stumble upon new ways of organizing self perceptions and concepts about the nature of reality. Others observe and copy the promising leads of those who are surviving well. Then one culture, and perhaps eventually, the world, shows new forms, unless the scope of on-coming catastrophe is overwhelming and everyone succumbs.

During major devastation and catastrophe people are

reduced to savagery and the children born to such people—like those in Kaplan's (1996) dramatic pictures—are truly new savages and must learn to survive in environments that never before existed. That is why I pointed out in an earlier chapter that writing off the hordes of "undisciplined" people living in urban ghettos or third world frontiers as mere savages who contribute nothing to the world, is probably a serious mistake. Just *to be able to keep on living* under some of these conditions requires ingenuity and the ability to develop disciplines that might well lead to new System-concepts that a future Spengler would some day see as the basis of an entirely new civilization. But, as I also pointed out earlier, we don't have the most rudimentary information about what could be called "new thinking" in these hell holes because nobody, to my knowledge, expects anything constructive to originate there.[146] The one related topic of study—of so-called "hardy children"—still hasn't revealed much about *how* they are different. What we do know suggests that under extreme conditions when learned habits are no longer functional we fall back upon our instinctual behavior reservoir—overlapping with, or identical with, what Powers called the *intrinsic system*. In the process reorganization is also frequently triggered and—because of its random component—can produce either successful adaptation or psycho-social pathology.

Animal research in the Skinnerian tradition led to the discovery that instinctive behavior gradually returns to break through conditioned training, apparently when the trained behavior is especially unnatural for the animal and is only sustained by being associated with its food supply. (Breland and Breland, 1961) Training that diverges too far from our biological inheritance—or clashes with it—results in reorganizations because our control of intrinsic variables begins to fail. Whether a populace faces catastrophe in the form of natural disaster, war or stupid or corrupt tyrannical governance some individuals find ways of changing their habits to survive.

Others then copy what proves to work. When central governments have attempted to train habits of action derived from philosophical premises—as in the Soviet Union—they essentially created tests of how well the philosophy read the nature of human nature. The outcomes have regularly showed that nature is more comprehensive, more complex and more subtle than intellectual schemes can apprehend. The Soviet leadership's supposed Marxist doctrines evolved to where they eventually required a citizen to defer his or her own survival needs in the interest of "the State." The result was increasing non-compliance, shadow economies or—from the point of view of the rulers of Soviet society: corruption. Ordinary people fell back on instinctual techniques of survival in preference to being doctrinally correct and starving. This resort to whatever works for surviving is the root of common sense. In cultures that are intact, or at least partly so, people evaluate a prescribed line of behavior—perceptual variables specified by laws, regulations or bosses—in terms of consistency with higher principles but finally—and unconsciously for the most part—with personal judgments as to whether one could survive by carrying out the commanded actions.

When survival begins to feel critical one's personal assessment of the situation is comprised of what has been called a sense of natural law by some thinkers. It can gradually lead a person to oppose rules that feel more and more artificial or unjust. I see this sort of process behind the rage of our own anti-government extremists whose ways of making a living are threatened by laws and appeals to greater "goods." Prior to such extreme steps you often see creative experiments in re-interpretations of laws and the first principles from which they are supposed to derive. An example of this sort, that arose in China of all places, was related in a *Wall Street Journal* article (Johnson, 1999). The writer described how large numbers of Chinese peasants—

joining class action lawsuits against local governments—have begun making inroads against tyrannical actions by local officials. " . . . class action lawsuits have proliferated rapidly in the past few years, as China's frustrated masses have discovered mass litigation." The article details how lawyers and politically informed local citizens have been pressing courts to uphold clauses in the communist state's civil and administrative laws aimed at preventing official abuse and environmental damage. "Although local officials resent having their authority challenged, central authorities see class action lawsuits as useful outlets for rising tensions in society . . . top leaders cautioned their local counterparts against using 'crude' and 'dictatorial' methods for dealing with dissent . . . they said the country's . . . judges and prosecutors should change to accommodate an increasingly assertive populace."

Similarly, there are innumerable examples of the power of ordinary people demanding new laws or enforcement of existing laws here in the U. S. Mothers Against Drunk Driving, the anti-gun lobby founded by the wife of Pat Brady and Senator Kennedy, women's groups against domestic violence, the various ecology and environmental groups and many others, illustrate the power ordinary people wield when they unite in efforts to obtain changes in conditions they perceive as harmful. Often these groups must struggle against the very governmental agencies officially designated to control the problems, but failing to do so. Still, opposing parties in such cases share a common feature in that each contender, as an individual, is controlling his or her perceptual variables at his or her own reference values. The agencies, courts, committees, legislators have reached their accommodations with the phenomena at hand as a result of compromises between proponents and opponents of whatever rule or law was originally there. Gradually over time a *status quo* is arrived at that tolerates a condition that the new opposition finds intolerable. They differ because of status differences and personal perspectives. Officials of government or business are not ordinary people, they are exceptional in terms of their social roles. In any society I have ever heard of the people in those roles provide themselves special treatment that protects them (to greater or lesser extents) from the conditions that constitute the problems addressed by the new lobbying groups.

The interesting feature of the operation of reform groups of all sorts is that almost invariably they apply to the commonly held Systems-concept of the nation. They argue from the sacred principles of the society, demanding that those in power live up to the precepts to which they are committed by virtue of the offices they hold. Those in power frequently oppose changes in the *status quo* in the same terms. They argue that the sacred principles are already being maintained as much as possible "under current conditions" or that the "troublemakers" are misreading them, or that they are all in agreement and remedy is on the way but it needs more time. When those in power blithely laugh at constitutions and traditions, as with the Nazis under Hitler or the communist party elite under Stalin, the sacred principles degenerate and the ground is laid for radical reorganization of the society although the control of brute force by those in power might succeed in delaying it for a long time.

Interestingly enough the bloodless revolutions that occur gradually as a major portion of a populace begins to slip around, then dilute, then ignore and finally confront unlivable control from above are the ones that usually are most effective. Bloody revolutions, such as the French and the Russian seem, at least for a time, to open the route for psychopaths to improve on the predations of the previous tyrants.

The sexual revolution throughout most of Western Civilization is still one of the best examples of such bloodless revolutions. There have been isolated instances of celebrated or notorious individuals living "freelove" lifestyles for a very long time. But, they only got away with it through being somehow lovable for other reasons (like popular heroes or famous actresses), and/or possessing high enough status to have the power to fight off attempts at sanctioning them. Why did the sexual revolution occur at just the point in time that it did? One source was certainly the chronic pressure of human physiology. The intrinsic Reference signals involving lust had become more critical sources for triggering reorganization by virtue of the postponement of the typical marriage age in the lengthening out of maturation that accompanied modern industrial society. Furthermore, it could not really have escaped the notice of ordinary people that kings and queens and princes and princesses frequently disregarded the strictures on adultery and bigamy. In fact Henry the eighth practiced both combined with opportunistic murders while claiming to be God's representative on earth. Most ordinary people at such times knew enough to keep their opinions about such things to themselves, but some of them must have concluded that what those exalted people did must be what humans in general are predisposed to do if no one is coercing them into other paths. Finally, the time came when no one was coercing them with enough force to prevent the breakdown of old patterns the hypocrisy of which anyone could hardly be blind to any longer. Thus, when "the Pill" reduced the sanctions imposed by nature the artificial ones of moral opinion had already suffered considerable deterioration.

Ordinary people are gaining power in other ways besides the reorganizations occurring from intrinsic-system error states in vulnerable members of humanity.[147] As young people begin to realize the once hardly imaginable implications of new technology their mastery of it has catapulted many into positions of power that formerly would have taken a lifetime for a few to achieve. Davidson's and Rees-Mogg's (1997) thesis on this point seems persuasive—where they argue that new technological developments have tipped the balance of power in favor of the small against the large on several fronts. The two most important scales are those of the vastly superior development of small weaponry compared to massive weaponry, and, even more far-reaching, the power that the internet affords to almost anyone with discipline and creativity. They see the end result of these developments as a net increase of the power of individuals *vis a vis* that of large, unwieldy organizations such as, especially, national states. Another source of power of ordinary people is the growth of popular, and self directed, education. Through the availability of information of all sorts—how to do it, whether home repairs, or self training in everything from foreign language to science, or one's own health care—anyone can acquire the equivalent of a university education. The process has now greatly accelerated because of the internet, people are gaining greater power to control more and more aspects of physical and intellectual growth and survival.

The internet, itself, has proven a liberating instrument for creativity as young people, in almost playful moods, have produced programs and systems and then simply given them away, sometimes out of idealism, sometimes out of insouciance, sometimes out of calculated strategies to enroll future patrons. Petzinger (1999) in an article about "Four Web Rebels" tells how some young internet experts challenge corporate America to grasp that the Internet is a communications medium, not simply a marketing tool. The writer refers to several instances of, "the Internet [possessing] such bottom-up power . . . [as] about the free Linux operating system, the MP3 music standard and the advent of on-line auctions, three of the hottest movements on the Net? All involve people to people conversations . . . ." The article, and scores of others like it, helps us recognize something that has perhaps always been true about the power of ordinary people and that is that people at large enjoy interacting with each other and when free of interference create a never ending supply of practical inventions and fertile ideas simply in the course of being playful and sociable.

Members of friendship and kin groups have always participated in "adult education" by sharing information, suggestions, advice and skill training. With the expansion of the number of such groups in the virtual relationships of the Internet the dissemination of all kinds of practical information and advice has exploded. All kinds of lore and useful rules of thumb formerly husbanded in various scientific disciplines are now disseminated to world wide audiences that any one can employ in personal improvement programs. Dieting advice, workout and strength building information, health food information, and a host of other things are now part of the common treasury of practical information. (Regrettably also, recipes for such things as bomb making.) For another example, I would like to offer a small contribution of my own, passing on a little formula for training someone to do something. It comes from the psychology of learning, and unlike a lot of academic theory of learning, I have found it useful in many ordinary situations. In addition it provides one more practical illustration of the explanatory power of the newer view. Edwin R. Guthrie, in his "theory" of learning (before the advent of PCT), described many concrete instances of behavior from which he drew a generalization that: *We learn what we do*. What he meant by that is that concrete behavior—entailing actual movements of the body in skilled performances—is learned through the exact recording of the particular perceptual signals of the original actions. These then are drawn from memory as the References for subsequent performances of what we would call the "same" behavior. Thus, it is essential actually to "make the moves" that bring the desired result, and to avoid as much as possible incorporating any non-essential or mistaken moves.

One of Guthrie's examples showed how he helped a mother train an adolescent daughter in a new habit of hanging up her street clothes, instead of throwing them on the floor when she came in. Guthrie advised the mother to be sure to be present when her daughter came in, and upon seeing the clothes thrown on the floor to insist that the daughter put them back on, back out the door, come in again and then take off her coat and immediately hang it in the closet. It worked.

Guthrie's "theory" of learning was of the most elementary sort of science. It essentially consisted of a generalization from a series of observations, which he then tested out by applying it in practical situations like the one above. Nevertheless, he had hit upon something that I could later make sense of, and extend, with perceptual control theory. A repeated act or behavioral habit occurs via the activation of a hierarchy of control systems each one having its own form of "memory." For the overall action to occur there must already be a recording in memory that the highest order (in this case, Program) supplies as the Reference condition for its subordinate level. (And so on all the way down to the muscle tension intensities in moving arms and legs.) Each subordinate level must have its own type of memory to supply the reference commanding the system below. Learning or training *consists of* making the whole sequence of correct actions, including all the required movements, so as to build the necessary memory recordings. If any of the necessary movements fails to be executed, some Reference values will fail to be recorded. Hence, to issue an abstract command like, "next time please hang up your clothes," is a different type of behavior. It stays wholly on the ideational level. On that level the answer, "Oh, yes, I'll do that." seems fully appropriate. One idea is matched verbally with the other, but no changes in the pre-existing muscular movement recordings have taken place.

I made a personally satisfying practical application of this analysis on my first job after my master's degree. I was working as a combination counselor/foreman in an industrial training shop employing welfare recipients. They had been judged to need training because of not having work habits appropriate to the kinds of simple factory work that could help them get off welfare. We supervisors came from two different kinds of backgrounds. One type were former actual industry foremen and the other were "college kids," like me. There was a certain amount of rivalry between the groups as to who really knew the most useful things for achieving our goals. One day our boss threw up his hands in frustration over the fact that a new job—assembly of a mechanical toy—was way behind schedule because the trainees kept making mistakes and had piled up more scrap than usable items. The foreman-type supervisor maintained that the job was too complicated for the trainees to learn. The boss asked me if I wanted a crack at it. I saw it as an opportunity to apply a "scientific" approach to the problem. I watched the supervisor train a new trainee, noting that it took him about an hour to train one person, who then made about 50% scrap. I asked to be trained myself, taking notes about each step in the sequence of moves. Then I set out to employ my version of the Guthrie-Powers approach. The first error I saw in the prior training program was that the supervisor and trainee sat facing each other, thus causing the trainee to see every movement in mirror-image. Next, the trainee did not always understand the shoptalk words that the supervisor used so that he sometimes had already made a wrong move before being ordered to correct it.

It occurred to me that the trainees would not need to be shown anything initially. That would eliminate the wrong mirror-image perception. All the movements could be instructed verbally by saying things like, "First, take the large round piece and set it in front of you with the holes-side up. Then put each of the four springs, one in each hole," etc.

That made it possible to have twelve people sitting in a circle around a large table all doing the same thing at the same time, hearing the verbal instructions. That gained a further advantage that had not occurred to me. They looked at each other, insuring that each one was doing the same actions as his peers. This made the person who grasped the correct move first into a spontaneous leader. As they perceived and copied the right move all were spared the embarrassment of making a wrong move. Within an hour they had produced 24 functioning toys with no scrap and with no wrong moves needing redirection. Clearly a win for "science."

 I tell this story as a concrete instance of the way "lore for living" is spread through all our kinds of communication events. I also hope you might find it useful when you want to show someone how to do something, if you weren't already aware of "Guthrie's principle." I have since used the same approach to train computer-illiterate graduate assistants in programming and or word processing by standing behind them and telling them what keys to press until they have produced a recognizable product. Thereby you can completely eliminate the "watch-me" phase that almost guarantees some misperceptions of what is to be done. The biggest problem with allowing any misperceptions is the one that Guthrie had come upon empirically. A wrong movement, once enacted, continues cropping up to frustrate the learner. Powers's contribution was to show why. It doesn't apply only to movement skills. I have found it also applies to learning a foreign language. When in the foreign country the phrases and sentences that actually come to mind when they are needed are the ones I have heard myself say *out loud* during learning. That kind of drill recorded the sounds that I needed to hear from myself in the real life situation.

 A second reason for telling this story was to illustrate how exchanging concrete information enlarges the general fund of knowledge of all of us. Especially when we nowadays enhance this process with knowledge gained from "scientific method."[148] This method, developed painstakingly from Aristotle on, was given a great boost by Galileo, who showed the value of using modeling to get at the underlying mechanism of how a process works. It is coming to be a part of the repertory of more and more ordinary people, no longer a tool of scientific specialists. PCT contributes to this development. It does so by virtue of going from generalizations about observable phenomena to plausible mechanisms for *why* they work as they do. More fundamental understandings give more grasp of where and how the generalizations apply.

Another personal experience illustrates the value of looking for the generalization *after* making the mechanical moves routine (so you don't have to be thinking about mechanics while examining the underlying principles). After starting high school algebra with a teacher who had us copy exemplary problems and then discussed how they were alike I moved on to another teacher whose method consisted of stating the principles involved verbally. My grades went from A to D. I couldn't understand what had happened. I concluded, like so many others after an initial setback, that I didn't have any aptitude for math. Years later, after learning PCT, where it helps to know a little math, I struggled to get deeper into it by making another sortie into algebra.

I made a surprising discovery, reflecting back on my high school experience. I realized that with the second teacher, when he gave his verbal explanations I pictured in my mind the conditions he outlined and thought to myself, "OK, I understand that." But I was not laying down in memory the concrete sequence of steps that you must go through when you actually write out a problem. Getting any step out of order is fatal. But that is all too easy to do when you are only remembering what you hear without actually going through the moves you make in writing it out. There are countless examples of this. Watch kids learning to play chess. They actually pick up the pieces and move them around above the board to see what the pattern looks like. Only after a period of doing that concretely can they perform it purely in their head. Or, when kids are learning to read—when practicing pronouncing the words—they can't remember what the story was about. They were busy recording the mechanics of pronunciation. Only when enough of those recordings have been stored does it come automatically, so that attention can shift up to the next level. In my second venture into math I did not neglect to "make the moves" even when I was sure I understood the steps involved. It worked.

You might notice that the above discussion was an example of the point being made. I tried to illustrate my admonition about being specific by relating actual experiences. Instead of giving you the generalization and allowing you to flesh it out with what ever of your own experiences my words would elicit, I asked you to understand my propositions in terms of the experiences from which they were formed. General semanticists used to call that, "going down the ladder of abstraction." As an illustration of controlling perceptual variables I would describe it as my desire for you to have the same pictures in mind as I had so that we would be talking about the same things on a concrete level. You might go on to draw different generalizations but at least we shared the same starting points.

I had not thought of it until writing this but I have suddenly gained a little more sympathy for the people on TV talk shows. I have often wondered what the audiences are looking for, besides the satisfaction of feeling superior to the dysfunctional humans on display. After talking about the value of concrete recordings of behavior, I moved on unconsciously to generalize that, *specificity enhances communication*. My next step, again unconscious, was an error signal—or, cognitive dissonance—from the inconsistency between that formulation and something I must have been harboring about seeing a snatch of one of those shows on TV. Still reflecting on the question of why people watch that sort of thing, it occurred to me that they show, in an indisputable fashion, what thoughts and acts people are capable of that formerly many of us would have thought were unique to ourselves. Perhaps that is enlarging everyone's understanding of the range of possible human behavior. The participants—seeing that the audience has not immediately pounced upon them and torn them to shreds for being disgusting beyond belief—might actually experience some healing in finding that they remain a part of human society. If there is anything to these speculations it would be that the voyeurism of watching social pathology of seemingly ordinary people is a *possible* additional avenue by which ordinary people enhance power to survive—by increasing the range of knowledge of what is human.

One other instance of the power of ordinary people is that anyone can think of explanations for a process interesting to her-or himself, that might simplify some aspect of reality. Each attempt at doing something is an experiment potentially enabling a step forward into the unknown. More often than not these speculations turn out to be wrong. The experiments fail. This is just as true for the great minds of the world as for the average person, yet if one is open to disconfirmation, the failure of an insight to satisfy the objective toward which it was aimed may start the reorganization process that leads to further progress. My personal satisfaction of this sort comes when I have thought I could see an underlying unity among phenomena that seemed unrelated on the surface.

Just as Isaak Newton found an underlying "something in common" in water flowing downhill, apples falling from trees and the moon and planets staying in their respective orbits, and then proved it out with mathematics, I have thought to find a common element in the decline of cultures and the birth of new ones in the human process of ordinary people controlling their own perceptions under the ultimate tutelage of the "drive" to survive. Bork, Kennedy, Lukacs, Ortega, Davidson and Rees-Mogg and all the other prophets of the decline of Western Civilization have offered differing proposals as to why and how it happens. But, for me they are all surface aspects of Spengler's and Kuhn's more profound theses that first principles in any system of thought have a finite capacity for useful implications and eventually become exhausted as members of the culture keep drawing derivations from first principles to arrive at new rules for the normal conduct of affairs. This view, in turn, seemed further illuminated by the explanation that behavior—including what we ordinarily call thinking—is a control process in which the most abstract principles ("Systems-concepts") limit the scope of lesser control systems in an interlocking hierarchy. All subordinate control systems act to maintain the superior ones in minimal error condition and thereby their freedom of operation is limited by the requirements of "truth" (minimal error state) of each higher order in the system.

We can so far not check these speculations mathematically as Newton did for his. However, adherents of PCT (most notably Rick Marken and Tom Bourbon) have begun to model hierarchical control system networks and have confirmed the first point: that superior systems limit the scope of subordinate systems that they control. They have done this using computer programming to model simplified aspects of behavior using the mathematics of control theory that Powers applied to explicate the nature of behavior. This new paradigm helps us move from philosophical speculations about such things as "historical forces" and prompts us to look at how humans, functioning as living control systems, both extend and limit their power in the real world.

In the following chapters I want to give examples of applying informal analyses in going about the search for individual solutions to difficult problems, using the applications that have been developed so far. This starts with the practice of formulating *the desired state of affairs* as a starting point for thinking about any conditions that one might hope to see changed. My thesis for the present chapter has been that simply by doing that and sharing it with whomever you can we will exert the maximum effort toward bringing about changes that humankind needs to keep moving ahead. Even if neither of us has the political or economic power to force others to do what we want we will accomplish the maximum benefit simply by accomplishing our personal goals and communicating what we learn in doing so. For that is wherein the power of ordinary people lies. When those with the political or economic power to enact laws do so on the basis of what everyone agrees-to coercion is minimized. When that is not so coercion is ultimately ineffective, because, in the longest run, it rests upon a view of behavior that is not how behavior works.

Chapter 17

PERCEIVING THE FUTURE

In Part One I reviewed the issues various writers perceive as a crisis in Western Civilization that simultaneously constitutes a world crisis. Then I focused upon the role of thought—its adaptability or lack of it—as a basic factor in many of the issues. I adopted Spengler's thesis on that point: The most fruitful implications of the basic premises of our culture have been drawn out to the point where they are beginning to conflict with each other. Basic assumptions or first principles are re-interpreted again and again until they begin to defy common sense, as different individuals and groups contend with each other to realize their own desired versions of specific states of affairs. I proposed that that notion of Spengler's makes more sense when understood within a new paradigm of behavior as control of perception. I sketched out this paradigm shift in the psychology of behavior informally and gave a brief outline of the basics.

In Part Three I expanded the most distinct version of the new behavior paradigm in more formal theory terms and began to draw its implications for new insights about individual and social conduct. Among other things I attempted to show further how the phenomena Spengler discerned actually come about via the control efforts of individuals attempting to maintain their personally desired conditions against disturbances from others' initiatives in society. In this last part I continue to demonstrate how a better understanding of behavior holds promise of improved efforts to marshall practical action—how ordinary people often spontaneously find their individual efforts harmonizing for overcoming obstacles to survival in difficult times. As ordinary people begin to employ new paradigms for perceiving reality—along with the new intellectual and material tools currently being developed—they will simultaneously create the groundwork of a new civilization. What that will turn out to be holds many possibilities at this point.

Consider the future envisioned by Davidson and Rees-Mogg (1997). It appears to forecast a modern version of the Dark Ages in which powerful, "sovereign individuals," or modern barons will compete with each other beyond the control of any supervening government. They argue further that ordinary people who master niches in the cyber revolution are gaining a new form of power—becoming the new information elite. Their knowledge would be to the new baron's as Galileo's was to the princes of his day. Perhaps we are seeing the first wave of such a phenomenon. Witness the surge of youthful Silicon Valley millionaires whose ability to affect political and cultural developments is at present mainly unrealized. What will be their conception of how the world should look when they begin turning their attention to that question?

However, I am confining my attention to derivations from PCT as a resource for attempting to deal individually and collectively with the impact of crisis in our own lives. It is also presently mainly untapped and unrealized, but it better explains something that psychotherapists, Zen gurus, and other coaches of personal efficiency, have been urging for the last generation or two, but without understanding the mechanism underlying their pragmatic observations. Namely, that *talking about* goals, fantasies, dreams, and wishes for improvements accomplishes two kinds of objective. First, acts of communication, themselves, promote well being and insight. Second, it constitutes a form of perceiving the future that—when shared by others—begins to function as self-fulfilling prophecy. When a person experiences a creative notion as desirable it becomes a Reference perception; the "idea"[149] begins, even automatically and unconsciously, to effect its own realization. And when ordinary people, en masse, share both their perceptions of current reality, and their Reference perceptions for a desired reality they are beginning jointly to bring about the future.

I emphasize the role of ordinary people in creating and developing the shape and future of culture and civilization in contrast with the "great man" or crucial-event theories of cultural evolution. I don't dispute that particular individuals, who made outstanding contributions at various junctures in history, might have been specially gifted. Nor that the challenges of climate, topography, history and human competition are important facts in understanding the evolution of a given culture. But, such theories subtly perpetuate the tendency to see things from the external, or "objective" frame of reference. They don't encourage one to focus attention on *how* individuals struggle to master crisis situations, controlling their environments in new ways. The environment does not *cause* behavior. Environment is the aggregate of conditions that people control *with* behavior.

We control it to our specifications, to the extent that is in our power.[150] When we are in good control of the environment we tend to keep things constant. When it changes we must exert effort to correct the error between what we now perceive and what we intend to perceive. When the environmental challenge is beyond one's control capacity we are forced to reorganize. When that is successful we have learned something—we are able to do something that we could not previously do. When many members of the society adopt the new practice and benefit we have the innovation that can be looked back upon as a crucial turning point.

For a somewhat parallel view, compare page 244 and following in Jared Diamond's (1998), *Guns, Germs and Steel*:

> THUS, THE COMMONSENSE view of invention that served as our starting point reverses the usual roles of invention and need. It also overstates the importance of rare geniuses....

This author devotes himself to the question of why, throughout history, one society and culture won out over its competitors. In a masterfully presented series of arguments he makes the case that multiple, interacting factors—climate, geography, the kind of food supply available or able to be developed, the amount of traffic with neighbors and their relative power, and such—can be intensively analyzed to account for the likelihood of the competition coming out as it did in each case. In the section referred to above he documents many instances of innovations—which for one reason or another, were not recognized or taken up—even though comparable and often prior to those that have gone down in history as turning points in the progress of civilization.

Underlying Diamond's argument, as in almost all contemporary writing in the life sciences, is what I call the Cartesian-paradigm assumption about the nature of behavior. Namely that factors of the environment determine human behavior. We see cause and effect the other way round. The qualities of the environment constitute the variables which any organism's control-hierarchy must bring to the organism's specifications. For example, if the environment is very cold, control activity must result in maintaining warmth. If the environment is very hot, temperature at the body boundary must be kept down. There are often many alternative ways to do each of such tasks.

Diamond's tacit depiction of environment as the causative agent does not pose an obstacle to appreciating his work. I am used to reframing automatically "factors" that supposedly determine behavior. I see them, instead, as the material or source of perceptual variables that humans (and other animals) maintain at values appropriate to survival.

How this bears upon the relationship between ordinary people and invention is as follows. All the various conditions that Diamond outlines in showing how one society has gotten a better shake in the distribution of opportunities than another, are both the challenges to their survival and the natural resources for dealing with them. From the external point of view inherent in the Cartesian paradigm the traditional conception of cause and effect leads one to perceive these conditions as compelling the particular coping behavior that resulted, as stated above. The internal point of view—how the individuals in a given group perceive environmental contingencies—has to do with the nature of their thinking. How members of a society control their environment (indirectly as a function of controlling perceptions), is a function of how they perceive, formulate and conjure with it. All that depends upon both innate intellectual ability and the resources already part of their particular culture.

"They" in this instance refers to the group as a whole, and simultaneously the individuals in it separately. We are all individually attempting to control the various features of our environment that comprise our living conditions. Some do better than others. When one organizes new behavior that solves a heretofore insoluble problem, that makes her or him an innovator. Until then he or she was often just an ordinary person.

No one thinks that every human being would perceive the same environment in the same way. Neither is there usually one and only one solution to an environmental challenge. That is not to deny that some individuals might possess superior thinking ability, although many other considerations enter into the question of who gets perceived as a genius in a given place and time, as Diamond suggests in the material cited. All the members of the society share, though probably unequally, the ways of thinking that are inherited from one's culture. That is one of the two types of resource for confronting challenge. That is what Spengler was talking about. But this resource has limitations that Spengler noted: a given culture's forms of thought contribute both resources and restraints to the ingenuity with which members of a culture meet challenges.

The other influence—the one identified by Powers—is the role of chance in reorganizations in the face of uncontrolled challenges. Because of the random element in individual reorganization different persons come up with different solutions to challenges for reasons that can not be identified. When different members of a society innovate different approaches to a given challenge, other factors besides efficiency enter into the determination of which one gets adopted.

Diamond (1998) relates various examples of peoples seemingly resisting tools and techniques that could have benefitted them. He even found instances of giving up tools and techniques that a people already had. He does not explore deeply into why that might be, nor for that matter how it comes about that someone does develop a successful solution to a challenge, because that is not where his focus lies. But, it is our focus here, though only in a general sense. The explanation is found in taking Spengler's and Powers's points together. Techniques for researching questions about why anyone, or no one, in a given culture perceives a solution to a given challenge lie in studies of creativity, as modified by the idea that innovations are accepted or rejected by a society in terms of their consistency with accepted basic notions about reality, and further modified by understanding that it might not be possible to nail down the role of chance in the reorganization of a person's brain circuitry that results in the "Eureka."

What we have developed so far, especially in the last century, are various procedures and rudimentary rules of thumb for fostering innovation or creativity rather than simply waiting for successful reorganization to occur. The title for this chapter is meant to emphasize this view. Behavior is an active process not a reflex mechanism caused by "forces" of the environment. As I treat the crises pointed up in Part One as the challenges currently affecting the quality of individual and group survival in our culture what we perceive—the way we perceive this looming future world—constitutes the environment that we must learn to master. If I have made my point so far you can see that what one perceives—in a given crisis—becomes, itself, the challenge that one's behavior attempts to control. Let us examine further the applications that we might begin to draw from thinking about behavior in that way.

Recognizing and formulating goals—Reference values—out loud, so to speak, is the first step. The reason I say, "Out loud," is that we often do not recognize clearly what we have been thinking until we hear ourselves say it (whether in speech or writing). It highlights the cultural value of letters to the editor, political discussions in parks, living rooms or bars, and other ways of stating in public one's view of how one would like the world to be. Anyone who thinks, "My ideas are not important because I have no political or economic power," needs to recognize each such instance as a tiny increment in the intellectual atmosphere that creates the broth of ideas in which new insights gel.

It is also essential to have a clear perception of how things are. This leads automatically to recognizing the degree of match or mismatch between the perceived condition and the desired condition. One of my criticisms of current lawmaking practices is just this neglect of necessary elements for control. The desired state is all too often left to be inferred in the wording of laws and rulings. Likewise the perception of the existing or current condition is ordinarily not defined. That allows for serious mismatches between what legislators intended and what public servants execute. Worst of all, there is ordinarily never any means provided for detecting the match between desired and existing conditions.

If it were to become a legislative habit for laws and regulations to be formulated so as to make each of these elements explicit in measurable terms it would be a big step toward the elimination of useless, nonproductive legislating. As things are now we as a society pay a large cost in terms of disrespect for meaningless legislation. Disrespect not only for the particular law or regulation but also for those behind such silly or insincere endeavors. The issue of gaining compliance with meaningful laws and regulations is closely related to a body of social science research, going back over a couple of generations, that convincingly shows that the best way to secure compliance is to satisfy the needs of both the promulgators and subjects. When that is not the case you have a power issue—between those trying to control others and those intended as the subjects of control. Recall that control systems resist disturbance to the conditions that they control. The only way that one control system can bring a variable under control by another control system—to a different Reference value—is with overwhelming force. In human terms that always means violence.

The resort to violence has short-run appeal in many situations because overwhelming force enables the dominator to control a perceived condition to his specification no matter what the dominated party is trying to control it to. We all learned about that as toddlers. It did not occur to us then that there could be consequences to just grabbing what we wanted from another child. As one becomes socialized one learns the value of mutual benefits. And, as civilization has progressed in the West, people have begun to create new definitions and new consequences pertaining to violence. The concepts of *war crimes* and *genocide* are beginning to shape the definition of civilization on the part of the most powerful nations. We have never before in history seen such an effort to set limits upon the use of violence.

The U. S. as the currently dominant world power is exerting some influence in this direction on the whole world. A cynical view would note that the rule makers do not rigorously apply the rules to themselves. But, I would argue that the implicit principle—that any *people* in the world may not be extinguished with impunity—has the quality of a goal for the future of the world that will not likely ever be rescinded. It has the appeal of "natural law." It appeals to anyone who can foresee the possibility of being less powerful than someone else *sometime* whether or not at present. I would think that applies to anyone who understands the notion of *consequences*; that is, everyone, except psychopaths and primitives.

Thus, simply by virtue of formulating and acting upon such a principle, as was developed at Nurenberg, or applied recently in the former Yugoslavia, even those adversely affected by it at the moment, would not appeal that such a rule should not exist. They might argue that it is incorrectly applied to themselves, but it is hard to imagine anyone saying that it is a lousy rule. This is one of the most powerful demonstrations that "ideas have consequences." Someone had to have that idea, and say it out loud, and have it repeated by others, and have many more think and say, "That makes sense." Thus, a desired perception was born and began to reshape the nature of the world's future. I would suggest that this is the process by which consensus—the jelling of opinion that is found in paradigmatic revolutions—comes about.

The concept of war crimes, as it was developed at the end of World War II, conformed, however imperfectly, to all the elements of effective control. The perceived condition—the extermination of an entire ethnic group (almost) could clearly be compared to the desired condition. And the allied forces possessed the effective mechanism for resolving their own error—although that was not actually implemented until fifty years later in Bosnia and Kosovo.

What would be a comparable situation when many citizens of a nation perceive themselves as relatively powerless in regard to their own rulers? Some critics (like Davidson and Rees-Mogg, 1997) argue that that already obtains currently in the United States of America. First the perception: that the government is only minimally responsive to the needs of ordinary citizens (as was the case with the Roman Senate in the time before Caesar was proposed for kingship). Next, that the current situation departs seriously from the desired state of affairs; in fact it threatens the survival of those holding that perception. Finally that the control system in question has the capacity to reduce the error state.

We have several versions of individuals attempting to reduce the error state in their personal perceptions of the present political situation. There are continual calls for "greater accountability" on the part of members of congress, in the media and in the everyday thinking of ordinary people. There is also an increasing lawlessness—not only on the part of business leaders, but also of private citizens, when they begin to think that conditions vital to their survival are jeopardized and no one else can be counted upon to correct them. In what follows I shall proceed by examining instances of good and bad attempts to achieve control over out-of-control aspects of our present national life. Then in the final chapter I describe some tactics to survive at the level of individual and family in a wider world that I am sure will not conform very well to my preferred image nor that of many other ordinary persons.

The Macro Scale

Though I accept the argument that our civilization is in some sort of crisis, as I look at the living conditions of my family, friends and neighbors I find myself wondering whether the apparently increasing numbers of random murders, global warming, the gradual degradation of the environment, the growth of ethnic and religious strife, the proliferating predictions of imminent recession—whether the gloomy pictures of such conditions are in fact real danger signs, or really reflect the tendency of communications media to report negative conditions almost exclusively. As some counter-critics argue, the average living conditions are improving gradually around the globe and local setbacks keep being resolved in the long run. The very fact that I can't answer the question satisfactorily is a source of unease despite my sense of personal well-being as "good enough."

At any one moment in time most victims of man-made disasters—from stupid resource management, pollution, genocides, random murders, such as Oklahoma City, and Columbine, drunken drivers, etc.—have seemed to have their lives sufficiently under control like almost everyone I know personally. Then in the twinkling of an eye have had it all overturned, ending up devastated and homeless almost overnight. Or, led by psychopaths or scam artists into bankruptcy or worse like death traps, Jonestown or Waco. The statistics might suggest that becoming a victim of any one of these tragedies is no more likely than being hit by lightning, or killed in a plane crash. However, unlike being hit by lightning, all these catastrophes directly or indirectly resulted from human behavior. In principle, different behavior in those instances would not have resulted in the disaster.

This reminds us of Farmer's (1977) thesis, that humans' power to affect our future has grown so greatly in recent decades that we have come to have extravagant expectations about it especially in dominant countries like the U. S. But, I find this incomplete. The material successes of our culture might have helped produce these extravagant expectations, but if you accept the contention of Soros (1998) that Capitalism has finally produced human problems that it is not capable of resolving, it looks like a case illustration of Spengler's hypothesis about the decline of a tradition of thought. The Western World's fundamental principles, that provided the groundwork for Capitalism, can not produce the cure for its faults. The real failure might not be in the theory of Capitalism itself, but in the fact that it is only an effective practice for the production and distribution of goods. It has no means of dealing with all the other considerations of full human life. It has evolved, like the concept of science as "value neutral" within the Western tradition of analytic thinking that produced the separation of ethical and esthetic feelings from the strategies for controlling the environment.

The notion of value neutrality in science, while initially productive, has allowed the creation of, among other horrors, atomic bombs. Yes, if the U. S. had not produced them first, Germany would have. But, that is no argument; both are Western countries and their scientists operated on the same philosophic principles. Is it possible to imagine a civilization dominating the world in which it would be unthinkable to *any* scientist (or national leader) to produce such a thing? Yes, it is possible to *imagine* it, just watch enough Star Trek programs. Whether it could be a human civilization seems like an unanswerable question at the present time. The overextended development of this principle is more easily criticized in business and law, I think. In recent years the newspapers and TV expose shows such as *60 Minutes* have featured over and over legal decisions that go against the human feelings of masses of ordinary people.

The argument that implicitly excuses these outrages is a variant of value neutrality: that the abstract principle must be preserved even when it results in insane consequences in particular instances. In business decisions a different variant results in frequent instances of degrading the physical environment as if the despoilers had some other place to live with the profits gained from destroying the earth. It is coming into focus presently as we see corporations losing suits in which they are found guilty of putting small gains in profit above potential loss of life. Still another variant is in the argument that violence in movies and television is not an influence in the behavior of those individuals who display violence in real life. Research in developmental psychology has shown that imitation is one of the earliest forms of learning and continues to be influential throughout life. You don't have to be an expert in this research. Most observant parents have realized this and use it in training children. Likewise, the video games in which youth can get real practice in aiming guns and the like have recently been shown to have been used by young men implicated in several school massacres. However, the arguments against restricting these forms of merchandising, as with the publication of books on bomb building or how to commit murders, rest basically upon the separation of the valuing of the quality of life from the valuing of selling anything anyone will purchase. At its core value-neutrality has turned out to be a form of linear one-dimension-at-a-time thinking.

I do tentatively accept Soros's critique. I don't have the economic skills to evaluate the argument, so I defer to his judgment for the moment as to the economics. But, I find his position on the divorce of human values from the conduct of commerce well taken. After all he has what I consider superior credentials in this subject. Though our distant hunter/gatherer ancestors were more vulnerable than we to natural disasters, and sometimes conquest by heartless invaders, the several aspects of their lives were much more integrated than are the corresponding aspects of present day lives. Their very inventions didn't turn against them.

This line of thought brought me back to my personal sense of things, where my argument began. Though I'm at present reasonably comfortable myself, I'm disturbed that the numbers of homeless people do not seem to be declining, that the numbers of drug addicts are not decreasing, that random massacres seem to be increasing even while "normal" murders are on the decline, that the world seems a more chaotic place than it was before the war to end all wars. I am affronted that so many members of the U. S. congress seem to be captives of powerful special interests with the result that initiatives to solve many different problems are stymied year after year. I worry that future historians will look back on these years and speculate about just when the United States ceased to be a democracy.

Our legislators are for the most part not malevolent people. I see them controlling their contingencies within the environment that they perceive, as any good control systems would. I firmly suspect you and I would likely do about the same in their place. If this is true, we live our lives by habits that apply to a system that is beginning to malfunction. And the most serious aspect of the malfunction is that efforts at correction malfunction as well. While this view of things might sometime prove contrary to the "real facts" it is the fact for all who perceive it that way, for as long as we do. It comprises the field of disturbances to the conditions that we control routinely in normal living.

The apparent intractability of our political-economic system is the fault of the leaders of our society, if you accept Warner's (1941, 1953) view that society is one large quasi-hierarchical control system. The social class hierarchy corresponds roughly to the hierarchy of control. The members of the upper-upper class (in Warner's terms) have the most power. They exercise it, for the most part, by enunciating/formulating/defining the conception and values that differentiate our nation (and more remotely our civilization) from others. Their values supply the highest level of Reference values. The outputs constitute the qualities that define the national identity. National "interests" are derived as the conditions necessary to preserve the national identity. They function to define the objectives of policies that are embodied in the passage of laws and the interpretations of the courts.

Let me emphasize, however, that, contrary to what some liberal critics and media insinuate, it is a mistake to view the members of the highest social class as selfishly sacrificing the well-being of the rest of us. Selfish, yes, to the same extent that each of us is. Each of us, organized as a hierarchical control system maximizing control of one's own perceived environment, automatically functions to achieve and maintain one's own values. To do otherwise would mean going into internal conflict, some sub-systems neutralizing the function of opposing ones. Good control systems do not function that way for very long. Control systems only change their own organization—reorganize—when existing structure fails to reduce error in intrinsic systems, that is, in our biological survival mechanisms. In everyday parlance: we don't change unless we have to. "Have to" in highly organized social systems occurs in natural disasters, wars, revolutions or responses to radical changes in the physical environment like persistent earthquakes, floods, ice ages or global winter, or occurs in personal catastrophes perpetrated by the consequences of particular legal and business decisions.

This immediately suggests two weaknesses in any approach to reform in a highly organized society like ours. First of all, most reformers work like lobbyists (which they often are) to mobilize the aspirations of a mass of ordinary people—their constituents—to impinge, especially, on judges and legislators. But those people by and large function in a manner that corresponds to the level of Programs in Powers's theory. One can infer at least two levels higher, that on which Principles/policies are propounded, and above that the level controlling System concepts, the *source* of Principles and policies. Maybe a few legislators, and fewer judges, are members of what Warner called the Upper-upper class—the level whose members define what the proper nature of our civilization is. But, most are not; they are members of the next layer down. Upper-upper class members function by suggesting to the legislators and judges what the basic identity and principles of our society *are* and what policies ought to be pursued to keep them intact.

Occasionally a member of the highest social status perceives the development of serious flaws in the fabric of society, and, as did Count Leo Tolstoy, advocates radical changes. This can provide powerful support to reformers (who mainly originate from the upper *Middle* Class in Warner's analysis), but only in regard to specific issues. If the structure of the civilization begins to be riddled with internal contradictions, that constitutes the kind of turmoil that the majority of the Upper-upper class find themselves compelled to suppress. Even though many individuals might personally feel great sympathy for people who are adversely affected by the current dysfunctions, their personal organization is predisposed by tradition and training to resist radical changes in the images and concepts that define society.

Members of the upper-upper class have reason to identify their personal lives and values with the traditions of their culture to a greater extent than members of any other class. Their names include those of the founders of the society. Their lands and business properties have histories traceable back to its beginnings. Their family traditions consciously or unconsciously reinforce notions that they *should* interpret the basic axioms and define the practical values/Principles—giving commands, however subtly—to the "official" governors of society, such as members of the government.[151]

So, the first obstacle to effective reform in a highly structured society is that it creates errors in the variables under control by the most powerful citizens—in the sense of monitoring the highest order of Reference signals. Thereby reform efforts inevitably incur their opposition. The second weakness is that the efforts for change most commonly do not even impinge directly upon the intrinsic systems of those who occupy the loftiest positions in society. In everyday terms, the most powerful members of society are going to be the last ones to feel the impact of its dysfunction. (*Power*, in this context could be defined in terms of relative ability to neutralize errors—that is, to resist disturbance to one's familiar state of affairs).

The usual efforts of reformers, whether by petition or violence, fail even to make contact with members of the upper-upper class. Instead, they generally address legislators, judges, bureaucrats and officials, whose decisions affect everyday living in either remote or immediate fashion. The *way* that they address them is either to assert "rights" defined by the constitution, or sometimes to imply notions of natural law that the constitution failed to cover. In either instance the remedies called for must not only survive the competing interests of partisan groups but then must be run through the filter of the traditional perceptions of those who define the highest level concepts. Since those at that level are not usually experiencing the distress of the petitioners it is most natural for them to control for the least change in the perceptual variables that they monitor.

Let me digress for a moment to suggest how this view of things suggests an explanation as to why violence is generally ineffective in bringing about change in society unless it is total as in a conquest or a revolution. Even a casual review of the effects of terrorists can hardly fail to indicate how little their efforts lead to the changes they claim to want. This is hardly a mystery, except possibly to themselves. In the first place their efforts generally affect the common people, the ones who are going about their daily business in the streets and buildings to which anyone can have access. The higher the status of a given member of society, the less chance that he or she will ever be in such places, except under special circumstances with some form of police control. Not only does the work of the terrorist hurt, and arouse hatred in, those members of society who have the least ability to bring about any change that the terrorist might want, but it is least likely to impact the only members of a society that influence its basic policies and programs. Overt action (of which violence is paramount)does not ordinarily impinge on the abstract level where the sources of public policy originate.

However, from the point of view of a psychotherapist, used to working with intentions of which a person is usually the least aware, there is still another insight to consider about the nature of terrorists. That is the "transferential" quality of their endeavors. I believe that a careful examination of most sincere terrorists justifies a surmise that—usually unbeknown to themselves—their true aims are best identified by what they actually accomplish rather than by the rationalizations they employ.[152] (I say "sincere" to differentiate the intentional terrorist from the professional killer who most often has been hired by someone for a more mundane purpose than to effect political/social change.) When we see innocent, ordinary people being maimed and killed by terroristic acts we should consider that that is what is really intended, despite the pious rationalizations. (Though the perpetrator ordinarily represses that fact from his own consciousness.) "Transference" in the psychological sense would suggest that the terrorist experiences some kind of emotional satisfaction upon observing the injury to the victims—who stand as scapegoats for his unconscious displaced retribution to real abusers of his own childhood.

I see the question of terrorists as simply a more concrete and more dramatic example of the general paradox of bringing about fundamental changes in first principles. Those members most in a position to redefine the highest level of goals have the least reason to do so. Further, the more highly differentiated the system the less likely are members at different status levels to have any but the most superficial personal contact, read: any shared experience or basis for empathy. Finally, those most negatively impacted may come in time to be in biological crisis in which instinctual rather than rational goals become their main objectives. But, this is the very condition in which random reorganization is triggered. It can result in the iconoclastic concepts by which revolutions—paradigmatic, first, then political—occur. All the aspects of social life in which these processes play out transpire over long periods of time in a civilization, and constitute what historians like Spengler and Toynbee perceived as the evolution of the civilization.

If you are inspired to join the various critics of contemporary life, reviewed in Part I, in attempting to identify the nature of deterioration in our current situation we might approach it by taking a look at some of the problems that we could agree must be dealt with more adequately than is currently the case in our civilization. We need to look for the presence or absence of all the elements of effective control in the various attempts at reform. I have hinted earlier at my belief that some of these problems can not be solved under our current social structure and will eventuate in some kind of cultural crisis and then some revolution as Soros (1999), e.g. thinks is needed. It might be in a fashion such as Davidson and Rees-Mogg (1997) predict but I view that as only one possibility. They have gone further than any others I know of to hypothesize about the process/mechanism by which they think their vision of a new society will come about.

I don't have a position on their prophecy, but I have a further thought about why attempts at reforming our current system fail. Besides the difficulty reformers have in affecting those most influential in defining the goals of society proponents of reform are also not yet likely to construe their plans in terms of the elements of good control. They, like the legislators they want to influence are not yet in the habit of thinking that way. We seem at present to be in a state of destructive chaos in which current structures are deteriorating. Probably there are individuals already thinking in terms of new ways to organize their individual lives who have not yet spelled it out like Davidson and Rees-Mogg. But there is no paradigm shift to a new way of organizing society. Until the conception of the nature of control is sufficiently widespread that people, in general, are used to think in such terms we are not likely to see pragmatically oriented types taking the time to think in such terms. With that surmise in mind let us turn to examining the following large scale problems as case illustrations.

Problems our Civilization Must Solve

PREJUDICE. Already the Islamic faith, and to some extent then, Islamic civilization has attracted the loyalty of several million Afro-Americans because they perceive the possibility of more equality there than from establishment circles in the United States. Lurking in the background of this fact one can see the larger scale of competition between civilizations for the hearts of people. Add other facts like the gradual darkening of the American complexion, and the antagonism to that expressed in calls for changes in immigration policy and it is not hard to understand how a valuing of diversity comes to be viewed as a critical reform.

But, what is actually happening in regard to this value? It is touted by intellectuals but many hard statistics point to increased segregation, ethnic hostilities and scapegoating as current problems.

Just recently there has been a flurry of protests against the practice of "profiling" used by many police departments in which they identify people with certain characteristics (invariably minority members) as more likely than average to commit crimes. The result is the arrest of many innocent members of that group on trivial charges so as to be able to check them out for the more serious crimes. The flaw in this procedure is failure to contemplate the long-run consequences of the attitudes that form in innocent people once they feel victimized. The old, coercion-based theory of policing seems to assume that "profiling" victims either do not retain any resentment of the treatment upon being let go, or else that it doesn't matter because they don't have enough power (political, economic or military) to pose effective consequences for mistreatment. The evidence is mounting that such assumptions are dangerous.

Against these hard, practical practices, often tacitly approved by the "silent majority," we have government and liberal organizations sponsoring various educational programs aiming to sell the idea that we would all be better off for valuing diversity and treating all human beings with equal respect. If the proponents of such programs were applying good control methods to obtain the conditions they want to perceive we would see more detailed spelling out of the concrete results intended, detailed descriptions of the current state of the condition of interest, and concrete definitions of the means whereby perceived conditions would be brought to match the desired state. Instead we see over and over again, people getting money to pursue goals that might be well conceived, but with poorly identified current conditions and little or no mechanism for adjusting the output to decrease the mismatch between desired and existing conditions. If that requirement is not being monitored and met, no good purpose is served by the reform program. When such programs fail to reach their announced goals it is not just a waste of time, money and human energy. It strengthens the argument of so-called ultra conservatives—that human engineering is mostly boondoggle, or beyond human abilities, and better "let nature take its course."

The related problems of police brutality and prosecutorial misconduct don't remain simply with the direct victims. They damage the sense of community, and the faith that members have in society's systems, with many serious wide-spread consequences that are becoming more and more apparent. The cure for uncontrolled misfeasance on the part of servants of the state could be in making them liable for conduct not directly identifiable with the defined function of their job. The distinction between mistakes in discretion and lawlessness resulting from a perception of impunity would need to be subject to higher levels of review. This problem area is one of a few that is going to benefit from advances in technology—such as having video cameras constantly running, monitoring the face to face behavior of public servants and citizens—without major changes in thinking about it. Given the advances in the means of implementing the control of such interactions, specifications for the desired state become easier to define in concrete terms.

TORTURE and GENOCIDE: As the world becomes more and more of a global village we all have more and more stake in what goes on everywhere. One can't simply be a passive audience. Knowledge of it makes us passive participants in defining acceptable mores on the world stage. Attempts to bring mass violence under control, as the UN is gradually beginning to address, will be influenced by the attitudes of all who express views whether directly via the media or indirectly by not visiting certain places as tourists, or boycotting certain imports and the like.

What could I as a common citizen have done about national policy on such things as the Nato war with Serbia? Our country has taken what seems an erratic position on "genocidal" situations over the last several administrations. We condemned Iraq for its inhumane treatment of its Kurd minority, but seemed to turn our backs when our ally, Turkey has done something similar. We looked away from genocide in Rwanda, but mobilized NATO to oppose it in Yugoslavia. Yet, even there our policy has failed to follow the well known principles of stopping violence—that you inundate the to-be-controlled area with so much force that opposition is patently useless. Does thinking about what conditions are being controlled contribute anything to analyzing these situations, given that I can only infer what the national leaders are intending from what is reported in the media? The answer to this and all comparable questions is Yes. If you find a state of affairs that seems to remain unchanged despite all sorts of external influences, that is a good candidate for a controlled condition. Clearly, then, in this case some other condition than the use of violence is what our government is attempting to control. Some skeptics have already identified that as perceived economic interests of the largest U. S. and multinational corporations. As I perceive such poor control over violence both within our nation and on our part within the world, I tend to withdraw my interest from the subject. It is an area of living which seems still to be in the condition of every man for himself. Thus, I see the topic as one where my only contribution could be to state out loud what I consider the desired condition and hope that everyone else will do the same. Whatever comes to be the majority Reference-value will only then begin to arouse the other components of good control.

I am opposed to genocide, under any name, but I would

like to see a country flooded with radio and air-dropped messages and finally demonstration bombings (hopefully of uninhabited locales) before going to the real thing. I also want the UN to execute the world's values regarding the mores of using force. The UN is the only body where, in principle at least, everyone participates in making the rules that everyone is required to follow. When the U. S. or a group like NATO undertakes to fill such a role it boils down in the end simply to coercion by the dominant force with the consequences that we are coming to know so well. In place of this the UN would seem to need an army of its own. At present that looks like an insoluble problem.

I would endorse the methods of the late Carl Rogers who introduced opposing groups to each other and reflected their mutual complaints until they reached some shared understandings. I know that many national leaders perceive their personal stake in maintaining their positions as antithetical to such a process, but I seem to recall that his procedures were sometimes accepted and had good results. The best chance for them would be when a politician is less psychopathic than the average, is matched by opponents of roughly equivalent power, and is realistic enough to recognize that. I would hope some leaders in the UN would subscribe to ideas like that enough to promote them.

DISTRIBUTION of VITAL SERVICES. The experiments of the last few generations seem to have shown that capitalism works most effectively with the fewest interferences from government during a period of increasing markets. But what happens when we achieve a period of overproduction? Capitalist theory calls for leaving the markets to adjust this situation. The problem that sometimes arises with that approach is that it tacitly assumes that people who are negatively affected can go into suspended animation while the corrections gradually take place. While not many homeless people starve outright in our society it would be hard to argue that most of them have a life. When that statistic increases, *especially* in a time of maximum employment, it is apparent that the current structure of society is failing to secure the needs of significant numbers of people.

We as a nation must decide whether or not to retain entitlements like social security and Medicare as rights like protection from fire or invasion. As various statistics make clear insurance companies take a quarter of each dollar spent for health care, and one has to ask whether that money would not care for all the people who are currently not covered with any medical coverage. Yet, someone has to manage the provision of care, and the only ones who would do it without being paid are the consumers themselves. But, that is the old system before there were second-party payers. The new system is reportedly lower in cost than the open ended system that preceded it when there were no bounds upon the continual growth of medical costs. Would it be possible to solve both ends of this dilemma? As with all the issues I have referred to the approach to a solution must incorporate the features of good control: Input from all who have a stake in the outcome, and must be negotiated until a common perceptual variable is defined; next, the desired condition must be defined in terms of the same measurable variables; and finally, the means of driving the perceived condition to the desired condition must be applied and accurately measured. When there is an imbalance of power among the contenders, the old human tendency to reach a solution satisfactory to the dominant power and enforce it upon the rest results in the perpetual violence that has until now always been accepted as the human condition.

DISTRIBUTION of VITAL SUPPLIES. Marx's dictum, From each according to his abilities, to each according to his needs—actually obtains in many families, to greater or lesser extents. Although some parents distribute their gifts and endowments on a strictly equal basis no matter what the different levels of prosperity their various children might enjoy, others subsidize those with lower disposable incomes to help them enjoy living standards more nearly equal to those with greater resources. A wealthy parent might well buy a house or a car for a son or daughter poet while never thinking to do so for a physician or lawyer offspring, and feel that in so doing he or she is contributing to the quality of life of the family as a whole. The legends of the early Christian communes present a further extension of the same idea.

The mistake Marx made was, in my opinion, to endorse such action as a desirable way to organize the communal life of people who do not know each other and have weak personal commitment to each other. That is, the citizens of a nation. What is the fundamental difference, from the point of view of how people control their own perceptions? It involves matters of instinctual—intrinsic system—functioning. Psychobiology research suggests a tendency to inherent benevolence between individuals sharing the same genetic stock, in humans and some animals. This tendency does not extend to members of the species not sharing a large endowment of common genes. Various communes, like some early Christian communities, seem to have succeeded in simulating this condition. But they seldom last more than a few generations at most, and never achieve a much broader population than one where all members can be perceived in a single gathering. Whether or not such perceptions of common identity gain support from instinctual sources they at least have limits determined by the capacities of lower order control systems such as what the eye can take in—in one glance—or something of the sort.

There is an equally serious mistake inherent in our current economic situation, even though it can't be identified with any particular thinker as in the case with Marx. That is the gradual violation that has come about in regard to what I would like to call "natural law of survival" even though that might stretch the concept. I mean the situation in which the rules of property ownership, competition for money, the very adherence to *rules* as of prime importance has led to a condition that thousands of families within our borders live on the very edge of starvation in the midst of the most unequaled plenty in human history. I call it a violation of natural law in the sense that prior to civilization human families and clans lived *in* nature and were all occupied in gaining daily sustenance. True, they were dependent upon the stability of their environment and natural disasters could result in annihilation. But, we now have some members of society in a condition of near annihilation in the midst of plenty. Instead of being at the mercy of nature they are at the mercy of man-made rules and definitions. That indicates faulty thinking, the kind of degeneration of once-effective ideas such as Spengler hypothesized.

The immediate cause of this condition is supposed to be that *these people* have no claim upon adequate sustenance because they have no skills of the sort needed by *those who own* the requirements for living. However those who own only own by virtue of rules and definitions. True, those rules and definitions were formulated gradually over time as more creative and aggressive people strove to secure their own survival by their efforts in a gradually integrating social structure. General acceptance of rules and definitions served the function of replacing continual combat for possession of the necessities of life. However, now the thinking has become overextended. There is an incipient clash between a primitive sense that might reside in all of us—that we all, as children of the earth, are provided for on the earth—and the definitions of property which have finally come down to say, "there's nothing left for you" to millions of people.

We are beginning to witness a new form of consequence from this development. Thousands of children are growing up with little or no adult supervision. In most cases the only adult or adults who care directly for them are not there. Either they go off to work everyday, or they have deserted them, or, in the big cities the children have migrated to the more exciting, substitute parentage of gangs. This is not a natural condition. Human evolution has not progressed far enough for children to be self-sufficient almost from birth like cattle. And our human society has evolved a dysfunctional condition that runs counter to what nature requires. Instinctual needs are not being supplied. We can speculate that genetically set reference signals are failing to be met, and that constant error signals precipitate continual reorganization efforts, the random effects of which produce internal chaos, experienced as severe anxiety, or when a genetic predisposition is also present: psychosis. While the outcome of some instances of reorganization is the positive one of the creative individual who comes from the slum, the increasingly frequent result is the random violence that has begun to baffle our sense of social harmony.

PRESERVATION of the WORLD ENVIRONMENT. A few years ago I read an article about how some lumber operators in Brazil challenged a U. S. advocate of forest preservation with the idea of paying them not to cut down trees in the Amazon forest. Under the circumstances I doubt they were in earnest. Their proposal was probably motivated by the desire to show the north American that he was hypocritically trying to get them to give up their self-interests for his. Yet, it struck me as an eminently reasonable idea. Cast it in the terms of a global community value. All things being equal the lumbermen might well agree that species diversity and survival is not a bad thing. Likewise, the arguments that reduction of the rain forest would leave the lumbermen without a job in the next generation and might also result in desertification because the soil would quickly lose its richness without the rain forest, might well be worth considering, *if* the lumbermens' need to eat today were not in question. What have we in the U.S. to gain from such payments, besides the satisfaction of seeing a world treasure preserved? Oxygen for breathing, for one thing. Less smoke in the world's atmosphere for another.

If one accepted the idea that it might be profitable to not cut down trees in the Amazon rain forest, how could such an idea be implemented? The lumbermen and ranchers currently cutting down the trees would have to be paid to do something else. Being paid to do nothing is welfare, and we think we already know what is wrong with that. Things like forestry products harvesting (which I understand is successfully practiced in an experiment in Costa Rica) comes to mind. I have no expertise in this subject, but the geniuses in the World Bank who recently stopped subsidizing the destruction have, or they can find who does. They might have stopped too soon. Stopping subsidizing the destruction should be only part of a package of finding something more worthy of support. I can visualize someone who might create a career for him or herself designing global scale problem solutions. Maybe such already exists. If so, I hope they start a fund drive or get foundation backing. The whole argument can be seen in terms of several different areas of wholistic thinking. The best known is the ecological approach. The advocates of this approach propose that every possible ramifying contingency needs to be added into the equation before a decision is implemented for World Bank funding.

Closely linked to the issues of the preservation of the earth as a human environment are the issues of the rapid population expansion of the present era. So far, predictions about humanity running out of food and water have not been borne out except for local and temporary instances. However, the threat remains. About twenty years ago, when the uses of space were still exciting to many people the *Futurist* magazine ran a series of articles depicting the designs for satellite colonies that various space engineers were envisioning. They struck me as promising in two regards. If enough people found satisfying living conditions in satellite colonies not only would that provide relief for the population problem but it would simultaneously reduce the invasion of the last natural habitats on earth. I have some friends who don't particularly revel in a glorious sunset, mountain scape or primeval forest. They seem perfectly happy in totally man-made environments. Their contribution to the better survival of the earth as an environment might well be to move onto a satellite.

How do you know that you have added all contingencies into the equation for a world bank investment or a new pilgrim voyage to uncharted quarters, and with the proper weightings? If you start with a description of the state of affairs of interest (what is perceived) and formulate the desired goal state in the same terms (the Reference perception) the discrepancy between the two states becomes more readily apparent. Then the effort to reduce the discrepancy has a specific target. The same variable (whether composite or simple) that is being perceived is simultaneously the *condition under control* and the *measure of the control effort*.

The application of that kind of thinking will be necessary, I believe, if the drug and tobacco problems are ever to be solved. Current efforts have the net tendency to drive coca farmers and processors and tobacco growers out of a livelihood. If they had got into their business fully knowing the murderous potential of their products that might be a justified course of action. But, that is not the case with many of them at least. When those enterprises were inaugurated they satisfied legitimate desires. What they were doing was not then known to be harmful and was not illegal. To turn against them after they have entrenched a heavy investment in their enterprise is a form of territorial assault, if you take a sufficiently instinctual view of it. On the other hand, to let them continue undisturbed is like shutting one's eyes to carnage. The solution to conflict between opposing control systems is to find perceptual variables that both sides can control at the same values. Or, at least, to converging values. You would have to find something for which to pay coca farmers more than they stand to lose.[153] I do recall reading some time back that tobacco and coca have potential medicinal components. This might be a place to start. It calls for creativity of course. The first step, however, needs to be a reorganization of thinking that permits us to value more global benefits more highly, and accept paying for them.

THE PROBLEM OF GUNS. No other issue demonstrates so clearly the disintegration of values in our society as that which revolves around public policy on guns. The arguments over the second amendment in some ways masks a national disaster that we are having difficulty facing as a nation. That is the subject of violence. Advocates of a government hands-off policy regarding guns, and their opponents are both overlooking or failing to read deeply enough into the real issue. Why do so many people nowadays want free access to guns? Because it is commonly held that crime with guns is an ever present danger everywhere and that criminals have unfettered access to guns. And why do criminals have unfettered access to guns? Because of the fervency of second amendment activists. The real issue is the widespread perception that we are almost continually surrounded by people who would do us harm. Is this the description of a healthy society? I say, No. The definitions of society conveyed implicitly by scholars when I was in school included the idea of a common set of values, a sense of group identity, unconscious and automatic cooperation on matters that affected the welfare of the whole. Few present day first world nations fulfill such definitions very fully any more.

Fear of violence from people around you is only one among many symptoms of the loss of community. One feels more crowded, on the street in big cities and on our roads and expressways, more of a sense of competition with other drivers for the freedom to get where one is going as one sees fit. Complaints about the loss of courtesy in public is another symptom. The media give us a sense that we are rubbing shoulders on any given day with murderers, rapists, child deserters, swindlers and other criminals who have escaped the clutches of the justice system. No wonder then, that we collectively feel so insecure in our person in company with our fellow citizens. For a long time members of the middle and upper classes soothed themselves with the idea that such things were only to be feared in the "concrete jungles" of the inner cities, but no more. Children in upscale schools around the country are showing that no part of society is immune. Remember Erik Erikson's thesis that the types of problems experience by "disturbed" children represent unsolved problems of the society.

Just tonight I happened to see one of the many TV programs depicting lawyers involved in the issues common in our society. In this case they were suing gun manufacturers for willingly advertising and selling guns that, by any standard of common sense, they would have to know would gravitate to criminals. It was played out as a conflict of values: freedom versus security. And in a certain sense that is true. But if you think more deeply about it, the underlying issue is that some people make a living by a means that ends up being deadly to other members of the society. Cigarette manufacturers have been targeted in the same way. The mafia's image is that they provide a service to a part of the public that a majority, or a politically influential minority wants to keep from them. The real difference between gun and cigarette manufacturers on the one hand, and the mafia on the other, is that someone has managed to restrict the freedom of public consumption of the mafia's products and not of the others. The deeper problem is that the question of how to make a living has gotten separated from the question of the kind of social climate the collectivity wants to live in.

The question we all need to be asking is why we as a nation are so immersed in a culture of violence. Our news media report real crimes all across the country every day, but, as if that were not enough, television and the movies inundate us with fictional versions as regularly. Why? It seems clear that the media not only set provocative examples and even provide training for the commission of violence, but in a superficial way the second amendment supporters and libertarians—who want no interference with either the availability of the means of violence nor the availability of the depiction of violence—are right. There would be no market for guns or violent movies if they did not appeal to large numbers of people. This is the real issue. Why do such things appeal to large numbers of people? I have already pointed out above the circular systems whereby the fear of violence functions as a self fulfilling prophecy in the activation of violence. But, why the interest in the fictional portrayal of it, as if the horrors occurring in real life were not enough? I have a hunch, but only that, that our average daily lives have become routine to the point where many, especially the young crave the rush of feeling greater excitement than one can experience in most of the rest of daily living. Movie violence is one cheap and ready way to achieve that. Add to that the frontier mentality that forms part of our history and the kind of anxiety reduction in the reassurance that comes at the end of the movie when the villain gets his just due and we have the two sided mechanism of arousal and relaxation. This situation is like a runaway train. Something will have to give. This is one more condition that I believe will provoke reorganization in enough people that we shall eventually have a cultural change.

The Seeds of Solutions

Although noöne can predict the form the future will take as a result of the new technological developments and their demands on human development, this development is already providing enough challenge and excitement especially for many young people that we may be glimpsing one form that the change may take. We have a resource never before available for propelling it. That is the rise of planning in its various forms as an occupation of its own. Communities, corporations, foundations and universities now have planning departments. There are future studies disciplines, a Futurist Society, and ordinary people are urged to plan for our own futures. I hope to see people taking this movement one more step—to advocate that anyone interested in not only his or her own future but the future of the world practice formulating how you would want the world to be. Never mind that we, ordinary people, do not have sufficient breadth of view nor sufficient facts to flesh out the picture you want to perceive; neither do the "experts."

What we do have, that nobody realized until relatively recently, is that formulations of the desired perception automatically sets in motion actions to bring current perceptions to the desired state. The beauty of this realization is that it entails less work than anyone previously realized. It is important before choosing to act on any matter to have as much factual information at hand as possible. It is also important to be alert to the trap of fantasy solutions—the way that reference signals output by higher order control systems can call up imagined perceptions from memory storage. They bypass the work of difficult control tasks. Just knowing this should be helpful in spreading "the scientific method" more and more into everyday thinking. For the heart of the scientific method is acknowledging and counteracting the human tendency to self-delusion.

Taking these considerations into account, the process of formulating how one would like things to be is using the mechanism of the self-fulfilling prophecy to good effect. In the same way that one is advised to keep your eye on the ball in order to be effective in hitting tennis-, or base-balls, so turning conscious attention to formulating a desired image of the future of the world begins the process of setting Reference values all down the line starting from the Principles that one formulates (already and automatically deriving from one's current concept of reality). Currently, remedies for various problems all too often take aim at the symptoms of the problem without any analysis being made of the underlying mechanism of it. As a result of the feedback nature of behavior we have the cascade of unintended consequences that bedevil so many remedial programs. One result of this may be increasingly radical proposals beginning to appeal to more and more people. As examples I have heard a rumor that in the old Soviet Union the problem of teenage unwed parenting was solved by taking the children into orphanages and putting the parents into prison. I don't know if there is anything to the rumor, but the important thing about it was that it was considered seriously by some people in America who felt the problem was becoming desperate. Likewise we are seeing the building of ever more prisons to house hardened criminals who got that way through gradual escalation of irresponsible behavior that met with no consequences in its early stages. The gruesome "solution" that we are beginning to see is the incarceration of children at younger and younger ages whose early indications of trouble went untreated.

I would like to see more of my tax dollars go toward good-control experiments that fill all the gaps in identification and treatment of children upon their first delinquent offense. I would also like to see our country turn once more to space exploration, both because it will be necessary to consider it as one possibility for dealing with the future of the population explosion, but even more immediately because of the value of having a larger national purpose with which people, especially youth, can identify, as we do in war. I would get the funds for such efforts by putting fewer taxes toward the foolish, non-productive "drug war." I would rather some of my taxes go to buy the coca farmers' product and burn what can't be used for medicines or research, until someone finds a product they could farm more profitably. I perceive the so-called "drug war" as insidiously supporting irrationally high prices which accomplish greater profits for distributors than anything else. I would like to see the people now employed in drug interdiction helping to increase the protection of normal activities on our city streets. I would also like to see a change in our cultural values along the lines pursued by the French in which conversation, music, art and the like are given more hours and the "normal" work week fewer hours in our value system. This doesn't affect me personally very much, as I am of retirement age, but I would like to see my sons with more time to interact with their children.

    I am opposed to casual abortions, but I am equally opposed to militant efforts of any group in society to impose its will on people who think differently. I think that problem will only be solved by those members of genuinely good will in both camps formulating together the desired objective—decreasing (toward zero) destruction of viable human fetuses. They need to accomplish this end by finding common grounds such as decreasing unwanted pregnancies by birth control, and adoption rather than moralizing, threats and punishment of the desperate.

    Ordinary people are coming increasingly to be more instrumental in advocating non-zero sum processes just because of the democratization of knowledge that has been a product of Western Civilization over the past few centuries. The world is becoming more and more filled by self-made specialists of all kinds who often have more breadth of scope for their thinking than the specialist experts who have careers to nurture and peers to compete with, processes that can militate against perspective. The very fact that we have seen a concept such as "war crimes" formulated in this century is an indication of the gradual emergence of life enhancing values on the part of many people around the globe. In previous eras genocide was an accepted practice of many cultures. I believe that the thinking behind the abhorrence of genocide has roots in common with the so-called "pro-life" movement, even while I suspect the possibility of cynical and dishonest motives on the part of some of its advocates.

We are at a juncture where I think opponents about the future, like Lester Brown and Julian Simon, could meet. Ordinary people are beginning to pay attention to the warnings about the future of the earth from people like Brown and Ehrlich and as a result beginning to fulfill Simon's prophecy that when people become aware of a problem they begin out of self-interest to find ways to cure it. What we learn is that deliberately describing for oneself how we want things is a more profound activity than merely wishing or hoping that things get better. For that reason I have described some of my own images, and invite you to do the same, believing that they become more articulated simply in the process of making them conscious.

I'm not concerned at the moment about what is feasible and what isn't. The process of "brainstorming," developed from the sensitivity training movements of the 60s and 70s has been shown to work best when imagination is temporarily turned loose from criticism. Neither do I worry about not having any direct influence over the political decision making process. People get ideas from each other, in conversations with kin and friends, or overheard in the plane, train or bus, or the bar or the park. Most of the great ideas for which politicians take credit, rightfully if they bring them to fruition, come from assistants who got them on the street or in the letters to the editor, from friends or constituents or think them up themselves—being immersed in the atmosphere of public discussions.

Chapter 18

INDIVIDUAL STRATEGIES: THE MICRO LEVEL

As I have come to the end of my argument I have discovered that the pursuit of my three purposes—of reporting those scholars worried about the decline of our civilization, Spengler's argument of why it comes about, and PCT as a theory that shows *how* it comes about—has, itself, been subservient to an even more basic purpose of which I did not become conscious until my prior task was accomplished.[154] Consider it a desire to find and communicate (at least symbolically) with other ordinary persons sharing the view that world conditions and social organizations are experiencing critical conditions. Thus, it would be wise to search actively for effective coping strategies rather than passively hoping to be taken care of by leaders of governments and other traditional institutions. Call it, if you will, a yearning to be part of an intellectual-vigilante posse on a lawless frontier of history.

The question whether Western Civilization is or is not crashing is not finally answered, as I see it. What is clear, however, is that a vast multitude of people around the earth perceive it in a crisis state. In our own country we are daily assaulted by images and reports of inexplicable violence, poverty in the midst of the greatest plenty in human history, financial insecurity in the face of immense prosperity, insane interpretations of laws, and a political process often out of control. We are frequently perceived by non-western peoples as destroyers of their cultures and exploiters of their resources, according to reports fed to us by our own media. The immediate, tangible, result is a feeling of unease. When simply contemplating touring in a foreign land we sometimes need to think whether one might be taken as a scapegoat for the world's ills by some terrorist or other.

Even developments that should be seen as positive—the almost unimaginable potential of a world wide web, the promise of ever increasing world trade, the hope for technological solutions to abundant energy—are regarded by many as coming on too fast. Or, are met with fear that it could all turn sour. Or, by the impression that it requires more ability to reorganize one's thinking and skills than one can handle. Or, by the concern that others will reap such benefits while one finds oneself excluded from them. Finally, dire warnings that environment protection might be losing the race with environmental degradation may be a likely source of the background level of basic anxiety that gated communities and Roth IRAs can hardly assuage.

. These facts seem to fit the picture of cultural upheavals that Spengler, a hundred years ago, and Davidson and Rees-Mogg today, suggested to occur with paradigm shifts in peoples' perception of the nature of reality. A few exceptional individuals formulate these revolutionary perceptions and become the leaders of the cultural revolution, but masses are swept along and often submerged in the upheaval that accompanies such events. I have reviewed the arguments in earlier chapters that this is what we are observing today, in both the flood of new inventions and discoveries—and the pioneers who are riding the crest of this new wave—and in the various cataclysms flooding over masses of others.

What might this mean for ordinary people? We can stand by and hope that our descendants will reorganize so as to survive in whatever future develops. We can hope that whoever has the ultimate power in the future will have more global perspective than most business and political leaders seem to have today. And one can determine to be among those ordinary people who keep right on living through major upheavals—the ones Haywood (1958) was talking about in *The Myth of Rome's Fall*. There are no guarantees, of course, but many ordinary people survive man-made catastrophes with foresight, creativity and keeping a low profile. You do have to have the luck not to get caught by natural catastrophes. For those willing to adopt new paradigms there are powerful new tools for individual survival.

The growth of information both on-line and in the libraries of many countries is still another tool helping to enhance the power of individuals as witness the increasing effectiveness of autodidacts in many technical enterprises. Still another factor is the spread of all the various means of communication whereby like-minded individuals discover each other and pool their efforts for mutual goals.

Some communities do solve problems that tear others apart. Some nations and peoples eventually contend successfully with conditions that go from bad to worse. Some families survive catastrophes that destroy others. Some businesses expand while competitors collapse. Is all this just a matter of luck? I think not. There might be genetic factors in creativity, but clearly, the concepts with which one tries to understand a problem determine the nature of the solutions one can derive.

Take a down-home, everyday example. If you have kids in school and you attend a school board meeting aimed at resolving some serious issue, what do you notice about proposals for solutions? Are they typically framed in terms of the desired state of affairs, or in terms of "here's what we ought to do"? I venture to guess that nine times out of ten it is the latter. Defining outputs as the goal toward which to work, rather than depicting the desired end-state, is conducive to a vast range of unintended consequences such as we have considered in earlier chapters. How much might you shake up that tired process by formulating action plans in terms of the desired end state while leaving the means of achieving them open to variation—as much as needed to achieve the desired end result? Specifying a course of action automatically curtails all other possible approaches. It also requires assuming that all participants agree on the desired end and are acting in good faith in moving to achieve it. That is, itself, not always a justified assumption.

Things become much more complicated when that is not the case. It might well be necessary to decide what is the nature of the social system operating in the situation? Are promising experiments really welcomed, or is there already an underlying course of action which the "powers that be" want to impose, or for which they hope to gain acquiescence? For example, in a school board meeting, when you are uncertain about the conditions that the superintendent, your principal or the chairman of the school board are intending to control, how do you judge whether your own intentions are likely to be facilitated or stymied? We all know how often window dressing is employed by authorities to mask intentions that are unlikely to be favored by an audience. Then it is useful to apply the "test for the controlled variable."

What anyone is perceiving/paying-attention-to constitutes the perceptual variable(s) he or she is trying to control. It would be useful if you can identify whether the authorities' perceptions match your perceptions. That comes clear in what they talk about and don't talk about and how they answer questions about what they haven't talked about. One can look for ways of disturbing what you think might be under control—whether by asking a question or proposing an action. If those in power immediately counter the purport of your efforts, it suggests you are hunting in the right area. If there is no opposing effort you can at least be sure that your ploy did not disturb whatever perceptual condition the authority is controlling for. Finally, when many proposals are offered and considered and presumed action is taken, whatever condition remains unchanged reflects the condition that is truly under control by the entity (person, committee, agency, body) that possesses the effective power in the situation. Never mind whether he, she or they are controlling it consciously or unconsciously.

This way of analyzing the interactions in a meeting does not apply only to school board meetings of course. That is simply one among many examples I might have chosen. The point is that one might easily be in a situation where others of higher status exert so much influence that one's own influence is of little consequence. If you perceive the condition that is under control to be inimical to your own interests there are really only two choices. One is to assess the possibility of marshalling a counter force of suitable magnitude. Ordinary people often do that. That is one of the chief virtues of American society whether or not we any longer have any true democracy in much of our political process. Think of the surprising success of many grass roots movements that have taken place in recent generations. If mobilizing grass roots influence does not succeed it might be best to treat the uncontrollable (from your point of view)condition the same way you would respond to news of an oncoming tidal wave, hurricane or earthquake.

Can you conceive of any condition under which you would move to another country? What might have been the difference between those Jews who left Germany before 1939 and those who didn't? It would be impossible to do a survey now to answer that question factually, but one can simulate it to some extent by asking oneself the question above. If you can't conceive of *any* condition, you might be implying that your highest priorities are in controlling some other variable than the optimal existence of yourself and your family. I'm not advocating emigrating from the United States, as Davidson and Rees-Mogg do in some of their publications. They are not in the class of ordinary persons; they are extraordinarily wealthy, and appear to conceive of their best interest in other terms than national identity. They have begun to perceive themselves as Sovereign Individuals, not subject to the laws of any country. You don't have to be in their socio-economic position, however, to appreciate that their attention is on something more concrete, more biological, than an abstract concept like nationality. It might only be retaining the maximum of their wealth, something many survivors might consider trivial, but it is at least a more substantive goal than preserving a definition that they claim is losing its significance.

You don't have to have great wealth and power to devalue definitions like nationality. This is happening at the opposite end of the power hierarchy as well. People like those in citizen "militias" in places such as Montana and Idaho hold similar points of view, with varying amounts of success. Obviously these people have already reorganized some higher level settings in their personal control-system hierarchies. Their most abstract conceptions of reality seem no longer to control identification with a nationality, nor do they seem any longer to maintain Principles like "patriotism," in reference to a nation, although some of them seem to give high priority to identifying with their concept of the white race. If they do value a perception like "patriotism," their patriotism is directed toward a nation the existence of which they perceive as under attack or already in the past.

Whatever personal stress—from a perceived threat to survival—led to this development is difficult to tell without studying the individuals specifically. These movements can be thought of as experiments illustrating personal reorganizations. From our point of view they represent experiments for surviving what the individuals perceive as societal degeneration—however dysfunctional the examples we have seen so far might be. Personal power is thus not beyond the means of ordinary people. Nor does it require affiliating with groups whose actions appear anti-social within the larger context. Many people actively choose to identify with a nationality or an ethnic identity or a more biological one like family and clan. One might also develop a sense of world membership. In time it could come to dominate one's other identifications, as most people place home community, state and national identifications in order of importance now.

A third option, the one I favor personally, is one that I suspect many people are already following as a commonsense measure. Partial out your sense of virtue. Adhere most strongly to laws and customs where they seem more or less consistent with "natural law" (i.e. conditions conducive to survival) and attempt to join with others to get the ruling powers to modify those that seem antithetical to survival. A good example of that currently seems to be our national struggle to make it harder for unsocialized people to obtain guns. Or the struggle to obtain reasonable medical care for all citizens. These are deadlocked in congress by conflicting interests, so cities and states are coming up with different answers according to the dominant groups in different places. Private parties are additionally recognizing that there might not be any consensus for broad scale solutions and therefore take individual steps to minimize their loss of personal power. Talking, complaining, proposing plans and programs supplies the ferment that ultimately produces solutions, maybe not in the form of influencing legislators who no longer view voters as their constituents, but in the various legal and informal end-runs that large numbers of individuals are coming up with—often without even a centrally organized movement.

This creates the atmosphere in which the perceptual signal reflecting one person's concerns begins to converge toward that of another and another until many people are beginning to attempt to control variables that are very similar. This is a form of social power. (See McClelland, 1994.) Consider again a concrete example of how the perceptual variable is simultaneously *what* is controlled and the *evidence of* control. If I want to raise my hand even with eye level, my perception of where-it-is is simultaneously the means of knowing whether or not it is where I want it to be. It is essentially the same with my perception of my congressman. He votes the way I want on certain measures and not on others. His voting record provides my perceptual and feedback signal. I get help from an organization called *Vote Smart* that publishes voting records of legislators. I send them money from time to time, to help them stay in business. Meanwhile, knowing how my congressman votes on various issues tells me when I can perceive him as working for me and when I am on my own and must take care of myself. If a competitor comes along and offers a better program, I will switch my vote.

Even when large numbers of people perceive the legislative process failing to serve the public will—winning election through the power of advertising that confuses people momentarily as to their own best interests—ordinary people have found ways to get the courts to solve problems by finding new perceptions of a situation that make it fall under constitutionally protected rights. Roe Versus Board of Education was a classic example. I believe we can anticipate like instances in the future. One that comes to mind is the case of factory pig farms that have been castigated from time to time on various TV exposé shows. Ordinary people report feeling physically assaulted by the overwhelming stench that some of these farms create. But there is at present no precedent in the law for controlling a phenomenon that has so far been defined merely as an annoyance. The owners of such farms defend the "slight inconvenience" as a small price to pay for cheaper pork. But, that line of reasoning will eventually be vulnerable. *Soilent Green* was a science fiction scenario of an even cheaper means of securing protein, with still greater profits (and without the noxious odor, I believe). Why wouldn't anyone then found a business on that basis? Because it exceeds the bounds of *ideas* that we can tolerate. Once we are in the realm of ideas, control becomes a matter of definition. It boils down to where you draw the line, and that is subject to argument.

Here is another example of immediate results from learning to think about behavior as the control of perception. It seems a small matter but made a significant difference to the individual involved. One of my former students had been in a dispute with some bureaucrat over a frustrating and seemingly unnecessary regulation. The discussion was becoming heated as each became emotionally involved. As my student felt her emotions surge she paused mentally and asked herself the question she had learned to apply in such situations: What do I want to perceive here? She immediately realized that she had subtly shifted her reference perception from her original goal to that of *winning the argument*. She reset her reference perception back to her initial objective and achieved it.

You could view this example as an instance of thinking about thinking in a fashion similar to manuals on problem solving in more quantitative realms. It is an example of using an understanding of how behavior works to solve a problem in interpersonal relations. Another application of the theory in personal affairs is using the concept of reorganization to counter anxiety. We all tend to dread the feelings of anxiety—being out of control—that can arise in tension-filled or life threatening situations. But, I have found personally, and have had others confirm from their experience, that simply remembering the idea—that control systems throughout the body are disturbed by the effects of random signalling as the reorganizing system kicks in—has often had a reassuring effect. I have found myself calming down and tolerating the anxiety that accompanies reorganization. Simply giving this theoretical explanation of what they might be experiencing has also been useful to some of my patients. Having an acceptable explanation of their discomfort enables tolerating it until a new internal organization occurs, oftentimes with newfound ability to solve a previously insoluble problem. We don't yet have the neurological and behavioral research to evaluate the hypothetical concept of reorganization, but, as you see, it is useful even taken as a metaphor.

Another example is one I observed many years ago in a rehab institution where a champion table tennis player happened to be in treatment. Staff members seized upon his presence there as an occasion for an informal tournament. In the course of it I noticed an interesting phenomenon that had all the earmarks of the theoretical definition of reorganization. A severely outclassed player would show a typical sequence of performances. As it began to become apparent that he was over his head he would begin to play more and more cautiously, to increase his control, until it became clear that he had no chance. Then, when winning was clearly hopeless he would start to play "wild." His play would dramatically shift to a freer, more audacious play. He would fall behind even faster but occasionally would successfully execute moves that were above his normal level of skill. The concept of reorganization was a good one for understanding this situation. When a person would look at his wild play in this way he would change his attitude from one of frustration to one of confidence that he was on the way to improving his performance.

Still other types of applications involve analyzing situations where you find yourself wondering how much control, if any, you can exert. You view the variable that seems under control, and look for ways to apply the test for the controlled variable. When the seemingly controlled variable appears to be a society-wide condition your ability to perform "the test" might be similar to the case of astronomers, biologists and geologists. The phenomenon is too large for any one, or all, humans to affect directly. Then you have to wait for natural experiments. You can do something from the underdog's position. Whether it be to move from a hurricane prone area or a street gang dominated neighborhood, you make a cost benefit analysis in terms of staying or moving. You make it with a mind set forming an image of what you want to be perceiving under various alternative solutions.

We can anticipate developments in the future that would increase the personal power of individuals. When nearly everyone (I would like to think, everyone, period.) has interactive, online capacity it will eventually be used not simply for polling but for voting. There will need to be safeguards against impulse driven, hysterical votes that fail to consider long run, and unexpected consequences. Our constitution already provided for this safeguard in the difference between senate and house. We could do it again in regard to wide scale referenda as an introductory step in the legislative process, already provided in a few states. In the mean time we can grumble and complain about the lack of legislative responsiveness to the popular will. We are beginning to see certain legislators competing for votes by offering to be more responsive. True, when they get in office they generally perceive the task of staying in office in a new light. But, some of them are holding fast, and voters will eventually find a way to reward them.

Meanwhile on a private scale the task is to learn how the system really works, as against being gulled into false perceptions like we were in high school civics courses. (Being taught only the formal and not the real process of government.) Criminals are not the only ones who learn to "work the system." There continue to be people like the late Saul Alinsky who taught a generation of reformers how to torture "the system" into enacting its own precepts. I have a friend who created a career for herself by forming an organization, mostly of mothers, to force governments to fulfill their legislated promises to handicapped children. When I get the various solicitations for environmental defense organizations I recognize the same process at work. Some people have created careers for themselves in organizing individual preferences into political forces to cure unresolved problems of our culture by private endeavors when governmental efforts are stalled. I feel empowered by those whose objectives I endorse when they are successful. When I subscribe to them it is because their announced objectives stand in reasonably well for reference values I hold.

Understanding how specifying goals automatically begins the process of moving toward desired conditions helps to make sense of various quasi-control systems at many levels of human organizations. Not that that would be a cultural innovation in itself. Planning departments in large organizations and governmental agencies already attempt to function in this manner. But, because not everyone with influence in a given control process understands the concept of a control system, planning often still winds up in dead ends. Yet, even when subject to the whims of larger social entities, some individuals successfully counteract deleterious influences, via supporting voluntary organizations, as noted above. As Kripner et al. (1998) suggested in their review of the fate of Easter Island the crucial difference between us today and previous peoples is that we have at least the beginnings of knowledge of how individual and collective destinies work out. Some members of our culture, at least, are in the process of extrapolating analyses of past processes into the future to facilitate facing it less randomly than could ever be done previously.

That suggests an amplified role for thinking processes at the present stage in the evolution of culture. Overt action is ultimately guided to conform to abstract concepts and principles. While I have no problem acknowledging the importance of the hypothetical "forces" posited by various writers as the engines of cultural evolution, I see such "forces" as perceptions that particular humans in particular places and times have imposed on their environment. They are abstract perceptions. You can't see them, whether as "forces" or as constructs about how reality works. They are perceived insights coming from someone's thinking. Talking about the ultimate impact of ideas on the environment is another way of saying that humans act upon environmental features to create optimal living conditions in accordance with the abstract perceptions they have created of optimality. Abstract variables exist entirely within the mental realm that we call thinking. Our lives are affected in large ways by manipulations of words and numbers by people whose main activities consist in studying charts and tables of numbers or getting reports from underlings who do that. Clearly the way that such people think about how behavior works will affect the way that they interpret their figures and propose goals based upon them.

Here are two illustrations of analyzing a behavioral event and coming out with a different conclusion as to what went on than the conclusion which people ordinarily would draw. The first comes from an article I read in the newspaper many years ago, concerning two bridge players being disgraced and kicked out of an international tournament. It happened somewhere in South America I believe. The particular complaint was that some judges, or referees, believed they had observed the two partners giving each other secret signals during play. The accused were highly indignant and protested their innocence. They had been partners for many years, in many such tournaments and were never previously indicted with such a charge. You might already have come to the surmise to which I came. My surmise was that they did indeed use secret signals—without knowing it. Thinking in terms of the hierarchy of control systems behind any behavior we can infer that lower order systems function automatically to achieve the reference conditions specified by the highest order involved. If the highest order is a Principle such as "Try to think like my partner," (or whatever) lower order perceptions detect and record, over the course of time, a myriad of sounds, movements, facial expressions, etc., that serve this aim. Since these partners had been together for a long time they might have acquired a large, unconscious repertoire of such recordings. In addition they would also have accumulated, unconsciously, reciprocal expressions that would elicit certain tactics in given circumstances. These would be the "secret signals."

Clearly the authorities in this episode were not prepared to conceive of the idea that the players in question might be both guilty and innocent at the same time, depending upon one's allowance for unaware, unintended actions. If they were, an appropriate correction for the problem could have been something other than disqualification.

Another example, possibly involving the same behavioral phenomenon, has a closer personal significance for me. When my kid brother was in his first year of college, preparing to become the chemical engineer that he eventually did become, he sent off an idea for improving an industrial process to a large manufacturing company. They sent back a polite letter thanking him for his idea but declaring it to be impractical. Two years later that company patented that idea. One hears many similar instances and of course, it provides a lot of work for lawyers. We tend to see it as theft of intellectual property. And, indeed, some companies are ruthless and immoral in their pursuit of the bottom line. But, that is not the only possible explanation of events like this. Following the same line of reasoning as in the case of the bridge players, we can put ourselves in the shoes of the engineers in the company who might have been asked to evaluate the idea. It is not a difficult guess that their highest order reference values would have been more focused upon their own expertise than upon furthering the career of some unknown kid. They already "knew" that the idea wouldn't work, because otherwise they would have been using it. But, then, sometime later, in another context, one focused, let us say, on the relevant process rather than on an evaluational task, one or another of the engineers might well have "thought" of this idea, never having a clue that he was *remembering* it.

What difference does this way of thinking about it make? For one thing, it can raise a question about the malice that we so often tend to perceive when someone else's pursuit of his or her goals conflicts with one's pursuit of one's own goals. Perceiving malice we often attack or defend. That, in turn, prompts a like response. It takes greater effort to introduce negotiation into a situation that has already taken on the qualities of battle. Certainly, an acquaintance with PCT should, in my opinion, remind one in advance to approach a potential ally/rival in terms of trying first to imagine what variables he or she is controlling that would affect his/her perception of one's own action. In the absence of such a view of the nature of behavior we too often naively tend to think that our own goals are perceived similarly by others whom we approach.

In a different kind of decision process, like buying a house, it can be useful in thinking about the multitude of variables that must somehow all be controlled simultaneously. Attempting to define for yourself just what you intend to perceive in a home and then looking at *this* house to determine how well it matches can take the place of a random assortment of considerations like, "Can I afford it?" "What will my relatives, friends, think of it?" Such considerations are taken into account automatically in their hierarchical order when viewed from the question of what you want to perceive as evidence of meeting your goals.

The concept of chance in the reorganization process makes comprehensible why different human beings arrive at quite different solutions to what appear to be the same problem. The same is true for problem solving within groups or societies regarding mutual control of general conditions. One can court chance. The concept of "brainstorming" a couple decades back, was one such view. On a larger scale Diamond (1998) in *Guns, Germs and Steel*, makes a persuasive case for the way that a combination of environmental conditions could produce *the* differences in the conditions of the various competing civilizations that resulted in the present dominance of Western Civilization. He was writing in the Cartesian psychological paradigm, but, if you make the proper adjustment to view his conditions from the perspective of individuals developing control hierarchies to maximize their living conditions it becomes possible to transform his insights from a purely explanatory mode to an action mode. One can brainstorm about various tradeoffs between assets of different groups—families, companies, communities, societies—to turn competitions into non-zero sum—win/win propositions.

One can place oneself in challenging situations so as to invite reorganization and thereby foster one's versatility and creativity. That may well be one of the motives behind the various daredevil pursuits like mountain climbing, sky-diving and so on, that people pursue. It is a form of gaining an appetite for facing the unknown and mastering unforeseen challenges and thus courting activities that inevitably incur reorganization of one's control hierarchy.

It may well be that the nature of what we currently think of as human nature is continuing to evolve under the impress of the developments we have considered above. Consider in this light Whyte's (1948) *The Next Development in Man*, and

Gorney's (1968) *The Human Agenda: How To Be at Home in the Universe Without Magic*. You can regard each of these books as an assessment of how individuals are changing as a result of the developments that have been occurring in our world cultures. You can also look at them as presenting what the writer would *like* to see people developing. It is his proffered cultural insight, available to become a self-fulfilling prophecy should a sufficient number of people find it congenial with their own Reference values for *society* or *culture*. Even more modest offerings sometimes function in the same way. Signs like "Do an irrational act of kindness," while they might seem trivial, apparently sometimes focus perception on higher values. A couple of people have remarked to me that upon seeing such a sign they decided actually to perform some charitable act they would not otherwise have thought about.

Another social innovation that was startling at first in terms of my tacit assumptions about private property came in a story about a succession of students who pooled funds to buy a house that will get to be owned by the last person to pay off the mortgage, without concern for their own contributions. Other such innovations include ordinary people starting movements out of their personal pain like Mothers Against Drunk Driving; Anti-gun people etc.

An ordinary citizen vis a vis large political and economic "forces" is like a private in a war zone trying to foresee how the war is progressing. You can only maximize your comfort in a very small way in the narrowest of circumstances. Yet if some tiny difference determines whether you survive or not, controlling that becomes all powerful. In the various examples I have cited, someone has gone ahead and created a solution that could not have been foreseen and that proved valuable for others even though it was only designed by one person for one immediate situation. When I was in graduate school my teachers stressed that science is "value free." It pursues the facts about nature. It has no information, or conclusions about what to do with those facts. There were thought to be no facts that could help one determine good or bad. The developing social sciences followed this view which they inherited from the philosophers who studied the nature of the hard sciences. This premise has worked out in some strange ways in applications of social science to advocacy and reform movements. The only real difference between a beneficial association, devoted to soliciting funds for charitable, humanitarian or ecologically wise purposes, and the most outrageous scams and confidence games depends upon who receives the benefits from their solicitations. The methods for appealing to the public and soliciting funds are essentially identical. However, this stance is coming to be questioned as we become aware of its negative by-products. Questioning it might sometimes also lead one to question one's loyalty to abstract principle when it conflicts with survival. Many privates do survive even at the front, and not always simply by chance. I like to think that one factor, among the many, might be the recognition that your highest—most general—perception will automatically set the values on down the line for the actions that you take.

I did not set out to write a self-help book. I intended to present the perceptual control view as a resource for analyzing the dysfunctional approach of making external efforts to control human behavior, and to explain why any conceptual system inevitably migrates over time into dysfunctional forms and finally to demonstrate how this point of view seems to imply that when social systems degenerate it is not those who control for the traditional concepts that most influence the new direction taken in the evolution of culture. However, making the case for the last point has brought up examples of how ordinary people do cope, and that, in turn, becomes a kind of self help idea exchange for coping. While writing this last chapter I came across a new book that might exemplify that point.

The Cost of Living by Arundhati Roy (1999) seems an unlikely choice at first glance. Her first essay, sarcastically titled, "The Greater Common Good," details the devastation wrought in thousands, not to say, millions of lives in the course of India's development of 3500 dams on the rivers of the country. The victims are rural people who have followed traditional lifestyles almost unchanged for centuries. Having lived in the same ground that their ancestors occupied for generations, and often illiterate, they had not been incorporated into the legal system of private property and other law-regulated activities common to the urban classes. Roy's description of these people sounds like the condition of indigenous peoples in America who met settlers moving westward. Their cultures have been ripped apart and themselves either left to starve, to survive on their own or to be moved to welfare slums near metropolitan areas, in the process of clearing for the development of a dam.

The picture is one of destruction of large numbers of individuals' lives for an abstract principle of *the greater common good*. The greater common good, of course, is implicitly assumed to be the benefits of electric power and all the aspects of modernity for which it is essential. Roy argues, however, that these people survived perfectly well in their traditional life styles. They grew their own food, were not dependent upon any form of welfare. They obtained medicines and tools in the forests in which they lived. They were in other words self sufficient in regard to the larger society surrounding them. They were not in need of, nor in consideration of, the greater common good that supposedly was used to justify uprooting their lives. It was someone else's good that was being promoted at their expense.

Of what concern is this to Americans? I have pointed out along the way that small farmers, as well as working class city dwellers in the paths of up-scale developments have encountered experiences not entirely different from those of the people in India that Roy documents. In some circumstances they have sold their land at a profit. In more instances they have first gone bankrupt as their previous means of making a living fell apart. But, one resource has been an appeal to higher law. Roy describes how the local people were mobilized to take their complaints to court by people like herself, acting out of moral instincts. They successfully held back the development of the dam for over ten years. In the course of it, misguided engineering and economic flaws were uncovered and the proponents were revealed to have been, themselves, misled by mistaken assumptions, poor planning and incorrect analyses. Delays like that permit kids to grow up and some of them to acquire educations in modern standards. Some even go eventually to law school and contribute to the defense of their traditions. It is an imperfect process but one that enables at least some doomed people to reorganize and not only fit themselves into the dominant culture but help to change it as well.

Another process, more subtle and less focused, is the slow process of change in the concepts and values of a large number of people. The reformers and advocates like Roy, and founders of new agencies aimed at attacking intractable social and governmental conditions, like those we have discussed above, succeed in mobilizing numbers of ordinary people by articulating concepts which give voice to inchoate perceptions of malaise—error signals within individual control hierarchies. Formulating the concept lends readily to defining the desired state of affairs from which the currently experienced error states diverge. That becomes the first step in the process of resolution.

The condition prior to the articulation of the important concept by the leader-to-be is a general state of complaining and grumbling on the part of the mass of people affected by the situation in question. There is often much confusion in the perceptions of the situation before a coherent picture begins to jell. This is where we can see how the conception of reality held by the public affects the process of jelling. In our society we have long had a tendency to *assume* the desired state of affairs and move directly to expressions of proposed actions to realize it. I tested out this tendency in myself by attempting to review conditions that I believe should be remedied in our society. I found that I often had to discover my reference values by backtracking from my proposals for action.

For one example, I tend to favor restricting the availability of guns in our society. When I began to analyze my position I soon experienced conflict in my belief that the second amendment was, and is, a valuable safeguard against the kind of easy usurpations to which many nations fall prey. Yet, tracing still further back the desired state of affairs was a no brainer: I want to perceive a steady and more rapid decline in the rate of homicides in our country. It then became clear to me that I do not know how to bring that about. The various proposals about guns should be seen as proposed experiments toward that end. But, when tried they need to be accompanied by measures of effects, time limits for evaluation, and an on-going process of germinating further experiments to replace failing approaches as immediately as possible. And, the whole panorama of potentially relevant variables, like moral education, the limitations of poverty and parental absence, ought to be recognized as the larger context in which specific experiments are formulated. That the first step in mobilizing general sentiments is public grumbling, and granting that that process will be improved when we get into the habit of grumbling in terms of describing the conditions that we desire to perceive. I found it easily extends to other desired conditions. I want to perceive a decrease in world population, without a decrease in the human population. At present this seemingly contradictory pair of goals is theoretically resolved when linked to another condition that I desire, namely, to perceive successful human colonization of space. I also want to perceive an increase in the area of "wild" space on earth. In that context I fantasy our descendants living in space and viewing the whole earth as we now view national parks—as space in which to "camp out" and indulge the instinctual tendencies that we still possess for living in harmony with nature. I also would like to perceive education of my grandchildren and their descendants that—like bilingual training—promotes the greatest possible understanding of the science underlying our technology and still also promotes appreciation and competence in living within at least one of the natural environments of an undevastated earth.

I do not know how many people share values like these. I would like to find out. I hope that we will increasingly advocate publicly the conditions we want. We shall then find the common denominators that majorities of us, at least, espouse. Of course, there are possibilities that some valued scenes are unrealizable, some are incompatible with others, and some might not be what we wanted if we get them. I don't contend that humans haven't always done this to some extent, but I do believe that cooperative efforts are more readily gained by publicizing goals than means.

Chapter Notes

(Notes in text follow continuously from beginning to end.)

Notes to Chapter One

1. I hesitated about putting the word, "expert" in quotes, as the subject of expertise is, itself, under contention by the competing experts.
2. The facts about Easter Island cited by Krippner et. al. resemble those reported by Jared Diamond in an article, "The Last Day of Easter Island: Science reveals the unwitting suicide of an entire society," which appeared in *Discover* magazine in 1995, although they did not cite this as a reference.
3. Compare Erik Eckholm and Lester R. Brown "The Deserts are Coming," *The Futurist*, December, 1977, p. 368, "An ecological phenomenon, desertification, is a human problem. People cause it, people suffer its consequences and only people can reverse it ... people undermine their own futures only when they can see no alternative ... what is essential to the short-term survival of the individual who lives on arid lands often flies in the face of what the long-term survival of society dictates."
4. Consider the cover subtitle, APOCALYPSE-NOT? Skeptics Challenge Prophecies of Environmental Doom in January-February, 1995 issue of The *Futurist* magazine, and compare with

the various articles in *State of the World*, 1995. In the area of investment, among innumerable examples, compare *The End of The American Century*, Why the Party's Over and What You Can Do To Protect Your self, by Rick Popowitz,—with a competing investment view by Dan Bruce, "Dow to Hit 7000 by Year 2000—after Dropping to 3000," etc.

5 I need to insert a comment here about how the material which follows relates to scientific versus exhortative writing. The model of organisms as environment control systems, that I describe in Parts II & III, is in the process of being increasingly well established by a growing body of psychological and biopsychological research. The implications of this model for personal and public decision making must initially be speculative. Speculation about the potential consequences of an idea is the first step in scientific testing of it. The next step, ideally, is the derivation of policy for practical action. While that, too should be tested in tentative, experimental fashion, the final test must be evaluation of its results (if any) in the real world.

6 In this connection consider the article by Paul J. McNulty, Juvenile Crime Rate Soars into 21st Century, in the Chicago Sun Times of Saturday February 11, 1995. Citing the *Survey of Youth in Custody*, McNulty reviews statistics such as, "From 1985 to 1991 homicides committed by boys in the 15-19-year old age group jumped 194% [and] ... In the final years of this decade ... America will experience ... a population surge [in this age group.]" While it is true that most recently (1996-1998) there has begun a significant decline in violent crime in the United States we must take that in concert with the fact that before that decline began we had reached a level far beyond the level of earlier generations in this century.

7 For example, Wolf, 1988, *Parallel Universes* The Search for Other Worlds.

Notes to Chapter Two

8 (1.) See A. Gore (1992) *Earth in the Balance*. Whether the fact is that

concern for the environment led him into politics in the first place, or that as a politician he became concerned with the fate of "spaceship earth," I believe it demonstrates a serious interest of a significant portion of the general public.

(2.) Brown, L. R. 1995 Vital Signs, page 15.

(3.) Ibid.

(4.) I trust the reader is familiar with the multitude of articles in newspapers, journals, books, conferences and activities of organizations like the Sierra Club, The Club of Rome, The U. N. and other organizations concerned with the future of the planet. One brief sampling of some of the older predictions which have begun to be borne out: "The Population Problem in 22 Dimensions," Brown, McGrath & Stokes (1976); "The Deserts are Coming," Eckholm and Brown (1977)—documented the spread of deserts in sub Saharan Africa, Asia, Australia, and the Americas which subsequent events have confirmed. In their report they also note continuing efforts in various places to reverse the process. Also compare, "Global Issues to Watch, The latest report from the Millennium Project," *1997 State of the Future*. [It] "identifies 15 important global issues to look out for and their implications for action—Fresh water is becoming scarce; the gap between the world's rich and poor is widening; the threat of new and reemerging diseases and immune micro-organisms is growing; the capacity of policy makers to make decisions is diminishing . . . ; Terrorism is growing in intensity, scale and threat; The severity of religious, ethnic, and racial conflict is increasing; Organized crime groups are becoming sophisticated global enterprises; Nuclear power plants around the world are aging." Also compare "The Coming Crisis in third World Cities," by Rashmi Mayur (1975), with Kaplan's (1996) reports on cities in the developing countries of Africa and the republics of the former Soviet Union.

(5.) Wall Street Journal, Monday, March 2, 1998; page A16. See also, "The Wreak of Russia," a World Report, in U. S. News & World Report, pp. 40-55, December 7, 1992.

(6.) Wall Street Journal, February 27, 1998; page A13.

[14] (7.) Kaplan, 1996

[15] (8.) However, I consider this single dimension of concern as too simple. For many people, myself included, the subject of cruelty to animals is also a consideration of no little significance. Indifference to suffering of others, including that of animals, has often been an early indicator of severe psychopathology, as in the case of mass murderer Jeffrey Dahmer. Beyond that, many people find such indifference to diminish oneself, morally and ethically. And finally, there is an entire potential area of biological research that has not yet been sufficiently developed, namely research on the possible connection between stress hormones produced in animals under conditions of extreme duress and any effects on humans from eating their meat over a long period of time.

Notes to Chapter Three

[16] (1.) I have to admit that this statement limps a little bit when we take tobacco into account.

[17] (2.) The victims' heirs could sue for damages. But, at least there is the threat—giving pause to the unscrupulous.

[18] (3.) Notice an article, "Environmental risks perplex government," by Beth Azar, 1995, "Scientific analyses of environmental risks tend to look at data—morbidities and mortalities... But such data leave out social, cultural and political factors such as the potential for catastrophe, issues of control, and equity and fairness of exposure that research has found to be central to peoples' risk evaluations."

[19] (4.) See also Howard's, 1995, article of the same name in U. S. News and World Report of January 30, and in the same place, "How Lawyers Abuse the Law," by Budiansky, Gest and Fischer.

[20] (5.) I have yet to see critics of Paul Ehrlich's views answer him specifically on the logic of his most salient arguments. For example, in a 1991 interview in the *Calypso Log* he states, "We can only support the 5.3 billion people we now have by constantly getting rid of soils that are manufactured on a time scale of inches per millennium but are being destroyed on a scale of inches per decade

... [and when critics] told us ... Technology will [enable the earth to feed, house educate, etc. five or 10 billion people] We would always reply, "Why don't we take care of 3.5 billion people properly? When we see that we can do that, then it will be reasonable [to consider allowing the expected population boom]." See also the articles by Robert Costanza and Beth Kneeland, ibid.

Critics like Julian Simon (1995a, 1995b) do indeed refute such arguments by pointing out previous, dire predictions that have (so far, at least) not come to pass. But, to counter Ehrlich's, Brown's and others' forecasts, with a general faith in human creativity, is not dealing with the specific logic of their predictions. It also does not adequately consider the implied warnings of catastrophe theory (Cf. Thom, 1975; Zeeman, 1976; Poston & Stewart, 1978) that indicates how slight increments in the control parameters of a trend can result in a sudden breakdown of the trend. Much literature (e.g. Kaplan, 1996) is currently showing that the nations of the earth, including even the U. S., are failing in the effort to provide a decent living for a growing worldwide underclass.

[21] (6.) From Eric Berne's book, *Games People Play*.

[22] (7.) Just today after I wrote this I happened to chance on a program called, "The Justice Files" on the Discovery Channel which featured the story of a young man who spent 7 years in prison on a false conviction. At the end of the program an expert civil liberties lawyer was quoted as estimating that there are in all probability about 30,000 innocent people in prison in the U. S. today as a result of mistaken identity, prosecutor intransigence, or other failures of the criminal justice system in this country. A sidebar stated that 80 people executed for crimes in this country were later proven to have been innocent.

[23] (8.) A random sampling in my collection of "ain't it awful" articles going back over several decades dredges up criticisms of all sorts of remedial programs that ended up going astray. I suspect that a general impression that the various New Deal programs had genuinely helped ease the depression for many people fueled expectations that government could and should sponsor programs to realize the

dreams for a better society that helped to inspire the GI's returning from WWII. And, indeed, the GI bill that spurred the growth of a university trained middle class seemed to justify such expectations for many of us. However, as such thinking accelerated many new programs initiated by government failed to meet their goals, either because of insufficient prior planning, inadequate initial funding support, mutually inconsistent objectives, limitations in scope or unrealistic basic assumptions. An article in Harper's magazine from the early 1960's is illustrative. Titled, "Learning to be Unemployable," it argued that, "imbalance in our educational system [has] concentrated on the 20 percent of students who go through college [while] the other 80 percent has been either ignored or sabotaged by an archaic system of job training [that results in] training young people in obsolete skills" [because of generous government funding of vocational and technical schools promoting archaic techniques]. This article can be taken as prophetic of the outcome of many well-intentioned government programs that lacked built-in safeguards against abuse. The ultimate in such programs was the naive early days of Medicare that many see as directly responsible for the national health care mess which we face currently. There is probably nothing really new in such critiques. I have occasionally seen articles illustrating criticisms of government policies in the nineteenth and eighteenth centuries, showing that there is nothing really new about criticisms of government. What does appear to be changing gradually is a growing understanding that failures of programs aimed at societal problems are mainly the result of inadequate abilities to control complexity rather than malevolent intentions of villainous people. That does not mean that some individuals have not exploited various systems. Rather, we are more ready to see that over and above some out and out criminals, many abuses result more often from ordinary individuals looking out for themselves more than identifying with ideals that might not be realizable anyway because of contradictions in the regulations.

[24] (9.) February, 1991 issue.
[25] (10). I remember that my grandparents made an agreement with the

city to turn their home over to it after they died in return for such welfare as existed. My grandparents survived on this plus what my grandfather derived doing odd jobs after he retired before there was social security.

[26] (11.) For additional views on welfare and homelessness see: From Boys Town to Oliver Twist (Shealy, 1995); Wisconsin's lesson in Welfare Reform (Roberts, 1995); Welfare The Myth of Reform (Whitman et al., 1995); Calling all data to inform welfare-reform debate (DeAngelis, 1995); Homelessness (Jones, et al. 1991).

[27] (12.) I also call it an example of the "dishwasher repairman problem." One time when our dishwasher flooded the kitchen floor, my wife hired a repairman who, after working a while, assured her that the problem was fixed. After he departed she turned it on and it again flooded the kitchen floor. When she called him to report that fact he became angry and insinuated that she must be at fault somehow. He returned, threatening a large increase in his fee for a second visit. He went through his motions again and before leaving my wife again turned it on and again it began to flood the floor. His first reaction was to say, "It can't be, I did everything the manual says."

[28] (13.) See my views on status and power in quasi control systems, such as "society," in part III below.

[29] (14). See Chaos Theory and Catastrophe Theory on the effects of tiny deviations upon the ultimate trajectory of developing processes.

[30] (15.) As I considered whether to cite some specific examples here it seemed to me that the reader will have current instances of his or her own to illustrate this point. These events were not isolated one-time things. They will always be occurring because this is part of our nature. The closed mind is something that all of us possess in matters that tie closely with our personal sense of survival. Why this is so will be taken up in part II.

[31] (16.) page 493.

[32] (17.) Kaplan, R. 1996, pp. 43-436.

[33] (18.) Food Scarcity An Environmental Wakeup Call, by Lester Brown, *The Futurist*, January-February 1998, pp. 34-38.

[34] (19.) Crozier, 1970, Preface.(Italics mine.)
[35] (20.) ibid., p. 94
[36] (21.) And even newer, multi-national individuals, "Sovereign individuals," as Davidson and Rees-Moog (1997), call them.
[37] (22.) Tharp, M. & Holstein, W. J., 1997, page 24 ff.
[38] (23.) For more details see a 1995 Anti-defamation Special Report, The Militia Movement in America.

Notes to Chapter Four

[39] (1.) Lukacs (1970), page 3.
[40] (2.) Ibid., p. 5.
[41] (3.) In fact this sentence is redundant or self-descriptive. For those of us who fancy ourselves to be educated, the amalgam of scholarly information with personal perceptions *is* the process of making sense of the world.
[42] (4) Compare David Riesman, (1950) on *The Lonely Crowd*.
[43] (5.) Namely, modern liberalism.
[44] (6.) See Richard Weaver's (1948) book of that name.
[45] (7.) Lukacs (1970) P. 7.
[46] (8.) Ibid., p. 9.
[47] (9.) Compare Kaplan (1996) and Davidson and Rees-Mogg (1997).
[48] (10.) Bork makes it unmistakable in a letter to the editor of the *Wall Street Journal*, July 22, 1998, when he says, "Mr. Jenkins . . . took my obvious joke that I had been concerned more with the decline of Western Civilization than antitrust as a confession that I had been out to pasture." I read this *not* as a declaration that he was not concerned with the decline of Western Civilization but that he had used irony to put in proper perspective his necessary involvement with practical matters of making a living as well as with his more profound concern about the future of civilization.
[49] (11.) Ibid, page, 40.
[50] (12.) Reich, Early Writings, Volume 1, The Impulsive Character: A Psychoanalytic Study of Ego Pathology (1925), Farrar, Straus 1975.

⁵¹ (13.) Davidson and Rees-Mogg, (1997), pp. 276-277.
⁵² (14.) Herman (1997), pp., 152 ff.

Notes to Chapter Five

⁵³ (1.) In the background lie the broad patterns of human development—childhood dependence, adolescent struggle for independence, adulthood challenges of achievement and generation, and the necessary compromises of old age—the universal stages posited by Freud and so beautifully detailed by Erik Erikson. (But, explicated and revised from the different venue of perceptual control theory by Plooij and Plooij, 1996, see below.) This is to draw attention to the fact of life scientists who study lives in the historical method, as an alternative method of science, like that of Spengler and Goethe.

⁵⁴ (2.) An interesting sidelight on this point comes from a by-product of my doctoral dissertation by my advisor, Desmond Cartwright. (Cartwright, D. S. and Robertson, R. J. 1961, Membership in cliques and achievement. *American Journal of Sociology*, 66, 441-445.) Cartwright found that the recognized leaders in a group of cliques engaged in a common enterprise were those whose achievement norms most resembled the average within their own group.

⁵⁵ (3.) I regard the lack of an "s" here as Not a misprint.
⁵⁶ (4.) Spengler, 1918/1926, p. 105.
⁵⁷ (5.) Op. cit. p. 47.
⁵⁸ (6.) And he hardly even had quantum theory to consider here!
⁵⁹ (7.) Op. cit. v.1 p. 59 ff.
⁶⁰ (8.) I was attracted to Jacob's book by a review in SCIENCE, shortly after it originally was published. Unfortunately the American publisher never went ahead to put the book out here, so far as I know. Rather than attempt to produce a literally correct interpretation I have taken some liberties in translating Jacob's words in terms of the message I get from his book as a whole.

[How could I overlook that all the "selfs" of my past have played the biggest role, the earlier the more so, in the development of that unconscious self-concept which ... dictates my values, desires and decisions? From our earliest times our imagination/ingenuity seizes the people and things it meets to abstract attributes of an ideal model of reality, a schema that becomes one's frame of reference, one's code for deciphering the world of one's own experience. Thus, I have carried within me since childhood an internal "statue"/model that forms my character and provides the continuity of my existence.]

[61] (9.) There were several articles on brain organization [hardwiring] in SCIENCE 5-10 years ago, that proposed that development in a given environment predisposes early development of hardwiring and that, in turn produces a restriction of later possibilities. Best common sense example: infants babble reproduces all sounds of all human languages, but eventually adult humans can not make certain sounds of foreign languages.

[62] (10). Compare here Lukacs's (1970) comment on Spengler in *The New Dark Ages*, page, 180: "We ought not apply biological rules to civilizations: this is where Spengler went wrong. Still there exist similarities, . . . a civilization, in its last stages of decay, shows symptoms of primitivism and of infantilism which reappear from within."

[63] (11.) Op. cit. v 1., p. 8, ff.
[64] (12.) Op. cit. v. 1, p. 86.
[65] (13.) Op. cit. v. 1, p. 88.
[66] (14.) Op. cit. v. 1, p. 141.
[67] (15.) Op. cit., v. 1, p. 314.
[68] (16.) Lukacs (1970), p. 171.

Notes to Chapter Six

[69] (1.) "Perceived" in this case is not limited to conscious awareness. The organism perceives any pattern of sensory input whether consciously, as in noticing a sunset, or unconsciously, as necessary for maintaining balance.

[70] (2.) The reason I say, "bring about and/or maintain" a condition is,

itself, a demonstration of how describing correctly what feedback systems do requires complex formations of language. Regarding the example of steering the car, there is more than one feedback principle involved. Your desire to get someplace is the specification for the whole series of actions involved in driving. The first actions upon the steering wheel must comply with how to get the car in the proper lane. After that the same mechanisms keep it there, but to the different specifications required to keep it there.

71 (3.) Realize that the definition of "constancy" has a range of meaning. Something like body temperature has *constancy* in that various readings of it fall near the same point on the thermometer, normally. However, if I follow the same route to work everyday there is a constancy to that also, but of a more abstract kind. It isn't continuously occurring; nevertheless an observer would see a constant habit. The great father of American Psychology, William James, already recognized the need for considering this aspect of behavior in saying, a hundred years ago, that the hallmark of *life* is the achievement of repeatable ends by variable means. "Repeatable ends" implies something keeps constant, even though by means that adapt to any changes in circumstances. "I go to work every day," contains a constancy that is not violated if one day I take street A, and another day I take street B. Unfortunately, James's insight was lost in psychology until Powers revisited it.

72 (4.) See Powers, 1973, and subsequent publications.

Notes to Chapter Seven

73 (1.) Spengler made a distinction between these terms, reserving "civilization" for the end stage of a culture—after the members carrying the creative force move from their physical homeland into cities. Modern historians at whom I've looked don't seem to see the necessity of this distinction, in most instances. Therefore, I tend to use them as more or less synonymous.

74 (2.) Op. cit. p. 7.

[75] (3.) I like Kuhn's use of the word, "paradigm" here. It could be thought of as a concept of concepts, or a pattern or mold within which concepts are constrained as they are being developed.

[76] (4.) Erikson (1970) p. 29.

[77] (5.) Op. cit. pp. 99-100.

[78] (6.) Ibid.

[79] (7.) Ibid., p. 101.

[80] (8.) To get a much more thorough feel for this, get Richard Marken's computer demonstration of a three-level control hierarchy and run it to see how interconnected systems adjust weights (Reference settings) in harmony to create virtual values for lower order systems to come to. See Appendix A.

[81] (9.) This observation, which is seconded by several researchers in the Perceptual Control Systems group, incidentally makes sense out of a pragmatic discovery of Sigmund Freud. He hit upon the therapeutic method of "Free Association" apparently by trial and error, but found it to be a reliable tool for psychoanalysis. In it the subject is advised to relax, not attempt to concentrate on anything in particular and then simply verbalize whatever thoughts come into awareness. Freud found that when patients did this, the spontaneous associations reliably cast up personal issues in which (in our terminology) there were unresolved error states.

[82] (10.) I think it was in Harper's Magazine, but unfortunately I have lost the citation.

[83] (11.) Spengler, 1918/1926, v. 1, pp. 68-69. Italics are from the original.

[84] (12.) Notice that this variable, expressed by the chain of words, hot/warm/comfortable/cool/chilly/cold has no name in our language. We refer to "temperature" meaning by that a variable in the physical world that we measure with a thermometer. But we do not have a particular name for our awareness of this continuum of sensation.

[85] (13.) Erikson (1950) op. cit. p. 28.

[86] (14.) Kuhn (1970) pp. 73-74.

Notes to Chapter Eight

[87] (1.) Freud's observations about early development were of course greatly refined and expanded by several of his followers, most notably by Erik Erikson in the sphere of personality development and by Wilhelm Reich in regard to character development.

[88] (2.) It was disputed by B. F. Skinner and his followers who were essentially committed to the view that anyone can learn anything at any time, if only there exists a sufficiently tight relationship between reward and the desired behavior. However, their work is applied only to a single habit at a time. A further limitation is that the desired change must be consistent with the overall organization that already exists in the person. It has been further called into question by some animal psychologists who have found that instinctual behavior gradually re-asserts itself in trained animals when the training was counter-instinctual. See the subject of "instinctual drift" in any elementary psychology text; or, specifically, Breland and Breland (1966).

[89] (3.) Obviously not a conscious intention. If the output were fixed, rather than the (physiological) intention, it would mean that the exact pattern of nerve impulses would travel to the cheek muscles under any and all circumstances. The smile would then be mechanical, always exactly the same. What you can actually see when observing an infant showing this behavior is that the smile emerges from whatever pattern the checks were just previously arranged in. Hence the smile, in order to match the "intention" would require different efferent patterns—at different times because of different starting points—to the cheek muscles to achieve the same set of afferent signals.

[90] (4.) What intervenes between these two events can be explained either by assigning it to magic, or by attempting to construct a model that works to give the same result. The first step in constructing such models was supplied by Powers. He called it "the test for the controlled variable." Spitz's experiment (or series of experiments, if you prefer) is an example of the Test. From his point of view the

test revealed what would, and would not, be followed by the designated change in the child's expression. That still does not tell us anything about the mechanism in the infant, but it is a jumping off point for studying that. It is from PCT research results that have already been garnered in other research that I proposed the cheek-muscle tension mechanism in the paragraph above.

[91] (5.) Quoted in chapter five, from Jacob (1987).

[92] (6.) To avoid the possible ambiguity of leaving room for an assumption of any "little man in the brain" to set the Reference levels, we might re-phrase Powers's words as, "suppose he has n-1 already-specified reference levels . . . ."

[93] (7.) Italics mine, RJR.

[94] (8.) Ibid. pp. 231-234.

[95] (9.) See Calhoun (1962) as one of the best known of a group of studies on this subject. He put laboratory rats into a large cage and allowed the population to increase naturally, while continuing to supply sufficient food for the size of population. Eventually the natural behavior patterns in the colony began to break down into various pathological conditions, different animals showing different patterns and a few of the strongest ones taking over the lion's share of the space and continuing in the most nearly normal patterns.

[96] (10.) I am aware here that by using the word, "evoke" I am at least coming close to falling into the stimulus-response way of thinking that pervades our communication. I accept that risk in cases like this because it would get me far off the path I am pursuing to speculate right now as to what would be the various perceptual variables the jury members might be controlling that the lawyer is hoping to get them to change their desired settings for. Hoping to change them in a direction favorable to his cause, that is. We know that in fact lawyers do influence the desired values of certain variables jury members are controlling—not always in the direction the lawyer hopes for.

[97] (11.) As an illustration of control that is less obvious than the one of keeping the car in its lane on the road: To maintain oneself upright

in the face of gravity, and other influences like wind and terrain, certain motor centers in the spinal cord must continually perceive the constantly varying kinesthetic feedback from muscles and joints in the legs as part of control systems that can continuously vary outgoing signals to the muscles to tense or relax when the incoming signals are not matching the specifications coming from superordinate control systems involving the balance mechanisms of the middle ear.

98 (12.) Cf. *Self Consistency* by Prescott Lecky, and Leon Festinger's (1957) *A Theory of Cognitive Dissonance*.

Notes to Chapter Nine

99 (1.) I continually stress that a condition under control is "perceived" by, or in the control system because that is what control does. It maintains the perception matched to its specification or reference value via its (the system's output "machinery") ability to affect the perceived condition so as to change its value. E.g. To pick up a pencil you must see where it is and you must also see (or feel) your hand moving to it. Seeing that distance shrinking is controlling the perception.

100 (2.) I hope it is clear by now that "feedback mechanism" is synonymous with "control system" as I use the terms. I will gradually phase out the term feedback because control is the active concept.

101 (3.) By template I am suggesting that we have had to learn from very early experience how to "see" patterns such as faces, scenery, etc. Think of Spitz's work on the infants smile, or many of Piaget's experiments.

102 (4.) There are many conditions in which we maintain something constant by continually varying something else. For example, you maintain the relationship of the car in its lane constant by continually varying the direction of the wheels.

103 (5.) That is, he proposed that there is a different *type* of variable controlled at each level, such that the next lower types of variables can be seen as components of the next higher level, as, e.g. the way

in which tactics or routines are components of strategies or programs of action.

[104] (6.) The reason that the term, "variable" is synonymous with "condition" here is that, by definition, a controlled condition refers to something that can vary. It if lacks a range of values the concept of control is meaningless.

[105] (7.) Some people who have extremely fast reaction times are able to mask the initial bounce, but it then might still show up with repeated trials.

[106] (8.) Powers's theory offers a way of explaining from the origin of the intention to the execution of the action within the same theoretical framework.

[107] (9.) See Richard Marken's feedback model of a fielder catching a fly ball.

[108] (10.) I proposed in IMP (Robertson and Powers, 1990) that the reticular formation of the diencephalon looks like a good candidate for the random signal generator of an intrinsic system.

[109] (11.) However, you can derive from Powers's postulation of an intrinsic system that it would be experiencing many error states during early development. The intake of food is still poorly regulated, likewise temperature and other homeostatic conditions. Hence, according to the theory he proposed, there would be frequent bursts of generalized signals into the higher brain where the learned hierarchy presumably develops.

Notes to chapter ten.

[110] (1.) A branch of social psychology continues to be devoted to this subject—how to detect underlying motives (intentions) from observable behavior. However, without the use of Powers's Test for the controlled variable, the current yield of this endeavor continues to be rather slim.

[111] (2.) In Western languages, at least.

[112] (3.) "60 Minutes," Feb 5, 1995.

¹¹³ (4.) See Philip K. Howard, *The Death of Common Sense* (Random House, 1995), reviewed in January 30, 1995 U. S. News and World Report, and "The Death of Common Sense in America."

¹¹⁴ (5.) Technically, attention shifts down to the perceptual variables controlled by the lower order systems that deal with the more immediate experience. A good illustration is when in driving with a strong side wind you come into a tunnel, or pass a thick woods, or a cliff. There is often a sudden lurch as the correction being maintained is no longer needed. Attention drops down momentarily to the steering process even if you were previously immersed in listening to the radio or in conversation with a passenger.

¹¹⁵ (6.) Pvs-perceptual variables. I remind the reader that control systems only control variables and are only perceived by the sensory equipment of the control system.

¹¹⁶ (7.) It was not faced by traditional psychologists either, although it should have been. But, psychology was already entrapped in the Cartesian paradigm, especially via Pavlov, Watson and Skinner. Hardly anyone was interested in understanding intention, seeing it as only an epiphenomenon of a human tendency for how a person experiences his reaction to external stimuli.

¹¹⁷ (8.) One can regard a good bit of what goes on in psychotherapy as a process of bouncing self-attributions off the therapist, while simultaneously reflecting on what one is actually accomplishing, to tease out and then put into words, intentions that one has been realizing without being conscious of them.

¹¹⁸ (9.) While economists formulate generalizations about the results of masses of individual commercial actions, and sociologists formulate generalizations about the aggregate of masses of social actions, we engage in them individually as we control whatever form of perceptual variables we have developed that apply in the cases in point. Even though economists sometimes refer to an abstract generality as a "law" it is not a law like the "law" of gravity.

Economic and sociological "laws" are generalizations about the results of masses of individual acts. As such their ability to predict future phenomena are only probabilities based upon extrapolations. A homely illustration is seen in a recent national election. The party that spent the most money—based on the rule that the most money generally wins—was checked by the other party's concentration on getting individuals to the polls.

[119] (10.) See, for example, Greene (1991a), (1991b), (1998), and many other articles in the Chicago Tribune in intervening years. Also, see Taylor (1998).

Notes to Chapter Eleven

[120] (1.) William James, the father of American psychology, and John Dewey, another of its pioneers, apparently grasped the inadequacy of linear logic for understanding behavior. Dewey in fact, noted the circular logic inherent in full explanations of behavior. But, their thinking was swept aside, probably under the influence of the philosophy of logical positivism as it entered into John B. Watson's attempt to employ Pavlovian conditioning as a foundation for all psychology as a "scientific" discipline.

[121] (2.) As far as I know he never cited Lecky's book, and I don't know whether he was unaware of it, or perceived it as different from his own researches.

[122] (3.) See, Robertson, et. al., 1987/1999, Testing the Self as a Control System.

[123] (4.) Buckley, 1968, pp 93-94.

[124] (5.) Bloom, op. cit. pp. 29-30.

[125] (6.) Weaver, op. cit. pp. 1-3.

[126] (7.) Even when as clinical psychologists we try to suspend our objectivity and learn to practice empathically, it entails the effort to counteract much of what we have learned as the "scientific" part in our academic training.

Notes to Chapter Twelve

127 (1.) I put the term, *instinctive* in quotes to indicate that I am using it loosely to refer to the whole class of human behavior that is coming to be seen as manifesting the sociobiological, or coevolutionary heritage.

128 (2.) *Encyclopedia Britannica*, 1970 Edition, v. 16, page 104.

129 (3.) *Encyclopedia Britannica*, 1970 Edition, v. 8, page 764 ff.

130 (4.) *Encyclopedia Britannica*, 1970 Edition, v. 16, page 104.

131 (5.) Sagan (1977) pages 57 and 64.

132 (6.) The trouble with calling something irrational or illogical is that—while it might truly fail to conform to an externally posed syllogism—the more significant consideration is finding what condition is under control. Calling something irrational is simply a cute way of saying that the behavior is not understood.

Notes to Chapter Thirteen

133 (1.) Warner, 1941, Volume 1.

134 (2.) Williams, Bill in a research study reported to the Human Systems Group annual conference, early 1980s.

135 (3.) I have too many references to the growing disparity of wealth and power between the upper classes and the rest of the U. S. population, and of the unhealthy consequences of that fact to cite them all in the text. As a sample of further references consider "Perpetual paranoia of the rich," a book review by Scott Sanders of Heinrich Böll's novel, *The Safety Net*. "The Safety Net presents a moral critique of... all affluent Western countries. The terror that haunts [the protagonist] is the shadow side of his power." Or, "The Rich in America—How they made their money—The populist assault on them." Feature articles in *U S News and World Report*, November 18, 1991. The article reviews the figures about the widening wealth gap in the 1980s—"Salaries of those earning $20k-$50k went up 44 percent; pay of those earning over 1 million went up 2184

percent...[and] the share of the nation's wealth held by the richest 10 percent climbed from 67.5% to 73.1% between 1979 and 1988." It is considerably greater now. Another reflection of the disparity in the application of justice between those of high and low status is reported in the journal, Civil Liberties of November, 1975, "A guy in Albuquerque got six months for wrapping the flag around his head but all Racquel Welch got for wrapping it around her behind was her picture in the newspaper." The disparagement of the rich goes back at least to the New Testament, and doubtless beyond. But the particular turn it is taking in current interest suggests the growth of further dysfunction in society as a quasi-control system.

[136] (4) Davidson and Rees-Mogg, 1993, p. 108 ff.

Notes to Chapter Fourteen

[137] (1.) I believe I owe credit for this idea to a science fiction book, *Startship Trooper*, written, I think, by Robert Heinlein. But the exact reference is, I regret to say, lost in my personal ancient history.

[138] (2.) It would be an interesting study to see if one could derive the history of this kind of national hypocrisy from the first principles of Western Civilization, or those of the systems-concept of United States. It might turn out that it is a generically human characteristic, although I get the impression that the ancient Greeks were more forthright about their selfish interests in discussing affairs of state, if Thucydides could be taken at face value.

[139] (3.) We don't need to attribute any malevolence to people for many of the kinds of torts that I am discussing here. We are all constructed so that we control those variables that are most important to our own functionimg, and in the process we often fail to pay attention to things we do that we would not like to take responsibility for. Since they result from controlling higher level variables they can be performed completely unconsciously—like the person who is aware of being in a hurry and hence only marginally aware or even unaware of parking in the "handicapped" slot. When made aware of it, a person might say, "Oh, I just wasn't thinking." In other cases of course the person feels

defensive and acts as if attacked by any would-be critic. But, even that person didn't park there with the thought, "I want to block out a handicapped person." Instead, if aware of the sign he or she will be thinking, "I'm in a hurry and there is no handicapped person here needing that spot, and anyway, there is another spot, if one shows up."

Notes to Chapter Fifteen

[140] (1.) Davidson and Rees-Mogg (1997), p. 12-13, 40.

[141] (2.) As I gathered from a lot of conversations that many did.

[142] (3.) I hope that it is clear that I am using words from everyday speech to describe what more precisely I would call "Program-level output controlling a Principle, like: We must get rid of him." I find it can sometimes be awkward to insert a technically correct PCT description in referring to events that are common knowledge and about which people are generally thinking in the terms of everyday usage. And yet, I don't want the reader to lose sight of the fact that my way of perceiving the event in question is structured by my employment of PCT as the proper way to understand any behavior.

[143] (4.) For more information about Edward Ford's program and publications see his RTP World Wide Web site.

[144] (5.) When the current perspective begins to fail, either because of implications that were not fatal when first adopted—but were not flexible enough to serve as the system gained increased complexity—or because of failure in dealing with a competitive entity (of the same level), disintegration sets in. This will either lead to a more effective reorganization or demise.

Notes to Chapter Sixteen

[145] (1.) I can illustrate this point and also do honor to two men whose personal convictions led them to what I consider extraordinary experiments in living that could eventually benefit us all. One is Vic Dufour, former chairman of my department at the university, who gave it up to invest his life and that of his family on an organic

farm in Indiana. The other is Greg Williams, mechanical engineer and talented computer programmer who did the same in Kentucky. I have heard of small groups and individuals doing similar things in this country and some others. While many may ultimately fail or require serious modifications the result of their efforts will help all of us learn things about making life on earth more sustainable.

[146] (2) Just after writing this my wife happened to rent a videotape copy of a last year's movie, *Bullworth*, a somewhat silly parody about a corrupt politician who becomes a populist hero by exposing his cynical, selfish machinations in selling out common people to greedy capitalists for their financial support. Beneath the thinly disguised liberal attack on the heartlessness of the rich one could find a panegyric to the survival skills and cultural integrity in black urban ghetto society.

[147] (3.) What I have said about ordinary people so far would seem to equate them with the lower classes in society. That is not what I mean. There are ordinary people among all classes, including the very rich among whom are the rulers of society.

[148] (4.) Observe, generalize, hypothesize the underlying mechanism, test, and refine the generalization.

Notes to Chapter Seventeen

[149] (1.) I put "idea" in quotes here because we do not have a well established word for that which is controlled by higher order neural control systems. Our closest term is "thought." But, when used for the concept I mean here we have to make clear that the "thought" might be a remembered or constructed word or image—visual, verbal, tactile, odorous—or, as Einstein stated when asked about the usual form of his thought, it might not be experienced in any sensory modality. The British philosopher, Locke, understood this, I believe. His term, "idea," conveyed this broad sense of meaning.

[150] (2.) We get our specifications from previous, successful perceptual "readings," according to Powers's hypothesis in BCP. The meaning of "Success," remember, in this case, is defined essentially as the

achievement of control that satisfies some basic need; i. e. that reduces error in the intrinsic system. That permits reorganizing to stop and the current neural "reading" to be stored in memory. Evocation of that memory serves as reference signal for subsequent control targeting in like circumstances.

[151] (3.) My point is illustrated, I think, in a story told by one of my roommates in graduate school. His family were Quakers who traced their roots to William Penn's settlement in Pennsylvania. Though his immediate parents had settled in Indiana their traditions were recognized by the leading members of their current community. His father had died prematurely at a young age, leaving his widow and son financially challenged. Sympathetic prominent citizens puzzled over how she might best support herself, seeing that she had no commercial skills. They settled the matter by appointing her director of the public library.

[152] (4.) I am trying to make a fairly general point here. However, if it seems too subtle let me say directly that—in spite of the skeptics—Freud was not far off in suggesting that at least some violence directed toward authorities or abstract entities, like "American society," is motivated by an unconscious aggression towards one's father or principle caretaker.

[153] (5.) I am thinking here primarily of the farmers. The drug lords who are becoming rich via a criminal enterprise are, in effect, being enabled, or if you will, subsidized, by the criminal definition of their endeavors. Experts in the subject of prohibition have pointed out that it is only the fact of criminalization that keeps the price of the product outrageously high.

Notes to Chapter Eighteen

[154] (1.) How that entails an application of hierarchical PCT with its implication for a reworking of Freud's theories about the unconscious might be an interesting topic at this point, although perhaps only to the psychologically minded. In any case it would be a digression from my present path, so I will reserve it for appendix B.

Bibliography

Azar, Beth "Carnegie report details cost of neglecting youth." *Monitor*, July, 1994, The American Psychological Association.

Azar, Beth, "Environmental risks perplex government," *Monitor*, March, 1995, The American Psychological Association.

Bailey, Robert *Eco Scam: The False Prophets of Ecological Apocalypse*, 1993. St. Martin's.

Bailey, Robert Seven Doomsday Myths About the Environment IN: *The Futurist, A Journal of forecasts, trends and ideas about the future.* Edward Cornish, Editor. January-February, 1995 pp.14-19.

Bassuk, Ellen L. 1991, "Homeless Families," *Scientific American*, December, 1991.

Bloom, Allan, 1987, *The Closing of the American Mind.* New York: Simon and Schuster.

Bonner, Bill, 1994, Listed as president, though of what is not given. TAIPAN Special issue, Fall 1994, published by Agora, Inc. 1217 St. Paul St. Baltimore, MD.

Boot, Max, 1998, editorial feature writer, "America's Worst Judges" *The Wall Street Journal*, Thursday, May 28. Adapted from, *Out of Order: Arrogance, Corruption and Incompetence on the Bench*, by the same author, Basic Books, 1998.

Bork, Robert H., 1996, *Slouching Towards Gomorrah, Modern Liberalism and American Decline*. Regan Books, Harper Collins.

Bower, Bruce, 1993 "Delinquent Developments," *Science News*, v. 143, p. 282.

Breland, Keller and Breland, Marian, 1961, The misbehavior of organisms. *American Psychologist*, 16, 681-684.

Brown, Lester R., McGrath, Patricia, L., Stokes, Bruce, "The Population Problem in 22 Dimensions," *The Futurist*, October, 1976 Edward Cornish, ed. The World Future Society, Bethesda, Maryland 20814.

Brown, Lester R., Flavin, Christopher & Postel, Sandra, "A Planet in Jeopardy," *The Futurist*, May-June, 1992, Edward Cornish, ed. The World Future Society, Bethesda, Maryland 20814.

Brown, Lester R. *State of the World*, 1998, 1995, A Worldwatch Report on Progress Toward a Sustainable Society. Lester R. Brown Project Director, Christopher Flavin and Hillary R. French, associate directors. New York, W. W. Norton & Co.

Brown, Lester R. *Vital Signs 1995* The Trends that are Shaping Our Future. Linda Stark, ed. The Worldwatch Institute, Lester R. Brown, President. New York, W. W. Norton & Co.

Bruce, Dan, 1995, Editor *Insightful Investor*, Special Issue Winter.

Brzezinski, Zbigniew, 1993, *Out of Control: Global Turmoil on the Eve of the 21st Century*. Charles Scribner's Sons Macmillan Publishing Company, New York, NY

Buchanan, Patrick J., 2002, *The Death of the West* St. Martens Press: N.Y.

Buckley, William F. Jr., 1968, *Up From Liberalism*, New York: Brosset & Dunlap, Inc. Bantam Books.

Budiansky, Stephen; Gest, Ted and Fischer, David, 1995, "How Lawyers Abuse the Law," *U. S. News and World Report*, January 30.

Cahill, Thomas, 1995, *How the Irish Saved Civilization*, Anchor Books, Doubleday. New York, London, Toronto, Sydney, Aukland.

Calhoun, John, B., 1962, Population Density and Social Pathology. *Scientific American*, v. 206: 139-148.

Chase, Edward T., 1963 Learning to be Unemployable, *Harper's Magazine*, April.

Cleckley, Hervey, 1982, *The Mask of Sanity*. New York: New American Library, Mosby Medical Library. Original publication date, ca. 1941.

Davidson, James D. & Rees-Mogg, Lord William, 1993, *The Great Reckoning*, Revised and Updated Version, New York: Touchstone division of Simon and Shuster, Inc.

Davidson, James D. & Rees-Mogg, Lord William, 1997. *The Sovereign Individual*. New York: Simon and Schuster.

DeAngelis, Tori, 1995, "Calling all data to inform welfare-reform debate," *Monitor* The American Psychological Association, February, p. 38.

Descartes, René, 1637, *De Homine*. Translated by T. S. Hall, 1972. Cambridge MA: Harvard University Press.

Diamond, Jared, 1998. *Guns, Germs and Steel*. New York, London: W. W. Norton.

Diamond, Jared, 1995, Easter's End, *Discover*, August, Vol. 16, #8. Paul Hoffman, President/Editor in chief. The Walt Disney Company.

Dowd, Ann Reilly, 1997, "Look who's cashing in on Congress," feature, Money and Politics, *Money* Magazine, December.

Eckholm, E. and Brown, L. The Deserts are Coming. *The Futurist*, December, 1977 Edward Cornish, ed. The World Future Society, Bethesda, Maryland 20814.

Ehrlich, Paul 1991, Stemming the Human Tide, in Mary Batten, ed., *The Calypso Log* Population and Environment, v. 18, #1.

Ehrlich, Paul & Anne, 1990, *The Population Explosion*. New York: Simon and Schuster.

Ehrlich, Paul & Anne, 1998, *Betrayal of Science and Reason: How Anti-Environmental Rhetoric Threatens Our Future*. Washington, D C: Island Press/Shearwater Brooks.

Erikson, E. 1950, *Childhood and Society*. New York: Norton.

Esquire Magazine, March 1974, Do Americans suddenly hate kids?

Farmer, Richard N., 1977, *Why Nothing Seems to Work Anymore*. Chicago: Henry Regnery Co.

Festinger, L. A. 1954, A theory of social comparison processes. *Human Relations*, 7, 117-140.

Festinger, L. 1957. *A Theory of Cognitive Dissonance*. Stanford, Calif.: Stanford University Press.

Fialka, John J.,1998, "Global-Warming Debate Gets No Consensus in Industry" *The Wall Street Journal*, April 16, p. A24.

Fill, J. Herbert, 1974, *The Mental Breakdown of a Nation*, New York: New Viewpoints, a division of Franklin Watts.

Ford, Edward E. 1994, *Discipline for Home and School*. Scottsdale, AZ: Brandt Publishing Company.

Ford, Edward E. 1989 *Freedom from Stress*. Scottsdale, AZ: Brandt Publishing Company.

Frank, Robert H. & Philip J. Cook, 1995, *The Winner-TAke-All Society*. N Y: The Free Press

Freedman, Jonathon, L., 1975, *Crowding and Behavior*, San Francisco: W.H. Freeman and Co.

Goodman, George, W. see Smith, Adam.

Gore, Albert, 1992, *Earth in the Balance*, New York: Houghton Mifflin.

Gorney, Roderic, 1968, 1979, *The Human Agenda: How To Be At Home in the Universe Without Magic*. Los Angeles: The Guild of Tutors Press.

Greene, Bob, 1991a, "Something Just Seems Wrong," *Chicago Tribune*, Sunday February 24. Section 5, pp 5-6.

Greene, Bob, 1991b, "Sarah Wins: 'Justice at Last,'" *Chicago Tribune*, Sunday, April 21. Section 5, pages 1 & 7.

Greene, Bob, 1998, "Parents Take First Step to Get Children Back," *Chicago Tribune*, Sunday, September 20. Section 1, page 2.

Hardin, Garrett, 1968, "The Tragedy of the Commons," *SCIENCE*, 162: 1243-1248.

Harr, Jonathon, 1995, *A Civil Action*, New York: Vintage Books, A division of Random House, Inc.

Hauser, Hillary, 1991, in Mary Batten, ed., *The Calypso Log* Population and Environment, v. 18, #1.

Haywood, Richard Mansfield, 1958, *The Myth of Rome's Fall*, NY: Thomas Y. Crowell Company, Inc.

Holden, Constance, 1975, "Drug Abuse 1975: The "War is Past, The Problem is as Big as Ever," News and Comment, *SCIENCE*, v. 190, November 14, p. 638.

Howard, Philip K., 1995, *The Death of Common Sense: How Law is Suffocating America*. New York: Random House

Hubbard, Harold M., 1991, "The Real Cost of Energy," *Scientific American*, v. 264, #4, p. 36.

Huntington, Samuel, 1996, *The Clash of Civilizations and the Remaking of the World Order*. New York: Simon and Schuster.

Ivins, Molly, 1996, "Rip-offs and Hissy Fits," *The Progressive*, Matthew Rothschild, Ed., Madison Wisconsin, v. 60, #7.

Jacob, François, 1987, *La Statue Intérieure*. Paris: Éditions Odile

Johnson, Ian, 1999, "Mass Leverage Class-Action Suits Let The Aggrieved in China Appeal for Rule of Law." *THE WALL STREET JOURNAL* V. 103, No. 58. Thursday March 25.

Frank, Robert H. & Philip J., 1991, Special Issue: Homelessness. *The American Psychologist* v. 46, #11.

Kaplan, Robert D., 1996, *The Ends of the Earth: A Journey to the Frontiers of Anarchy*. New York: Vintage Books, A Division of Random House Inc.

Kennedy, Paul, 1987, *The Rise and Fall of the Great Powers*. New York: Random House.

Krippner, S., Morifee, A. & Feinstein, D. New Myths for the New Millenium. *The Futurist*, March, 1998. Edward Cornish, ed. The World Future Society, Bethesda, Maryland 20814.

Kuhn, Thomas, 1970, *The Structure of Scientific Revolutions*, 2nd edition. Chicago: The University of Chicago Press.

Lasch, Christopher, 1995, *The Revolt of the Elites and the Betrayal of Democracy*. New York: W. W. Norton & Co.

Lind, Michael, 1995 Sr. Editor, "To Have and Have Not—Notes on the Progress of the American class war," *Harper's Magazine*, June, p. 35 ff.)

Lublin, JoAnn S., 1998, "Executive Pay—Pay for No Performance," *The Wall Street Journal*, The Wall Street Journal Reports, Lawrence Rout, Editor. Section R1, pp. 1-18, April 9. Additional quotes from, "A Better Way," an interview with Jerre L. Stead, CEO of Ingram Micro Inc. and Prof. Charles O'Reilly, Stanford Business School

Lukacs, John, 1970, *The Passing of the Modern Age*, New York, Evanston, London: Harper and Row.

Martine, Sara and Murray, Bridget, 1996, "Social toxicity undermines youngsters in inner cities," *Monitor*, The American Psychological Association, October, p 27.

McClelland, Kent, 1994 "Perceptual Control and Social Power." Sociological Perspectives, v. 37(4):461-496.

McNulty, Paul Juvenile Crime Rate Soars Into 21st Century—Commentary, *The Chicago Sun Times*, Dennis A. Britton, editor, Saturday, February 11, 1995.

Morris, Desmond, 1969, *The Human Zoo*. N Y: Dell Publishing Co.

Nietzsche, Frederich, 1883, *Also Sprach Zarathustra*. Reprinted, N. Y.: Frederich Ungar. English translation by Thomas Common, 1960, N. Y.: The Modern Library, Random House.

Nietzsche, Frederich, 1901/1906. *The Will to Power*, 1968, A New Translation by Walter Kaufmann and R. J. Hollingdale. New York: Vintage Books, A Division of Random House.

Ortega y Gasset, José, 1932, *The Revolt of the Masses*, New York: cited in Lasch (1995).

Ortega y Gasset, José *An Interpretation of History* (tr. by Mildred Adams) New York: W.W. Norton & Co. Inc., c. 1973 A lecture series given in 1948-49.

Pavlov, I. P., 1937, *Experimental Psychology and Other Essays*. New York: The Philosophical Library.

Perelman, Michael, 1998. *Class Warfare in the Information Age*. NY: St. Martin's Press.

Petzinger, Thomas, 1999, "Four Rebels Try to Make Managers Talk Like Human Beings," *The Wall Street Journal*, section B1. Friday April 9.

Phelps, Robert, 1965, (Ed.) *Twentieth-Century Culture The Breaking Up*, New York: George Braziller, Inc.

Plooij, Hetty van de Rijt—and Frans X., 1996, *Why They Cry* (A child development book, outlining the growth of nine levels of perception during the first year.) London: Thorsons Tel: +44 181 307 4403, Fax: +44 181 307 4629.

Popowitz, Rick, 1994, The End of the American Century "Why the Party's Over and What You Can Do To Protect Yourself" Advertising supplement to the investment advisory letter, TAIPAN, December.

Poston, T. & Stewart, I. 1978. *Catastrophe Theory and Its Applications*. London: Pitman.

Powers, W. T., Clark, R. A., and McFarland, R. L. 1960a. A general feedback theory of human behavior: part I. *Perceptual and Motor Skills*, Monograph Supplement 7, (1),71-88.

Powers, W. T., Clark, R. A., and McFarland, R. L. 1960b. A general feedback theory of human behavior: part II. *Perceptual and Motor Skills*, Monograph Supplement 7, (3), 309-323.

Powers, W. T., 1973, *Behavior: The Control of Perception*. Chicago: Aldine Publishing. Co.

Powers, W. T., 1989, *Living Control Systems: Selected Papers of William T. Powers*, Gregg Williams, coordinator, Gravel Switch KY: The Control Systems Group, Inc.

Powers, W. T., 1998, *Making Sense of Behavior: The Meaning of Control*. New Canaan, CT: Benchmark publications.

Rachlin, H., 1970/1976. *Introduction to Modern Behaviorism*, 2nd edition. San Francisco: W. H. Freeman & Co.

Rauch, Jonathon, 1998, "Demosclerosis Returns," *The Wall Street Journal*, Tuesday April 14.

Riesman, David, 1950. *The Lonely Crowd: A Study of the Changing American Character*. New Haven: Yale University Press.

Roberts, Steven, 1995, "Wisconsin's lesson in welfare reform," in Science and Society, *U. S. News and World Report*, July 3, p. 56.

Robertson, R.J., Goldstein, D.M., Mermel, M., & Musgrave, M.,1987/1999. "Testing the self as a control system: Theoretical and methodological issues." *International Journal of Human-Computer Studies. 50, (571-580).* Revision and update of a paper presented at the *3rd Annual Control Theory Conference*, October 7-11, Kenosha, Wisconsin: The Haimowoods Center.

Robertson, Richard and Powers, William T., 1990, (Eds.), *Introduction to Modern Psychology: The Control Theory Approach.* Gravel Switch, KY: The Control Systems Group, Inc. Reprinted, 1998, New Canaan, CT: Benchmark Publications.

Roy, Arundhati, 1999. *The Cost of Living.* NY: Modern Library.

Rosenthal, R., 1976. *Experimenter Effects in Behavioral Research.* (Enlarged Ed.) New York: Irvington.

Rosenthal, R. 1977. The Pygmalion effect lives. (In: Schell, R. E., (Ed.), *Readings in Developmental Psychology Today,* 2nd ed.) N. Y. Random House.

Rosenthal, R., and Rubin, D. B. 1978. *Interpersonal expectancy effects: The first 345 studies.* Behavior and Brain Sciences. 3, 377-415.

Sagan, Carl *The Dragons of Eden* 1977. New York: Random House.

Schiavone, Aldo, 2000, *The End of the Past: Ancient Rome and the Modern West* Harvard U. Press.

Shealy, Craig N., 1995, "From Boys Town to Oliver Twist—Separating Fact From Fiction in Welfare Reform and Out-of-Home Placement of Children and Youth." *The American Psychologist*, v. 50, #8, 565-580.

Simon, Julian L. 1995a, (Ed.) *The State of Humanity 1995*, Cambridge, MA: Blackwell Publishers, Inc.

Simon, Julian, 1995b, Why Do We Hear Prophecies of Doom From Every Side? IN: *The Futurist*, A Journal of forecasts, trends and ideas about the future. Edward Cornish, Editor. January-February, 1995, pp. 19-24.

Simon, Julian, 1996, *The Ultimate Resource*, Princeton, NJ: Princeton University Press.

Simon, Roger, 1975 "Is Prison Problem Really Solvable?" *Chicago Sun Times*, April 13, p. 5.

Skinner, B. F. 1938. *The Behavior of Organisms*. New York: Appleton-Century-Crofts.

Smith, Adam (pseudonym of, Goodman, George W.), 1981, *Paper Money*, New York: Summit Books, Simon and Schuster.

Soros, George, 1999, *The Crisis of Global Capitalism*, New York: Public Affairs.

Spengler, Oswald, *The Decline of the West*. In two volumes: 1. Form and Actuality, 2. Perspectives of World History. Originally published in 1918, as Untergang des Abendlandes, and translated by Charles Francis Atkinson and published in 1926 by Alfred A Knopf, Inc.

Suro, Robert, 1999, "Gore presents anti-drug plan. Says abuse 'spiritual problem'" *The Chicago Sun-Times*, Tuesday, February 9, page 16. Reprinted from the Washington Post.

Taylor, T. Shawn, 1998, "Boy's 2 years could fill book of tragic tales, People, system failed William." *Chicago Tribune*, Sunday, October 18. Section 4, Pp 1-2.

Tharp, Mike and Holstein, William J., 1997, "Mainstreaming the Militia," *U.S. News and World Report*, April 21.

Thom, R. 1975, *Structural stability and morphogenesis: An outline of a general theory of models*. Reading, MA: W. A. Benjamin.

Time Magazine (no author identified) 1970, "Why Nothing Seems to Work Anymore," feature article, March 23 issue.

Toynbee, Arnold J., 1947, *A Study of History* Abridgment of volumes I-VI by D. C, Somervell. New York and London: Oxford University Press.

Warner, W. Lloyd, 1941, *The Social Life of a Modern Community*, New Haven: Yale University Press. The Yankee City Series, Vol. 1.

Warner, W. Lloyd, 1953, *American Life: Dream and Reality*, Chicago: The University of Chicago press.

Warren, James, 1996 In "Sunday Watch," *Chicago Tribune*, October 6, Section 2 p. 2.

Weaver, Richard M., 1948, *Ideas Have Consequences*, Chicago: University of Chicago Press.

Whitman, David with Dorian Friedman, Mike Tharp and Kate Griffin, 1995, "Welfare The Myth of Reform," Cover story in: *U. S. New and World Report*, January 16, p. 30.

Whitman, David & Friedman Dorian, with Amy Linn, Craig Doremus & Katia Hetter, 1994, "The White Underclass," Special Report, *U. S. New and World Report*, October 17, 1994.

Whyte, Lancelot, L., 1948, *The Next Development in Man*. New York: New American Library, Mentor Books.

Williams, Bill ca. 1988-1989, Overlapping boards of directors of major American corporations. A computer analysis. Reported to *Control Systems Group* annual conference. Haimowoods, Kenosha, Wisconsin.

Wolf, Charles, 1999, "A Quantum Leap," *The Wall Street Journal*. Book review of George Soros's *The Crisis of Global Capitalism*.

Zeeman, E. C. 1976, "Catastrophe Theory." *Scientific American*, 234, #4, pp. 65-83.

Appendices

Appendix A. Resources for Learning More about Perceptual Control Theory

A simplified version of Powers's major opus (1973) is "Making sense of Behavior" (1998).

For online resources see:

>the Control System Group homepage, http://ed.uiuc.edu/csg/csg.html
>W. T. Powers's web site, www.home.earthlink.net/~powers_w
>Richard Marken's web site, MindReadings.com
>Dåg Forssell's homepage, www.Forssell.com
>other members' web sites, via links on CSG homepage.

Appendix B. The Unconscious as I View it in terms of Hierarchical Control Theory

Although the concept of unconscious mind had already been proposed before Freud his name is most identified with it historically because he made considerable use of the concept in theorizing about the nature of mental malfunctioning. He postulated that the unconscious is a repository of instinctual urges that strive for direct satisfaction and must be supervised by an ego that administers achievement of instinctual desires in harmony with the strictures of society as represented by the individual's superego, roughly equivalent to one's conscience.

He viewed instinctual urges as primal, preverbal or subverbal impulses. They would not be immediately available to consciousness except as transmitted by the ego in its function of "civilizing" them to obtain satisfaction in socially acceptable forms. Thus, the need for psychoanalytic interpretation to enable the individual to realize the more primitive, selfish aims underlying the conflicts between conscious intentions and their instinctual origins.

Within PCT it is also possible to understand that one might not be consciously aware of all the sources of a particular intention. However, the nature of such unconsciousness, as well as the mechanisms involved, appear quite different. One view of consciousness would be that systems acting to maintain Reference specifications from higher levels are monitored by the higher level that is setting the References signals in question. Examples might be: Listening to a program on your car radio while driving effortlessly in easy traffic, then suddenly finding your awareness focused on the line of red brake lights in front of you; or, the hostess of a dinner party suddenly deaf to the words of a guest with whom she was talking while hearing, instead, the baby crying upstairs. In each case of this sort a good understanding of PCT raises the suggestion that consciousness is comprised of perceptual signals from a lower order system that is being adjusted by systems above. In the driving instance we might assume that the Program for skillful driving is monitored by Principles such as (for example) "Avoid accidents," or the like. And in the instance of the mother in conversation the Program of polite small talk would be monitored by higher order systems like a Principle such as "Keep the party running smoothly," plus "Be alert to the baby," or the like.

Taking the view of consciousness, or awareness, as suggested above we see that at any given moment all of the systems that are working automatically—not having their Reference settings currently being reset—are unconscious but potentially able to become conscious, as Freud might have called preconscious. But, for any system to become conscious it must be adjusted and/or monitored by a level above. In that case systems of the highest level would never be in consciousness since, by definition, there is no higher level monitoring them. This suggests an interesting interpretation of certain social psychological phenomena, including a function of friendship interactions. Studies of friendship interactions have shown that at least part of the activity consists for many people in helping to define and confirm one's self concept, self perceptions or self attributions. For example, the work of George Herbert Mead in social psychology involved his view that self identity is a product of the individual's transactions with his/her social environment.

If you tentatively accept the view that a person *needs* interaction with others to build a picture of who one is from the mirroring of one's associates the above view of consciousness suggests why one might need such interaction. That is, if there is a *self-system* controlling your *self-image*—your perception of who you, and there is no higher system monitoring the functioning of the self-system then its functioning would be invisible to the individual. It would be unconscious. One would have to infer what it was doing. It would have no counterpart of the experience you have when your awareness "donwshifts" from (say) what you are saying to a listener to whether your voice sounds hoarse or tremulous while you are saying it. So, to build a picture or image for yourself of who you are you would need to add to your awareness of your principles or values (of which you are mostly conscious) your inferences about your own functioning and those attributions you hear from others that you accept as consistent with the image you want to hold of yourself.

Appendix C. William Powers Proposed description of a Human Control System Hierarchy*

(Presented here in descending order of generality or abstractness.)
(All quotes are from Powers, 1998.)
Note that the perceptual variable of each level is conceived as something that is independently perceived as a phenomenon/condition in itself, but which nevertheless comes about by the simultaneous control of some set of lower level perceptions.)

11. System concepts—the broadest view of an entire system, such as Government, Science, Society, Self, etc. Each one controlling a set of Principles controlled in combination to achieve the perceptual variable maintaining the system concept.
10. Principles—Often made synonymous with personal *values*, such as Honesty, Integrity, (being) well organized, cooperative, etc.
09. Programs—"A structure of tests and choicepoints connecting sequences" For example the Program of driving to work in the morning might involve the following sequences of action:
08. Ordering in time, for example to implement the Program mentioned above: Get dressed, go to garage; open car door, slide in, turn key, place left foot on brake, move gearshift into reverse, apply mild pressure to accelerator with right foot (etc.)

Perception of Reality and the Fate of a Civilization

07. Categories—A term representing a class of objects or perceptions that have something in common as signalled by the class name. For example, *Dog*, to represent a group of current and/or memory perceptions of four legged creatures that bark, etc.
06. Relationships—a perception of independent lower level perceptions existing at the same time. For example, the perception of something being *On* something involves perceiving both objects, in three dimensional space such that the visual angle from horizontal of the object depicted as On is greater than the visual angle of the other object (which can be depicted as *Under* in a complimentary relation) with no side to side displacement and with no discernable space or object between them.

    Note the complimentarily of the relationships involved.
05. Events—"A familiar space-time package of perceptions that follows one particular pattern" such as the bounce of a ball, or the ring of a bell, etc.
04. Transitions—"A series of different configurations, if they are similar enough and occur rapidly enough (but not too rapidly) introduce the sense of motion into a scene . . . . The second hand on a clock creates a continuing impression of rotation."
03. Configurations—the simultaneous control of a set of sensations, such as the lighter/darker differences in shading that comprises perception of a line, edge, corner, or, a shape or form of anything, or a musical chord, etc.
02. Sensations—the experiences derived from neural signals that we recognize as hot or cold, pressure, roughness, smoothness, etc. Or, the separate components of a musical tone such as pitch, loudness, timbre, etc.

01. Intensities—consider the components proposed as the composition of sensations, taken individually.

---

* Adapted and summarized from Powers, 1998.

Author Index

Aristides, 13
Azar, 440
Bailey, 43-45
Bassuk, 62
Bloom, 26, 84ff, 87, 103, 110, 113, 237, 257, 260, 454, 461
Bonner, 40
Boot, 343
Bork, 19, 84ff, 87, 103, 110, 113, 124, 257, 258, 374
Bower, 65
Breland, 270, 361, 449
Brown, 22, 36ff, 39ff, 43, 45, 49ff, 55ff, 60ff, 71, 412, 437, 439, 441, 443
Brzezinski, 87ff
Buchanan, 11, 19, 93
Buckley, 124, 255ff, 454
Cartwright, 445
Calhoun, 269ff, 450
Chase, 225
Clark, 131
Davidson, 23, 42, 73, 84ff, 88ff, 92ff, 98, 116, 120ff, 302, 308, 327, 333, 341, 343, 365, 374, 377, 385, 394ff, 415, 419, 444ff
Descartes, 20, 84, 115, 131ff, 141, 197, 203, 223, 255
Diamond, 379ff, 429, 437

Dowd, 301
Eckholm, 437
Ehrlich, 22, 37, 43, 49, 52, 412, 440ff
Erikson, 27, 150ff, 157ff, 167, 236, 276, 407, 445, 448ff
Farmer, 56, 75ff, 79ff, 113, 225ff, 387
Feinstein, 12
Festinger, 250, 451
Fialka, 56, 59
Ford, 352ff, 457
Freedman, 181, 269
Goodman, 115
Gore, 309ff, 319ff, 438
Gorney, 430
Greene, 454
Hardin, 60
Harr, 67ff, 343
Hauser, 61
Haywood, 94ff, 344, 416
Holden, 65
Holstein, 444
Howard, 59ff, 75, 110, 113, 122, 203, 225ff, 238, 244ff, 262, 322, 343, 440, 453
Hubbard, 58
Huntington, 98, 103
Ivins, 62ff
Jacob, 110ff, 175, 445
Johnson, 366
Jones, 443
Kaplan, 39ff, 43, 70, 95, 239, 358, 361, 439
Kennedy, Paul, 23, 103, 354, 374
Kennedy, Sen. Ted, 363
Krippner, 12, 84, 87, 437
Kuhn, 24, 26, 54, 69, 104, 108, 124, 129, 133, 138, 148, 159, 164ff, 176, 185ff, 259, 374, 448
Lasch, 90ff, 110, 302ff, 341

Lind, 300
Lublin, 301
Lukacs, 79, 85, 87, 89, 92ff, 95, 98, 103, 121, 125, 131ff, 148, 199, 374, 444, 446
Marken, 207, 374, 448, 452
McClelland, 448, 452
McFarland, 131
McNulty, 438
Morris, 269ff
Mortifee, 12
Newton, 27, 121, 165, 360, 373ff
Nietzsche, 84ff, 115, 119
Ortega, 84ff, 90, 341, 374
Petzinger, 366
Phelps, 82ff
Phillips, 26
Plooij, H., & Plooij, F.X., 174, 217, 445
Popowitz, 438
Poston, 441
Powers, 29, 129, 131, 177, 179, 185, 191, 197ff, 203ff, 210, 215, 217, 231, 257, 272, 283, 285, 289, 332, 361, 369-70, 374, 381, 391, 447, 449ff, 452, 458
Rachlin, 203
Rauch, 72
Rees-Mogg, 23, 42, 73, 84ff, 88ff, 90, 92ff, 98, 116, 120ff, 302, 308, 327, 333, 341, 365, 374, 377, 385, 394, 395, 415, 419, 444, 456ff
Riesman, 444
Roberts, 443
Robertson, 445, 452, 454
Rosenthal, 53, 189, 251ff
Sagan, 276, 278, 455
Schiavone, 13, 14
Shealy, 443
Simon, 22, 44ff, 48, 50, 52, 65, 79, 80, 323, 412, 441

Skinner, 204, 449, 453
Smith, Adam (AKA George Goodman)77, 115
Soros, 331ff, 387ff, 394
Spengler, 21, 24, 26, 29, 85, 100ff, 107, 109ff, 115ff, 119ff, 124ff, 129, 132ff, 137ff, 142, 144ff, 149, 153, 158ff, 164, 167ff, 168, 177, 185, 187ff, 191, 236, 246, 258ff, 271, 280, 296, 309, 319, 356, 360ff, 374, 376, 381, 387, 394, 402, 414ff, 445, 446ff
Stewart, 441
Suro, 309, 317, 319, 321
Taylor, 454
Tharp, 444
Thom, 441
Toynbee, 100, 394
Viscusi, 45, 46
Warner, 28ff, 282ff, 288ff, 302, 319, 389, 390ff, 455
Zeeman, 441

Subject Index

"1929 type" depression, 40
21st Century, 438
60 Minutes, 60, 64, 152, 224, 327, 387, 452
abandonment of democracy, 90
abortion(s), 236, 322, 411
abstract principle(s), 28, 66, 69, 109, 168, 245, 343ff, 346, 374, 388, 431ff,
academic freedom, 255
adult education (informal in friendship and kin groups) 367
advertising, 25, 40ff, 244, 261, 263, 296, 310, 407, 421
advocacy(ies), 54, 76, 80, 261, 431
Africa, 16, 39, 70, 77, 350, 356, 439
African, 279
    Afro-American(s), 395
        jury, 342ff
Agee, 83-4
ALAR, 47ff,
Alarm(s), 70
Alpha males, 277
Amazon rain forest, 403ff
America(n, ns),
    40, 65, 70, 74, 76, 79, 83, 97, 121, 141, 152ff, 186, 236, 242, 273, 276, 292, 298, 300, 324, 344, 395, 403, 410, 432, 438

    century, 438
    cities, 39
    class war, 300
    corporate, 366
    government, 72
    historians, 97
    Indians, indigenies, 63, 154, 155, 432
    life, 83
    militia movement, 444
    principle(s), 90, 152, 311, 334ff, 354, 418
    rich, 455
    taxpayers, 59
    workers, 62
Amicus Brief, 323
analyzing, 112, 205, 398, 418, 423, 426, 431
anarchy, 67, 229, 258, 307, 346
animal crowding, 269
anomaly(ies), 40, 133, 138, 159, 165, 168, 185, 187, 259, 294
Anthropologist(s), 200, 282, 293
anti-children attitude, 237
anti-drug plan, 309
archaeologist(s), 147
Aristarchus, of Samos, 158
Aristides, Aelius, 13ff
Aristotle, 271, 371
assumption(s) about reality, 21, 22, 24, 29, 83, 84, 102, 111, 124, 137, 154, 223, 273, 376, 379, 442
Atlantic Monthly, 39
attention,
    31, 32, 49, 103, 106, 109, 129, 153, 198, 202, 223, 242, 257, 284, 332, 339, 419
    shift, 226, 372, 378, 410, 453
authority, 18, 58, 81, 88, 89, 140, 224, 241, 259, 280, 289, 313, 327, 363, 418
average citizen, 22, 298, 373

axiom(s), axiomatic, 26, 107, 112, 124, 133, 135, 145ff, 149, 158, 159, 167, 168, 185, 188, 236, 360, 392
Ayn Rand, 295, 359
Babylon, 97, 120
"Bare Knuckles and Back Rooms, " 66
basic human nature, 267
basic premises, 23ff, 104, 113, 139, 376
Beatrice Foods, 67
behavior(s), 15, 19ff, 25ff, 55, 68, 91, 129, 133ff, 141ff, 149ff, 161ff, 171, 173, 189, 195, 203ff, 207ff, 213, 220, 222, 226ff, 232, 246, 250, 254ff, 260, 271, 278ff, 295, 308, 311, 315, 318, 322, 331ff, 334, 358, 361, 373, 375, 377, 380, 386, 388, 397, 426ff,
    control aspects, 22, 27, 104, 129, 130ff, 134ff, 140, 143ff, ff, 164, 170, 172, 176, 187, 189, 197, 202, 211, 232, 253, 317, 319, 336, 348, 422
    deviant, disturbed, pathological, 159, 181, 186, 219, 255, 269ff, 275, 277, 410
    mass, 27, 138, 188
    nature of, 9, 103, 131, 263
    sexual, 25
    sinks, 270,
    two ways of viewing, 132, 224, 250
    unethical, 65, 123
Behaviorism, 268, 271
Biological approaches, 267
Black Hills, 151
Black Muslims, 319
Bloody revolutions, 364
body of ideas, 110
Britain, 89, 98, 354
British upper class(es), 122
Brown versus Board of Education, 258
business, 17ff, 37, 51, 58, 64, 113, 166, 171, 186, 200, 242, 261, 312, 364, 385, 387ff, 390ff, 393, 405, 416, 421, 422

    businessmen, 40, 58, 157, 190
    corporations, 260
capitalism, 75, 166, 331ff, 387, 399
Carcinogen, 46
    or Toxin of the Week Phenomenon, 47
care manager(s), 262ff
Cartesian, (ism), paradigm, fallacy, view of behavior 21, 121, 141, 204, 213, 248, 250, 260ff, 268, 319, 347, 349, 352, 379ff, 429, 453
catastrophe(s), 11, 13, 35, 40, 150, 344, 360ff, 386, 390, 416, 440, 441
Catastrophe Theory, 323, 443
Category(ies), 60ff, 121, 162ff, 190, 201, 210, 244, 277, 479
Cathedrals, 106, 107, 115, 167
Causality, causation, 116, 125, 131ff, 141ff, 223
Central Asia, 70
centralization, 355ff
CEO(s), 50ff, 57, 285, 301ff, 323, 354
    challenges to, 24, 36, 49, 74, 76, 104, 138, 146, 149, 158, 163, 190ff, 225, 274, 291ff, 315, 320ff, 324, 349, 351, 359, 363, 366, 378, 380ff, 403, 409, 429, 437, 445, 459
chance, 97, 104, 147, 243, 248, 290, 355, 381ff, 423, 429
child-
    development, 150, 238
    hood, 274
    lessness, 242
    rearing, 16ff, 65, 75, 110, 116ff, 123, 150, 159, 174, 235ff, 239ff, 252, 279, 335, 352, 384, 394, 407, 446, 450
    smile of child, 173ff
    hardy child, 220
children, 16, 27, 40, 65, 75, 90, 92, 123ff, 130, 150, 168, 235ff, 241ff, 251, 258, 261, 276, 352ff, 361, 388, 401ff, 407, 410ff, 425
    growing up with little or no adult supervision, 402ff

lower class children growing up under parental stress
and abuse, 238
chimpanzee and human infant development, 217
Chinese
    civilization (13th to 15th centuries), 354ff
    peasants, 362
Christian,
    born-again, 319
    early communes, 401
Christian defenders of the poor, 295
chronic error, 201
chronic issue, 229, 232, 325
    cost of law enforcement, 325
    chronic problems, 350
    chronic reorganization, 159
Chronic Social Issues, 229
circular causality, causation, 42, 132, 199, 204ff
citizen(s), 13, 22, 59, 78, 80, 103, 122, 139, 152, 154, 187, 210, 235, 276, 279, 285, 287, 298, 304, 308, 310ff, 324, 332, 339, 345, 353, 362ff, 385, 392, 397ff, 401, 407, 419ff, 430, 459
    responsible citizenship, 227
    citizenship seen as bsolete, 93
civil rights, 25, 124ff, 242
civilization(s), 9, 12, 16, 18, 20, 23ff, 28, 36, 53, 70, 73, 78ff, 83ff, 88ff, 92, 94, 96ff, 100, 103, 106, 111, 115, 121, 132, 138ff, 144ff, 147, 153, 164, 168, 177, 188, 195, 214, 241, 246, 248, 254, 261, 273, 280, 295, 305, 342, 344, 349, 356, 361, 364, 378, 387, 390, 394, 402, 412, 446, 456
    contemporary, 48
    create the groundwork of a new, 377,
    crisis in, 27, 190, 376, 386
    decline, 11, 13, 15, 21, 120, 133, 142, 149, 158, 191, 296, 341, 374, 414, 444

    definition of, 384, 391
    great advances in, 359
    idea of, 273
    modern phase ends, 333
    revolution in, 331, 345
    turning point in progress of, 379
clash of Islamic and Western cultures, 11
class action lawsuits, 363
class interests, 302
Class War, 297, 299ff
Classical,
    Civilization/culture, 84, 97, 107, 114, 117, 119, 158, 167
    science, 108, 159
    society, 114
clergy, 66, 183, 285, 313
Clinton, President, 287, 334
    administration, 309
closed mind, 68, 69, 443
    closed mind set, 337
cognitive
    abilities, 183
    behavior, 162, 186, 279, 299, 338
    boundaries, 132,
    dissonance, 28, 189, 250ff, 259, 262, 326, 339, 341, 343, 372
    function, 92
    structure, 163ff
    systems, 174
    tolerance for inconsistency, 343
colonial people, 98
Columbine, 386
common abstractions, 109
common element(s), 52ff, 146, 241, 343ff, 348, 373
common identity, 104, 401
common interest(s), 333, 353

common sense, 17ff, 28, 60, 65, 69ff, 75, 92, 103, 109ff, 118, 120, 123, 136, 149, 200, 245, 259, 261, 271, 322, 349, 362, 379, 407, 446
    anti-commonsense, 113
    defy, 75, 143, 346, 376
Communal Control of the Environment, 297
communal life, 104, 283
    of people who do not know each other, 401
communist(s)(istic), 140
    countries, 166
    party elite, 364
    state, 363
community(ies), 17, 41, 62, 83, 122, 133, 147, 150ff, 159ff, 176, 200, 238, 246, 283ff, 290, 292, 303ff, 325, 354, 356, 358, 397, 403, 409, 420, 429, 459
    Christian, 401
    gated, 41, 415
    loss of, 82, 407
    meetings, 123, 293
    passing of, 82
    purpose of, 70
    scientific, 58
    solve problems, 416
    of Woburn, 70
competence, 27, 146, 148, 176, 179, 182ff, 190, 435
competition, 23, 40, 50, 73, 76, 98, 109, 134, 137, 138, 144, 179, 180, 246, 274, 278, 294, 299, 300, 303, 336, 350ff, 356, 378ff, 395, 402, 407, 429
    of ideas, 55
competitive, 290, 312, 354ff, 357
competitor(s), 135, 137, 139, 379, 416, 421
Computers, 85, 205, 208, 215, 227, 276, 326, 333, 351, 370, 374, 448, 458
conception of reality, 19, 31, 145, 154, 175, 434
conditioning, 166, 203, 268, 454

Congress, 25, 57ff, 72, 75, 122, 154, 225, 238, 285, 301, 303, 334, 355, 385, 389, 420
congressman, 52, 421
consciousness, 14, 83, 87, 100, 110, 116, 156, 167, 202, 232, 234, 275, 393, 476, 477
    self-, 84, 87, 223
consequences, 37, 59ff, 95, 98, 225, 293, 299, 316, 346, 349, 390, 396, 455
    of ideas, 438
    of random action, 215ff
conservative, 13, 25, 138, 153, 182, 219, 289, 300, 315, 335, 397
conservative action, 52
Conservative political attitudes, 267
Conservative writers, 19
contemporary life, 79, 394
contemporary psychology, 141, 249, 254
control, 15, 22, 27ff, 37ff, 42, 52, 62, 70, 72, 76, 87ff, 91, 102, 121, 130ff, 135, 142ff, 149, 159, 162ff, 168, 175, 184, 198, 201ff, 213ff, 217, 228, 232, 238, 259ff, 279, 282ff, 286, 288, 294, 311, 315, 335ff, 354, 366, 377ff, 383, 395, 418, 425, 431
    controlled condition(s), 199ff, 206ff
    controlled perceptions, 28
    of perception, 29, 104, 129, 138, 161, 171ff, 176ff, 183, 189, 246ff, 284, 401, 427
    of violence, 42
    over resources, 183
    system(s), 20, 28ff, 130, 140, 147, 155, 161, 169ff, 174, 176, 179, 199, 202, 204ff, 208, 211ff, 216, 219, 220, 227, 233, 235, 251ff, 266, 270, 272, 277ff, 300, 304, 311ff, 340ff, 258, 374, 385, 389, 406, 423, 427, 438, 443, 451
    system hierarchy(ies), 29, 134, 144, 153, 156, 178, 190, 209, 226, 253ff, 265, 290, 324, 344, 379, 390, 419, 433, 448
    systems group, 9

theory (systems theory), 9, 27, 197, 229ff, 250, 267ff, 339, 368, 345
  controlled variables, 145, 174, 183, 189, 210, 213, 233, 239ff, 243, 263ff, 277, 285, 292ff, 295, 297, 299, 307, 312, 317, 323, 346, 352, 421, 453,
conversion to a spiritual group or religion, 319
Copernicus, 158, 185, 187
corruption, 15, 17, 19, 76, 110, 124, 152, 169, 245, 259, 261, 328, 337, 345
  of implications of Marx's [ideas], 166
  of thought, 120
  from psychologist point of view, 16
  point of view of the rulers of Soviet society, 362
  corruption of heart, 303
creating community, 82
creative potential
  exhaustion of, 148
  of the first principles, 145
Crime(s), 18, 38ff, 41ff, 56, 62, 64ff, 77, 90, 123, 219, 224, 255, 309, 317, 325ff, 346, 352, 396, 406, 408, 438, 441
  war crimes, 384ff, 412
crime dramas, 345
crises, 60, 81, 129, 148, 150, 182, 190, 344, 382
crisis, 18, 20, 27, 52, 148, 150, 159, 165, 182, 187ff, 190ff, 232, 243, 324, 332, 335, 376ff, 382, 386, 394, 414, 439,
  intellectual, 169
crisis state, 414
Crusades, 52, 115
culpability, 349
  question of, 349
culture(s), 11ff, 24, 26ff, 29, 36, 40, 80ff, 84, 90ff, 97, 101ff, 111, 117ff, 123, 132, 139, 142, 146ff, 164, 166ff, 170, 176ff, 185ff, 191, 235ff, 255, 159ff, 266, 274, 283, 303, 309, 333, 335, 342, 356, 358, 360, 362, 373ff, 376, 378ff, 387, 391, 412, 415, 425ff, 430ff, 447

    Asian, 98
    decline, 82, 97
    disintegration, 342
    development, 116,
    forming period, 167, 272
    history of, 21, 112, 138
    Japanese, 247
    non-western, 143
    cultural violence, 408
cybernetic, 131
    cybernetic revolution, 20
Dakotas, 150
Dark Ages, 86, 93, 327, 346, 377, 446
dawn of time, 211
decadence, 335
Declaration of Independence, 124, 271, 273, 285
decline, 13, 15, 21ff, 26ff, 48, 80ff, 87, 89, 93, 95, 97ff, 101, 103, 109, 114, 120ff, 133, 142, 145, 149, 188, 236, 296, 327, 373ff, 387, 389, 414, 444
    definition of, 99
    of natural resources, 49
defense mechanisms, 174
degenerate moral positions, 113
degeneration, 48, 124, 191, 302, 402
    cultural, 15, 236, 271, 296
    ecological, 16
    environmental, 386
    of Western paradigms, 167, 188, 334
degeneration of 19th century liberalism, 267
degradation, 16, 18, 81
    of scholarship, 87
degrees of freedom, 177ff, 185, 191, 257
democracy, 90, 153, 279, 311ff, 389, 418
Descartes, 20, 84, 115, 131ff, 141, 197, 203, 223, 255
desertion of the elite, 303

destiny, 101ff, 116ff, 132, 144ff, 256
    concept of, 223
    sense of, 110ff
deterioration, 21, 30, 55, 71, 188, 334, 394
deterioration of the culture, 188
development, 93ff, 114, 146, 170, 309
    human, 31
    of competence, 176, 183, 185
    of culture, 51, 116ff, 147ff, 175, 272, 280, 297, 377
    scientific, 97, 187, 255
    theories of, 27
developmental,
    crises, 159
    learning, 216, 388
    malfunctions, 150
deviant behavior, 269
Dewey, John, 357
dirty play (by athletes), 123
DISTRIBUTION of VITAL SERVICES, 399
DISTRIBUTION of VITAL SUPPLIES, 400
disturbed behavior, 159
division of labor, 55, 58, 296, 319
    unintended defect of, 57
Do Americans Suddenly Hate Kids?, 236, 242
Dr. Bruno Bettlheim, 237, 242
Drug addicts, 315ff, 389
drug free society, 315
drug lords, 346, 459
drug problem, 318
    the spiritual aspect, 319
drug war, 77, 309, 318, 411
dysfunctional,
    approach of external efforts to control, 431
    habits, 319
    people, 275, 372

early development, 171, 174, 175, 446, 452
    Freud on, 449
earth as a human environment (preservation of), 404
Easter Island, 31ff, 40, 84, 425, 437
    Easter Island culture, 12
ecology, 47, 350, 363
Ecological experts see the world in danger, 11, 39, 45, 359, 404, 431, 437
economic(s), 22ff, 30, 37, 39, 42ff, 45, 61ff, 71ff, 74, 81, 83, 93, 98, 101, 107, 115, 117, 119, 136, 210, 296ff, 302, 323ff, 331, 338, 351, 375, 382, 388, 389, 396, 398, 401, 419, 433, 454
    chaos, 88
    condition, 277
    development, 40, 166
    force(s), 11, 25, 430
    historian, 76
    opportunity, 309
    revolution, 354
    theory, 49
economists, 40, 49, 55, 59, 298, 453
education, 74, 238, 240, 257, 267, 274, 279, 326, 350, 351ff, 366ff, 434ff
effective reform (obstacle to), 392,
effector mechanism, 385
egalitarian societies, 332
electors, 312ff, 315
Energy, 21, 35, 49, 58ff, 79, 204, 241, 280, 290, 297, 338, 397, 415
environment(s), 16ff, 22, 26, 30, 37, 39ff, 45, 47ff, 52, 56, 61ff, 79ff, 104, 106, 138, 140, 142, 145, 150, 170ff, 175ff, 182, 188ff, 198ff, 212, 217, 219ff, 222, 245, 256, 281ff, 286, 288, 290ff, 299ff, 304, 306, 308ff, 313, 350, 358ff, 361, 378ff, 386ff, 402ff, 415, 426, 435, 438ff, 446

environmental, 20, 22, 30, 37, 39, 45, 51, 173, 214, 277, 280, 311, 380, 426, 429, 437, 440, 443
   activists, 40
   "causes" of behavior, 204
   challenge(s), 57, 70, 104, 274, 478, 381
   damage, 363
   pessimists, 51
   policy, 81
   societies, (groups), 16, 47, 49ff, 363
   variables, 268, 291
   villains, 50
epigenetic rules, 271ff, 274ff, 281
equality, 124ff, 301, 395
Error, 67, 156, 172ff, 183, 186, 202, 212, 229ff, 234, 251ff, 287, 326, 349, 360, 369, 374, 378, 385, 390, 448, 452, 459
   chronic, 201
   signal(s), 199, 206, 209, 225, 230, 275, 304, 313, 372, 403, 433
   state, 216, 270, 284, 291, 294, 311, 315, 319, 365
establishment, 25, 67, 395
   educational, 241
ethologists, 269
ethology, 172, 267, 269ff
Euclid's system, 111
Euclidean geometry, 108
Europe, 98, 354, 356
European(s), 12, 85, 294
evolution, 23, 104, 113, 115, 139, 142, 167, 170, 180, 217, 307, 350, 403
   course of development, 107
   cultural changes (in), 15
   in brain structure, 276
   of civilization, 140, 394

of culture, 21, 29, 142, 164, 166, 176, 274, 378, 426, 428, 431
of thought, 103, 109, 133, 259
theory, 69
experience of reality, 105
experiment(s), (-al), (-ation), 54, 71, 165, 172, 181, 189, 208ff, 212, 236, 240, 249, 251ff, 264, 268, 309, 336, 359, 362, 373, 399, 404, 410, 417, 420, 424, 434, 438, 449, 451, 457
extreme derivation (of a principle), 112
faith in government, 13,
faith in the system, 115,
family farmers, 298, 324
Far East, 351, 356
fear of brutality, 123,
feedback, 27, 31, 42, 131ff, 134, 140, 143ff, 157, 187, 195, 197, 294, 351, 410, 421, 447, 451ff
   machines, 204
   mechanism, 198, 205
"feel good" legislation, 75
Ferguson's view, 303
feudal,
   baronies, 346
   order, 94
   system, 346
first principles, 105, 109, 112, 125, 132, 133, 135, 140ff, 143, 145, 148ff, 195, 280, 360, 362, 374, 376, 394, 456
Ford, Edw., 352, 353, 457
formal laws, 272
formative axioms, 188
formative development, 190
formative principles, 164
Free will, 117,
freedom, 63ff, 97, 121, 151, 178ff, 261, 374, 407ff
   academic, 255

concept of, 119
of thought, 120
French, 71, 354, 364, 411
French revolutionary motto, 124
fundamental
    axioms, 246, 257, 387
    changes, 20, 26, 31, 73, 195, 394
    Christians, 69, 289, 300, 315
    principles, 24ff, 113, 132, 134, 174, 176, 185
    process, 28
    religions, 321
    tendencies, 107
    understandings, 84, 371
    values, 61, 64, 112
fundamentalistic religion, 19
future, 12, 14ff, 24, 26, 35, 39, 42ff, 45, 47ff, 58, 71, 80, 88, 90, 97, 103, 117, 137, 216, 228, 245, 321, 325, 333, 377ff, 382, 384, 387, 409ff, 412, 416, 421, 424ff, 437, 439
Galileo, 84, 204, 371, 377
genetics, 65
genetic endowment, 274, 401
    evolution, 266
    predispositions, 175, 270, 403
genetically given control systems, 170, 172ff, 231, 267
genocide, 273, 384, 386, 397ff, 412,
geographic areas, 356
geographic factors, 98
German(s), 96, 105ff, 167, 241, 258, 344
    raids, 95
    thinkers, 101
Germany, 98, 387, 418
global,
    benefits, 406
    change, 87

famine, 43
warming, 37, 43ff, 54, 56ff, 386
globalization, 354
Goethe, 102, 445
Gore, VP Albert, 309, 310ff, 319ff, 438
Gothic
    Cathedral(s), 106ff, 115, 167
    concept, 114
    thought, 115, 118
Goths, 115
governance, 13, 56, 73, 308, 325, 331, 361
government(s), 13, 17, 27, 46ff, 49, 54, 62, 71ff, 122, 190, 273, 279ff, 285ff, 298ff, 308ff, 319ff, 325, 327, 333, 339, 343, 362ff, 377, 385, 392, 396, 398ff, 406, 440ff
    agents, employees, 152, 156
    failure, 60,
    leaders of, 425
    national, 354
    world, 16
great depression, 61
Great Powers, 86
Greek and Roman countrysides, 106
Greek or Roman temple, 106
Greek scientists, 223
group as a whole, 380
group identity, 104, 343, 406
group power, 343
Gulf War, 59
Guthrie, Edwin R., (theory of learning), 367ff,
habits, 102, 112, 119, 147, 154, 170, 176, 219ff, 234, 316, 350, 359, 361ff, 368ff, 383, 389, 395, 434, 447, 449
    coping, 149ff
    of thought, 319
Hammurabi, 120

Harvard law,
    faculty, 67
    professor, 69
hierarchy, (ies),
    control system, 29, 129, 136, 164, 170ff, 174ff, 189ff, 209, 214, 216ff, 226ff, 229, 235, 242, 246, 253, 272, 285, 311, 340, 368, 389, 419, 427, 429, 433, 448
    (other hierarchy, as source of disturbance to one's own), 226
    of bureaucracy, 153
    of an individual, 179, 293, 324, 344
    of interlocking control systems, 202, 374
    of purpose(s), 129, 134ff, 139ff, 146
hierarchical
    control system(s), 134, 144, 153, 207, 255, 265, 276, 284, 290, 313, 319, 390
    model, 157
    social organization, 300, 306, 326
    variables, 266
highest controlled perception, 340
Higher education, 255
higher,
    priority, 166, 238, 240, 245, 266, 342, 343
    perception, 247
historical perspective, 89, 302
history, 13, 26, 40, 43ff, 49, 89, 92, 95, 101, 103, 109ff, 112, 117, 121, 125, 137, 139, 145, 149ff, 153, 155, 166, 176, 222, 247, 256, 259, 268, 272ff, 300, 304, 307, 334, 350, 378ff, 384, 402, 408, 414, 456
    British and American, 344
    of civilization, 13, 29, 100, 142, 177, 190
    of science, 104, 138, 148, 164, 187
    underlying principles in, 94, 97
    writing in Classical and Western terms, 114

Homeless, 61ff, 386, 389, 443
homeless shelter, 245
hopelessness, 90
hopeless quest for compliance, 227
Hugo Grotius, 272
human behavior, 19ff, 104, 131, 140, 149, 204, 207, 211, 218, 221, 246, 250ff, 268ff, 373, 379, 386, 431, 455
    instinctive, 271
human being(s), 25, 69, 88, 104ff, 145, 168, 170, 195, 226, 244, 248, 256, 263ff, 268, 272, 276, 303, 313, 380, 396, 429
human development(s), 31, 217, 409, 445
    take people by surprise, 31
human fallibility, 46
Human ingenuity, 43, 45, 239
human nature, 19ff, 28, 30ff, 49, 64, 85, 146, 202, 267, 268, 270ff, 274ff, 299, 362
    continuing to evolve, 429
human qualities, 273
    necessary for survival, 272
human race, 70,
human rights, 273
human thinking, 103, 111, 133, 259,
Human-Resources-Management, 301
humility, 289
idea(s), 55, 80, 97, 106, 108, 110ff, 116ff, 119, 121, 132, 138ff, 141, 143ff, 148ff, 170, 175, 188, 191, 195, 197, 203, 214, 221, 247, 261, 264, 267ff, 271, 280, 288, 325, 349, 351, 367ff, 382, 396, 401, 403ff, 406, 422, 427, 428, 446, 456, 458
    consequences of, 85, 384, 438
    of death, 160,
    of grace, 117
    great, 413
    of private property, 151,

of progress, 27ff, 96, 114
ideals, 43, 75, 182, 293, 301, 336, 366, 442
illegal drug usage in the U. S, 310, 322
    by upper middle class and upper class, 320
impeachment (debacle), 334ff, 338, 340ff
impervious to control by U. N., 16
India, 98, 114, 432ff
Indian(s) (indigenous Americans), 150
    agent, 154, 156
    chief, 155
    law, 151
    secretaries of Indian affairs, 153
    treaties, 152
indifference to rules, 92
individual crisis, 335
individual freedom, 97, 151
individual responsibility, 29, 61, 64, 255
industrial and technological revolutions,
    rectify the injurious consequences of, 349
industrial revolution, 241
infinitesimal calculus, 108, 114, 195
inflation, 15, 77, 121
information, 12, 15, 24, 47, 84, 121, 132, 165, 212, 233, 243, 262, 296, 319, 335, 337, 340, 351, 361, 366ff, 370, 409, 430
    growth of, 416
    information elite, 93, 377
    scholarly, 444
information-age, 94
inhuman, 15, 398
inhumane outcomes, 113, 158
innocent fraud, 263
Input, 173ff, 199, 206, 211ff, 230, 400, 446
insider information, 337
instinct, (ive)(s)(ual), 28, 92, 117ff, 170, 172, 231, 269ff, 278ff,

281, 288, 299, 338, 344, 346, 361ff, 394, 401, 403, 405, 433, 435, 449, 455, 476
drift, 269, 449
tendencies, 51
intellectual
    ability, 380
    crisis, 159, 169
    games, 296
intellectual-vigilante posse, 414
intention(s), 26ff, 62, 71, 119, 134, 136, 139ff, 155ff, 182, 188ff, 208, 210, 213, 221, 223, 226, 230ff, 234, 266, 268, 277, 295, 315, 334, 353, 393, 417, 442, 452ff, 476
internal conflicts, 307
internet, 333, 351, 366ff
Intrinsic system, 159, 172ff, 216ff, 231, 269ff, 272, 274, 276, 361, 392, 401, 452
    intrinsic variable, 274, 361
    intrinsic-system error, 218, 278, 365, 390, 459
investment, 405, 428
    advice merchants, 41
    newsletter, 43
invisible hand, 323
Isaac Newton, 373
Islamic,
    Baghdad, 120
    civilization, 350, 351
    faith, 11, 395
    young people, 321
Japan, 45, 354
Japanese movie, Kagemusha, 247
Jeremiahs, 13, 22, 31
Jesus, 117, 305
Jews,
    American, 321

who left Germany, 418
Jewish liberals, 300
John Holt and Jonathan Kozoll
    books of, 353
John Stuart Mill, 257
Jonestown, 386
jury
    decision, 183
    nullification, 341ff
    tampering, 122
justice, 67, 69, 92, 122, 154, 156, 271, 280, 315, 335, 343, 407, 441
Kafka-esque true stories, 327
lack, of common sense, 60
    of compliance, 22
    of even basic consensus about what the problems are, 15
    of foresight, 91
    of legislative responsiveness to popular will, 424
    of power does not annul individual responsibility, 29
    of values, 238
Laissez faire, 55
late stages in a cultural process, 92
lawmaking, 224, 246, 383
legal reasoning, 135, 261, 347
legislators, 17, 72, 224, 280, 301, 311ff, 318, 350, 363, 383, 391ff, 420ff, 424
    not malevolent people, 389
legislators and executives,
    members of the insulated classes, 350
lessened responsibility, 347
liberal, 19
    critics, 390
    organization, 396

Liberalism, 255, 257, 444
liberals, 13, 63, 219, 267, 300, 342
linear causation, 204
Linear Logic, 22, 27, 195, 225ff, 239ff, 242, 250, 261, 318, 319, 323, 454
    psychology, 268
    linear thinking, 225, 243
living organism, 20, 130ff, 141, 195, 200, 203, 231, 306
local community, 284
logical extremes, 103, 168
Lutherans, 289
malevolence, 233, 265, 456,
malevolent, 155, 263, 389, 442
manufacture of stuff, 255, 264
Market, 40, 47, 67, 93, 115, 399, 408
Marx, 118, 268, 295, 400, 401
Marxist theory, 166, 167, 362
mass movements, 54
mass production, 195, 241, 246, 248, 254, 261, 264, 345
Maxwell, 165ff
media, 15ff, 23, 44, 46ff, 49, 60, 65, 77, 80, 91, 238, 241ff, 296, 302, 309, 327, 337, 339, 341, 385ff, 390, 398, 407ff, 415
media abuse, 123
medicine, 206, 264, 411, 432
members
    of congress, 285, 385
    of primitive horde, 132
    of ruling class, 14
Meso-America, 356
Mexico city, 38, 86
Michelangelo, 110
Middle Ages, 84, 271
Middle East, 16

mind readers, 347, 349
Missionaries of Charity, 245
Modern Age, 79
    waning of, 89, 120, 334
modern ethic, 258
modern historians, 100, 109, 447
modern state, 89, 93, 347
    growing powerlessness of, 93
moral dilemmas, 150
Morale, phenomenon of, 119
mother-love, 117
Mothers Against Drunk Driving, 363, 430
multinational companies, 346
multinational corporations, 18, 95, 398
mural or multigraph, 356
Nappy Hair, 279
narcissism, 87, 169
national identity, 92, 286, 302, 343, 390, 419
national Principle(s),
    that all men are born equal, 289
    inconsistencies between, 342
    when unclear, 317
nationality, 25, 73, 419ff
Native Americans, 154
Natural Resources, 45, 49, 98, 351, 380
    Defense Council, 323
natural law, 28, 271ff, 344, 362, 384, 392, 420
natural law of survival, 402
nature of human nature, 85, 268, 271, 275, 362
    Lenin's mistaken view of, 64
nature of Nature,
    rival views of, 190
    Spengler's view of, 146

nature of reality, 21, 29, 103, 132ff, 137, 139, 147, 154, 159, 186, 320, 360, 415
nature/nurture debate, 267
Nazi(s), 364
    Germany, 98
Near East, 356
new learning, 218, 232
new social order, 93
New York,
    City, 86
    Times, 279
    publisher, 66
news media, 44, 408
Newton, 27, 165
Newtonian physics, 226
Newtonianism, 121
Nikita Krushchev, 157
nineteenth century, 114, 257
Nobel winner, 175, 110
Nordic Ting, 124
normal science, 148, 154, 165, 187
North Africa, 356
nuclear age, 226
nullifying actions, 225
    decisions, 228
number-worlds, 107
Nurenberg, 273, 384
nurture, 267
Oceania, 356
Oklahoma City, 73, 299, 324, 386
opting out, 92, 343
ordinary people, 13, 25, 81, 337, 341, 347, 350ff, 360, 365, 371, 377, 458
    and survival, 334, 344, 358, 362, 373, 416, 431
    and caveat emptor, 296

and dependence on popular media for information, 15
and impeachment, 278
and self-directed education, 366
did not experience "Fall of Rome", 344
government officials are not, 364
in bringing about, or constituting wave of, the future, 80, 378, 380, 409, 411ff
patronage of, 354
perceive government, 280
perceiving crime in terms of common sense, 18
power of, 363, 375, 420, 433
Soviet view of, 268
ordinary person(s),
    desire to reach, 414
    great persons [who] started as, 360 380
    how does he evaluate facts? 13
    view of, as impotent in face of "social forces, " 25
organized crime, 439
organisms,
    act to realize their intentions, 199
    and environment, 47
    living, 130, 141, 231, 306
    microörganisms, 439
out of control
    aspects of our present life, 385, 415, 422
    dread of feeling out of control, 422
    environment in third world, 37ff, 87ff
    people seen as, 304
    political processes, 415
    systems, 123
Output, 156, 173, 198ff, 201ff, 206ff, 211ff, 215, 226, 231, 264ff, 298, 313ff, 390, 396, 409, 417, 449, 451, 457
output mechanism, 202, 211, 213ff
overcrowding,
    in animals, 181

paradigm(s),
    basic, 84
    cultural, 96, 152, 354,
    explained, 448
    falling apart, 159, 187, 259
    new, 98, 376ff, 416
    political, 85
    psychological, 268, 429
    Western, 167
    revolution, 24, 73, 103, 129, 133, 148, 164, 169, 188, 276, 331
    shift, 13, 23, 25ff, 29, 54, 121, 280, 341, 394ff, 415
parallels with our own times, 14, 18
paranoia, 123
    of the rich, 455
passengers on the Titanic, 37
pathology(ies), 160, 181, 269, 275, 361, 373, 440, 444, 450
PCT, 27, 143, 197, 206, 218, 283, 339, 371
    as a theory, 414
    as revolutionary, 351
    applied, applying, 217, 235, 317, 334, 352, 377, 428, 457, 476
    demonstration(s) of, 227
    research in, 220, 374, 450
perceived condition, 131, 240, 383, 385, 396, 400, 451
    and reference/desired condition, (mismatch between), 383
    Intention as synonymous with reference/desired condition, 229
perceived variable(s), 201, 299, 316, 348
perceptual set, in language recognition, 186
perceptual variable(s), 29, 145, 155, 162, 171, 174, 182, 184, 189, 190ff, 201ff, 209ff, 226ff, 232, 234ff, 241ff, 250, 260ff, 263, 265ff, 279, 283, 285, 290, 292ff, 295, 313,

317, 322, 334, 362ff, 372, 380, 392, 400, 406, 417, 421, 450, 453, 478
personal logic, 102, 111
personal power of individuals, 293, 420, 424
personal powerlessness, feeling of, 255
personality
    development, 104, 171, 449
    differences, 265
    psychopathic, 91
    reorganization, 263
philosopher of history, 101, 167
philosophy
    liberal, 19
    of exploiting the earth, 36
    of government, 280
    of logical positivism, 454
    of "Win at Any Cost, " 122
physical environment, 88, 138, 176ff, 201, 282, 286, 288, 292, 388, 390
physical law, 101
Piaget's work, 174, 217, 451
plaintiff(s), 70
    attorney, 348
Plato, 108
police brutality, 397
political issues, 257
political process, 336, 415, 418
political scene, 261
politicians in power in Illinois, 355
popular media, 15
Population, 12, 18, 30, 36ff, 44, 47, 61ff, 65, 67, 77, 91, 94, 138, 240, 242, 257, 302, 322, 350, 401, 404ff, 411, 434, 439, 441, 450, 455
    growth, 48, 98
    surge, 37, 438

position-control by Configuration-control system, 213
post-citizen savages, 78
pre-ordained goal, 336
prediction tools, 36
prejudice, 30, 152, 281, 395
preprogrammed control systems, 270
preservation, 55, 168, 287, 311
PRESERVATION of the WORLD ENVIRONMENT, 403ff
president, 45, 58, 81, 224, 241, 285
President Clinton, 276
    impeachment of, 287, 334, 336ff
primal horde, 146
prime assumptions, 124
primitive
    experience, 106
    Gothic thought, 115
    horde, 132, 170
    man, 116
    people(s), 200, 222, 280
    principles, 117
    society, 61, 288
    view of reality, 104
principle, 17, 24, 28, 51, 58, 66, 69ff, 84, 87, 94, 96, 101ff, 105ff, 109, 112, 117, 120ff, 124ff, 132ff, 137ff, 140ff, 148ff, 152, 154, 156, 158, 161, 164, 166ff, 177, 179, 182ff, 188, 195, 201, 207, 210, 212, 214ff, 222, 226ff, 245ff, 248, 252, 257ff, 261, 275, 277, 280, 283, 286ff
Principle level PV, 289
    conflicts of, 297
    of equal justice, 124
    like "patriotism", 419
private citizen, 80, 385
private property, 61ff, 64, 151ff, 430, 432
processes going out of bounds, 122

Program(s), 201, 210, 212ff, 275, 287, 292, 294, 307, 314, 332, 342, 368, 391, 457, 476, 478
progress,
    and decline, 42, 97
    eletist view of, 359
    idea of, 96, 114
    manifestations of, 257
    of civilization, turning points in, 379
    of thought in [a] culture, 185
    of technology, 138
    pace of, 56
property rights of Indians and Philadelphia lawyers, 152
providers, 262, 264
psychic stimulus, 160
psychological,
    experiments, 254
    assumption that all subjects are equivalent in research plan, 254
    growth, 309
    theories of development, 27
psychologist(s), 16, 21, 26, 53, 91, 101, 141, 157, 189, 197, 203, 213, 250, 254, 265ff, 449, 453ff
psychology, 102, 130, 134, 141, 174ff, 203, 213, 215, 220, 249, 254, 260ff, 268, 303, 376, 388, 447, 449, 452ff
    of learning, 367
    revolution in, 131
psychopath(s), 16, 259, 364, 384, 386
"psychopath's law, " 123
psychopathic, 18, 28, 91ff, 399,
psychopathology, 440
psychotherapist(s), 26, 82, 101, 218, 377, 393
psychotherapy, 67, 264, 453
Public policy, 140, 279ff, 393, 406
public rituals, 284
Pygmalion Effect, 189

Pygmalion in the Classroom, 253
pyramid of control systems, 212
quasi-control system, 28ff, 170, 179, 200, 283ff, 292ff, 302, 304, 306ff, 313, 319, 356, 389, 425, 443, 456
quasi-organism, 283
quasi-person, 261
random actions, 218, 220, 231
rationalization, 258, 293,
    capacity for begins to break down, 159
    mechanism of, 156
    political, 273
real indian, old Dakota Souix as, 150
reciprocity,
    between the board and the CEO, 301
redistribution of wealth, 62, 304
Reference, (as technical term), 199, 206, 209, 211, 221, 234, 243, 245, 318, 368
    levels, 178, 450
    perception, 378, 405
    settings, 207, 212, 268, 297, 319, 448
    signal(s), 214ff, 220, 230ff, 234, 270, 272, 275, 312ff, 367, 392, 403, 409, 459, 477
    specification, 229, 476
    values, 186ff, 198, 201, 216, 218, 232, 246, 252, 265, 274, 284, 293, 295ff, 307, 314, 319, 322, 358, 363, 382ff, 390, 398, 410, 425, 428, 430, 434
references group, 257, 297
reflexes, 203, 214ff
reform(s), 11, 20, 22, 72, 81, 89, 240, 257, 304, 318, 323, 350, 390, 392, 394ff, 397, 431, 443
    of welfare, 62
    political and economic, 30
reformers and advocates, 50, 353, 390, 391, 392, 395, 425, 433
regulatory horror stories, 245
rehabilitation, 218, 265, 314

Relationships, (as technical term), 210, 213, 294, 479
relationship(s),
    between global economy and earth's ecosystem, 55
    of causes and effects, 125
    with one's superiors, 154
relativistic philosophy of space, 165
reliable observations, 249, 254
religious fundamentalism, 19
remedy(ies),
    [that] appear not to be working, 18
    dubious, 12
    for earth degredation, 81
    ineffective, 26
    must survive competing interests, 392
    new types [of], 359
    perceived as wasteful, 238
    paid by managed care only for symptom relief, 263
Renaissance science, 159
reorganization(s),
    and paradigm revolution, 276
    chronic, 403
    cognitive, 169, 406
    countering anxiety, 219, 422ff
    in members of a group, 307
    individual, 29, 185, 187, 217, 220, 271, 291ff, 305, 309, 315ff, 320ff, 331, 340ff, 344, 351, 353, 359
    of learned behavior, 171, 174, 216
    of power, 73, 365
    of thinking, 226
    on going, 160, 173
    personality, 263
    periodic, 190
    process, 373
    random (chance) aspect of, 175, 191, 220, 232, 274, 360ff, 381ff, 394, 429

social, 317, 333, 364, 409
  theory of, 148, 218, 270
restitution, 346ff, 349
Roman conquests, 167
Roman empire, 13, 18, 93ff, 97, 327, 345
Roman Senate, 385
Roman underclass, 345
Rome, 335,
  fall of, 13
rules of thumb for fostering innovation, 367, 382
ruling class, 14, 19, 302,
ruling legal fiction, 262
sacred principle(s)/value(s) of the society, 191, 364
  of "freedom of speech, " 211
  of the U. S., 285
Santa Fe, 63, 337
Saul Alinsky, 425
savages,
  German, 258
  new, 361
  present day, 94
  produce Ur-concepts, 360
scapegoate(d)(s)(ing), 280ff, 396,
  for world's ills (by terrorists), 415
  unconscious, 394
scare, 12, 47, 50
  tactic, 42
scholarly
  historical approach, 42
  information, 444
  opinion, 58
  writers, 96
science,
  a "win" for science, 370
    alternative method of (knowledge), 435

ancient, 95
as system concept, 190
as value free, 387, 430
basic axioms of, 133
classical, 159
decay of, 87
Greek, 108
hard science investigators, 9
history of, 24, 104, 109, 138, 148, 164
life, 188, 379
modern, 53
natural, 102
normal, 154, 165, 187
one of two forms of understanding reality, 101
physical, 141, 248
rules of, 54
social and social research, 49, 294, 346, 358ff, 383, 431
Western, 255, 354
science fiction movies, stories, 422, 456
scientific crisis, 159, 187
scientific ideas, development of, 187
scientist(s), 55, 175, 183, 387
SCIENCE (the journal),
    articles on brain organization, 446
    review of Jacob's book, 445,
secessionist movements, 74, 308
secretaries of Indian affairs, 153
Seleucid kingdom, 97
Self fulfilling prophecies, 28, 30, 53, 250ff, 336, 378, 410, 430
Self system, 183, 252, 477
self-consistency, 22, 189, 250ff, 258, 451
self-image, 154, 210, 213, 247ff, 252, 264, 314, 335, 477
Self-fulfilling prophecy, 28, 30, 250, 251ff, 336, 378, 408, 410, 430
sense of justice, 154, 156

sensory receptor, 206
"separate but equal, " 258ff
Sequences, 210
sequences, 213, 478
sex, 289
    and violence, 66, 274, 321
sexual abuse, 238
sexual revolution, 25, 322, 364ff
Seychelles Islands, 44
shared environment, 288, 299
shared perceptions, 104, 286
short term sensationalism, 242
short term survival, 437
short term values, 50
Sierra Club, 16, 359, 439
Sioux, and Sioux culture, 150ff
Skinnerian tradition, 361
small farmers, 229, 432
smile, 172ff, 449, 451
Smith, Adam (on economics, invisible hand), 115, 328
social action, 15, 26, 235, 453
social class, 28ff, 282ff, 288, 293, 297, 332, 353, 390
social class hierarchy, 302, 389
society, as hierarchically organized, 28ff, 283ff, 286, 305
    as morally bankrupt, 169
social climate, 96, 408
social contract, 308
social crises, 325
social engineering, 28, 267ff
social fabric, cracks in, 332
social life, 56, 394, of Modern Community (the book), 283
social reorganization, 317
social status, 288ff, 294, 304, 326, 346, 350, 391
Socialism, 119
socially undesirable behavior, 219

societal
- contradictions, 150
- degeneration, 48, 420
- demise of, 116
- functioning, 294
- reorganization, 316
- rules, 158, 164
  - inconsistent demands from, 158, 164

societies,
- advanced, 71, 304
- affluent, 38
- complex, 293
- doomed, 12, 84
- egalitarian, 332
- European, 294
- history of, 103
- new, 188
- primitive, 61
- simpler, 290
- Western, 88, 333
  - Non-western, 321

sociobiology, 269ff, 455
sociological theory, 67
sociologist(s), 71, 256, 293, 299, 320, 453
Socrates, 83, 135
South America, 426
Sovereign Individuals, 93, 308, 327, 377, 419, 444
Soviet leaders, 268
Soviet Union, 16, 61, 350, 362, 410, 439
Space,
- concept of, 114, 116, 159, 167
- conquest of, 195, 321, 411, 435
- paradigm for, 166
- reality of, 195

specification(s), 20, 189, 198ff, 205, 208, 215, 229, 235, 245, 283, 311, 378ff, 383, 397, 447, 451, 458, 476
sport-utility vehicles, 61
standardized product, 241, 264
standards,
    discard of, 87
    moral, 19, 120, 333
state of the world, 20, 39, 43, 45, 53, 55
statistical analyses, 80
statistical arguments, 20, 37, 80
statistics of concern only to specialists, 37ff
Statistics on murders, 16
statistical studies, 45
Status Mobility, 291, 345
status roles, 306
status striving, 289, 291, 297
stimulus-response, 131, 223, 349, 450
stimulus-response language, 206, 212
stimulus-response research, 220
stress, 12, 219, 269, 291, 294, 309, 324, 419
stress hormones, 440
superior systems limit scope of subordinate systems they control, 374
superordinate system, 209
Supreme Court, 259
survival, 20, 29, 58, 91, 103, 109, 146, 246, 258ff, 271, 272ff, 292, 294, 321, 332, 341, 358ff, 362, 366, 380, 382, 385, 390, 402ff, 405, 416, 420, 431, 437, 443, 458
Swiss tradition, 312
Synanon, 280, 319
System Concept, 278
systems and environments, 199
systems running out of control, 123
Systems-concepts, 210, 278
Systems-concepts of reality, 185

technical inventions, 85, 148
technique(s),
    of research, 359
    shared in primal horde, 146
technological development(s), improvements, 10, 72, 94, 138, 303, 321, 333, 366, 409
technology, revolution in, 23, 36, 42, 341, 349, 351, 359
teleological principle of economic development, 166
terrorist(s), 42, 46, 54, 73, 190, 393, 415
testing the limits, 151
Teutonic chieftains, 93
The Postman, (movie), 78
The President, could improve reading scores, 241
    facing charge, 334
THE PROBLEM OF GUNS, 406
theft of intellectual property, 427
therapeutic, 150, 171, 448
therapy, 267
    clients, 234
third world, 16, 36, 39ff, 81, 94, 153, 322, 361, 439
thought, 85, 97, 101, 103ff, 108ff, 112ff, 119ff, 124ff, 146, 159, 163, 182, 185, 259, 261ff, 271, 319, 351, 373, 376, 381, 387, 458
time(s), 14, 21, 42, 77, 96, 99, 114, 267, 305, 335, 346, 377, 446
Time Magazine, 74ff
To Sir With Love (the movie), 352
tobacco,
    company, 25, 51, 261
    farmers, 318
    smoke, 54, 405
totalitarianism, 307
traditional,
    conceptions, 21, 431
    cultural structures, 276

    institutions, 414
    life styles, 432
    Psychology, 27ff, 174ff, 453
    solutions, 56, 189
    values, 23, 321
    view of behavior, 332
    ways falling apart, 358
Tragedy of the Commons, 60
trained behavior, 358, 361
turmoil, dilemmas in confronting social turmoil, 26
    compulsion of upper-upper class to suppress, 391
TV talk shows, 325, 372
twentieth century, 11, 85,
    principle character of, 121
types of tasks, 285
tyranny, 260
U. N.,
    inability to stop wars, 16
    publications of, 37
    treaty on CO_2 and global warming, 56
U. S.
    children, 16, 244
    cities and crime, 77
    citizens, 276
    congress, 25, 154, 334, 389
    corporations, 398
    culture, 151
    generals, 151
    government, 308, 327
    history, 97
    homelessness, 61, 441
    law, 152
    seen in decline, 80ff
    society, 87, 294

unanticipated consequence(s), 75, 225, 245
unconscious assumptions, 111
unconscious "research" into human nature, 275
unconscious repertoire, 427
unconscious self-concept, 446
uncooperative patient, 265
under class, 91, 94ff, 441
unemployment, 26, 62, 77, 354
unintended by-products, 61
United States,
    and violent crime, 438
    its evolution as a system, 288
    seen as unraveling internally, 11
    will historians wonder when it ceased as a democracy? 389
unnatural substances made by chemistry, 350
upper class, 38, 89, 122, 283, 285ff, 300, 304ff, 320, 455
upper-upper class, 385, 390ff
ur-concept(s), 360
US NEWS, 73ff, 324
use of violence, effort to set limits on, 384
value neutrality, 387ff
verbal contortions, 113
violence, 12, 90
    appeal of in media, 16
    culture of, 408
    debate as to effect of movies, 388
    Fear of, 152, 407ff
    ineffective in bringing about change, 77, 392
    heretofore accepted as human condition, 400
    limits upon, 384
    toward authority as unconscious aggression toward parent(s), 459
visceral reaction, 279, 304, 339ff
Vital Signs, 36

W. R. Grace Co, 67
Waco, 386
Wall Street Journal, 14, 38, 72, 286, 301, 331, 362, 439, 444
war crimes, 384ff, 412
weapons of offense, defence, 333
welfare, 62, 230, 239, 244, 277, 295, 316, 339, 355, 369, 404, 406, 432, 443
West Africa, 39
Western Christian's idea of Grace, 117
Western countries, 332, 387, 455
Western development, 117
western elites, 90
Western history, 97, 118
Western ideas, 97, 115, 121
Western man, described as abandoning belief in transcendentals, 258
Western psychology, 248
Western science, 102, 255, 354
Western society, 23, 88, 124, 143, 321, 333ff
Western spirit, 108
Western thinkers, thinking, thought, 97, 113, 119, 159, 262, 308
Western World, fundamental principles of, 387
whistle blowers, 156
Why don't we all... form of advocacy, 54
will,
    concept of, 118
will-to-power, 115
World Bank, 43, 229, 404ff
World Futurist Society, 52
world membership, a sense of, 420
world of the Hellenes, 114
world trade, 415
World War II, 211, 285

world wide water usage, 37
world wide web, 415, 457
Worldwatch Institute, 36ff
Wounded Knee massacre, 151
"Yankee City" series, 283
Zen gurus, 377